CHINESE SOCIAL HISTORY

AMERICAN COUNCIL OF LEARNED SOCIETIES
Studies in Chinese and Related Civilizations
Number 7

The series of which this volume is a part is published through the generosity of the late Margaret Watson Parker, of Detroit, who wished to honor the memory of Charles James Morse, a pioneer collector and student of things Oriental, but who, during her lifetime, preferred that her gift remain anonymous.

CHINESE SOCIAL HISTORY

Translations of Selected Studies

By

E-TU (ZEN) SUN and JOHN DE FRANCIS

1972

OCTAGON BOOKS

New York

Copyright 1956 by American Council of Learned Societies

Reprinted 1966
by special arrangement with American Council of Learned Societies
Second Octagon printing 1972

OCTAGON BOOKS
A DIVISION OF FARRAR, STRAUS & GIROUX, INC.
19 Union Square West
New York, N. Y. 10003

LIBRARY OF CONGRESS CATALOG CARD NUMBER: 66-19731

ISBN 0-374-97657-0

Printed in U.S.A. by
NOBLE OFFSET PRINTERS, INC.
NEW YORK 3, N. Y.

INTRODUCTION

The present work is intended to provide a sampling of modern Chinese scholarship in the field of the social history of traditional China.

What we mean by the term "social history" can be indicated, negatively, by opposing it to humanistic studies and political history, and, more positively, by suggesting a general affinity with what James Harvey Robinson long ago called the New History.* This sort of history has attracted a not inconsiderable number of practitioners among Western scholars dealing with their own past. Its application by Westerners to the Chinese scene has, however, been much more restricted, and compares unfavorably with their relatively advanced work in the humanities.

On the other hand Chinese historians have for some time been writing prolifically along lines which for them are more genuinely new than in the case of their Western counterparts. The extensive use of this approach only coincidentally dates from shortly after the initial appeal for a New History. It represents, rather, in its historical context, a modern phase of China's response to the West, plus a reaction to internal developments which have evoked a general revaluation of almost all aspects of Chinese life.

The first phase of China's response to the West, initiated in the seventeenth century by the proseletyzing activities of Jesuit missionaries, was marked by the curiosity of a few men of letters in some limited aspects of Western culture. The second phase, which grew out of the nineteenth century defeats of China at the hands of industrially more advanced powers, was characterized by the desire to import the material achievements of the West without disturbing the basic fabric of Chinese society. In the twentieth century, however, a combination of internal and external factors had the effect of expanding the range of Chinese interest. World War I and its aftermath added new foreign influences to those already emanating from the West. At the same time the failure of the republican revolution of 1911 to cope with internal disintegration and external weakness created a greater willingness to seek out more drastic cures for China's manifold ills. It was in the course of

---

*James Harvey Robinson, The New History: Essays Illustrating the Modern Historical Outlook. New York, 1913.

this search that interest in the social sciences began to develop
widely in the 1920's.

For three decades thereafter Chinese historical scholarship
was dominated by the attempt to apply diverse aspects of Western
social science to the study of China's past. Working under the influence of Bruno Hildebrand, one scholar wrote of China's middle
ages as characterized by a "natural economy." Another bisected
Chinese history into two civilizations in the manner of Arnold
Toynbee. Others presented diverse historical interpretations each
of which was advanced as the true reflection of the views of Karl
Marx. In the case of many others the debt was less to a specific
individual than to the general corpus of Western scholarship. It
should be noted, however, that although the original stimulus may
have come from the West, its path of entry into China was frequently via Japan, so that the concept of "Western influences"
should not be thought of in too limited a geographical sense. Nor
should it be forgotten that there has been a good deal of modern
Chinese scholarship possessing a purely indigenous character, or,
at best, only a remote connection with Western thought.

Most recently the beginnings of still another phase in the study
of Chinese history can be discerned as the victory of the Commu-
nists has begun to exercise its influence on Chinese scholarship.
It would appear, therefore, that the three decades following World
War I constitute a unique period in Chinese historical study. Its
termination suggests that the time is ripe for a closer look into
the scholarly production of this period both as a source of information on the past and as a basis of comparison with subsequent
trends.

In seeking to make a contribution along these lines we have
chosen, from among the many tasks which need to be done, that
of presenting a sampling of studies on the social history of traditional China. Our first step was to discover what was available in
this field. Proceeding on the belief that the largest and perhaps
least known body of useful scholarly information was to be found
in the standard academic periodicals, we began by compiling a
list of significant articles which have appeared in Chinese learned
journals in the course of the past three decades. In making the selection we attempted to use scholarship as the sole criterion, and
to accept only those articles showing evidence of solid research
behind them. Our search through twenty-seven journals resulted
in the compilation of a selected and critical bibliography of 176
items, for which we provided notes indicating the amount of material available, the value of the articles, and other information
useful as a guide for further research. The annotated list, which

we published under the title Bibliography on Chinese Social History,* was then used as the basis for a further selection of twenty-five articles. It is these articles, totalling seven hundred-odd pages in the original Chinese, which we now present in translated and summarized form as examples of what modern Chinese scholars have produced on the social history of China.

In our present effort we are conscious of having been able to cover only a small part of the ground. By confining ourselves to periodicals we have doubtless put aside much that is valuable in books dealing with Chinese social history. The limitation to learned journals has likewise resulted in the exclusion of valuable material in the truly enormous but frequently ephemeral periodical literature. A really complete survey of modern Chinese scholarship would doubtless have to take into account the material contained in books and other sources excluded from our limited sampling.

Topically the material which we have selected follows the interests of Chinese scholars as reflected in our Bibliography. In the course of compiling this list of articles, which were selected without any preconceived detailed topical plan, we found that the material could be conveniently arranged under fourteen subject headings, such as Agrarian Relations, Social Structure, Population, and so on. From each of these topical divisions we have taken care to select at least one item for the present book. Of course the Chinese have not devoted equal attention to all subjects, and our selection reflects their preponderant interest by its emphasis on various aspects of economic history.

Chronologically the contents of the articles range from the earliest authenticated dynasty in the second half of the second millenium B.C. to the end of the empire, which was moribund in the nineteenth century but not officially pronounced dead until 1911. Needless to say, there is no thought of being able to cover this long expanse in any detail, or even to give an adequate balance to the various phases of Chinese history. We have sought merely to select items falling within at least the major divisions which have attracted the interest of Western students.

Purely for the convenience of the reader, especially one not thoroughly familiar with the sequence of Chinese dynasties, we have arbitrarily imposed on the chronological arrangement of the articles a further grouping into three periods each of which contains roughly one-third of the material. The first period extends

---

*E-tu Zen Sun and John De Francis, Bibliography on Chinese Social History: A Selected and Critical List of Chinese Periodical Sources. New Haven: Far Eastern Publications, Yale University, 1952.

for roughly 1,500 years, to the third century A.D.; the second, somewhat more than 1,000 years, to the fourteenth century; and the third, about 500 years, to the last part of the nineteenth cen- tury. Hence although a good deal of attention is given to what we loosely call Antiquity, relatively more is devoted to subsequent eras, especially to that period which in Western history is labelled Modern, but which we hesitate to designate thus for fear on the one hand of suggesting unwarranted associations and on the other of arousing equally unwarranted expectations for the last word on the latest developments. In short, our division into periods is a matter of convenience, not of historical analysis.

It may also be of interest to note the chronological distribution of the articles on the basis of when they were published. More or less accidentally, our choice fell on articles published chiefly in the second half of the period encompassed by the articles in the Bibliography. The earliest item selected appeared in 1930, and the last in 1947. It is not quite so accidental, however, that no less than eleven of the articles happen to have been published in the years 1935 and 1936 alone, for the mid-thirties were a period of particularly intense intellectual ferment and scholarly activity. The sharp drop in output thereafter is melancholy testimony to the blow inflicted on Chinese scholarship by the succeeding years of defensive war and civil strife. The situation here is remini- scent of that in the field of archeology, where a brief period of sci- entific excavations was likewise ended by the Japanese invasion, though not before leading to the brilliant discovery, or at least authentication, of a dynasty previously regarded as in the shadowy realm of pre-history. In view of how much was accomplished in so little time, one is tempted to speculate on what untold riches await discovery in the earth and in the library.

Of the twenty-seven journals dealt with in our Bibliography, nine are represented in the present work. It is not surprising that the largest number of articles, six, happen to come from Shih- huo, a journal which took its title from that of the economic trea- tises in the dynastic histories, and which elected to describe it- self also by the English name Chinese Social and Economic His- tory Semi-Monthly Magazine. Four other items derive from the Bulletin of the Institute of History and Philology, an organ of the government-supported Academia Sinica, and a like number come from the lively journal published by Tsing Hua University. The remaining items are scattered one or two each among six other journals.

In our handling of the material in the Chinese articles we have proceeded on the conviction that the study of Chinese history is a task which must involve not only professional sinologists but also social scientists who do not read Chinese. For the benefit particularly of the latter we have adopted the device of rendering part of the material in summarized form in the hope of making a more readable product than is possible in a full and close translation. The latter has been reserved, for the most part, for passages of major importance, where it is desirable to have as close an approximation as possible of the original ideas. Even in our summarized sections, however, we have sought to extract most of what was valuable in the original, and to present this largely in the author's own style and language. Sometimes the summary is in extenso, actually a mixture of direct translation and close paraphrase, with only occasional minor omissions and condensations. Sometimes the summary is drastic, as in the case of the second article, the original of which consists almost entirely of an analysis of hundreds of archaic Chinese characters. In all cases, however, we have sought to render the original faithfully, without significant additions or subtractions.*

Such minor additions as have been made are along the lines of dates for individuals or reigns, rough contemporary geographical equivalents for place-names, and other aids for increasing the intelligibility of the material. The major subtraction has been the documentation, particularly that of a purely bibliographical nature, as this is available in the original for the occasional sinologist who might be interested and is of rather limited utility for the non-specialist. On the other hand, in order to spare the sinologist the trouble of searching out the frequently not very accessible originals in order to check on every crucial point, we have sought to provide an indication of the sources and at least a few of the characters for some of the key terminology used by the authors of the articles.

Such compromises, particularly in the matter of documentation, are admittedly not entirely satisfactory. It is conceivable, for example, that the importance of an article may lie not so much in the argumentation as in the documentation, so that to omit the latter is to omit what is most valuable. Yet a mass of technical footnotes is hardly the most appetizing fare for any but highly specialized readers. Our decision to solve the problem by omitting most of the documentation is a draconian solution which leaves us by no means entirely happy.

We are also aware that other solutions might have been made

---

*See the Explanatory Note on page xviii for indication of how translation, summary, insert, and omission are handled typographically.

to the thorny problem of exactly which articles should be selected
for inclusion in a book of this sort. It was not easy to limit our
selection of items for the Bibliography to less than two hundred
articles, and it was even more difficult to make the further selection of twenty-five for the present work. Despite the fact that,
with such a limited number of articles, a fully representative
cross-section of the literature was out of the question, we have
sought to provide at least a little diversity, not alone in the topics
dealt with and the periods covered, but also in authorship, interpretation, presentation, and other aspects. As an inevitable result, however, the articles sometimes express conflicting interpretations, differ in readability, and are of uneven value. These
facts are by no means necessarily all to the bad, and in any event
they can hardly be avoided completely, though they might be altered in a detail, by a different selection of articles.

In view of the above-mentioned diversity in the articles it
seems hardly necessary to point out that their selection does not
imply acceptance on our part of the statements of fact or opinion
expressed by the authors. On the contrary, disagreement or dis-
approval exist with respect to many points of major and minor
importance. We have, for the most part, resisted the temptation
to note these points and to comment extensively on the diverse
subjects treated in this volume. We prefer to leave this task to
specialists in the various fields.

To be sure in such matters there is likely to be considerable
disagreement even among specialists, as illustrated by the fact
that a number of scholars who were invited to review our material
in manuscript form variously approved and disapproved the same
article, expressed a desire for both more and less generalization,
and otherwise made plain that a selection of this sort cannot hope
to satisfy all readers. More important, their reactions also serve
to underscore the fact, which should be pointed out with the utmost emphasis for the benefit especially of the non-specialist,
that many of our articles, far from being definitive, frequently
raise more questions than they answer, and in any case do not
exhaust the interpretations and data on the subject-matter under
discussion. Our material remains far from complete even in those
few instances in which we have been able to present opposing points
of view, as in the discussion on the well-field system, a subject
characterized by a paucity of primary data and an excess of that
sort of scholarship, especially typical of work on ancient Chinese
history, which is so highly interpretive as to remind one of Mark
Twain's reconstructed dinosaur--"three bones and a dozen bar-
rels of plaster." The views expressed on the subject of the well-

field by Wu Ch'i-ch'ang, who reflects the position of the "Doubt Antiquity School" of the 1920's and early 1930's, and by Hsü Chung-shu, whose work is a recent reaction against the earlier skepticism, reveal something of the dynamics of Chinese thinking on a problem far more controversial and complicated than has been indicated by our limited selections.

All this leads us to feel that the basic problem in arriving at a fuller knowledge and understanding of modern Chinese scholarship is simply that too little work is being done by Westerners in a field marked by new and yet prolific activity by Chinese scholars. The only real solution, to our mind, is an increased body of translation, plus a great deal more original research and analysis by individual specialists or teams of scholars. These are tasks which await the attention of both the sinologist and the social scientist.

The contribution which both groups are able to make toward the advancement of the study of Chinese history is well indicated by the variety of helpful comments and criticisms made on the material by numerous specialists. Some of the comments have been incorporated in the notes. Many more helped to guide us toward improvements in our translations. Still others, especially some by Professors Wolfram Eberhard of the University of California and Robert Sabatino Lopez of Yale University comparing Chinese and Western institutions, opened up subjects beyond the scope of this book. It is our hope that all these matters will be taken up later in greater detail by these and other scholars.

Apart from Professors Eberhard and Lopez, other scholars whose generous assistance it is a pleasure to acknowledge include the following: Professors Herrlee Glessner Creel, Edward A. Kracke, Robert Redfield, and S. L. Thrupp of the University of Chicago, L. Carrington Goodrich of Columbia University, Jeremy Ingalls of Rockford College, William W. Lockwood of Princeton University, and Edwin O. Reischauer and Lien-sheng Yang of Harvard University. We are also indebted to the staffs of the Library of Congress and the libraries of Columbia, Harvard, Johns Hopkins, and Pennsylvania State Universities for their cooperation in making available the numerous Chinese periodicals needed for our work. Acknowledgement is also due to the American Philosophical Society and the Economic Cooperation Administration for grants which made possible the initiation of this work.

John De Francis
E-tu Zen Sun

CONTENTS

III. THE LAST DYNASTIES (1368-1911)

LIST OF MAPS

CHRONOLOGICAL TABLE
OF PERIODS ENCOMPASSED BY THE ARTICLES

I. Antiquity

Shang or Yin		ca. 1523-1028 B.C.
Chou		ca. 1027-221 B.C.
Western Chou	ca. 1027-771 B.C.	
Eastern Chou	771-221 B.C.	
Spring and Autumn	722-480 B.C.	
Warring States	403-221 B.C.	
Ch'in		221-207 B.C.
Han		B.C. 206-220 A.D.
Western (or Early) Han	206- 9 A.D.	
Hsin Dynasty (Wang Mang)	9- 23 A.D.	
Eastern (or Later) Han	25-220 A.D.	

II. The Middle Period

Three Kingdoms		220-280 A.D.
Six Dynasties		222-589 A.D.
Tsin Dynasty		265-420 A.D.
Western Tsin	265-316 A.D.	
Eastern Tsin	317-420 A.D.	
Northern and Southern Dynasties		386-589 A.D.
Northern Dynasties	386-581 A.D.	
Northern Wei (also called Wei, Later Wei, Toba Wei)	386-535 A.D.	
Northern Ch'i	550-577 A.D.	
Northern Chou	557-581 A.D.	
Southern Dynasties	420-589 A.D.	
(Liu) Sung	420-479 A.D.	

Ch'i	479-502 A.D.	
Liang	502-557 A.D.	
Ch'en	557-589 A.D.	

Sui   589-618 A.D.

T'ang   618-906 A.D.

Five Dynasties and Ten Kingdoms   907-960 A.D.

Sung   960-1279 A.D.
   Northern Sung   960-1127 A.D.
   Southern Sung   1127-1279 A.D.

Liao   907-1125 A.D.

Chin   1122-1234 A.D.

Yüan   1280-1368 A.D.

III. The Last Dynasties

Ming   1369-1644 A.D.

Ch'ing   1644-1911 A.D.

EXPLANATORY NOTE

1. Material not otherwise indicated comprises paraphrase or summary of the original Chinese text.

2. Slant lines enclose direct translation of the original text.

3. Quotation marks are used a) in longer passages, to enclose material quoted by the author and translated by us, and b) in short phrases or expressions, to draw the reader's attention to special terminology used by the author.

4. Indented passages comprise translations of material quoted by the author.

5. Brackets enclose additions made by the translators. In passages of translation four dots enclosed in brackets represent our deletions. Four dots not so bracketed indicate omissions made by the author himself.

6. Our rendering of passages from well-known works, such as the Book of Poetry, follows with minor modification the standard translations, unless the author's intent demands a different interpretation.

7. Most of the original reference notes and bibliographical data are omitted in our translation or summary. These changes are not indicated, even in passages of direct translation.

8. Of the notes added by us, those of significance for the general reader are handled as footnotes. Those of a more specialized nature are placed at the end of each article.

9. In a limited number of cases Chinese characters have been inserted in the text in order to facilitate the reading of the material. Characters have also been supplied for some of the bibliographical data in the Notes at the end of each article. Much of the special terminology used by our various authors, together with many names of people, titles of books, and similar material, are provided with characters in the Index.

10. Chinese weights and measures have as far as possible been rendered by roughly corresponding English terms (indicated in parentheses below). In the following tables the chief units are defined in relation to each other and, where possible, by rough equivalence in English measure:

Length

ts'un	寸	(inch)	= 1/10 ch'ih
ch'ih	尺	(foot)	= 14 inches English measure
li	里		= 1/3 English mile

Weight

liang	兩	(ounce)	= 1/16 chin
chin	斤	(catty)	= 1-1/3 pounds English measure
tàn	擔	(picul)	= 100 catties

Volume

sheng	升	(pint)	= 1/10 tou = 31.6 cubic inches English measure
tou	斗	(peck)	= 10 sheng
hu	斛		= 1/2 tan
tan	石		= 10 tou

Area

mou	畝		= about 1/6 acre
shang	晌		= 6-12 mou (The shang was a land unit used in Manchuria with local variations)
ch'ing	頃		= 100 mou

Money

wen	文	(cash)	= 1/1000 string
kuan	貫	(string)	= 1,000 cash; a unit of paper currency
liang	兩	(tael)	= unit of about 1.3 ounces English measure, generally used for silver and having a fluctuating relationship with the copper cash

CHINESE SOCIAL HISTORY

I

ANTIQUITY

(ca. 1523 B.C. - 220 A.D.)

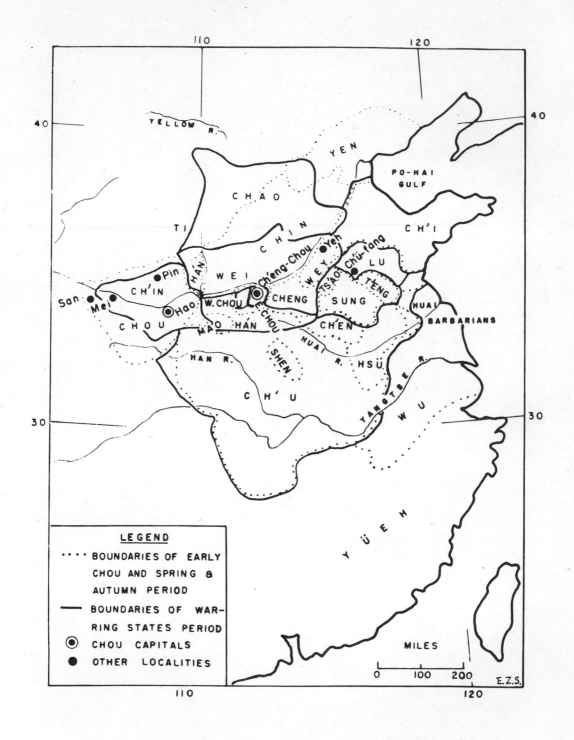

LEGEND

- ···· BOUNDARIES OF EARLY CHOU AND SPRING & AUTUMN PERIOD
- —— BOUNDARIES OF WAR-RING STATES PERIOD
- ⊙ CHOU CAPITALS
- ● OTHER LOCALITIES

MILES

0   100   200

E.Z.S.

Map 1. Feudal states during the Chou period

1

THE WELL-FIELD SYSTEM IN SHANG AND CHOU

by

HSÜ CHUNG-SHU

1. Earliest Meaning of "Field":
Hunting Field and Battle Field

The initial meaning of the word t'ien 田 ["field"] was "hunting field" and "battle field." This is a fact that scholars for over two thousand years have seldom realized.

The [ancient] lexicon Shuo-wen, in defining t'ien as "a place where grain is planted," derives this meaning by contending that the character represents the paths in a plot of land under cultivation. This is erroneous. In ancient times hunting was carried on throughout the year. It provided meat for food and fur for clothing, and it was also the most prevalent means of military training, as indicated by many accounts in the classics. In the oracle bone texts, our oldest extant historical records, the familiar sentence "the king went afield" often appeared together with the expression "the king hunted." These were followed by such phrases as "there were no accidents either coming or going," or by an account of the number of animals obtained in the hunt, but never by the mention of agricultural matters. Even in the Chou dynasty records, such sentences as "went afield and got three foxes" in the Book of Changes, and the use of the expression "afield" with military events in the Rites of Chou, clearly indicate that the organization of the hunt was similar to a battle formation.

Although the authenticity of the Tso Chronicle and the Rites of Chou has been the focus of controversy among scholars, they can still be considered reliable as sources of information on the institutions of the Spring and Autumn and early Warring States periods, when they were completed. The Tso Chronicle contains descriptions of hunts in which the strict formation and multitudinous forces are highly reminiscent of military campaigns. This bears out the descriptions given in the Rites of Chou. Of all the hunts, that held in the course of the winter was the most elaborately conducted. The exact details of this hunt, however, are now not known.

The Ku-liang Chronicle and the Book of Poetry also give descriptions of the hunt in later Chou. During the Spring and Autumn and the Warring States periods, the land of the original hunting preserves of the Chou nobility had been largely placed under cultivation, so that it was necessary to have boundary marks for the hunting party, beyond which it was not to proceed. In the course of the hunt specific detachments of the troops were assigned to different tasks. The form of the character t'ien 田 depicts the "right and left flanks" and "the upper and lower garrisons" in the hunting formation; these are enclosed by the boundaries of the hunting field.

2. Words with the "Field" Component that Derived Their Meaning from "Hunting"

The Shuo-wen further errs in defining all characters with the "field" component, with three exceptions, as having derived their meaning from agriculture.

Take the word ch'u 畜 ["domesticated animal"], which the Shuo-wen explains in terms of the agricultural field. The character actually consists of two parts, a top half, which in ancient times denoted "twisting, fibre, rope," and a bottom half which was the figure for "field." It obviously referred to the constraining of animals obtained in a hunt, that is to the domestication of animals. This word also reveals the progress of ancient Chinese society from the hunting into the pastoral stage.

Again, the character tang 當 ["at the place"] is explained by the Shuo-wen as meaning "adjacent fields." Tuan Yü-ts'ai's commentary on the same work holds that its meaning was derived from agricultural fields, whereas actually it was derived from meeting animals on a hunt. The top part of this word is the character shang, denoting royalty; the lower part is "field." It was the practice in ancient hunting to flush the animals so that they ran head-on toward the king's chariot.

More examples of such misinterpretations can be found in the terms liu 留 "to keep, to stop" (the lower part being "field," the upper part a symbol denoting the arrangement of banners on a hunt); miao 苗 "shoot of a plant" (in Chou times, the summer hunt was called miao, due to the luxuriance of grass and foliage); chiang 疆 "boundary," which has a "bow radical" clearly revealing its origin in hunting; and so on.

In fact, the story of the domestication of animals and pastoralism

in China can be told by analysing the forms of the characters for
"hunting," "doing," "fowl," "sheep," "cattle," and others.

3. A Society of Walled Cities, Hunting, Pastoralism, and Agriculture.

Although it would be an error to hold that in the later Chou period the Chinese people still remained in the hunting stage, it is
nevertheless clear that hunting was still a major element in the
life of the people. For instance, passages in the Book of Poetry
mention the pursuit of wolves and other beasts, and the Rites of
Chou describes the trapping of animals.

From the variety of agricultural objects as well as animals
mentioned in the oracle bones, and from the records of prayers
for rain and divinations for harvests, we may conclude that agriculture was already highly developed in the Shang dynasty. However, hunting and pastoralism were still widespread, and this situation prevailed without major change down to the Spring and
Autumn and the Warring States periods. For instance, though the
poem "Seventh Month" in the Book of Poetry is primarily concerned
with descriptions of agricultural work, yet in it the first and
second days are given to hunting by both the common people and the
nobility. Other contemporary evidences indicate the co-existence
of agriculture and hunting. The Book of Rites states that "when inquiry is made of the common people's wealth, the answer is in
terms of animals," indicating the importance of livestock as
property.

To contend that hunting, pastoralism, and agriculture existed
contemporaneously in ancient China may seem to contradict the
theory usually held by sociologists that they represent three successive stages of economic development. There were, however,
these special characteristics in the Chinese scene: The hunting in
pre-Ch'in times was carried on primarily by the nobility, who conducted it together with the masses by gathering the people in groups,
and was different from the general hunting-fishing economy elsewhere. Also, after the rise of agriculture the people began to build
and live in walled cities, and were unable to move about freely
with their animals. Therefore a city-hunting-pastoral-agricultural
society was developed. This, however, was not unique to the ancient Yellow River region. The Jurchen people of Manchuria retained the same system as late as the Ch'ing dynasty. This might
be considered as a remnant of the ancient Chinese system, since
the Po-hai Gulf separating Manchuria from Shantung was formed
only in historic times and the two areas were originally communi-

cable by land. That the Manchu emperors had special hunting parks, where hunts were conducted with battle formations, was itself a manifestation of ancient customs. With the transformation of hunting land into agricultural land in China Proper, it is to the peripheral areas that we have to look for evidence of the early culture.

Thus, during Shang and Chou the rise of pastoralism had not entirely replaced hunting, nor had agriculture replaced pastoralism. The result was a prolonged stagnation in social evolution. Critics usually glorify the nominal equal distribution of landed property under the well-field system*, not realizing that such a system was actually the tool with which the ruling tribes enslaved other peoples. It contributed little to agriculture, but succeeded in prolonging feudal society for centuries. It was not until the end of the Warring States period, when the system of the "public land" was abolished, that Chinese society began to enter a new cycle.

4. The Four Ranks in the Feudal System of Shang and Chou

In ancient feudal times there was no rigid system of uniform institutions. Of the five feudal ranks of later date--duke, marquis, earl, viscount, and baron--the terms for duke, earl, and viscount were derived from common expressions denoting seniority or respect, and only marquis and baron were actually the remnants of the four ranks of Shang times.

The four ranks of Shang were marquis, count, baron, and knight. According to the Book of History, these four were also known as the "outer ranks," that is, territorial officials, in contrast to other officials, known as "inner ranks," who served at the central government. The four constituted the feudal ranks of the time, and served a superior sovereign, for which reason they were called "governors of state." The "inner" and "outer" ranks of Chou were inherited from the Shang system. In all the reliable Shang and Chou sources mention is made only of these four feudal titles, not five.

The four titles have been defined by a commentary on the I Chou Shu as follows: marquis, to patrol for the king; count, to remit the land tax to the king; baron, to do the king's service; knight, to defend the king. The Rites of Chou contains definitions which parallel the above. Actually, what the commentary describes as "land tax" should be explained as "tax from hunting." The form of

---

*The name of this system, in which land was supposed to have been divided into nine equal plots, is derived from the resemblance of the divisional scheme to the Chinese character ching 井 "a well."

the character nan 男 ["baron"], on the other hand, is made up of
the elements "field" and "strength," which indicates that the position concerned agricultural enterprise.

In accordance with their specific functions, then, the distribution of fiefs was as follows: The knights' fiefs were located at the
capital, the fiefs of the barons farther out, those of the counts
were still farther away, and the fiefs of the marquises were situated on the borders of the country, since the function of the marquises was to patrol the borders.

The Tributes of Yü lists five feudal ranks and the Rites of Chou
lists nine. The sequence in the two works is different, that of the
Tributes of Yü conforming more to the arrangement of Shang.

5. Land System and Military System
of Shang and Chou

Shang and Chou, contrary to the opinion of some writers, had
distinct land systems and military systems. In the Shang period
the well-field system was used in the territories of counts and
barons. Eight families constituted a "well." Local administration
and military organization were both based on units of four and its
multiples. Thus, according to the Rites of Chou, four wells were
a "town," four towns were a ch'iu 丘 , four ch'iu were a county
[i.e. territory of a count], four counties were a district, four
districts were a tu 都 . In military organization, as indicated in
Military Regulations, a work of the Warring States period found
in a commentary on the Rites of Chou, each ch'iu had to provide
one war horse and three head of cattle; each county, containing
sixty-four "wells," had to provide one long chariot, four horses,
twelve head of cattle, three armored warriors, and seventy-two
foot soldiers with weapons.

Furthermore, under the Shang well-field system weights and
measures also were based on units of four. For instance, in linear
measure eight "feet" made one hsün 尋 . In volume four tou 豆 made
one ou 區 , four ou made one fü 釜, and ten fü made one chung 鍾
In weight there were sixteen ounces to a catty, which is a system
preserved to this day.

With the institution of the "tithe tax" in the Chou dynasty, local
administration and military organization came to be based on units
of five or ten. Various passages in the Rites of Chou testify to
this. For instance, "Five men make one 'company,' five companies
make one liang 兩 , four liang make one tsu 卒 , five tsu make
one 'brigade,' five brigades make one 'division,' and five divisions
make one 'army'."

That counting by the decimal system was a Chou practice is proved by accounts of the military forces of the states of Chin [in present Shansi] and Wu [in Kiangsu], both founded by members of the royal family of Chou. Chin instituted in 644 B.C. a system of local divisions based on units of 2,500 families. The troops of King Fu-ch'ai [495-473 B.C.] of Wu were divided in groups of 100 and 10,000. The military organization of the state of Ch'i [in Shantung] showed the same method of counting.

Such were the differences between the Shang and Chou systems. After the fall of Shang the Chou people moved into the eastern part of North China as conquerors, and the two systems then co-existed among the two peoples. When Mencius [390-305 B.C.] advised Duke Wen of T'eng [in Shantung] on the well-field system, he said, "Let the one-ninth tax [chu 助] be instituted in the more remote parts of the country, and let the levy of one-tenth [fu 賦] be imposed in the more central parts of the country." The more central parts of T'eng were inhabited by the Chou people; the one-tenth tax, ch'e 徹 , involved what Mencius called fu 賦, a character which from its composition means the paying of military service and of sums for armaments. Such payments were the privilege of the con- querors, a practice still to be found in the time of the Six Dynasties [220-587 A.D.]. The periphery of T'eng, on the other hand, was inhabited by the conquered Shang people, who were responsible for the one-ninth tax in grain and cloth, known as the chu.

The parallel existence of the two tax systems continued until the end of the Spring and Autumn period, when an amalgamation took place. For instance, three changes took place in the tax sys- tem of the state of Lu [in Shantung] in 593, 590, and 482 B.C. Af- ter the last change, both the Shang and Chou peoples in the popula- tion were held responsible for the payment of a land tax as well as for military levies. In the state of Cheng [in Honan] a similar change occurred, as recorded in the Tso Chronicle for the year 542 B.C., when Tzu-ch'an instituted the fiscal reforms.

The result was the organizing of the original Shang well-field system into units that were counted by the decimal system. As shown in the Military Regulations, the system was as follows: 100 mou 畝 was to provide one man; three men were one wu 屋 , and three wu were one "well." Ten "wells" made one t'ung 通 , which was to provide one horse, thirty families, one warrior, and one foot soldier. Ten t'ung [100 "wells"] made one ch'eng 成 ; ten ch'eng [1,000 "wells"] made one chūng 終 ; and ten chūng [10,000 "wells"] made one t'úng 同 . The latter comprised 100 square li 里 , and had to provide 30,000 families, 100 chariots, 1,000 warriors and 2,000 foot soldiers. Thus, the well-field

institution was re-organized on a decimal basis, and was gradually
losing ground even [in the original Shang territory] in eastern North
China.

6. The Well-Field and the
Granting of Fiefs

After receiving their fiefs the feudal aristocrats heaped up earth
into mounds and planted trees on them as border marks. This practice is plainly indicated by the form of the word for feng 封 ["fief"]
in the oracle bones and bronze inscriptions. When earth was heaped
up into mounds, it follows that ditches were made at their bases.
Therefore the "fief establishment" was sometimes called "ditch-
enfeoffment" and "ditch-establishment." A similar practice is maintained by the Mongols, who sometimes heap up a stone pile, called
obo, in the desert to mark boundaries. This seems to point to the
fact that the making of mounds had originated in hunting and pasto--
ral times. At that time the land was covered with wild growth and
high mounds and deep ditches were the only means by which boundary lines could be made visible.

Thus, the granting of fiefs occurred in the time of hunting and
pastoralism. The square borderlines in hunting areas served as
enclosures for animals in the hunt, and as fief boundaries in regard
to enfeoffment. It follows that ancient fiefs were marked out in
square shapes. This was also the best way to insure against wastage of land on the vast Yellow River plain. Therefore in the feudal
period the fiefs of the nobility were referred to in terms of "so
many square li." With the rise of agriculture the practice of division
into square areas was continued and led to the establishment of the
well-field. Thus, the square shape of the well-field was evolved
from the systems of the hunting society, and not due to anyone's
accidental "bean-cake"-like [i.e. rectangular] design.

The terms mou 畝 , lung 壟 ["dyke"], ch'iu 邱 ["mound"], and
ch'ien-mo 阡陌 ["paths between fields going north and south, east
and west, respectively"] used in the Chou, Ch'in, and Han periods
were relics of enfeoffment in the times of the hunting economy.
That they pertained to the division of land into square areas is testified by many passages in [the ancient dictionary] Erh-ya and the
Book of Poetry describing the straightness of the roads made up
from the paths and dykes, and also by the due north-south or due
east-west directions of the roads.

It has been maintained that the square shape of the "well" was
unnatural. The fact is that the system was used only on the broad
plains of North China, while in regions where the natural terrain

was unsuited to such rigid markings other systems were used. The hills, forests, marshes, and coastal areas were under the control of special officers [who were not concerned with the well-field system]. The sacrificial fields of fifty mou, and the fields of twenty-five mou allotted to men who were beyond the eight-member norm of a household, both of which are mentioned by Mencius, were also field divisions that were not square. In other words, land boundaries followed both artificial and natural lines. Furthermore, the well-field system was limited to the former Shang counties and baronies in the lower Yellow River region. It is erroneous to hold that it was either a generally prevalent system or a utopian dream of the ancients.

The Shuo-wen makes the further error of confusing the "well" of "well-field" with the "well" of "well-spring." Actually they are words of different origins. This is evidenced by the inscriptions on the oracle bones, in which "field" was often represented by the character 田 , a square enclosing nine subdivisions of space, and "well-spring" was represented by the character 井 , the dot indicating the center of the shallow wells of antiquity that resembled animal traps. Hence it is that the characters for "trap" contain the "well" component. The early existence of the confusion between the two is indicated by the Book of Changes, in which the well-field and the well-spring were made to appear as identical characters with different meanings. But from the later significance of chǐng "well" as "orderly," from the word keng 耕 ["to plow, to farm"], and from a number of characters pronounced hsíng which were derived from it (e.g. 刑 "criminal law," 形 "shape," 型 "type"), we may conclude that the bean-cake-like well-field actually had existed in ancient times.

7. Landed Estates and the Periodic Exchange of Land

Agriculture flourished during Chou. However, it was not intensive but extensive agriculture, with the people moving elsewhere once the resources of a cultivated area were exhausted. Therefore the Chou people had such distinctions as "year-old land," "two-year land," and "three-year land." References to these appear in the Book of Poetry, the Book of History, and the Book of Changes, and were defined by Ehr-ya among other sources.* It seems that

---

*Most sources agree that the terms were as follows: "year-old land," tzu 菑 ; "two year land," hsin 新 ; "three year land," yü 畬 . This is also the definition that seems to have been favored by the author. A commentary in the Book of Rites, however, differs in defining "two-year land" as yü, and "three year land" as hsin.

the area under cultivation had to be shifted at least once every three
years, a custom that was continued down to the Spring and Autumn
period.

With the shifting of fields the people's dwellings also had to
change. The Book of Poetry mentions "a hut in midfield." Other
sources bring forth the evidence that the Chou people lived in huts
in their fields during spring and summer. During autumn and winter
they lived in loess caves before their eastward conquests, and in
cities of their own construction after moving east.

The Kung-yang Chronicle describes the division of the 900 mou
of a "well" as follows: each of the eight families in a "well" had
100 mou for their own cultivation, worked ten mou as the lord's
land, and had two and one-half mou for the building of huts. It also
reports that the people lived out in the fields during spring and summer, and went in to protect their cities during autumn and winter.
The same was recorded in the section on "Food and Money" in the
Han History.

A great deal of land was needed for fallow and new land in this
extensive agriculture. The uncultivated land was ownerless and was
known as "gathering ground" because the people gathered wild vegetables there to supplement their diet. Now all other land belonged
to the rulers, so that when estates were given to the ministers and
tai-fu 大夫 [i.e. the minor lords], the "gathering land" was the only
source available. Hence the estates became known as "gathering
land." The estate owners then brought together people to cultivate
the land for them, and lived off the rent from it; the grants were
therefore known as "provision estates." This resembles the practice of present-day Mongol princes who live on rent from their Chinese tenant farmers.

With the "gathering land" put under cultivation the supply of unused land became scarce, and the problem arose of land exchange.
Consequently, the periodic exchange of land was instituted. Under
this system land was classified into three categories--good, medium, and poor. Good land was cultivated every year, medium land
every other year, and poor land one out of every three years. As
to the actual method of exchange, various sources differ in their
interpretations. The Kung-yang Chronicle seems to indicate that
exchange was to take place once every three years between those
having different grades of land so as to equalize the benefits; on
such occasions the people's dwellings also would change. Tuan's
commentary on the Shuo-wen, on the other hand, holds that the
changes took place every year, so that in three years a person
would have cultivated all three grades of land, and at the end of the
three-year cycle each person would have rotated back to his original place.

This shifting of the population from poor to better land was carried over into the policy of population removals after the Chou conquest of eastern North China, where the land was more fertile than
that of the western parts. In the process the conquered Shang people
were moved west, that is from a fertile to a less fertile area. In
effect this was similar to exile in later ages. The Book of Poetry
plainly indicates that the Shang people when moved west were still
given land and dwellings--a proof that it was a manifestation of the
periodic exchange of land. The practice was later continued by
Ch'in during its conquests. However, as the latter's forces got farther and farther away from the original area of Ch'in [in Shensi],
there was evident among its people a reluctance to move. Therefore in order to carry out the policy of land exchange it was necessary for the Ch'in government to grant noble ranks to those who
moved, or to send pardoned convicts to the new areas. After the
founding of the dynasty occurred the celebrated removal of the
120,000 wealthy families of Chou to Shensi, and other large-scale
removals. It is plain that the exchange of land was considered a
usual practice, although it was an ancient custom.

The exchange of land was also instituted in the state of Chin as
an emergency measure. Good crown land was granted to the ministers as a means of rallying them in a state crisis. Again, when
Shang Yang was the minister of Ch'in, he took the fiefs of the ruling
house and distributed them among meritorious military officers,
so that the legal status and way of life of the aristocracy and the
common people were determined by their military merits alone.
Almost identical measures were instituted by Tzu-ch'an in the state
of Cheng, beginning in 542 B.C. This resulted in Tzu-ch'an's being intensely hated by the aristocrats, who vented their anger in
ditties wishing for his death.

Beginning with the authors of the Early Han History, it has been
held by historians that Shang Yang was responsible for the destruction of the well-field system. Actually he merely based his measures
on the old custom of exchange of land, but the result was a thorough
breakdown of the old feudal aristocracy. Because status was determined by military merit, the erstwhile aristocrats became equal
with the common people and were subject to legal sanctions. The
rigid feudal class system was thus destroyed, and a new class of
wealthy landlords began to emerge. Therefore the effect of Shang
Yang's reforms was the destruction of the feudal class structure
and not of the well-field system.

Tzu-ch'an and Shang Yang introduced a revolution by forcing the
aristocrats to accept the [common people's practice of] exchange
of land; this earned their enmity and led to Shang Yang's death.

However, the need for land still existed. It was at this juncture that the method whereby a person rotated his land without change of residence was put into practice. According to the Rites of Chou, land that did not need to lie fallow was allotted at the rate of 100 mou per household; land that was to be cultivated once every other year, 200 mou per household; and land cultivated once every three years, 300 mou per household. The Rites of Chou, being a compendium of the various practices during the Spring and Autumn and Warring States periods, deals with both the well-field system and the land exchange and rotation system that were based on decimal organizations.

The Lü-shih ch'un-ch'iu states that in the state of Wei [in Shansi] the rate of land distribution was 100 mou [per family]. Yeh [in northern Honan], having poorer land, had a 200 mou rate. That the rate could be fixed at 100 mou in Wei meant that the land was good land which could be cultivated without rotation. It signified the existence of intensive agriculture in this area. Subsequently agricultural techniques, notably that of irrigation, steadily improved in Ch'in and Chin. During this transitional period, however, the practice of rotation still prevailed in areas where the land was medium or poor. According to "Food and Money" in the Early Han History, Chao Kuo [active in the reign of Emperor Wu] initiated a method whereby each mou of land was divided into three parts, with each part cultivated in annual rotation. This was known as the "fallow" or "alternate" system in the Han dynasty. At this time also the place of residence had become fixed. Passages in the Book of Poetry describing the wives of farmers sending food to the latter working in the fields seem to indicate that the rotation of land no longer entailed a change in residence.

8. Ch'e and kung 貢 Taxes

From his very vague description of the kung, chu, and ch'e taxes, it appears that even Mencius was unable to know the detailed distinctions among these taxes.

With an extensive agriculture that changed little down to the Spring and Autumn period, and with the continued use of caves as dwelling places, the economy of Chou was quite simple. The Book of History records that King Wen [father of the founder of the Chou dynasty] himself worked in the fields. This was due to the fact that in early agriculture the people were able to produce barely enough for subsistence, and had little surplus to pay the king as taxes. The staple crop was millet, which indicates a primitive agrarian economy. The taxes paid by the Chou people in the early days were probably less than one-tenth.

The original home of the Chou people was an area in the west,
where the terrain, unlike that of lower Yellow River valley, was
rough and hilly. From the inscription on the San bronze salver,
dated in the reign of King Li [prior to 841 B.C.], the following information can be deduced on the land situation in San and Mei,
south of the Wei River in modern southwestern Shensi, though the
full meaning of the inscription has not yet been deciphered: After
the conquest of San the King of Chou moved the local population
from that region, where the terrain was hilly, to Mei and gave
them land there, exchanging their former land for new land in units
of 1,000 mou. The latter was an indication of the decimal system
of Chou. One thousand mou was the land allottment of ten men,
and also was related to the ch'e tax, which was computed on the
basis of 100 mou.

The poem "Hsi-hsi" in the Book of Poetry describes King
Ch'eng [11th century B.C.] leading 10,000 men to farm in a thirly-
li area. Thirty li square was equivalent to the allotments of 10,000
men. When such a large area consisted entirely of the people's
land, the well-field system obviously could not have existed.

The ch'e tax followed the expansion of the royal Chi family [of
Chou] into other parts of China. Mencius' advice to Duke Wen of
T'eng on the one-tenth tax was one example. Another was the ac-
count of the enfeoffment of the Earl of Shen [in Honan]:

> The king gave charge to the Earl of Shao
> To institute the ch'e tax in the territory of the Earl of Shen.*

The states of Lu [in Shantung] and Han [in Shensi] were other instances.

Actually, there was no tangible line of demarcation between the
system of one period of the feudal society and that of another.
Where the Chou people went, the ch'e tax was introduced; where
the Shang people lived, the chu system was retained. It would be
an error to interpret Mencius' somewhat ambiguous account as
though the systems of Hsia, Shang, and Chou were entirely unconnected affairs.

There is evidence that the kung tax or "tribute" also existed in
Chou. There were several kinds. From accounts in the Tributes
of Yü we may gather that the "local kung" was a tribute of local
specialities paid by local rulers to the king. All the feudal rulers
of Chou had the obligation of paying "legal" tribute to the king;

---

*We here translate according to the apparent intent of the author. Legge has a
somewhat different rendering. He suggests, in addition, that the Earl of Shao was
Minister of Works under King Hsüan, and that the event described here refers to
colonization and the setting up of a new state, called Shen. (The Chinese Classics,
IV, 535-537)

this consisted mainly of supplying a labor force and provisions in
times of war. They also paid annual or periodic tributes to the
king, the amount being determined by the rank of the noble. Tribute
also was paid by tai-fu to the rulers of states. From the above it
is clear that kung was an affair of the aristocrats, and not a tax
paid by the common people. It was during the Warring States period
and the Ch'in and Han dynasties, when the [old] aristocracy had
been brought down to the level of the common people, that kung became a general name for the dues paid to the government by the
people.

As to the chu and ch'e taxes, their rates had begun to exceed
two-tenths at the end of the Spring and Autumn period. The Tso
Chronicle records that in 543 B.C. there was mention of the
people's paying two-thirds of their crop to the ruler in the state
of Ch'i. It seems that with the advancement of agriculture there
were parallel increases in the rate of taxation from one-tenth to
two-tenths and up to over one-half of the crop.

9. Land System and Colonization
of the Frontier Peoples

Chinese administrative policy regarding the frontier peoples
since the T'ang and Sung dynasties--the system of local chieftains
and self-rule, and the periodic payment of tributes--strongly resembled ancient feudalism. Various reports also reveal that the
frontier peoples, such as the Li-shu in southeastern Yunnan, still
practiced extensive agriculture accompanied by the per capita allotment of land, a system with many features similar to the well-
field system.

There is evidence that the land system outside Pyongyang in
Korea was very close to the systems of Shang and Chou. From descriptions written during the Ch'ien-lung period [1736-1795] the
"bean-cake" divisions of land still obtained there at that time;
this was apparently an old custom preserved among the northeastern tribes. Again, the land system under the Manchu Banner administration also showed a similar way of division by precise per
capita allotments.

A close parallel to the ancient system of allotments existed in
the land system of the Inca empire in South America. The same
was true of the Maya and Aztec land systems in Central America.
These seem to be additional proof that the ancient Chinese "well-
field" system and the "allotment of 100 mou per man" were not
just fabrications of later generations, since similar devices can
also be found in the history of other peoples.

10. Concluding Remarks

I have found that there is an immense body of information on social history hidden in Chinese etymology, which, when explored, can add much to our knowledge of ancient history and can be of assistance to sociologists.

According to sociologists, the life of early peoples was primitive and maintained on a subsistence level. Yet the Confucianists have established a tradition that glorified the institutions of Hsia, Shang, and Chou, especially the well-field system that allotted land on a per capita basis. While the Chinese could not have been an exception to the general law of social progress, there still, nevertheless, must be some explanation for the land distribution under the well-field system, if it was not mere fabrication of the Confucianists.

The well-field system first appeared in outline in Mencius and Chou-Kuan [i.e. the Rites of Chou], with more details gradually added to it in such works of the Han period as the Kung-yang Chronicle, Ku-liang Chronicle, and others. However, there were still gaps in the information, and in later ages no one was able to prove its existence by actual demonstration. Those in Chinese history who advocated the application of the allotment principle, such as Wang Mang [9-24 A.D.], the Northern Wei dynasty [386-535], and the Taiping régime [1850-1864], either failed in the attempt, or did not actually apply it, or did it only for temporary and specific purposes. For this reason Emperor Ch'ien-lung concluded that it was an impossible task for his government to attempt.

Though knowledge of the well-field system remained inconclusive, it was not until 1919 that its very existence was questioned by scholars, when Hu Shih expressed doubt on Hu Han-min's thesis that the well-field had really existed in antiquity. Soon a large number of scholars were involved in the controvery. Their debates were published in a special volume* in 1930, but neither side was able to gather sufficient evidence to prove the system's existence or non-existence. The present article has tried to throw some light on the subject by exploring the rich historical material contained in Chinese etymology. The land systems of the frontier peoples, and that of the Incas, also help to point to the fact that the accounts in Mencius and the Rites of Chou were not mere fantasies.

---

*Ching-t'ien chih-tu chih yu-wu (Discussion on the Existence of the Well-Field System). Shanghai: Hua-t'ung Book Co.

NOTES

徐中舒，"井田制度探源"，中國文化研究彙刊
Hsü Chung-shu, "Ching-t'ien chih-tu t'an-yüan," Bulletin
of Chinese Studies, IV, Part I (September, 1944), 121-156.

This article reveals something of what can be unearthed
by a specialist in etymology, but also displays the weakness
of excessive reliance on this approach, as when the author
attempts to date the creation of the gulf between Manchuria
and Shantung by literary rather than geological criteria. The
results of the attempt to draw parallels between the early
Chinese land system and that of other early societies are also not conclusive. Despite its shortcomings, the article presents a stimulating interpretation of the well-field problem.

2

SOME AGRICULTURAL IMPLEMENTS OF
THE EARLY CHINESE

by

HSÜ CHUNG-SHU

The oracle bones and bronze inscriptions both contain the character lei 耒 either as a radical or as an individual ideograph. There are somewhat different forms of the character, but the essential feature is plainly indicated in all. Passages in early works describe the use of the lei as a digging fork and also indicate its measurements.

The lei was made with a single handle and a forked, pointed end. Some ancient coins of about the Spring and Autumn period likewise had such ends in imitation of the agricultural tools. Early pictorial representations of the lei also reproduce these characteristics. From the oracle bone inscriptions it would appear that the lei was made of wood. Wooden lei survived until the time of Western Han. Bronze lei came into being at some time later than the date of the oracle bones.

The character ssu 㠯 , on the other hand, does not appear in the oracle bones. It does appear, however, in bronze inscriptions, where it has many variant forms. These show that some ssu were made of wood and others of metal. The main difference between the ssu and the lei was that the former had one single blade and the latter a forked blade. The shape of the ssu can also be detected through ancient coins. The ssu seems to have been the forerunner of the later hoe, of which the closest relatives are probably the various Japanese hoes.

Written sources are not consistent as to whether or not all agriculturalists needed to have both lei and ssu. But from various sources it can be concluded that (a) the lei was customarily used by the Shang people in the east, and was taken over by the states in the east after the defeat of the Shang dynasty; (b) the ssu was customarily used by peoples in the western part of China, and continued to be widely used in the Wei river region [in Shensi] after these peoples moved east.

Ancient coins with forked ends circulated in the area which during the Warring States comprised the states of Hán [in Shensi-Honan-
Shansi], Chao [in Shansi-Hopei]; Wei [in Honan-Shansi], Eastern
and Western Chou [in Honan], and Sung [in Honan]. It was here then
that the lei prevailed. From other sources we also learn that the
lei was used in the territories of Ch'i [in Shantung] and Yen [in
Hopei].

The fact that the character ssu does not occur in the oracle bones
shows that the ssu was not a Shang implement. Yet it can be established that agriculture in western China did not lag behind that of
the east at that time. The point is that the people in the west independently developed their own agricultural implement, the ssu.
It was the development of the lei and the ssu which made possible
the advances in agriculture in both eastern and western China.

In later ages lei and ssu were often incorrectly taken to be the two
parts of the same ploughing implement. The confusion began even
before Mencius mentioned "lei ssu" as though it were a compound
word. But a study of bronze inscriptions establishes beyond a doubt
that the two words had separate origins. The confusion arose out
of the existence of wooden lei toward the end of Shang dynasty, while
the Chou people in the west were already casting metal ssu. Consequently people mistook lei to be the wooden handle and ssu the metal
share of the same instrument. It is significant to note that it was
after the Chou people had developed this advanced metal implement
that they were able to increase agricultural production to a high
level.

A study of the written records reveals that the earth was dug up
with a lei by stepping on the upper unforked part and pushing it into the earth; this was called t'ui 推 ["push"]. Then the broken earth
was pushed forward as the lei was removed; this was called fa 墢
["to amass"]. A series of such repeated movements would turn
over the sod in a field and prepare it for planting. One account mentions the participation of the king, feudal lords, and officials in
the Spring, with the king allotted the least number of "pushes."

Before the period of the Warring States better results were
sought in "pair-ploughing," a system in which two men worked together with two ploughs. These men were also responsible for the
preparation of the tools beforehand so as to avoid confusion in work.
This system was easy to preserve in a society with fixed stratification of social and economic classes, wherein the agriculturalists were a hereditary class and static social conditions did nothing to change the method of ploughing. However, the gradual disintegration of the strict class system after the Warring States
tended to destroy pair-ploughing. By and large it had disappeared
in its original form during the Han dynasty.

The use of oxen in agricultural work was a relatively late development in all parts of the world. When oxen were mentioned in
ancient records for the Shang and early Chou periods they were used
to draw carts. Ploughing by oxen did not exist even at the time when
the Rites of Chou was written. There has been a historical controversy as to whether ploughing with oxen was invented by Chao Kuo
of the [western] Han dynasty or had existed earlier. Chia Ssu-hsieh
of Later Wei in his Essentials for the Common People and Chia
Kung-yen of the T'ang dynasty held the former view. Others, such
as Yeh Meng-te and Chou Pi-ta of Sung, held that it had existed
before that time, but that Chao Kuo probably popularized it. However, the written sources used by Chou Pi-ta were either unreliable or were misinterpreted by him. From available evidence we
can only conclude that ox-ploughing had been invented before Han,
but not any earlier than the beginning of the Warring States period
[fifth century B.C.].*

With the coming of ox-ploughing lei and ssu became only supplementary tools, but they did not entirely disappear. They survived
in the form of several later implements having different names,
as for example the curved-handle shovel and the long hoe mentioned in writings of the T'ang dynasty. However, by the Yüan dynasty these surviving forms had also become still less important
as major agricultural implements.

NOTES

徐中舒, "耒耜考", 歷史語言研究所集刊

Hsü Chung-shu, "Lei ssu k'ao," Bulletin of the Institute of History and Philology, II (1930), 11-59.

This article is extensively documented and copiously illustrated.
Many characters are reproduced from the oracle bones and the
bronze inscriptions. A detailed translation or summary is impossible without reproducing these illustrations. Hence only a brief
summary of the article has been presented.

For some further comments on this article and reproduction of
illustrations from it, the reader is referred to L.C. Hopkins, "The
Cas-Chrom v. the Lei ssu. A Study of the Primitive Forms of the
Plough in Scotland and Ancient China," Journal of the Royal Asi-
atic Society, Oct., 1935, pp. 707-716; Jan., 1936, pp. 45-54.

*Arthur Waley disputes Hsü's dating of the introduction of ploughing with oxen.
He doubts that there is any literary evidence earlier than a passage in the Han His-
tory which refers to ploughing with oxen as occurring about 90 B.C. (A. Waley,
"Note on the Iron and Plough in Early China," Bulletin of the School of Oriental and
African Studies, XII, Parts 3 and 4 [1948], 803-804.

3

FEUDAL SOCIETY OF THE CHOU DYNASTY

by

CHANG YIN-LIN

1. Introduction

The present article will describe the society of Chou for the period from about the eleventh to the fifth century B.C. The structure of the society of this period, for which comparatively detailed knowledge is available, laid the foundation of Chinese social history.

Strictly speaking, the word "feudal" applies principally to territory which is nominally ruled by a royal house, but which is actually divided into small sections, each having its hereditary political overlord who is also the owner of the land. Such was unquestionably the situation in the Chou dynasty, when the king had exclusive control over only his royal demesne, the rest of the land being granted to a number of states. Within each state, and in the royal demesne itself, only part of the land was the personal fief of the ruler, the rest being granted to a number of minor lords. Within his own territory each minor lord had his own tax system, labor force, army, followers, and capital city.

On the basis of their origin, there were three kinds of states: (a) Those which the king of Chou established from conquered territory at the beginning of the dynasty and placed under his own relatives, such as the states of Ch'i [in Shantung], Lu [in Shantung], and Chin [in Shansi]. These states showed the strongest support of the dynasty through the Spring and Autumn period. (b) Those established, long after those of group one, by subdivision of the original royal demesne. Ch'in [in Shensi] and Cheng [in Honan] belonged to this group. (c) Those which survived from the previous dynasty and surrendered their independence to Chou without having been conquered, such as Sung [in Honan], Hsü [in Anhwei], and Ch'u [in the Yangtse valley].

The minor lords in the royal demesne were almost exclusively members of the ruling house. Within the various states the lords originally came also from the sovereign's clan, but this exclusive

system began to break down some time in the seventh century B.C.
For example, Kuan Chung and Yen Ying, two famous ministers in
the time of the Ch'i dukes Huan [651-643 B.C.] and Ching [547-
490 B.C.], were not of the ruling house, and by the time of Duke
Mu [659-621 B.C.] "professional officials" were already extensively employed in Ch'in.

Minor lords in the states were called tai-fu 大夫, the highest
rank being that of the "minister." A state could have a maximum
of six ministers. By the Spring and Autumn period tai-fu did not
all possess land grants; Confucius is a case in point.

The family of a tai-fu was designated by the special term shih 氏.
This term could only be applied to the aristocracy, in contrast to
the "surname," which was used by every individual. Men were
known by their shih, and women by their surnames. After Ch'in
and Han the two terms became identical in meaning.

The structure of Chou society was as follows: The top stratum
consisted of the Chou king and the various feudal lords; next came
the officials andwarriors; next the common people, consisting primarily of farmers; and last of all came the slaves owned by the
aristocrats.

2. Slaves

Detailed and exact information on slavery is still lacking. Some
records exist of the granting of slaves; for instance, we learn that
as many as 1,000 families of Northern Barbarian slaves were given
to an official for his military exploits by Duke Ching [599-581 B.C.]
of Chin.* The wealthy tai-fu of the large states probably possessed
over 10,000 slaves.

The primary source of slaves was war. Except for a few who
were used for sacrificial purposes, most of the war captives became the victors' slaves. The joint campaign of the kingdoms of
Wu, Lu, and Chou against Ch'i in 484 B.C. yielded a booty of 800
war chariots and 3,000 warriors. The desire to acquire slaves
sometimes motivated acts of aggression. Slaves often constituted
the tributes offered by minor to major states, or by rulers of states
to the Chou king. Ransoms sometimes were paid, but they probably
involved only prominent persons among the captives. Aside from
war captives, convicts also became slaves.

One function of slaves was to serve as household servants. A

---

*We here follow the apparent intent of the author in rendering Ti ch'en as "North-
ern Barbarian slaves." James Legge (Chinese Classics, V, 329) has a quite different understanding of the passage, as indicated by his statement that the official was
rewarded "with the revenues of a thousand families with which the Ti ministers had
been endowed..."

more important function was production. Every feudal household, from the king down to the official, was a self-sufficient economic unit. Slaves produced all the necessary goods, from food, clothing, salt, and timber to chariots, weapons, and musical and ritual implements. Labor was supervised by a special official, and each craft again had its own superintendent. For example, the Chou king had a "Superintendent of Pottery."

Skilled slaves sometimes were used as gifts. All slaves could be mortgaged or sold, and the masters had the power of life or death over them. For instance, Duke Hsien [676-652 B.C.] of Chin once used a slave as a taster of food which had already poisoned a dog. It is difficult to determine, however, what proportion of those buried alive with the dead consisted of slaves.

All the members of a slave's family were themselves slaves. The status of slave was hereditary, and only under highly exceptional circumstances could a slave be freed. We find only two such incidents in recorded history within this period, apart from the common occurrence of newly enslaved prisoners being ransomed by their state.

3. Peasants

//In our above account of the life of slaves we left aside a very important question: What was the relationship between slaves and agriculture? In other words, what was the position of the majority of agriculturalists? Material is very incomplete on this point, and our present statements are mostly drawn from indirect inferences.

//Let us imagine the head of the [royal] Chi and Chiang clans in the course of founding the Chou dynasty leading their followers into the new territories in successive groups, occupying the cities, partitioning the land, and becoming lords and tai-fu. Of the land they occupied, a small portion was set aside for development by themselves; such land was tilled by slaves and the income was entirely appropriated by the lords. These were the so-called "public fields." The remaining major portion of the land continued to be cultivated by the peasants originally there, but exactions of grain, cloth, and corvée were imposed on them; tenancy was hereditary but not salable or transferable to others. These were the so-called "private fields." All fiefs probably included both public and private fields, but a few might consist only of private fields. The K'o ting-tripod of Western Chou records the Chou king as making seven grants of land, yet in only one of them is it specified "give unto him slaves and slave women." This indicates that in Western Chou the practice of granting serfs with land was already uncommon.

// Peasants working on private fields were the so-called common people. Their status was somewhat higher than that of the slave, but their life was no better. Though there were fixed quotas for the levies of grain and cloth, these certainly would not be low; in the Spring and Autumn period the tax of [only] a tithe still remained an unattainable ideal. Aside from the regular levies, the peasants had to make special contributions to weddings and other festivals in the nobleman's home. Moreover, labor corvée was an endless obligation, and the peasant's spare time was ordinarily all spent on jobs for the noblemen. If the latter wanted to build palaces, pleasure gardens, ancestral shrines, or city walls, the people could be conscripted at all times for hard labor. If a nobleman wanted to engage in warfare, the people had to provide him with supplies as well as with their own lives. In famine years their lot was worse than that of the slaves, who had some support, and in most cases "the old and weak starved in ditches, while the strong dispersed in all directions."

// The folk poem "Seventh Month" of the Western Chou period describes in detail the life of serfs on public land in the region of Pin (modern Pin-hsien, Shensi). According to this poem, a serf's daily life is as follows: In the first month he receives agricultural implements. In the second month ploughing begins; his wife sends his meals to the field, and the "field foreman" also comes with a smiling face. At the same time his daughter goes along the paths between the fields to gather mulberry leaves with a basket. In the eighth month the harvest is begun. At the same time the daughter is busy reeling off silk, which after being reeled is dyed black, yellow, or red to provide for the lord's clothing. In the tenth month rice is gathered, and wine is made in order to pray for the lord's longevity next spring. After the harvesting is all done, the peasants go to work in the lord's home, gathering thatch during the day and making rope at night. In the same month thanksgiving ceremonies and convivial parties take place, lambs are cooked, and everyone goes to present wine to the lord, shouting cries of "long life!" In the eleventh month they hunt for foxes to provide fur for the lord. In the twelfth month peasants receive military training together. In this month fattened pigs are presented to the lord, and ice is chopped and stored for the lord's use in the following spring and summer.*

// The poem "Seventh Month" was used by the aristocrats for musical entertainment, and must therefore have conformed to their taste. How properly content were the peasants in the poem to lead

---

*The material presented here does not follow exactly the text of this ode. Compare Legge, The Chinese Classics, IV, 226 ff.

an existence like horses and oxen! But the peasants and other common people sometimes did not behave properly when the aristocrats proved too callous toward their sufferings. King Li [878-
842 B.C.], the tenth monarch of Chou, lost his throne in a popular uprising when he was chased out of the capital. Feudal lords
whose fate was similar to that of King Li or worse appear continuously in the written records. In 634 B.C., during the rivalry for
power between the great states of Chin and Ch'u, the ruler of
Wèi, having offended Chin, decided to adopt a pro-Ch'u policy.
But Wèi was situated closer to Chin, and a pro-Ch'u policy would
invite frequent invasions by Chin, in which case the first to suffer would be the peasants. Even if they were fortunate enough to
escape death or captivity in war, upon their return home they would
find their crops cut down by the enemy, trees felled, houses burnt,
and even the wells filled. Thus the Wèi ruler's pro-Ch'u policy
conflicted basically with the welfare of the Wèi people. The latter started a great revolt, and drove the ruler into exile.∥

There are many more instances of popular revolts in the various states around the sixth century B.C. against oppressive
princes.

∥The recorded uprisings were the successful ones, wherein
the position and life of the aristocracy were affected. There were
probably many others that were unsuccessful and unrecorded. At
that time the common people were gradually asserting themselves,
and many an alert official began to recognize the importance of the
populace. They exerted themselves to give favors to the people and
rallied them for their own support, so as to strengthen their own
houses, weaken the ruling houses, and even take over the ruler's
position.∥

A number of historical incidents illustrate the foregoing statement. For instance, during the rule of Duke Ching of Ch'i [547-
490 B.C.] the peasants had to give up two-thirds of their harvest
as feudal dues, leaving only one-third for their own subsistence.
Thereupon the Ch'en family initiated the policy of granting grain
loans to the people with a new large measuring implement, but using the old small measure when receiving payments from the
people. This set the family in a favorable light in the latter's
eyes, and later the Ch'en family easily usurped the rule of Ch'i.
Similar cases occurred in several other states.

∥The above-mentioned people who participated in rebellions and
were utilized by the powerful families included of course various
groups of the common people. Among these the majority naturally
consisted of peasants; the remaining minority consisted of merchants and artisans. The major difference between the common

people and slaves was that the former could accumulate private
property and were free to change their place of residence. But actually the peasants seldom moved, except in times of famine. Although in the sixth century B.C. there existed in the memory of
the people the ancient tradition that "people should not move, and
farmers should not migrate," this nevertheless seems not to have
been an absolute restriction; tradition was after all distinct from
legal limitation.

4. Towns

//A place where people congregated to live was usually called
a "town." The towns can be divided into two main categories, the
walled and the unwalled. The walled towns again can be classified
into three groups: first, the capitals of the Chou king and of the
various states; second, the metropolises of feudal lords within
the royal demesne and the states; and third, the ordinary walled
towns.//
    The dimensions of the towns varied. Lo-yang, capital of East-
ern Chou, was said to have within its inner walls an area of 81
square li according to Chou measurement, which is equal to approximately 21.7 per cent of the area of modern Peking. The area
enclosed by the outer walls of Lo-yang was said to be twice the
area of modern Peking. Capital cities of states remained much
smaller until the end of the Spring and Autumn period. Towns of
officials were even smaller.
    Population statistics for the various cities are completely lack-
ing. But contemporary records indicate they were not densely
populated.
//When we consider the geographic distribution of the capitals of
the various states, a common feature is easily detected; so far as
we know, each one, almost without exception, was situated close
to some river. This was not necessarily for purposes of communi-
cation, since at that time the Yellow River was in this respect
more of a hindrance than a help. The main reason for the proximity of the capitals to rivers was the more fertile soil of river val-
leys, which made the food supply more dependable. The purpose
of a city was the protection of the life, property, and ancestral
shrines of the aristocrats. The principal inhabitants in a capital
city were the ruler and his guards, the artisans of the "hundred
crafts," and the ministers and tai-fu and their guards. Like the
royal court, most state courts had the following officials of importance: Grand Minister of War, in charge of military affairs;
Grand Minister of Crime, in charge of the judiciary and police;

Grand Minister of Finance, in charge of taxation and corvée; and
Grand Minister of Works, in charge of public works, such as the
construction of city walls, roads, and ancestral shrines [of the
ruling house]. Within the capital of a state the principal buildings
were as follows: The palace, pleasure gardens, hunting parks,
treasury and granaries, and ancestral temples of the ruler; the
she 杜 shrine for sacrificing to the God of Earth, and the chi 稷
shrine for sacrificing to the God of Grains; residences of the ministers and officials; and hostels provided for envoys of other states.
These buildings were located in the center of the city and were
surrounded by people's houses and market places. The markets
were most often found by the main streets close to the outer city
gates. Outside the outer gates were moats or ponds, the bridges
over which were probably movable. At the entrances of the outer
and inner city walls were "suspended gates" that could be raised
or lowered. The city gates were constantly guarded, and were
closed at night, with the guards "beating the watches" all night
long. Duties had to be paid on goods passing through city gates.
This constituted a large item of income for the ruler, who sometimes gave away as a gift the right of levying duties at a certain
city gate.

//Commerce at this time had in general not yet outgrown the barter stage. Shells were still used as a medium of exchange during
Western Chou. Inscriptions on bronze vessels of that period contain such records as "fourteen p'eng 朋 of shells were spent for the
casting of this precious vessel," and "thirty lieh 寽 of shells were
granted." A p'eng was probably a number of shells placed on a
string, and a lieh represented those strung into a circle. But shells
were not real money, for they were actually a kind of ornament,
either strung in a string or circle, or inlaid in implements or garments. Imitation shells made of bronze already existed in the Yin
period. Probably a circle of bronze shells was also called a lieh
(written with or without the "metal" radical), and the word lieh later
turned into a term for a unit of weight. In the inscriptions on
bronze vessels of Western Chou there were records of the granting of so many lieh or so many chün 鈞 (another measure of weight)
of "metal", i.e. bronze, and the imposing of a fine of so many
lieh of "metal." However, it seems that neither shells, nor bronze
computed in terms of lieh and chün, were widely circulated as
wealth. As late as the second half of the Spring and Autumn period
the various major or minor bribes which were given among the
states still consisted of land, chariots, horses, brocades, bronze
vessels, or jade articles, and not shells or "metal."

//The most convenient place for barter trade was the market

place. The so-called fair of this time was probably just some vacant land at the roadside where people periodically congregated. The "merchants" also were only itinerant peddlers who travelled between the various cities, the fixed, large shop apparently still not existing. Their merchandise consisted mainly of silk, hemp, cloth, and such agricultural products as grain, besides some products of family handicraft. Industry based on hired or slave labor had not yet emerged.∥

However, powerful wealthy merchants appeared in the large cities during the second half of the Spring and Autumn period at the latest. They were able to make bribes comparable to those of minor feudal lords, and sometimes succeeded in entering the preserve of the aristocracy, the field of politics. For example, in 627 B.C. a merchant of Cheng successfully turned back the invading army of Ch'in. Owing to a compact arrived at between the first sovereign of Cheng and the merchants, commerce enjoyed special protection and flourished in that state.

5. Marriage and Inheritance

Information on the life of the common people is lacking, since it had not been recorded by court historians. Only from folk songs is a certain aspect of the marriage system discernible: marriage had to be arranged by the parents and through the matchmaker. Socially men and women--at least among the aristocracy--were totally segregated. For example, in 506 B.C. a sister of the Duke of Ch'u insisted she could marry no other man than Chung Chien, because in helping her escape from the invading enemy he had carried her on his back and had therefore touched her.

A common phenomenon in aristocratic families was polygyny. In the families of the Chou king and the feudal rulers the custom prevailed whereby girls of a bride's house accompanied her to her husband's home. These girls, called ying 媵, were destined to become concubines. Other concubines could also be taken by the rulers. As a result intra-familial feuds and tragedies were frequent occurrences during the Spring and Autumn period.

∥The system of primogeniture prevailed among the aristocracy. (Ch'u, Ch'in, and Wu are known to have been exceptions to this rule. Ch'u used ultimogeniture at the beginning, and changed to primogeniture only in 630 B.C. Ch'in used fraternal succession, and changed to primogeniture after 620 B.C. Wu was subjugated in 473 B.C., but still practised fraternal succession through the first part of that century.) This system was frequently disturbed by internal strife of the ruling house--either the uncle usurped the

nephew's throne, or a younger brother replaced an elder brother,
or an elder brother replaced a younger brother. At the same time,
another contributing factor to internal strife lay in the ruler's giving special favor to the son of his favorite young concubine, thereby upsetting the institution of primogeniture. For example, the
above-mentioned Duke Hsüan of Wèi was killed by the followers of
[his sons] Chi-tzu and Shou-tzu [whom he had murdered].//

6. Warriors

Sacrificial ceremonies and warfare were the two most important
things in the aristocrat's life. Both were considered as of direct
concern to the existence of the state, and both required specialists
for their execution.

Specialists for war were called shìh 士 , a word originally designating a warrior and later a man of letters. The reason for these
diametrically opposed meanings goes far to explain one of the major differences between pre-Ch'in and post-Ch'in society. Throughout both periods the word referred to an educated person, but because the content of education changed from military skills to
literary pursuits, therefore the significance of the word also underwent change. The warrior's training included archery, chari-
oteering, the use of shields and spears, dancing, music, and ritual. Poems learned to music probably constituted the warrior's only literary education. Archery tournaments and group ceremonial
dances were important occasions for the warriors. In the former
certain rules of decorum had to be followed; the latter took place
mostly during sacrificial ceremonies or feasts, with each dance
having its particular narrative content, choreography, and musical accompaniment.

//The ideal warrior was supposed to be skilled in arms, possessed of the virtue of loyalty, willing to regard honor above safety
and duty above life, and always undaunted by adversity, even if
this meant going so far as to oppose overwhelming fate with his
mere body. Such was the tragic and magnificent spirit--a spirit
on which hung the life or death of nations--which was possessed
by the ancient warriors, although the object of their loyalty was
most often a single house or person. We give the two following
stories as illustrations.

//(a) During a war between the states of Lu and Sung in 684 B.C.,
the horse of Hsien-fen-fu, a chariot driver for a general [of Lu],
suddenly ran amok, causing the defeat of the Lu army. The Duke
of Lu fell to the ground, and when Hsien-fen-fu went to help him,
said, "This is because we did not have a divination." (Customarily

an officer's chariot-driver was chosen by divination before the battle.) Hsien-fen-fu answered, "We were not defeated on any other
day but today. It must be due to my lack of courage." Thereupon
he rushed into battle and was killed. Later, as the grooms were
cleaning the horses, they discovered an arrow in his horse. The
Duke of Lu, now realizing that the fault did not lie with Hsien-fen-
fu, ordered a eulogy to be written for him. This began the eulogiz-
ing of warriors after death.

// (b) In 480 B.C. there was internal strife in the state of Wèi, and
the minister, K'ung K'uei, was beseiged in his own house. One of
his household officials, Chi-lu (a disciple of Confucius), on hearing the news started out on a rescue mission singlehanded. On the
way he met a colleague who told him that such action was not required of him. Chi-lu replied, "Since I am employed by this person I ought to rescue him when he is in danger." When he reached
the K'ung house the gates were already barred, so he shouted
that he would burn down the house. Two professional fighters were
sent out by the men in the house, and in the subsequent fighting
Chi-lu was wounded in the head by a spear which also cut off the
tassel of his hat. Remarking that "A gentleman must not die losing his hat," he retied the tassel and then dropped dead.

// Sons of the king, feudal lords, and tai-fu received the education
of warriors. There was a "School Palace" in the royal household
where the prince and his aides learned archery, and in which the
Chou king and his officials also sometimes held archery tournaments. In addition there was an "Archery Hut" where the king
practised archery, music, and dances.

// The status of warriors was second only to that of tai-fu. They
possessed no fiefs, but had land for their own provisioning. In warfare the armored warriors rode in chariots and constituted the
main battle force. But under the warriors were large numbers of
rank-and-file soldiers. These were for the most part peasants
called up at times of need.

7. Religion

// The supernatural world of the Chou people is known to us in
more detail than that of Yin. Aside from the ancestors of the various families, there were gods of the sun, moon, and stars, who
controlled the seasonableness of snow, frost, wind, and rain, and
there were also gods of mountains and streams, who controlled
flood, drought, and plagues. But the most important ones on whom
people's lives depended were the God of Earth and the God of Grains.
The former had to do with the fertility of the soil, the latter with

the abundance of the crops. The God of Earth was called <u>she</u>* or
hou-t'u 后土 [i.e. Prince of Earth]; the God of Grains was called
<u>chi</u> or hou-chi 后稷 [i.e. Prince Millet]. The shrines where <u>she</u>
and <u>chi</u> were worshipped were likewise called <u>she</u> and <u>chi</u>. <u>Chi</u> was
merely one kind of grain, and its use as the name for the God of
Grains and the "Father of Agriculture" bespeaks the long-since
forgotten historical fact that millet was the first wild plant domesticated by man.

⫽ Just as feudal society was headed by a king, so were all the
gods ruled over by a Supreme God [shang-ti 上帝]. He was concerned with men's morality, and could reward the virtuous and
punish the evil. Like the king, however, he occupied a high position
but enjoyed little direct power, as he was seldom in touch with the
people's daily life, and did not require the people to go to expense
on his account. The sacrificial ceremonies for <u>shang-ti</u> were
called "Country Sacrifices"; according to historical records, only the Chou king and the Duke of Lu performed them. The term
<u>shang-ti</u> first appears in the Chou records. It seems that the con-
cept of <u>shang-ti</u> was the invention of the Chou people,** and therefore Country Sacrifices were performed only by the house of Chou
and its elder branch, the state of Lu. ⫽

The origin of the concept of the <u>shang-ti</u> is not known. The other
gods all had primitive origins, and were mainly anthropomorphous;
moreover, their positions in the supernatural world derived from
appointment by <u>shang-ti</u>, similar to enfeoffment.

<u>Chi</u>, the God of Grains, was regarded as the ancestor of the
Chou dynasty as well as the initiator of agriculture. It is not known
whether the Chou people had inherited the <u>chi</u> god, or had invented
this themselves. It is definitely known, however, that <u>she</u> was worshipped before Chou, and that in the capital of Lu there were
shrines for both the Chou <u>she</u> and the Yin <u>she</u>. We cannot ascertain,
however, whether the difference between these two shrines consisted of a difference in the gods worshipped, or in ritual only.

Each family from that of the king to the scholar-warrior had
its ancestral temple. There were two kinds: the "great temple,"
dedicated to all ancestors, and the "special temple," dedicated to
only one ancestor. The latter was destroyed after a certain number of generations. The <u>she</u> and <u>chi</u> shrines and the temples constituted the three sacred places of every capital city. Periodic sac-

---

*The character she社 was originally written t'u 土 [earth]; the 示 on the side
was a later addition. [Author's note].

**This is at variance with the view advanced by Herlee Glessner Creel in <u>The
Birth of China</u> (London, 1936), p. 342.

rificial ceremonies were performed with great solemnity. There
were also extemporaneous ceremonies on occasions that called
for them, such as sickness. Sacrifices to the spirits, such as animals, cloth, and jade, were in most cases actually destroyed,
and no substitutes were used. The major ceremonies, combining
grand architecture, dignity, colorful robes, dances, music, and
elaborate ritual, were extremely impressive affairs.

She was the god closest to the people. The annual grand ceremony of she occurred in the spring. Other sacrifices were performed at his shrine before and after battle and on the occasions
of flood, fire, eclipse of the sun, or insoluble legal disputes.

Besides these, there was a whole array of stray ghosts, spirits
of ancient heroes, etc., who acted through male and female mediums. Mediums often were supported by the feudal lords but they
did not become regular officials.

Four groups of officials at the courts of king and nobles were
specially assigned to deal with the supernatural. They were the
Officers of Prayer, the Officers of Ceremonies, the Diviners, and
the Historians. The head of each respective group in the Chou
court was called Grand Officer of Prayer, Grand Diviner, etc.;
the state courts had a similar system. From recorded incidents
we can infer that the Grand Diviner's position was very high in
the government, and that the Grand Historian was eligible for enfeoffment, which was presumably true also of the other three.
Lesser officers among the four groups were given land for their
own support; their holdings were sometimes large enough to invite forcible seizure by members of the ruling house. These four
categories of officials were needed for all major state affairs, and
their offices were hereditary. The result was that they became
highly respected officials at court.

8. Tai-fu

// The majority of feudal lords were of course the tai-fu. They
were the mainstay of the landlord-ruler class. Although the total
number of noble houses of the various states cannot be ascertained
for specific periods, yet we know that in Lu there were "three
houses of Huan" which descended from Duke Huan alone, and in
Cheng there were "seven houses of Mu" which descended from
Duke Mu. Around 609 B.C. there were at least twelve noble
houses in Sung. There were 48 "districts" in Chin around 537 B.C.;
of these nine alone had eleven noble houses. On the average, the
ratio between a ruling house and its noble houses was one to a
minimum of ten.

// The domain of a noble house was computed in terms either of
"town" [i 邑] or of "district" [hsien 縣]. When "town" was mentioned the land surrounding it was naturally included. A "district"
was originally a unit of land; when this term was used the city
lying within the area was included also.//

There is no definitive information as to the size of fiefs.
Records vary on this point. It seems that in small states only the
ministers could have as many as 100 "towns." In larger states,
however, transactions involving 300 "towns" were made.

The term "district" was used only in the large states like
Ch'in, Ch'i, Chin, and Ch'u during the Spring and Autumn period.
Originally it denoted a newly conquered territory, and "district
magistrates" were despatched from the sovereign's court to administer the area. This was the forerunner of the later centralized administrative divisions of commandery and district. In the
Spring and Autumn period, however, the district system was
neither uniform nor prevalent, and the sizes of districts varied
in different states. In states where neither districts nor commanderies were instituted, "administrators" were appointed by
the ducal and other great households for the management of their
fiefs.

// Now let us leave the digression and return to the noble houses
of the various states. Their land was originally all received from
the sovereign, who nominally remained the owner. People subordinate to the noble houses had the obligation of paying rent and
corvée only to them, but the noble houses had the obligation of
paying annual tribute and taxes to the sovereign; hence the saying
"the duke lives off tributes." The sovereign or administrators
could increase the quota of tribute, as illustrated by the following
incident: In 551 B.C. Tsang Wu-chung, the famous sage of Lu,
was sent on a mission to Chin. Caught by rain on his way, he
sought shelter with a tai-fu named Yü-shu, who was just then pre-
paring to drink some wine. Upon seeing Tsang Wu-chung, Yü-
shu said, "What's the use of being a sage? I'm happy with my
drinking. What good is there in being a sage, if one has to travel
even in the rain!" These words came to the knowledge of an administrator, who, considering that Yü-shu was an evil influence
in the state because he had held a state envoy in scorn though in-
capable of becoming one himself, as a punishment ordered Yü-shu's
tribute quota to be doubled.

// Tai-fu were free to dispose of their land. Some wealthy ones at
least set apart portions of their fiefs with which their younger
sons might establish new hereditary houses called "secondary lineage." Other persons favored by a tai-fu could also receive, or

petition for, land grants from him. For example, in 500 B.C.
Prince Ti of Sung gave five-elevenths of his fief to a favorite fol-
lower. Also, in 486 B.C. Hsü Hsia, the favorite of the tai-fu Wu-
tzu Sheng of Cheng, asked for a grant, but the latter had none to
give; Hsü then received permission to get it from some other
state, but when the Cheng army subsequently fought Sung at Yung-
ch'iu, it was completely annihilated. Tai-fu could also receive
land grants from tbe sovereign of another state. For example,
in 656 B.C., when Duke Huan of Ch'i led a joint campaign of several states against Ch'u, Shen-hou of Cheng proposed changing
the route of march on the way back, thereby greatly pleasing
Duke Huan, who granted the large Hu-lao district in Cheng to Shen-
hou. Also, in 657 B.C., when the tai-fu Tzu-shu Sheng-po of Lu
was sent on a mission to Chin, Ch'üeh-shuang, Minister of Chin,
wanted to give him a district as a means of influencing him, but
he refused. [....] Tai-fu also could desert to other states with
their fiefs. Thus in 547 B.C. Wu-yü of Ch'i took [his fief of] Lin-
ch'iu and fled to Chin.

// Aside from Fief Administrators, officials privately employed
by tai-fu were, so far as present knowledge goes, the Household
Manager in charge of household business, who was the equivalent
of the prime minister at the royal or ducal courts, the Officer of
Prayers, the Historian, the Director of Commerce in charge of
trade, and the Minister of War in charge of military matters. These
officials depended on the tai-fu for their livelihood. An estate was
granted to the Household Manager during his term of office; it was
to be returned to the tai-fu or handed over to the successor upon
retirement. A special code of morals prevailed among these
manorial officials: "A manorial official dares not administer state
affairs," and "It is the utmost crime for a manorial official to
exceed the lord's house in strength." //

No exact information exists for any period as to the comparative
military strengths of the noble, ducal, and royal houses. The
strength of the Chou court fluctuated, being very weak after the
move to the east [in 770 B.C.]. In the last part of the Spring and
Autumn period [562-482 B.C.] a first-rank state could command
a force of at least four or five thousand chariots, and a second-
rank state had at least one thousand. These figures were much
higher than that for the earlier period. As to the number of warriors per chariot, this is still an unsolved problem. Extant records
show that it ranged from three to thirty.

// Although nominally there was a difference in status between
the ducal houses and the noble families which possessed land,
people, and armies, actually they were opposing forces. The head

of a noble family acted as though he were the absolute ruler of a
certain area. The special powers of a ruler consisted only of the
following: (a) performing sacrifices on behalf of the entire state;
(b) receiving tributes from the noble house; (c) commanding the
armed forces of the state; and (d) granting and taking away fiefs
and ranks, and appointing and dismissing court officials. But in
most states, such as Lu, Ch'i, Chin, Sung, Wèi, and Cheng, the
strong noble houses sooner or later also gained control of the
last two powers.

9. Family and Clan

// Among the sons of a tai-fu only one could inherit his rank and
position. Of the others, one might establish a secondary lineage
and some others might be promoted to tai-fu by the sovereign.
But in the long run such opportunities could not but be limited. A
"fortunate" tai-fu would thus have a number of sons, not to speak
of grandsons and great-grandsons, who were without fiefs. Members of the subsidiary branches of the nobility who were closely
related to the hereditary tai-fu generally became his private officials or warriors; the distantly related became his plain soldiers
or common subjects. A tai-fu, his personal officials and subordinates, and his army thus constituted a big clan. Under his leadership the entire clan went with him when he went to war, and rebelled when he rebelled. His enmity toward another tai-fu became
the enmity between two clans. When he fled the state the clan
fled with him, and when he failed the entire clan might be destroyed.
// Under the noble houses were the common people, who lived in
clans. Above the nobles was the large clan composed of the ruler
of the state and the ministers and tai-fu bearing the same surname
[as the ruler]. Still above this was the large clan composed of the
Chou king and the feudal lords of the same name. In most cases
affinal relationships, equal [in significance] to lineal relationships,
existed between the Chou king and feudal lords of different names,
or among the latter themselves. It can be safely said that the
structure of this feudal society was based entirely on the clan-
family. //
    For a time, before the usurpation of Chin by the Hán, Chao,
and Wei families in 403 B.C., consanguinal and affinal relationships within the Chou political structure were sufficient to re-
strain the most disruptive forces against this feudal framework.
The status of the Chou king was thus preserved, and serious wars
also were averted between related states more than once, as in

the case of the withdrawal of the Ch'i army from Lu as a result of the persuasive arguments put forth by the Lu envoy. States ruled by sovereigns bearing the same family name seldom destroyed each other in the Spring and Autumn period. Within the states, usurping officials after seizing power usually established a puppet ruler in conformity to the idea of legitimacy.

∥Considerations arising out of consanguinal or affinal relationships faded with the lapse of time. Status differences between the sovereign and the subordinate were maintained by power; when that power was gone, the concept of status was nothing more than a paper tiger, which was bound to be torn apart. The more holes it had, the less influence it exercised. An organization depending solely on family relations and ruler-subordinate stratification of status for its support could not last long. How much more so, when we recall that for the Chou empire there were from the beginning both internal and external forces that could not be confined to these two concepts?∥

NOTES

張蔭麟, "周代的封建社會," 清華學報

Chang Yin-lin, "Chou-tai-ti feng-chien she-hui," The Tsing Hua Journal, X, 4 (Oct.; 1935), 803-836.

The principal source for this article is the Tso Chronicle (Tso chuan). Specific references for citations are given by the author in an appendix of footnotes.

Topical sub-headings have been added by us for the nine subsections demarcated by the author.

4

THE INVESTITURE CEREMONY OF CHOU

by

CH'I SSU-HO

1. Introduction

In the age of feudalism all land belonged to the king. The king
made grants of land to the feudal lords, the lords granted land
to the ministers and tai-fu 大夫 , and these in turn granted part
of their land to their followers and servants. These grants were
called fiefs. The making of the grants was accompanied by a solemn
ceremony called investiture. Further, because those who received
official positions were likewise given remuneration in land, the appointment of officials also involved an investiture ceremony. Owing to the lack of pertinent source material, the details of this
ceremony in ancient China were for many centuries not known to
students of antiquity. It was not until the ancient bronze implements had been unearthed in later ages that more exact knowledge
concerning the investiture ceremony became available. Thus the
Ch'ing scholar Chu Yu-fu, on the basis of information contained in
bronze inscriptions as well as in the written classics, was able to
write seven treatises on the various investiture ceremonies of Chou.
Nevertheless, his work still leaves many gaps to be filled. Yet a
clear idea of the functioning of the investiture ceremony is vital to
our understanding of feudalism in ancient times. It is the purpose
of the present study to attempt a fuller reconstruction of the investiture ceremony as an aid to those interested in the study of ancient
history.

In Europe during feudal times a ceremony called "investiture" was
also conducted on the occasion of enfeoffment. Although the details
of this ceremony varied according to time and place, the basic
elements were largely identical. Generally speaking, the European
procedure was as follows: The person to be enfeoffed knelt unarmed
in front of the one granting the fief and swore his loyalty to the latter until death. This was called the ceremony of "Homage" and of
the "Oath of Fidelity." The lord then formally conferred the fief

37

upon the grantee by the symbolic gift of a tree twig and a handful
of earth, signifying the land and forests granted, and by a light tap
on the investee's back, signifying the granting of the right to rule
in the fief. The lord also gave to the investee a formal order de-
tailing the latter's obligations and the amount of land and the number of households within the fief. This constituted the ceremony of
investiture.

After the ceremony had taken place, "feudal bonds" were
formally established between the invested one and the lord. Both
the seigneur, who was the lord, and the vassal had definite rights
and obligations with respect to each other. Such contractual relations were a special characteristic of feudal society. Briefly
stated, the vassal owed three kinds of obligations to the lord,
namely to give military service, to render advice, and to pay tribute. On the other hand the lord, aside from granting the fief to
the vassal, also had the obligations of protecting the latter and ad-
judicating his disputes with others. These contractual conditions
had to be strictly observed. If a vassal broke his contract the lord
could "forfeit" his fief, and if a lord broke his part of the contract
the vassal could "disavow" his relationship and transfer his services to another lord.

Since the feudal relationship was based on personal contract, its
duration was coincident with the lifetime of the two contracting
parties. Theoretically the lord was entitled to take back the fief
at the death of the vassal and grant it to some other person. This
was the practice in the early days of feudalism. As time went on,
however, the relationship gradually changed from the personal to
the hereditary. When a new lord acceded to the place of seigneur,
therefore, the vassal had to be invested anew by him. Likewise,
when a vassal died, his son and inheritor had to be reinvested by
the lord and to pay tribute to the latter. If the son had not yet come
of age the lord then was to manage his fief; the proceeds were to
go to the lord, who also arranged for the marriage of the vassal's
son.

Such were the general features of the investiture ceremony and
the lord-vassal relationship in European feudalism at its height
during the Middle Ages. As to the investiture ceremony and feudal
system of ancient China, these were by and large similar to the
European system. Because human cultures, although not identical in content or rate of development, nevertheless proceed through
paths that are on the whole similar, therefore if we disregard the
dissimilarities in minute detail and compare the major features
of Chinese and European feudalism, we shall be able to answer
many of the unsolved questions regarding the former.

2. Ritual of the Investiture Ceremony*

The term hsi-ming 錫命 ["to invest-appoint," "investiture"]
first appears in the Book of Changes. In the section on "Military
Campaigns" in this work is the phrase "the king thrice invest-appointed," and in the section on "Litigation" is the phrase "invested
him with a leather belt." According to the commentary of Yü Fan,
"invested" means "invest-appointed." In many old texts the characters hsi 錫 ["to invest"] and tz'u 賜 ["to grant"] were used inter-
changeably, since they both contained the same basic element, although one had the "metal" radical and the other the "cowry shell"
radical. Hence "investiture" was written either as hsi-ming ["to
invest-appoint"] or as tz'u-ming ["to grant-appoint"] in some
written sources.

When an investiture was made it was always accompanied by a
document; hence it was also called "document-appointing." The
Tso Chronicle reports for the year 632 B.C., for example, that
"The king ordered the minister, Yin-shih; his own brother, Hu;
and the Historiographer of the Interior, Shu-hsing Fu, to document-appoint the ruler of Chin as the chief prince." The terms
ts'e-ming ["to document-appoint"] and ts'e-li ["to document-establish"] were used exclusively after the Ch'in and Han periods.

The general outline of the ancient investiture ceremony is contained only in the Book of Rites. The passage reads:

> In ancient times an enlightened ruler granted noble ranks
> to the virtuous and stipends to the meritorious. He had to
> make these grants in the temple of the royal ancestors, to
> show that he dared not presume to be the sole dispenser [of
> such honors]. Therefore he offered worship to them, this
> being called "the first offering," and then descended to the
> bottom of the central steps [of the temple] and faced south.
> The investee stood facing north. The Historiographer, at
> the ruler's right, formally appointed him with a document.
> [The investee] bowed twice, knocked his head on the ground,
> took the document, and returned home. He then offered sac-
> rifices at his own family temple. This constituted the grant-
> ing of ranks and awards.

---

*The reader will perhaps find it easier to follow the discussion of the various
Chinese terms for "investiture" if they juxtaposed as follows:

  hsi-ming 錫命 to invest-appoint
  tz'u-ming 賜命 to grant-appoint
  ts'e-ming 策命 to document-appoint (i.e. appoint with a document)
  ts'e-li 冊立 to document-establish

Four notable features stand out from the above account: first, the investiture had to take place in the royal ancestral temple; second, the ruler stood facing south and the investee north; third, the Historiographer appointed the investee with a document; and fourth, the investee had to make obeisance before leaving with the document, and later to make offerings at his family temple.

In the Rites of Chou the functions of the Minister of Sacrifices, Assistant Minister of Sacrifices, Historiographer of the Interior, Master of Archery, and Banquet Supervisor on the occasions of investitures were all specifically defined. When a feudal lord was to be invested by the king, the Minister of Sacrifices acted as Usher for the investee; when ministers and tai-fu were invested, the Assistant Minister of Sacrifices served as their Usher. On both occasions, however, the document containing the order of en-feoffment was conferred by the Historiographer of the Interior. This information supplements that given in the Book of Rites. It is not true, however, that the latter describes only the investing of ministers by the feudal lords, while the Rites of Chou describes that of feudal lords by the king, as some historians have con-tended.

Records of investitures are contained in some of the three to four thousand Chou bronze vessels extant today, especially in those dating from Western Chou [ca. 1027-771 B.C.]. These bronze inscriptions are a good complement to written sources, and enable us to reconstruct the Chou ceremony in general outline. The following is a discussion of the several aspects of the cere-mony:

(a) The investiture took place in the royal ancestral temple. This point, which was indicated by the Book of Rites passage just cited, is due to the fact that in the era of divine authority all ac-tion had to stem from the will of the gods; hence the investiture ceremony had to take place in the ancestral temples. On this point the written sources have been corroborated by the extant bronze inscriptions. The study of these inscriptions, which has gained momentum ever since the Sung dynasty, has recently cul-minated in Kuo Mo-jo's authoritative Commentary on the Bronze Inscriptions of Chou, a study of the texts found on 323 historically invaluable bronze vessels. Of this number, 162 belong to the Western Chou period, and of the latter group, 55 contain rather detailed accounts of investitures by the king. Most of the vessels were cast by the investees to commemorate the occasion and to pass the honor down to their posterity.

With few exceptions, all fifty-five investiture ceremonies took place in the Chou royal temple. Seven vessels mentioning the

ancestral capital of Chou* indicate that the ceremony was carried
out at the capital city of Hao [near Sian in Shensi]. Twenty-three
mention Chou or Ch'eng-Chou [near Loyang in Honan]; the inscriptions regarding fourteen other ceremonies indicate that they
were carried out at the royal temples, that is, in these two capital cities. Nine vessels have no mention of locality. Only two mention places other than the Chou capitals; one of these places is
Cheng,** which became the capital of later kings, and the other is
Han-tz'u [?] 寒㽙, where the king performed the ceremony during a stop in his travels. Hence, during Western Chou investiture
was a function of the royal court, thus differing from the later
practice during the Spring and Autumn period, when the king sent
envoys to the feudal states to carry out the investiture ceremonies.
This proves the validity of the information given by the Book of
Rites that the bestowal of ranks and stipends had to take place in
the ancestral temple.

(b) The sovereign stood to the south of the main steps, facing
south, and the investee stood facing north. The bronze inscriptions
indicate that the investiture ceremonies took place in the central
hall of the royal temple. Eleven of the fifty-five bronzes contain
specific mention of the central hall as the locale of the ceremony;
although the others do not mention it, probably for the sake of sav-
ing space, the investiture probably invariably took place in the
central hall. The inscriptions tell us that the king took his seat in
the central hall and that the investee received the investiture
standing in mid-court. Many bronzes contain passages like the
following:

> The king arrived at the central hall and took his seat. Sung
> entered the gate, accompanied by Tsai Hung, and stood in
> mid-court.

> The king arrived at Mu Temple and took his seat. Shan-fu
> K'o, accompanied by Tung [?] Chi, entered the gate and
> stood in mid-court facing north.

The general procedures of the investiture ceremony as revealed

---

*Tsung-Chou 宗周 , which in Western Chou was Hao. There was also a second-
ary capital in the east, Ch'eng-Chou 成周 , which was built at the beginning of the
dynasty by the Duke of Chou and later became the capital of Eastern Chou in 771 B.C.
**Two different capitals received this name in Western and Eastern Chou. The
earlier Cheng was located east of present Sian in Shensi. The later Cheng or New
Cheng was located near Hsin-cheng District in Honan.

in these accounts are quite similar to those stated in the Book of Rites. Just what is meant by "mid-court," however, is a debatable question. Wang Kuo-wei maintains that it was the middle of the floor-space of the central hall itself, but that the inscriptions did not bother to record how the investee entered the hall, went across the floor, and so forth. At that date, he adds, the central hall in the temple was not walled in, and therefore could be called a "court." This explanation seems to be correct.

(c) The order of investiture was conferred by the Historiographer. The Rites of Chou states concerning the Historiographer of the Interior: "When feudal lords, vice-ministers, ministers, and tai-fu are invested, [the Historiographer] confers the orders on them." The inscriptions bear out this statement, as many of the bronzes record the king telling the Historiographer of the Interior to confer the order on the investee. In some cases this person is called simply Historiographer, the title being followed by the personal name, as for example Historiographer Hsü, Historiographer Mou, and so on. This appears to be an abbreviation of the title Historiographer of the Interior.

(d) Ushering was performed by the Minister of Sacrifices. One of the functions of the Minister of Sacrifices, as stated in the Rites of Chou, was "to act as usher when the king invests the lords." The Assistant Minister of Sacrifices, according to the same source, was "to act as usher when Ministers and tai-fu are granted positions and ranks." In the bronzes, however, only the Hsiao-yü ting-tripod contains the expression "ushering," but this was a record of reward to a victorious general, an occasion different from investitures. When investitures took place, the officials who assisted in the ceremonies were said to "accompany" the investee, as indicated by the texts of numerous inscriptions. This in fact was the equivalent of what the Rites of Chou called "ushering." Furthermore, while the Rites of Chou had the Minister and the Assistant Minister of Sacrifices act as ushers, the bronzes make no mention of these officials but designate a number of others serving under the king. This would seem to invalidate the assertions in the Rites of Chou.

(e) The investee made a double obeisance, and retired with the document of enfeoffment. This was the procedure set forth in the Book of Rites. The bronze inscriptions also nearly all end the account of the investiture with some such sentence as "[the invested person] bowed, knocked his head on the ground, and humbly praised the king's virtues." These examples are too numerous to cite further.

3. Contents of Investiture

An investiture usually comprised two aspects, the first consisting of the royal order of investiture, and the second of the things granted by the king to the investee. The Shih Tui vessel, for example, first records that Shih Tui was invested with the position of Assistant Equerry, and then notes down the gifts he received on the occasion.

The gifts granted to the investee varied according to the rank of the receiver. The Rites of Chou and the Book of Rites contain different accounts of the gradation of gifts. It would seem, however, that what these works have presented is a later idealized version of the Chou rites, which the Confucian scholars made more regular and systematic than they actually were.

As to the gifts granted to feudal lords, the [Han dynasty work] Han-shih wai-chuan and a passage quoted in the Book of Rites describes them as falling into nine categories, from chariots and horses for the highest or first rank to millet wine for the lowest or ninth rank. The two sources, however, differ as to the gifts for some of the in-between ranks. These accounts were the origin of what was later known as the "nine grants." A comparison with the bronze inscriptions shows that all the items mentioned by these books--chariots, horses, garments, bows and arrows, weapons, wine, and so on--were given as gifts at all times, but not according to so strict a scheme of gradation as indicated by the written works. Further, dozens of other things not mentioned in the latter, such as shell money, pennants, and jade articles, were recorded as gifts. On the other hand, two items mentioned in the Han-shih wai-chuan and Book of Rites, namely audiences and vermilion doors, are not found in the inscriptions. They seem to have been taken from Han practice and anachronistically attributed to Chou times.

On the basis of the data in Kuo Mo-jo's Commentary on the Bronze Inscriptions of Chou we can tabulate the gifts granted by the king at investiture ceremonies. The following are a few examples:

Bronze vessel	Gift
Chung chih	Horse(s)
Chung ting	Fief
Ling ting-tripod	10 ch'en 臣 [slave] families
Large Yü ting-tripod	1 medium jar of millet wine; cap and garment; ceremonial shoes; chariot and horses;

Bronze vessel, cont'd	Gift, cont'd
	400 pang-ssu 邦司 ["Admi- nistrators"], 659 common people, 1,300 i-ssu 夷司 ["attendants"] and wang- ch'en 王臣 ["royal officers"], 1,050 jen-li 人隸 ["slaves"].
Small Yü ting-tripod	1 bow, 100 arrows, 1 chariot ornament, 1 pei-chou 貝冑 [shell helmet?], 1 metal lance.
Small Ch'en Ching i	50 p'eng 朋 ["strings"] of shells.
Historiographer Sung yin	Jade sceptre, 4 horses, and chi-chin 吉金 ["bronze for ceremonial vessels"].
Shih-hu yin	Red shoes.
Mao yin	4 jade containers, 1 long chariot, 1 sacrificial [bronze] vessel, 10 horses, 10 head of cattle, 4 pieces of land.
Ta yin	2 horses, a roll of cloth.
Ta ting-tripod	32 horses.
Hsing yu	Land 50 li square.
Hsiao yu	20 strings of shells.
Pu-ch'i yin	1 bow, 1 sheaf of arrows, 5 families of slaves, 10 pieces of land.

From the inscriptions on seventy-five bronze vessels, of which the above are samples, we learn that the gifts ranged from one to more than a score of items on each occasion. They included every- thing from cowry shells and bows and arrows to land, people, and royal officials. As to apparel, the items most frequently given seem to have been red shoes, of which there are eight mentions. Such items are also present in some passages in the Book of Poetry. There are in the bronzes twenty-one references to silk banners, fifteen to horses, and one to cattle. Millet wine appears eleven times, cowry shells nine times, horse ornaments eight times, and "tiger kerchiefs" and jade sceptres a like number of times. Land is mentioned four times. There are references to several kinds of chariots and to innumerable varieties of accessories for these.

The point to note here is that in ancient times officials did not

receive any salary aside from their provision fields, and therefore
were given generous gifts whenever an investiture took place. However, since the gifts were not confined to nine articles, nor the investitures confined to nine titles, we may conclude the idea of
"nine grants" was the fabrication of scholars of a later age, and
not a system that actually prevailed in Chou.

4. The Investing of Royal Officials

// As pointed out above, both the enfeoffment of feudal lords and
the appointment of royal officials in Western Chou were signalized
by the ceremony of investiture. This was due to the fact that in
ancient times those with titles always held official posts, those
holding official posts were given remuneration, and those given
remuneration received grants of land. Enfeoffment and appointment actually amounted to the same thing. The only difference
was that the fiefs of royal officials lay within the royal demesne,
while those of the feudal lords were usually situated outside it.
There was no difference, however, between the two investiture
ceremonies.
// Generally speaking, in the investiture of a royal official the
higher the person's position, the more magnificent were the gifts
received. Among the bronze inscriptions, those on the Large K'o
ting-tripod and the Mao-kung ting-tripod contain the most solemn
and detailed accounts, which give us a view of the ceremony that
accompanied the investiture of high officials in Western Chou.
The second section of the Large K'o ting-tripod reads:

> The king was at the ancestral capital of Chou. At dawn the
> king arrived at Mu temple and took his seat. Shan-fu K'o,
> accompanied by Tung [?] Chi, entered the gate and stood in
> mid-court facing north. The king ordered Yin-shih to invest
> Shan-fu K'o, and said: "K'o, formerly I had ordered you to
> promulgate Our decrees; now I shall [....] invest you with
> a title. I grant you [....] land at Yeh and at Pei. I grant you
> farming households cultivating the land at Yung, to serve as
> your subjects and subordinates. I grant you land at K'ang,
> at Yen, and at Fu-yüan. I grant you servitors, drums, bells
> [....]. Be diligent day and night, and do not disregard Our
> order." K'o bowed and made obeisance, and humbly praised
> the virtues of the king [....]. //

Such was the ceremony conferring on Shan-fu K'o the position of
Provisions Master. This seems to have been an official of major

importance. He had the authority to "promulgate the King's decrees," and he was often mentioned together with other high officials at the Chou court. The interpretation given by the Rites of
Chou, that this official was in charge of the king's food and drink,
is obviously erroneous.

The ceremony is recorded in even greater detail and in more
elaborate language on the Mao-kung ["Duke of Mao"] ting-tripod.
In the text the king addressed Yin, the Duke of Mao, in a lengthy
oration, first on the Chou legacy in ruling the country, then on
the elevation of Yin to a high position to aid the king "by order of
the past kings [of Chou]," followed by an exhortation to the Duke
of Mao to rule justly and wisely in his territory. The gifts granted
to the Duke of Mao were then listed; these included wine, jade
articles, a metal chariot, various trappings for the chariot (many
of metal), horses, pennants, and so forth. The Duke of Mao then
gave praise to the king, and cast this ting-tripod to commemorate
the event for posterity.

Kuo Mo-jo's investigation of the Mao-kung ting-tripod establishes it as dating from the reign of King Hsüan [827-780 B.C.],
which is an acceptable conclusion. The state of Mao was situated
in modern Honan; its rulers were descended from the youngest
son of King Wen and, as the Book of History and the Tso Chronicle
attest, had a long history of aiding the kings of Chou down to the
Eastern Chou period. The investiture of Yin as a royal administrator was therefore extremely solemn, and the gifts to him
were particularly rich and generous.

5. The Investing of Feudal Lords

//In the bronze inscriptions there are many accounts of the investiture of high officials, but those on the investiture of feudal lords
are relatively scarce. This is because most of the extant bronzes
date from the middle of Western Chou, when the time had already
passed for the large-scale investing of feudal lords. There are,
however, many accounts of feudal enfeoffments in early Chou in
the Book of Poetry, Book of History, and the Tso Chronicle. A
general picture of these investiture ceremonies can be gathered
from a comparative study of these texts and the bronze inscriptions.
//The "Praise-Odes of Lu" in the Book of Poetry has the following record of the enfeoffment of the [son of the Duke of Chou, uncle
of the reigning king, Ch'eng, as the first] Duke of Lu:

> The King said, "Uncle,
> I will set up your eldest son,

And make him lord of Lu.
I will greatly develop your territory there,
To be of help and support to the House of Chou."

Accordingly he named him Duke of Lu,
And made him lord in the east,
Giving him the hills and rivers,
The lands and fields, and the attached states.

∥If we compare this with the bronze inscriptions, it appears to
be a paraphrase of the original document of investiture at the time
when the Duke of Lu was enfeoffed.∥

From supplementary information furnished by the Tso Chronicle
in an account describing the establishment of the state of Lu, it
can be seen that, because of the especially distinguished and influential position of the Duke of Chou, who was both the uncle and
prime minister of the king, the enfeoffment of his eldest son took
on a particularly solemn and comprehensive aspect.

∥Data from the two written sources just cited indicate that the
following things were granted to the Duke of Lu at his enfeoffment:

∥(a) Land: The Book of Poetry speaks of "giving him the hills
and rivers, the lands and fields, and the attached states." The Tso
Chronicle states that "lands were apportioned on an enlarged scale."
The expression "attached states" refers to small neighboring
states outside the boundaries of Lu for whose administration the
Duke was to be responsible. According to the same source the document of enfeoffment at the investiture of the first Duke of Ch'i
[traditionally 1122-1078 B.C.] also states: "Do you undertake to
punish [the guilty among] the princes of all five degrees, and the
chiefs of all the nine provinces, in order to support and help the
House of Chou. . . . [Rule over the land] east to the sea, west to the
[Yellow] River, south to Mu-ling [in Shantung], and north to Wu-
ti [in Shantung]." At that time, when the Shang and Yěn* [peoples]
had only recently been conquered and the frontier tribes had not
yet been subjugated, all the newly enfeoffed states had the responsibility of pacifying the frontier peoples and administrating the surrounding regions.

∥(b) People: Aside from the people of Yěn there were also the
six conquered clans of Shang. These six clans had to "receive
their orders at Chou, and work in Lu." A comparison with bronze

---

*We write the name of this barbarian group, which was located in Shantung, as
Yěn in order to distinguish it from the better-known Yen state, which was situated
in what is now northern Hopei.

inscriptions leads us to the conclusion that "Chou" here refers to
Ch'eng-chou [in Honan], rather than to Ch'i-Chou [in Shensi], as
some persons have inaccurately maintained. The conquered Shang
people had become slaves, who after having been registered at
Ch'eng-Chou were moved to live in the east. The possibility of rebellion was prevented by such dispersions, while at the same time
they could be used as frontier bulwarks.

//(c) Officials and administrators: Large numbers of officials
were needed for the administration of the newly conquered land and
people, and only the conquering Chou people could fill these posts.
Hence the Chou people became the aristocracy of the new states.
The officials can be classified into two categories: First, the
ceremonial and kinship officials indispensible to the founding of
a new state at that time, such as the Officers of Prayer, Officers
of Ceremonies, Diviners, Historiographers, and so on. Second,
the officials who ruled over the people; they were known as officials and administrators.

//(d) Bronze vessels: In Tu Yü's commentaries [on the Tso
Chronicle] these are explained as "bells, ting-tripods, and the
like, which were constantly used in the ancestral temples." Bronze
vessels were given to newly enfeoffed feudal lords by the Chou
court so as to help them in conducting sacrificial ceremonies; this
was known as "pacifying the altars of the tutelary deities."

//(e) Chariots,   clothing, and other articles of use: There were
precious items like the gem of the sovereigns of Hsia and the Fan-
jo [bow] of Feng-fu. There was the metal-decorated chariot and
the banner with the dragon design, which proclaimed the investee's
favored position. There were also archives and documents.

//Thus, officials, administrators, bronzes, and archival documents were all moved from the [original] Chou territory to the
East. In the process Chou culture also was brought to East China.//

The Tso Chronicle also contains an account of the ceremony at
the enfeoffment of K'ang Shu, founder of the state of Wèi [in Hopei].
The document of investiture, called "Ordinance to K'ang," forms
the chapter with this title in the Book of History. It is the only surviving document on early Chou investiture of feudal lords.

This document is very lengthy. The first part shows that the
event took place in Ch'eng-Chou, and that the "king" referred to
was the Duke of Chou when he was acting as regent after the eastern campaigns. The document embodies a detailed directive on
the governing of Wèi, especially with regard to such major aspects
as the careful meting out of penalties, the employment of men of
talent, and good treatment of the people. Obviously this was because K'ang Shu at that time had the important task of governing

the newly-conquered eastern territories and pacifying the Shang population, so that the Duke of Chou was particularly concerned and gave him very detailed instructions. According to the preface to the Book of History, two other chapters, namely "Ordinance on Drunkenness" and "Timber of the Tzu-Tree," also were instructions to K'ang Shu of Wèi; they deal with such questions as prohibition of drinking, diligent government, and good treatment of the people. These documents prove that in early Chou the feudal lords had to follow royal directions in the administration of their fiefs. In this respect they were unlike the quasi-independent lords of later Chou.

Another account in Tso Chronicle recording the investiture [in 506 B.C.] of K'ang Shu of Chin [in Shansi] shows that he was enfeoffed to rule over the frontier people in the northwest. The gifts he received were similar to those accorded the lords of Lu and Wèi--land, people, royal administrators, and bronze implements.

Most of the investitures of feudal lords took place toward the beginning of the dynasty, in the period of King Ch'eng and the Duke of Chou, when new lands were being added to the map. The lords were enfeoffed to rule over the conquered peoples and "serve as shields to [the house of] Chou." With the completion of the process of parcelling out the land outside the royal demesne among the lords after the period of King Ch'eng, investitures began to decrease in number. Subsequently, however, when King Hsüan [827-780 B.C.] was able to rally the declining royal fortunes and conquer new territories in the south, a new round of enfeoffments began as feudal lords were given the task of ruling the southern territories newly acquired by Chou. A number of poems in the Book of Poetry record the investiture of these lords. One such poem, an account of the investiture of the lord of Shen by King Hsüan, describes how the former was given land, people, and gifts, including a chariot, horses, a large jade sceptre, and ornaments for the horses. These poems tally well with investiture accounts found in bronze inscriptions.

Another poem describes the investiture [in 826 B.C.] of Duke Mu of Shao, whose personal name was Hu. Victorious from the conquest of the Huai barbarians, he was invested by King Hsüan to rule in the southern territory. The text of the poem again appears to be a paraphrase of the original document of enfeoffment. Parts of it read:

> On the banks of the Yangtse and Han rivers,
> The King had given charge to Shao Hu:
> "Open up the whole of the country,
> Institute for me the tax of one-tenth;

Do not distress the people, nor treat them harshly,
But make them conform to the royal state.
Make the large and small divisions of the land,
As far as the southern sea."

"I give you a large libation-cup of jade,
And a jar of herb-flavored spirits from the black
  millet.
I have made announcement to the Accomplished One,
And confer on you hills, lands, and fields.
In [Ch'i-] Chou [in Shensi] shall you receive investiture,
According as your ancestor received his."
He bowed with his head to the ground [and said:]
"May the Son of Heaven live forever!"

The gifts given to Hu were similar to the presents granted to the
lord of Shen. The last part, in which Hu gives praise to the King
after receiving the investiture, repeats the procedure recorded in
the bronze inscriptions.

From the above accounts of the enfeoffment of several rulers of
states, a general view of the early Chou feudal system can be gathered. At their investiture the feudal lords not only received titles,
but also large amounts of gifts from the king, including such important items as land, people, officials, bronze vessels, clothing,
chariots, utensils, weapons, and so forth. Among these, the jade
sceptre was of major importance, for it was a symbol of rank and
office. The Rites of Chou states that the king's sceptre was 1.2
[Chinese] feet in length; the duke's, 9 [Chinese] inches; the marquis' and the count's, 7 inches. The lords were required to hold
their sceptres in their hands when seeing the king. Other items
of special significance were the bronze vessels given to feudal
lords "to help them in sacrificial ceremonies."

6. The Investing of Feudal Heirs

The original feudal relationships based on personal contract
were supplemented gradually by the tendency toward hereditary positions. The king, the royal administrators, and the feudal lords
all came to have hereditary posts, a natural development in a society of patrilineal clans. The result was that at the death of the
king, the lords had to be invested anew by the new ruler, so as to
reestablish the contractual relationship between them. Similarly,
at the death of a feudal lord his heir also had to be invested by the
king before he could assume his father's rank. This was the system that prevailed in medieval Europe as well as in ancient China.

[The Han dynasty work] Po-hu t'ung, in its commentary on the sentence "When a feudal lord dies, his sceptre is returned to the king by an envoy," explains the essence of the procedure when it states that the original investiture extended only through the lifetime of the investee, so that at his death the sceptre had to be returned to the king, and his heir could not formally become his successor until he himself had been invested by the king.

In one bronze inscription, a record of the investiture of Po-ch'en as the lord of Keng, the king's proclamation "[I order you] to succeed your forefathers as the lord of Keng" is followed by a list of the gifts granted to the investee on this occasion; these included millet wine, clothing, horse-drawn chariots, chariot equipment, weapons, and so forth. In the poem "Grandeur of Hán" in the Book of Poetry, a paraphrase of the original investiture orders of the Marquis of Hán at his succession to the position, is a rather detailed account of the occasion. The following are some excerpts from this account:

> The king himself gave the charge:
> "Continue the services of your ancestors;
> Let not my charge to you come to nought.
> Be diligent, early and late,
> And reverently discharge your duties."
>
> With his four noble steeds,
> All very long, and large,
> The Marquis of Hán came to court.
> Holding the sceptre of his rank,
> He entered and appeared before the king
> The king presented to the Marquis of Hán
> A fine dragon-flag with feathery ornaments.....

Other poems in the Book of Poetry also contain accounts of the investiture of lords. Additional data from the Rites of Chou and the Kung-yang Chronicle with regard to the gifts of clothing point to the fact that the feudal lords could not begin to wear the garments denoting their rank until these had been formally granted by the king at the ceremony of investiture.

Another aspect of feudal succession is revealed in a passage in the Discourses of the States. Duke Wu [825-816 B.C.] of Lu, it is recorded in the "Discourses of Chou," took his two sons, Kua and Hsi, to see the king of Chou, whereupon the latter designated Hsi, the younger of the sons, to succeed to his father's title. This designation was made over the objections of the king's advisor,

Fan-chung Shan-fu. Duke Wu died soon after returning to Lu,
whereupon Hsi succeeded him [in 815 B.C.] as duke. Later, however, the people of Lu killed Hsi and set up Kua as their lord. Ultimately King Hsüan was forced to send an expedition against Lu,
defeat it, and establish Duke Hsiao as the ruler of the state. This
episode shows not only that the feudal heir had to receive investiture from the king, but that the latter even had the right to choose
the successor.

7. Royal Investitures during the
Spring and Autumn Period

⫽The above reveals that at the height of Chou power the feudal
lords had to be personally invested by the king and to receive the
document of enfeoffment and gifts of banners and garments before
they could assume sovereignty in their states. Later, however,
the king's power steadily decreased with the decline of the Chou
royal house, reaching a still lower state when King P'ing moved
the capital to the East [i.e. to modern Lo-yang, in 771 B.C.].
Outside his own demesne the king was devoid of authority and was
helpless against the feudal lords, who often perpetrated usurpa-
tions and assassinations in their states. The question of succession was certainly a matter beyond the power of the king to inter-
fere. The investiture ceremonies, therefore, were neglected as
royal control diminished in the country.
⫽Of all the feudal states, Lu had the closest relations with the
Chou court, and was also treated in greatest detail in the Spring
and Autumn. Yet of the twelve dukes of Lu [recorded in this work],
only three--Dukes Huan [711-694 B.C.], Wen [626-609 B.C.], and
Ch'eng [590-573 B.C.]--were invested by the Chou king. Among
these, moreover, Duke Huan was invested only posthumously.
Apart from these three there were only six lords of other states
who are recorded in the Discourses of the States and the three commentaries on the Spring and Autumn as having been invested by the
king. They are Duke Hsiang [543-536 B.C.] of Wèi, Dukes Huan
[685-643] and Ling [581-554] of Ch'i, and Dukes Wu [678-677], Hui
[650-636], and Wen [635-628] of Chin. Of these, Duke Hsiang of
Wèi was also posthumously invested. Moreover, all these investitures had taken place in the respective states and were officiated
by envoys sent from the Chou court for this purpose. The lords
in question did not go to the royal court and receive their investitures personally from the king.
⫽It is recorded in the Spring and Autumn, for example:

> First year of Duke Chuang [693 B.C.]: "In the winter the
> king sent Jung-Shu to invest Duke Huan with his title."

First year of Duke Wen [626 B.C.]: "In the summer the Son of Heaven sent the Earl of Mao to invest the duke with his title."

Eighth year of Duke Ch'eng [583 B.C.]; autumn: "The Son of Heaven sent the Earl of Shao to invest the duke with his title."

Only these three rulers of Lu have been recorded as receiving the investiture from the Chou king, and in each case the ceremony was performed by an envoy sent by the king. Moreover, the first person so invested, Duke Huan, was actually a usurper. The king not only was too weak to conduct a punitive expedition against him, but even had to invest him with the title after his death. Such was the extremity of powerlessness reached by the king's government.//

In its account of the investiture of Duke Ling of Ch'i the Tso Chronicle has preserved the original text of the document of investiture; this document refers to the aid that the early Ch'i rulers had given the house of Chou, and admonishes the present incumbent to follow in the tradition of his forefathers. The same work contains a rather detailed account of the investiture of Duke Wen of Chin. The gifts to the investee consisted of garments for riding in chariots, one red bow and 100 red arrows, one black bow and 1,000 arrows, one jar of millet wine, and 300 warriors; the ceremony ended with Duke Wen giving praise to the king. It seems that the procedures were the same as those of Western Chou, except that they were not presided over by the king.

In sum, during the Spring and Autumn period the investiture ceremonies were neglected owing to the decline of the Chou court. Even if the ceremonies were occasionally performed, they had by now lost their original significance and become a mere formality. The three dukes of Lu, for example, were invested because the Chou king wished to be on good terms with Lu; Duke Huan of Ch'i and Duke Wen of Chin were invested because they had given support to the royal house; and Duke Ling of Ch'i was invested because the king was about to marry a daughter of the Ch'i ruling house. In other words, investiture had become a sign of the king's special favor. Otherwise the Chou court dispensed with this ceremony for the sake of economy.

NOTES

齊思和, "周代錫命禮考," 燕京學報

Ch'i Ssu-ho, "Chou-tai hsi-ming-li k'ao," <u>Yenching Journal of</u> <u>Chinese Studies</u>, No. 32 (June, 1947), 197-226.

Professor Ch'i Ssu-ho, one of the leading students of Chinese feudalism, has also written on the subject in English, as in his "A Comparison between Chinese and European Feudal Institutions," <u>Yenching Journal of Social Studies</u>, IV, 1 (1938), 1-13. For studies on the subject by Westerners see Henri Maspero, "Le régime fé-odal et la propriété foncière dans la Chine antique," <u>Revue de</u> <u>l'Institut de Sociologie</u>, XVI (1936), 37-70 (reprinted in <u>Mélanges</u> <u>posthumes sur les religions et l'histoire de la Chine</u> (Paris, 1950), pp. 111-146, and Marcel Granet, <u>La féodalité chinoise</u> (Oslo, 1952).

The major sources used for this article are the studies of bronze inscriptions by earlier writers, especially those of Wang Kuo-wei and Kuo Mo-jo. These are supplemented by ancient records, chiefly the <u>Tso Chronicle</u> (<u>Tso chuan</u>), <u>Spring and Autumn</u>, <u>Book</u> <u>of Poetry</u>, <u>Rites of Chou</u>, and <u>Book of Rites</u>.

We list below a number of English terms used by the author himself as the equivalent of the accompanying Chinese expressions:

ch'en 臣 "vassal"
ch'en-fu li 臣服禮 "homage"
chün 君 "Lord"
feng-chien kuan-hsi 封建關係 "feudal bonds"
feng-chu 封主 "seigneur"
hsüan-shih shih-chung li 宣誓矢忠禮 "oath of fidelity"
shou-hui 收回 "forfeit"
shou-ming li 授命禮 "investiture"
ts'ai-i 采邑 "fief"
t'ui-fan ch'i shih-ming 推翻其誓命 "disavow"

5

THE CHINESE LAND SYSTEM BEFORE THE CH'IN DYNASTY

by

WU CH'I-CH'ANG

PART I. SOME IMPORTANT PHENOMENA IN THE FIRST PERIOD OF AGRICULTURE

1. Free Possession and Colonization of Virgin Land

⫻From the Chou period on China left the nomadic hunting-fishing age and entered the age of agriculture. The Shang were a nomadic fishing and hunting people; the Chou people were initiators of agriculture.* The revolution led by King Wu [of Chou against Shang] was not only political, but was also one of economic systems and social organization, as well as of culture and thought. It was, in reality, a revolution in dietary habits. Culture and thought stem from the form of social organization, social organization is based on the economic system, and the economic system in turn undergoes revolutions according to changes in dietary habits.

⫻At that time the word "field" no longer meant "hunting grounds," but land for planting, and "rice" was no longer used for wine-making, but had become a staple food. Man no longer lingered in the stage of "eating meat" and "feeding on distillery dregs and sipping on thin wine," but had rapidly entered the stage of "eating cereals." Therefore the consumption of grain suddenly increased, and land for the planting of grain (including rice, wheat, millet, legumes, and various cereals) was tremendously expanded; consequently the demand and desire for the ownership of land also were heightened. The small area around Ching and Pin at the upper reaches of the Wei River [in Shensi] was naturally insufficient for these needs. The people looked westward: mighty mountains lay

---

*These ideas are typical of those held by a large number of Chinese scholars, even in the face of earlier evidence that agriculture considerably antedates Chou, but they were largely abandoned following the excavations carried on at the site of the Shang capital shortly before this article was published.

one beyond another, and the prospects were absolutely nil. They
looked eastward: rich alluvial land spread alongside the river
banks, and every man could occupy and possess as much as he had
the appetite for. There was no limit on his taking, no restriction
on his staking out, and no need to pay a farthing for all this. This
was the so-called "virgin land." So, following the course of the
Wei River, the people expanded freely eastward. It was possible
to occupy as much land as one could cultivate. [.....] This was approximately the latter part of mid-Shang.

❡Except for the narrow belt along the Wei River, the wide eastern
plains had not yet been colonized by man. It was after a considerable period of time that man's efforts spread to the east of the
Yellow River. The level land on both sides of the river made the
crossing comparatively easy, but east of the Lü-liang and Lung-
men ranges [in western and eastern Shensi respectively], numerous mountains obstructed the way, and it was difficult for the
new agriculture to spread into this region. Not until the time
when King Wu conducted his campaign against King Chou [of Shang
about 1050 B.C.] was the way cleared. Therefore in the early
years of the reign of [King Wu's son] King Ch'eng the agricultural
way of life had not yet been adopted in the Loyang area [in Honan],
and instead of tilling the fields the people hunted in them. The
Book of History says, "and so at the city of Lo [-yang], exert your
efforts on t'ien 畋 in your fields." One commentary notes that,
" 'To take an animal' is called t'ien," and another states that "Tien
means 'to hunt'." Thus it can be seen that at that time the country
people around Lo-yang actually were exerting their efforts at
hunting afield, not raising grain crops. It was probably after the
reign of King Ch'eng, and the conquest of the barbarians of the
Huai River area and the reaching of Yĕn [in Shantung], that agriculture gradually was introduced to the central plain and the lower
Yellow River region. But even then it was limited to the areas
close to the banks of the Yellow River. In places of some distance
from the river banks we have not yet found any evidence of agriculture as late as the King Hsüan period [877-786 B.C.] of Western
Chou. To the contrary, we have discovered some counter-evidence
that the region had not yet reached the agricultural stage. For
instance, a poem in the Book of Poetry, in narrating the story of
Chüeh-fu marrying his daughter to the Marquis of Hán, enumer-
ates many of the products of Hán, but among all these not a single
grain is included:

> The military power of Chüeh-fu is strong,
> And there is no state which he has not visited.
> In selecting a home for [his daughter] Chi,

None seemed so good as Hán.
Very pleasant is the land of Hán,
With its large streams and meres,
Full of big bream and tench;
With its multitude of deer,
With its black bears and grizzly bears,
With its wild-cats and tigers.
Glad he was of so admirable a place,
And here Chi found rest and joy.

The territory of Hán must have been in the northwestern part of Shansi. //

The Book of Poetry and other written records prove that the area covered by Hán was not placed under cultivation until after it was granted to the Marquis of Hán during King Hsüan's reign.

2. Common Tribal Ownership of Land

// Since land was as free as air and sunlight, and anyone could occupy it without limit, without conditions, and without payment, then as a matter of course the right of possession followed after occupation. The first right of possession naturally belonged to the individual who was first in occupation. But this was not so in all cases. Historical evidence tells us that the first occupiers of land were not such-and-such individuals but such-and-such tribes. Therefore, while it is true that the earliest form of land ownership was "private ownership," yet it was tribal "private ownership" and not individual "private ownership." A particular piece of land would belong entirely to a particular tribe. In relation to outsiders the land was privately owned by the tribe; within the tribe the land was owned in common. This is a point that must be made clear.

// The reason for this is that at that time the colonization of un-used land was not carried out in the manner of the present Shan-tung people's "going to the East of the Pass" [i.e. Manchuria], that is, in an individual, unorganized, and wandering fashion. At that time people lacked such group identities as family, society, and state, but had only tribal identity. They had left the matrili-neal system only a short time before, and still preserved the tri-bal organization based on consanguinity. At that time in all mat-ters there was only action by the clan-tribe, not action by the in-dividual. But with the continued increase in the birth rate follow-ing the discovery of a new agricultural way of life, many small clan-tribes became large ones. By this analysis it is evident that enfeoffment was the result of colonization. The period when the

clan-tribes expanded eastward, unconditionally tilling and occupying unused land, was also the period when clan-tribes large and
small were colonizing in the east. Thus the ownership of the occupied and tilled land naturally belonged to clan-tribes and not to
individuals.

∥After a piece of land was occupied by a clan-tribe, except for
the "tilling of land," which was an obligation on every person from
the chief down, it was necessary to have division of labor owing
to the increase in the number of people and amount of work. An
experienced man was therefore elected, whose special duty it was
to manage all arrangements and plans pertaining to the land. This
man was called "tender of the land"; later he was also designated
as "the person who tends." From these titles we are able to tell
that land was commonly owned by tribes.∥

Among the bronzes a number of items inform us as to the Chou
emperors' "tenders of land"--the royal ministers of colonization.
Inscriptions on various bronze vessels indicate that the Chou emperors and heads of feudal states all had their "tenders of the land"
to take charge of the pioneering and colonization of their own
people. This proves that these actions were taken by the tribe as
a unit.

The poem "Gathering White Millet" in the Book of Poetry has
the following passage:

> They were gathering the white millet
> In those one-year fields
> And in the two-year fields
> When Fang-shu came to take command.
> His chariots were three thousand,
> With a host of well-disciplined warriors.
> Fang-shu led them on.

This shows that King Hsüan of Chou sent Fang-shu with a force of
three thousand to campaign against the enemy on the one hand, and
to colonize unused land and harvest grain on the other. It was a
case of occupation and colonization by the tribe. Other references
in the Book of Poetry give further proof of the thesis of the acquisition of territory by tribal units in the time of King Hsüan. An
instance is the colonization of territory in the south by the Earl
of Shen, whose subordinates oversaw the breaking of new agricultural land, the founding of a city, and the establishment of what
later in the Spring and Autumn period became the state of Shen
[in Honan]. The land unquestionably was possessed by the tribe
in common.

3. The System of Farming by Serfs in a Three-Class Society

//Free virgin land was occupied by various clan-tribes, and common landownership of the tribe was established. The individual of
that time had only the duty to cultivate the fields but not the right
to control it; on the contrary, he himself was subject to control
by the clan. From the emperor down, not to mention the minor
chieftains, every person had to till the fields. Thus one bronze
inscription reads: "The King and officials plough* the fields at
Ch'i-t'ien." The "King" here must have been King Chao [tradi-
tionally 1052-1000 B.C.] of Chou.

//This state of affairs was quite just, but it could not last long.
The expansion of the area under cultivation had reached the boundaries of the land of other tribes, while the population had increased to such an extent that it could not be contained within the
limits. Under these circumstances the only way out was "to fight."
Thereupon the history of the Chinese nation witnessed the beginning of wars for colonization and seizure of land. The curtain
went up on a tragedy of evil, cruelty, and violence. The victorious tribes gradually found they could eat without working and embarked on the road to aristocracy. The defeated captives escaped
the death penalty of human sacrifice, but fell into a life sentence
of equality with oxen and horses [....] and became a special class
of serfs. Thus the sole origin of serfs was captivity in war. The
cause-and-effect cycle was that the wider the area of colonization,
the more frequent the wars, and the greater the number of captives taken. The increase in the number of serfs affected them
personally, degrading their status and lowering their price so that
they were regarded as worthless by the victorious people, who
sent them around freely as gifts like horses and oxen. The bronze
implements contain an abundance of data on this problem. [....]

//The material informs us that (a) The unit of the serfs was the
"family," which means that serfdom was hereditary, a perpetual
bondage. (b) The emperor gave away serfs to officials, and officials
in turn gave away serfs to their followers, which shows the low
and unfavorable position of the serfs. (c) When serfs were given
away on a large scale, the unit was an entire conquered area.
Therefore once defeated, the whole population of a certain place
would all be turned from "self-cultivating farmers" into serfs.
For instance, the people of several localities mentioned in a pair
of bronze inscriptions were all ordinary people of these localities,

---

*The character chi 耤 symbolizes a man working with a plough in a flooded field.
[Author's note.]

who unfortunately sank into serfdom owing to defeats in war. On the basis of what were then "states," the serfs were definitely the "stateless wretches" of the time.

// Another point of importance is that, when calculated as individuals, the serf was referred to as fu 夫 ["person"] in the bronze inscriptions. Upon careful reflection, we can see that the nung-fu 農夫 ["farmers"] of the classics were probably all nung-nu 農奴 ["serfs"]. When this is made clear, then it is possible on the one hand to make sense of the classics, and on the other hand to reconstruct the system of serfdom according to these works. //

In the classics the farmer appears as one kind of captive of Yin [i.e. Shang]. Yin are the people of a state that had been subjugated. This proves the "farmer" was actually a "serf." The poem "Seventh Month" contains the following passages: *

> Alas, us farmers
> Now that our harvest is done,
> We go to perform labor at the palace.

> ...we go after badgers,
> And take foxes and wild-cats,
> To make furs for our lord.

> We make dark fabrics and yellow;
> Our red manufacture is very brilliant,
> It is for the lower robes of our lord.

But what of "us farmers"? The poem adds:

> Without the clothes and garments of hair,
> How could we get through the year?

This is solid proof that the "farmers" in the poem "Seventh Month" was a "serf."

Further evidence from the Book of Poetry shows the economic oppression of the landlord on the serfs and the latter's resentment against economic inequality. The poem "Extensive Fields" says:

---

*We translate these passages according to what seems to be the intention of the author. For a different interpretation, especially of the first three lines, see Legge, Classics, IV, pp. 226-233. On the interpretation of the phrase rendered as "farmers" see our Bibliography on Chinese Social History, item 22; for discussion of the poem as a whole see item 108.

> The landlord comes
> With his wife and children
> [......................
> ....]
> He dismisses his followers,
> And tastes the quality [of the grain].
> Good crops cover the fields,
> Good will they be and abundant.
> The landlord is not displeased,*
> As the farmers work industriously.

The poem "Cutting down the Sandal Trees" says:

> You sow not nor reap; -
> How do you get the produce of three hundred farms?
> You do not follow the chase; -
> How do we see the badgers hanging up in your court-
>   yard?
> Oh for a superior man
> Who would not eat the bread of idleness!

Inscriptions on bronzes reveal the following points: (a) The word fu 夫 denotes "slaves." (b) The serfs (ch'en 臣) were of a lower status than the common man, the farmers, and were distinct from them. (c) Serfs could be used as payment for debts or damages. (d) The mortgage value of five serfs was about "a skein of silk," "one horse," or "100 yüan [of coins]." (e) The total price for five serfs was probably "seven fields."

The bronze inscriptions further permit us to speak of either a "two-class system with serfs" or a "three-class system with serfs." In the former the serfs made up one class and were all cultivators of the land. In the latter the serfs formed two classes. The upper class managed the estates for the large landlords, that is for the kings, aristocrats, and officials. The lower class of serfs, called "field men" or "tenant farmers," worked in the fields under the control of the manager serfs; they were thus "serfs of serfs."

//From the middle of the Chou period, when the land along the Wei, Yellow, Huai, Han, Fen, and Yangtse Rivers was consider-

---

*Here too we follow the apparent intent of the author in our rendering of this passage. Legge (Classics, IV, 378-379) has quite a different interpretation, especially of the expression tseng-sun, which he renders as "distant descendant [of the Chou kings]" in contrast to Wu's interpretation as "descendants of landlords."

ably colonized, China tended more and more toward a situation in which the lowest serfs provided the livelihood of the middle serfs, and the middle serfs provided the livelihood of the officials and aristocrats. Aside from some partially self-cultivating farmers, the lowest stratum of serfs were the ones who shouldered the whole burden of production. Since the times of Eastern Chou, on the other hand, those above the shǐh 士 ["warrior-scholars"] class had all become parasites who lived off the lowest serfs and "could neither use their four limbs, nor distinguish the five grains."//

A frequently asked question is whether there was any possibility for a serf to elevate himself to the status of a self-cultivating farmer. On the basis of historical evidence from the bronzes it is possible to answer this question in the affirmative. The evidence concerns the story of Yu Wei-mu as given in the inscription on the Ko-ts'ung ting-tripod.

//This Yu Wei-mu was a serf of Ko-ts'ung, as proved by the charge, made against him before King Li by his master, that "You are the tender of my fields." Originally the land in Yu, given to Ko-ts'ung by his ancestors through the method of "division by shooting arrows," was tilled by the serf Yu Wei-mu, but the latter took possession of his fields and denied Ko-ts'ung's ownership--"It could not be given to Ko-ts'ung." The matter came to such a pass that Ko-ts'ung was helpless and had to appeal to the King. After an investigation ("the King ordered an inquiry"), Yu Wei-mu was made to swear in front of the King that he would subject himself to decapitation if he did not return Ko-ts'ung's land, and only thus was the land recovered. This story shows Yu Wei-mu's rise from serfdom into a self-cultivating farmer. It is a record of importance in the history of the ancient Chinese land system, even though his efforts ultimately failed.

4. Unchecked Abuses of the Right of Land Disposal

//As a result of prolonged large-scale free colonization of virgin soil, land became privately owned by the tribes. This in turn engendered two other phenomena: (a) Although the individual lacked the right to dispose of land, that of the tribe was unlimited. (b) Every man had to till the land; therefore in his mind land was a very precious thing. Later the expansion of tribalism led to conflict over land, and to decision by battle. Out of victory or defeat two separate classes emerged; those who became the aristocracy reaped the harvest without tilling, and those who fell into serfdom tilled the land without possessing it. These conditions engendered two additional phenomena: (c) Victorious tribes an-

nexed the land of the defeated ones, so that there was a temporary
surplus of land. (d) The aristocracy lived comfortably off the sweat
and toil of the serfs, without knowing the hardships of agricultural
work. At this juncture phenomenon (b) naturally disappeared,
while (a) became intensified. The inevitable result of the converg-
ence of phenomena (a), (c), and (d)--i.e. the tribe's increased
right of land disposal, coupled with a surplus of land and a lack of
appreciation for the value of land--was the extravagant use of
land.

//How could land be used extravagantly? It was due to the fact
that the aristocrats, who "neither sowed nor reaped," who worked
neither in young fields nor in old, but who nevertheless "possessed
a thousand granaries and ten thousand chests," and the practice
of exercising their right of disposal to the limit by wantonly giving
away the serf-tilled land and the serfs themselves to their followers so as to display their own wealth and lavishness.//

Instances of land awards are indicated in the classics and on
bronzes. For example, "The Duke of Lu was enfeoffed in the east;
he was granted land and rivers, fields and vassals." Again, "King
Ch'eng gave the Duke of Lu six clans of the subjugated people...
and distributed to him fields and vassals." These cases occurred
at the beginning of the Chou dynasty. Other passages in the Book
of Poetry, Tso Chronicle, Discourses of the States, Analects,
and the bronzes show that the practice of giving away land and serfs
increased greatly in scale toward the latter part of Chou. Not only
the monarch, but the high officials and aristocrats also were lavish in presenting fields and serfs to their followers, including
military officers and estate managers. Some of these grants far
exceeded in size those made by the monarchs of the Western Chou
period. For instance, the Tso Chronicle records: "Chao Chien-
tzu [died ca. 476 B.C.] swore that...to him who vanquished the
enemy, a higher tai-fu would receive one district; a lower tai-fu,
one commandery; and a 'scholar,' 100,000 fields." When the ruler
or overlord did not have enough surplus land to give away it could
be taken by force from others for that purpose. For example,
Duke Wen [635-628 B.C.] of Chin "gave the fields of Ts'ao and Wèi
to the people of the Sung." Also, starting with the middle of Western Chou, the mortgaging of land had already begun to flourish.
Such practices produced numerous cases of land litigation. The
Tso Chronicle contains a truly impressive record of the complexi-
ties of land entanglements, the confusions in the system, and the
evil brutality in the disposal of land. An examination of the material reveals seven cases of taking of land by violence, five of
forcible occupation, four of land disputes, fifteen of indiscrimi-

nate awards of land, four of bribery with land, three of using land
to barter goods, one of acceptance of land loot, and six of recovery
of stolen land by means of political pressure.

⫽In sum, the foregoing shows how in a situation of aggression the
newly risen aristocrats made extravagant use of the land, had not
the least love for it, and willfully abused the right of disposal of
land. They not only indiscriminately gave away land, but also cal-
lously robbed and occupied land by force; therefore there was also a profusion of litigations, mortgages, bribes, and barter exchanges. They also indiscriminately divided the loot, and sometimes arbitrarily took fields and serfs as a means of punishment
or of making amends--such as shown in a bronze inscription. In
terms of classes, these practices were common to the emperor,
the feudal lords, and scholar officials. In terms of time, they existed throughout Western Chou and the first half of Eastern Chou.
This was an inevitable state of confusion in the first stage of expansion of Chinese agriculture.

5. Complete Lack of any Concept of "Bound-aries" or Standard of Land Measurement

⫽How could there be fixed boundaries for land under this condition of great confusion and disturbances? Since primeval virgin
land was freely colonized by various tribes, moreover, how was
it possible to have a uniform standard for boundary delineation?
Bearing in mind the time factor, this was the era of initial en-
lightenment, and there was entirely lacking in the people's minds
even the shadow of any ideas such as "order," "system," "standard," and so forth; therefore how could they have the ability to
divide, measure or calculate the amount of land? Hence the bronze
inscriptions frankly refer to "five fields," "seven fields," "ten
fields," "fifty fields."⫽

"One field" meant simply "one piece of land"; "ten fields,"
simply "ten pieces of land." There was no limit as to the size of
the fields, and it did not matter whether they were round or
square. Our ancestors knew nothing of such things as feet, acres,
and so forth. Up until the Spring and Autumn period they were
still talking vaguely in terms of "100,000," fields," "700,000
fields," and "1,000,000 fields." There was no telling whether it
was a matter of 100,000 feet or 100,000 miles of fields.

⫽A very interesting question concerns the method of dividing
the land and estimating its amount. An illiterate rustic in the se-
cluded countryside, if approached with the question,"How far is
it from here to there?", would certainly have gazed around, made

a mental estimate, and answered, "Quite near, the distance of an arrow-shot." This concept of "an arrow-shot" was the only method our ancient ancestors had of estimating and dividing the land. The various forms of the character for "boundary" in the bronze inscriptions [....] show on examination plots of fields separated by paths; the boundary lines were all determined by shooting from bows, which is why the character has the "bow" radical. Therefore in later times "the land of one arrow-shot" was also called "the land of one bow." This is the first bit of evidence.

//That the boundaries of fields were determined by shooting an arrow from a bow is indicated by an inscription saying, "...if I do not turn over the fields and fiefs which were allotted to Ko-ts'ung's forefathers by shooting arrows...," which clearly informs us of the division of fields and fiefs by archery. "Shooting" took the place of surveying. This is the second bit of evidence.

//Some may ask: If in primitive times there were no definite boundaries or standards of measurement for land, how does one explain the word mou in the Book of Poetry?//

No word for mou has been found among the inscriptions on oracle bones and shells. This word first appeared on the bronzes with the meaning "luxuriant and fertile land." Later in written works, such as Chuang-tzu, Discourses of the States, and the Book of History, the meaning became different. Mou now neither meant the earthen path separating two fields, or was a synonym for mu 母 ["mother" or "source"]. In no case did mou denote a unit for land measurement in ancient times.

Further, the irrigation ditches and paths of that time were constructed according to the contours of the land. This is evident from bronze inscriptions giving accounts of boundary surveys, as well as from written records. This should completely demolish any notion that the "well-field" system, requiring sharp geometric demarcations and measurement, had existed other than in legend. As the Tso Chronicle shows, there were instances of revisions of boundaries owing to changes in ownership, to wars, or to a new administrator's efforts, but in general the state of land boundaries was one of confusion.

6. Complete Lack of "Rent," "Levies," and "Taxation"

//Were problems of rent, levies, and taxation involved with land in those days? This is another interesting subject of investigation. Judging from the above--Section 2: Common Tribal Ownership of Land, and Section 3: The System of Farming by Serfs in a Three-Class Society--the toilers in the fields at that time can be divided

into two categories. One was the self-cultivating farmer; he had
his own land and lived off his own labor, and naturally had no concern with "rent," "tax," and "levies." The other was the serf,
whose all, including his person, was the property of another tribe;
his status was that of horses and oxen, and he lived on a minimum
subsistence level.

// Such conditions did not allow the existence, or even the emergence, of such problems as "rent," "levies," and "tax." Furthermore, judging from Section 5--that there were no definite boundaries or standard measurements for land--there was no way of beginning the process of taxation and rent collection. Our answer
to the query therefore is simply a negative one.//

Although the words denoting "tax" and "levies" in later ages
were present on bronzes and in the early classics, their meanings were quite different. Up to the middle of the Spring and
Autumn period "levy" had meant "military duty," and "tax" was
synonymous with "to remove." No mention has been found of
rents, taxes, and levies in the Book of Changes, the genuine text
of the Book of History, or the Book of Poetry. Therefore it is
safe to say that during her first period of agriculture China did
not have rents and taxes or similar institutions.

// We can now sum up. It is very unfortunate that the well-field
system, presented in some late pre-Ch'in anonymous writer's
ideal "Outline of National Reconstruction"--the Rites of Chou--is
even today taken by some people to be the work of the Duke of
Chou, and to be the picture of land taxes during the time of [the
legendary] Yao and Shun. Such ideas have long since become ob-
solete and do not merit refutation. It is sufficient for us to understand the more reliable historical evidences presented above. If
we understand Section 1, that the free colonization and occupation
of ownerless virgin land was unconditional, unlimited, and without payment, then can the thesis of the well-field advocates that
all land belonged to the nation still be valid? If we understand
Section 2, that the ownership of land belonged to each tribe privately, that only the tribe could be a legal person and not the individual, then can the thesis of the well-field advocates that the
land was awarded to each individual at a certain legal age and returned at a certain legal age still be valid? If we understand
Section 3, that under the three-class system with serfs the victorious people could live without tilling the land, whereas the
serfs who had lost their country merely had their lives spared
and could only till the land without possessing it, then can such
assertions of the well-field advocates as the one that "eight families tilled the public field together" still be valid? If we under-

stand Section 4, that the right of land disposal was freely abused, with personal grants, bribes, mortgages, and forcible seizures leading to an extremity of confusion, then can the thesis proferred by the well-field advocates of a situation that was orderly, well-planned, systematic, step-by-step, and standardized still be valid? If we understand Section 5, that actually there were lacking definite boundaries and units of calculation for land, then the thesis advanced by the well-field advocates of a geometrically designed irrigation system is certainly ten thousand miles from the truth. Moreover, do not the well-field advocates say, "Each man had 100 mou"? But in those days people did not even know what a mou was! If we understand Section 6, that the so-called "rent," "tax," and "levies" were completely lacking, then the contentions of the well-field advocates regarding systems of "Hsia tax," "Yin tax," and "Chou tax" are even more groundless. (What Mencius described was the situation prevalent in the states of Chou and Lu. See below.)

∥Undoubtedly, we cannot ignore evidence of the opposing viewpoint, and we should look for it as much as possible. Now we have it. The "Great Fields" poem in the Book of Poetry, which contains authentic and trustworthy historical material on the early agricultural era in China, has a passage that can be used as a weapon by the well-field advocates in their counter-attack:

> May it rain first on our kung 公 fields
> And then come to our private ones.

∥What is the meaning of this passage? Does not "kung fields" show that eight families together tilled 100 mou of public land? In order to understand this passage, as a matter of fact, it is necessary first to understand the expression, "kung fields," but before we can understand this term it is necessary to know the meaning of kung. Let us begin with what kung means in the Book of Poetry.∥

On the basis of a statistical analysis of this source I find that, leaving aside the kung used in personal names and special terms, and considering only those used independently, this character occurs seven times initially, seven times as the second character, twice as the third character, three times as the fourth character, and five times at the end of a phrase.

Each of these many kung refers to a particular, definite person who is either a local leader or member of the landlord class. In no case, however, can the word be interpreted as designating the emperor, still less such abstract concepts as "public," "common masses," or "publicly owned." Therefore the well-field advocates are really seriously slandering the Book of Poetry when they take

"kung fields" to refer to the public ownership of the land by the country or the empire, or to the nationalization of the land, or to the
ownership of the land by the king.

// Apart from the poem "Great Fields," that entitled "Seventh
Month" provides another excellent example of "kung" and "private"
paired in a contrasting sense:

> The boars of one year are to be retained privately;
> Those of three years are to be given to the kung.

Here the word kung clearly had the same meaning as the kung-tzu
公 子 ["lord"] in "return with the kung-tzu," "furs for our kung-
tzu," and "the lower robes of our kung-tzu," the ending tzu having
been omitted for rhythmic purposes. Hence kung-tzu became kung,
meaning precisely the landlord class. The poem "Seventh Month"
describes exactly a situation of aristocrat-serf opposition, and is
just the right evidence [for our argument]. The poem "Great
Fields" also describes a situation of conflict between the two
classes of hereditary landlord and serf. The "kung fields," therefore, were none other than the fields belonging to the "landlord,"
the person mentioned by the Book of Poetry in "The landlord comes
with his wife and children" and "The grains grow up straight and
large, So that the wish of the landlord is satisfied."//

PART II. SOME DIRECTIONS OF CHANGE IN THE FIRST
PERIOD OF AGRICULTURE

// Like other phenomena, the above characteristics of China's
first agricultural period from around the end of the Shang dynasty
to the first part of the Spring and Autumn period [ca. 1200-700 B.
C.] could not last permanently. Hence changes gradually took
place in several directions.

1. From Common Ownership by the Tribe to
Private Ownership by the Aristocracy

// The land, originally colonized and occupied freely by each clan-
tribe, belonged to the clan-tribes in common. The special feature
of this period was "the equality of the tribal members"; from the
chief down to the lowliest member of the tribe there existed hardly
any class consciousness, and there was equal production and equal
consumption. In other words, everyone, including the tribal chief,
had to till the land. In later times the "Agriculturist School" of
persons like Hsü Hsing and Ch'en Chung-tzu sought to restore this

system, upon which they conferred the name Tilling Together.*
But such a magnificent system could not escape its inevitable doom.
In the first place, class consciousness gradually manifested itself.
Secondly, the tendency toward individual action became more pronounced. Thirdly, frequent wars led to the emergence of individu-
alism of military leaders. Fourthly, the system of garrison colonization fiefs overthrew that of free colonization and occupation.
Fifthly, and still more important, the stronger and larger tribes
gradually achieved statehood. Sixthly, as the weaker and smaller
tribes were annexed, their members became the serfs of warlords,
and tribal property became the latter's private property. The above
causes produced the following result: common tribal ownership of
land changed into private ownership by the aristocracy.

//There is no need to discuss the first cause. As to the second,
let us only look at the bronze vessels. One inscription records the
king's granting land to T'ai-pao as an individual; another, the
king's granting land to Shan-fu K'o as an individual; another, the
king's granting land to Wu as an individual; another, the king's
granting land to Shao as an individual; another, the king's granting
land to Ta as an individual; another, an aristocrat's granting land
to Pu-ch'i as an individual; another, an aristocrat's granting land
to Po as an individual; another, an aristocrat's granting land to
Mao as an individual. Also in the classics: Discourses of the States
records Duke Hui [650-637 B.C.] of Chin giving land to the individuals Li K'o and P'ei Cheng; the Tso Chronicle records the Marquis of Chin giving land to the individuals Ch'i Hsi, Tsang Ho,
and Kung-tzu Feng, and an aristocrat giving land to the Old Man
of Chiang District [in Shansi]. Were these not proofs that common
landownership by the tribe was gradually changing into ownership
by the individual owing to the latter's activities?

//The third cause was related to the second. For example, in the
above instances T'ai-pao, Pu-ch'i, Wu, Kung-tzu Feng, and so
forth, were granted land because of their military exploits. For
those backed by armed forces, however, it was even easier arbitrarily to take over the common property as their own. Such living dramas as the division of common property of the state and nation by military personages were still flourishing as late as the
Spring and Autumn period. For instance, the Tso Chronicle records for the eleventh year [562 B.C.] of Duke Hsiang [of Lu]:
"...in the first month of the year three armies were raised (by

---

*This refers to the doctrine that husbandry should be carried on jointly by the
ruler and his people. The doctrine was propounded chiefly by Hsü Hsing, a contemporary of Mencius (390-305 B.C.). See Legge, Chinese Classics, II, 246 ff.

Chi Wu-tzu); they divided the ducal domain into three parts, and each took possession of one part...". This was the record of the three families of Chi-sun, Meng-sun, and Shu-sun partitioning the public property of the state of Lu.

∥As to the fourth cause, the situation of peaceful and free colonization was entirely altered by the development of conflict and wars. If the people still wanted to colonize new areas, they had to do so with large armies as garrison colonies. Following King Wu's campaigns against Shang and the conquest of the Shang people of Central China by the Chou peoples of Western China, the people of Western China migrated to eastern and northern China in great waves. This was called "enfeoffment" at that time.∥

The following are some examples of "enfeoffment," which was mainly a sort of "garrison enfeoffment":

> Formerly, when King Wu conquered Shang and obtained possession of all the land, those of his brothers who received states numbered fifteen, and those [princes] with the surname Chi who received states numbered forty.

> When the Duke of Chou ruled the country, he established seventy-one states, of which fifty-three were held by members of the Chi family alone.

> Formerly the Duke of Chou....enfeoffed his relatives so that they could act as a protective screen for Chou.

∥The evidence for the fifth cause is inexhaustible.

∥As to the sixth cause, the annexation of weaker, smaller tribes by larger and stronger ones, and the turning of the former's land and people into private property and slaves of individuals, this is extremely well documented in the Tso Chronicle.∥

One passage in this work for the year 514 B.C. states that during the administration of Wei Hsien-tzu [in Lu], the land of the Ch'i family was divided into seven "districts," and that of the Yang-she family into three "districts," and lists the individuals who were made heads of these ten "districts."

Thus the land commonly owned by the clan-tribe gradually passed into the private hands of the aristocracy.

2. From the Basis of Serfs to that of Fiefs

∥In the serf-farming system of the three-class society described above, the lower serfs were the real producers and provided live-

lihood for the middle serfs, who in turn supported the aristocracy.
The nature of the middle serfs was similar to the "estate managers" of later times. In the time of imperial Chou [i.e. before the
rise of the states as political powers], such estates were still
known only by locality and not by any unit of measure. For instance,
one inscription mentions "the people of Yung," "the people of Ping,"
and "the people of Chou"; another mentions only "the people of
Keng" and "the people of Chin." As yet they did not use the terminology "the people of Yung town," "the people of Ping town," and
so forth. But in the Spring and Autumn period these private estates
gradually developed into larger villages and urban centers, which
the contemporary people called "towns." Such "towns" were the
source of food supply for the idle aristocracy; hence they were
known as "provision estates." The former granting of serfs and
bestowing of land were now lumped together as the granting of
"provision estates."

// As to the granting of serfs in the imperial Chou period, in terms
of territorial units the highest figure recorded in the inscriptions
was "three p'in 品 "; in terms of individuals the highest number
was 1,050 persons; and in terms of families the highest number
was thirty. As to the granting of fields, the highest figure recorded
was eleven. These were the maximum figures for the imperial
Chou period (so far as the most recently excavated bronzes indicate.) Compared to those in the Spring and Autumn period, however, these figures suddenly appear very small. During the first
half of Spring and Autumn, the general practice was to make grants
in terms of "one thousand families" and "one hundred districts." //

A typical record states that "The ruler of Chin gave Huan-tzu
one thousand families of Northern Barbarian slaves*, and also rewarded Shih Po with the district of Kua-yen [in Shansi]." The
"district" of that time consisted of less than a thousand families
and was smaller than a "town." Fiefs consisting of from three to
sixty "towns" were given by heads of states to their officials. There
was a great difference in the size of these "towns" as between
central and eastern China. Those in the Central Plain were larger
than those in eastern China [i.e. present Shantung], seven or eight
of the former equalling sixty of the latter. Hence a high official in
the Central Plain might receive eight "towns," as against a hundred
for a high official in eastern China. From the Spring and Autumn
period on there were also many cases of fiefs being acquired by
bribery, theft, violent annexation, and division.

---

*See the note on this passage on page 22.

⫽ Thenceforth there are no longer any records of the granting of "fields." True, this is partly due to the fact that the fields had now acquired units of measurement. But why then are there no records of the granting of this or that many mou of land? The main cause was the vogue of extravagance and rampant annexations prevalent at the time; the aristocracy was now ashamed of such a thing as the former niggardly "granting of fields." This situation informs us that the process of land concentration in the hands of individuals was progressing rapidly at that time.

3. Gradual Formation of Standards of Land Measurement

⫽ It has been noted above that in the time of imperial Chou--the first period of agricultural life of the Chinese people--there was neither a standard of calculation nor a unit of measurement for land, and that the word mou then had the meaning only of "flourishing field." Yet this first stage of new agricultural life was daily developing, expanding, and progressing, and naturally outgrew such vague concepts as "till five fields" and "till ten fields." Furthermore, the more complicated became the land relations, the more vexing became the standardless, unitless, and confused land accounts. Hence standards of measurement were gradually established under the pressure of circumstances.

⫽ But how were the first standards of land measurement brought into being? What methods did our ancestors use to estimate the vast boundless land? They employed two methods to calculate it.

⫽ First, if faced with a wide and boundless stretch of land, how would they measure it without tape measure or yardstick? They very ingeniously computed the land area according to the number of people that could be fed with grain produced from it. If the field was sufficient to feed five hundred people, which was the equivalent of a "brigade," it would be called the "land of one brigade." If it was enough to feed one hundred people, which was the size of a "company," it would be called the "land of one company." This practice was preserved down to the Spring and Autumn period. ⫽

The Discourses of the States in several places indicates the widespread use of group designations as units of land measurement, as in the passage "Shu-hsiang answered, '.... A chief minister of a large state [receives] the land of one brigade, and a taifu, the land of one company.'" The domain of the Son of Heaven was described simply as "feeding a million people with nine hai 畡 of land; " it was of no importance what the specific size of a hai was.

//Secondly, suppose that they came across a very small plot of
land which was easy to measure, but that they possessed no knowledge of inches and feet, did our ancestors have a way to cope with
this situation? Yes, they did. They carefully counted the rows of
grain in the field.//

There were special characters for one, two, and three rows of
grain. Three hundred rows were called a mou. In the smaller fields
the rows were counted off with the finger, but in the larger fields
they were paced off. One pace, made up of two steps, was the
equivalent of three rows and three furrows. An area of one pace
by a hundred paces was one mou. For the sake of uniformity, the
plough was used as the basic measure for the width of the rows
and furrows. But the size of the plough in itself was not uniform
in different parts of the country, varying from five and six to eight
[Chinese] inches. The important point is that there began to be a
generally adopted way of land measurement.

After a lapse of considerable time, new and more refined concepts of land area emerged to allow flexibility in calculations.
These were the wan畹 (30 mou), a narrow rectangle; the hsi 畦
(50 mou), a wider rectangle; and the ch'ing 頃 (100 mou), a square
area. This marked the first step of the progress from a general
concept of land area to a more complicated and detailed one, and
can be termed the ancient method of land measurement.

The next step occurred in the time of Duke Hsiao of Ch'in[361-
338 B.C.], when the traditional concept of 1 mou equals 1 x 100
paces was overthrown. The Ch'in regulations fixed 1 mou at 1 x
240 paces; the Ch'in mou therefore had an area two and one-half
times that of the old mou. This can be designated as the Ch'in
system of land measurement.

But the last step in the progress took place still later, probably
during the Warring States and after the reformed standards of
Duke Hsiao of Ch'in. Heretofore people's concept of land surface
was defective; they could think of an area of land only in terms of
30 or 50 or 100 mou, but a single mou was still represented in
terms of a line rather than an area. They only knew that 1 x 240
paces equals 1 mou, without realizing that the same area could be
achieved with other combinations of measurements. But with the
levying of taxes on land, methods for the calculation of land area
also improved. People became versed in the computation of land
plots of all shapes and sizes. They also learned that 12 x 20 paces,
or 15 x 16 paces, all equally constituted the area of one mou.
That is, the concept of land surface had clearly graduated from
that of "line" to that of "area."

4. Emergence of Taxes and Levies

Down to the time of the granting of fiefs, the private property of the tribal chief was indistinguishable from common tribal property, and there was no need for taxation. But as time went on and the larger tribes became states, the various political and military expenditures resulted in the emergence of a system of levies and taxes.

// Before discussing the system of taxation there is a point that must be made absolutely clear, namely that "levies" and "taxes" were two entirely distinct things in China's first period of taxation, and should not be confused together. "Levies" consisted solely of the requisition of military supplies and were a kind of special military levy. "Taxes" were the ordinary land and grain taxes. "Levies" were taken directly from the populace. "Taxes" were exacted by the government from the landlord class. The two must be discussed separately.

// Here let us discuss "levies" first. In origin the levies were somewhat similar to conscription and the requisition of weapons. They were also more or less akin to the organization of popular defense corps, being very similar to the systems of pao-chia 保甲 and pao-ma 保馬 of later ages [i.e. the systems for local defense instituted by Wang An-shih in the Sung Dynasty]. In sum, they were a sort of regular army for the country, a sort of law for the drafting of able-bodied men and the commandeering of war chariots. //

Historical materials tell us plainly that all levies were military requisitions, and that the word "levy" denoted primarily the requisition of war chariots. Hence relevant phrases were used to describe political units, such as "a state of one thousand chariots" or "a household of one hundred chariots." In addition, levies also included the soldiers, horses, and armaments that complemented the chariots.

The next question is, what was the method used to collect the levies from the people, and what was the standard? Although the details are not yet clear, we are informed by the Tso Chronicle that in 590 B.C. "the armed levies of ch'iu 丘 were instituted in Lu as a result of trouble with the state of Ch'i. Thus "the armed levies of ch'iu" were an arms expansion program which could in no way have been so heavy earlier. At one time a tien 甸 , which comprised four times the number of people in a ch'iu, had to contribute one long chariot, four war horses, twelve oxen, three armored warriors, and seventy-two foot soldiers. "This used to be the levy on a tien," said one commentator, "but now Lu took it from a ch'iu, and was censured for the heavy exactions."

But there are two other versions of the standard of collection; this indicates that actually a uniform standard was lacking at the time. Some of the figures are highly improbable, so that a final answer as to the rate of conscription is still wanting. However, there is definite evidence in the Tso Chronicle of an evolution in the unit size on which the levies were based. With the growth of population the number of people within the tien, ch'iu and other units increased, whereupon the government, in order to get the full benefit of the increased manpower, exacted from the ch'iu what it had previously taken from the tien. Later the exaction, called "the levy on fields," was based on the actual area of a household's cultivated land. This was instituted in the twelfth year of Duke Ai [482 B.C.], although Confucius had protested vainly against it as being too heavy.

// To return to our subject, it is clear from the above that in their origins the levies were military matters, that is the con- scription and collection of regular armies and military supplies. The source of these collections was the people, that is, the farmers. But in the later days of this system, the levies were made by some corrupt officials only in the form of raw materials for armament-- that is, in metal. This metal was not used to make weapons but was made into private treasure instead. The case of Yüan P'o in the state of Ch'en [in Honan] illustrates this:

> In the summer Yüan P'o of Ch'en fled to Cheng. Previ- ously, while he was the Minister of Education, Yüan P'o had made levies on the fields in fiefs on the occasion of the marriage of the Duke's daughter. He took what was left over for his own great implements (Tu's Commentary: " 'Great implements' are bells, ting-tripods and such like.") His countrymen expelled him, so he left.

This case, cited in the Tso Chronicle under the year 484 B.C., is very significant. It indicates the existence of an intermediate method in the transition from direct levies of armaments to indi- rect levies of property. After the time of Duke Wen [403-387 B.C.] of Wei and Duke Hsiao [361-338 B.C.] of Ch'in, the "levies" be- gan to be separated from military conscription and became "poll levy," an indirect collection of property like the "tax."

// Now as to the "tax," its nature was entirely different from that of the "levies." Ever since the ownership of land had gradually passed from common tribal possession to private ownership by the individual, the private property of landlords gradually increased in amount, and public land decreased proportionately. The out-

come was that the only common tribal land left was the domain of
the monarch, the rest having all been occupied by powerful aristocrats and other active individuals. Yet the state was gradually assuming definite form and increasing its expenditures, for which
the private domain of the monarch alone was of course insufficient.
It was necessary then to take a "tax" of a certain percentage from
the entire landowning class. Therefore the Erh-ya as well as Yen
Shih-ku's Commentaries in the Han History both have it thus: "Tax
--to donate." This means that the landlord class donated a part of
their harvests as a contribution to the ruler. The Spring and
Autumn Classic probably contains the earliest mention of the word
"tax" in ancient Chinese history: "In the autumn...of the fifteenth
year...the mou was taxed for the first time." (Fifteenth year of
Duke Hsüan [of Lu, i.e. 594 B.C.].)//

Records in the Kung-yang Chronicle, the Book of Rites, and
Mencius show that the first taxes in Lu were based on the mou as
the unit of collection. The accepted rate of the time was one-tenth
of the product, which was, however, later increased to two-tenths.
The one-tenth tax was also called ch'e 徹, which in ancient pro-
nounciation probably had the same sound as the word for "tax"
[shui 稅].

//After the lapse of a certain period, the taxes were doubled in
the time of Duke Hsüan's great-great-grandson Duke Ai [494-480
B.C.]. They now stood at two-tenths. But that was still not enough.
Thus, in the Analects we find:

> Duke Ai asked Yu Jo: "The year is one of scarcity, and
> [the returns for] expenditure are not sufficient. What is to
> be done?"
> Yu Jo replied: "Why not [simply] tithe the hundred families?"
> [The Duke] said: "I find two-tenths insufficient. How can I
> do with one-tenth?"
> [Yu Jo] replied: "If the hundred families have enough, how
> can the prince be in want? If the hundred families are in
> want, how can the prince have enough?"

//Besides informing us that the two-tenths tax-rate had been
started before Duke Ai's time, this bit of historical material also tells us that the "tax" was taken from the aristocracy alone.
This explains the statement "If the hundred families are in want,
how can the prince have enough?" The "hundred families" were
the aristocracy, meaning precisely the opposite of the "common
people" of today. In the slightly later "Institute of Yao" in the
modern text [i.e. Han dynasty] version of the Book of History, the
term "hundred families" was used in every instance plainly in

contrast to the "masses." The "masses" were the serfs and the
"hundred families" were the landlord class. [....]

// And so several decades passed by. By that time the tax rate in
excess of one-tenth was probably quite widespread in China. Not
only were the aristocratic "hundred families" taxed more than one-
tenth, but the serf "masses" were also made to pay the "tax." That
is, half of the "tax" was gradually shifted from the shoulders of
the aristocratic "gentlemen" to those of the common "rustics."
How do we know this? It is shown in the texts of Mo-tzu and Mencius:

> Now the farmer pays his tax to the official, and the official
> uses it for wine and grain to make sacrifices to the Supreme
> God and the spirits..." (Mo-tzu.)

// It is clear then that taxes were borne by the common people and
farmers after the time of Duke Tao [467-431 B.C.] of Lu. Therefore Mencius suggested with great vigor to Duke Wen of T'eng:

> Duke Wen of T'eng sent Pi Chan to ask (Mencius) about the
> well-field system...Mencius said, "...Although the territory
> of T'eng is narrow and small, yet there must be in it gentle-
> men and rustics. Without the gentlemen there would be none
> to govern the rustics, and without rustics there would be none
> to support the gentlemen. Let the one-ninth tax [chu 助] be
> instituted in the more remote parts of the country, and let
> the levy of one-tenth [fu 賦] be imposed in the more central
> parts of the country.

// This was Mencius' suggestion to Duke Wen of T'eng for the prevention of future troubles, but at the same time it was also a pro-
test against the practices prevalent in the whole empire. Mencius
saw that the one-tenth levy, formerly shouldered only by the
aristocracy, was now borne by the farmers (including self-cultivating farmers and serfs). Therefore he protested that the "rustics," who worked themselves to the bone, should not be responsible for the "tax" [shui]; their lot was pitiable enough after paying the one-ninth chu (i.e. tsu 租 ["rent"]) to the landlord. Mencius further saw that the former one-tenth tax on the aristocrats
had long since become two-tenths, but that even this was considered insufficient by the government. Therefore he suggested
that the highest tax on the aristocrats in the central parts of the
country ought to be "the levy of one-tenth," which should not be
exceeded. Note that in Mencius' time the word shui ["tax"] had
been changed into fu ["levy"] by common usage. Thenceforth

"levy" acquired two meanings: one was the original military levy, which later became the poll levy; the other was the levy that evolved from the land tax. This was entirely different from the narrow interpretation of "levy" in the time of Tzu-lu [one of Confucius' disciples].//

The main item collected as the "levy" at that time was of course grain. Mencius and Kuan-tzu give evidence of levies collected in terms of grain. The rate of the levies, however, continued to fluctuate. According to Kuan-tzu, there had been some attempt to increase it to three-tenths, but Kuan Chung was said to have suggested that such a rate should not be allowed except in a year of great plenty.

As to tsu ["rent"], it was a matter between the landlord and his serfs. In Mencius' time tsu was a word used exclusively for the rent paid by the serf to the landlord; this varied each year according to the harvest. But by the time when the Book Kuan-tzu was written, tsu was employed also to denote both "taxes" and "levies."

In short, "levies" were collected by the government from farmers; "taxes," by the government from aristocrats; and "rents," by landlords from the farmers. Thus a triangular relationship was established.

5. Methods of Changing Private Landownership

//Since landownership had gradually changed from common possession by the tribe into private possession by the family--that is, from the hands of the great majority of the people into those of a very small minority--the former tribes then became the equivalent of small states, with which the family could not compete. Large-scale mobilizations, war, and bloodshed were necessary, if land was to be taken by force from the tribe. The rise and decline of families were but short dramas, and it took little effort to scheme for the landed property of some declining family. Therefore the frequency of violent seizure and forceful occupation of land, as recorded in the classics of the Spring and Autumn period, is truly striking. For example, figures in the table given in Part I show that in the Tso Chronicle alone there are seven cases of the taking of land by violence, and five of forceful occupation. In Discourses of the States there are two cases of land dispute. Other evidence can be found in the Book of Poetry, which records the taking of another's land; in the Analects, which records Kuanchung's taking of the fief of the Po family [in Ch'i]; and so on.

//The above cases involved the annexation of the private property of families by military or political force. That is to say, the way

of changing private landownership was still limited to the two paths
of military or political seizure. It can also be said that there was
but one method--plunder. This was before the establishment of
the system of trading with money. In the period before Ch'in, with
the coming of the age of monetary trade, those possessing large
amounts of money naturally found it unnecessary to assume a bru-
tal face and resort to the taking of land by force, but could use
their economic power to oppress the common people at their own
leisure. Thus the method of changing private landownership gradually became a monetary transaction--buying and selling.

According to our observation, not a few great families had
risen through the purchase of landed property at the time when
Kuan-tzu* was written (or was it perhaps shortly after the usurpa-
tion of Ch'i [in 481 B.C.] by Ch'en Heng?). Therefore the following legend was recorded in Kuan-tzu: "When Duke Huan [of Ch'i]
campaigned against Ku-chu [in Hopei-Jehol], the grain in the Ting
family was sufficient to provision the entire army on a five-month
march..." It is eminently clear that this was not an actual historical fact of the time of Duke Huan, but rather that it was either
a fable invented by the author of Kuan-tzu, or a contemporary
story. But from the account that there were families with enough
to feed an entire army (number of men not known) for five months,
we can get a general picture of the vast concentration of cultivated
land in the hands of the powerful households.

//Furthermore, this practice of absorbing the landed property of
self-cultivating farmers and small landowners through buying and
selling was soon noticed and utilized in the Warring States period
by Shang Yang, a radical utilitarian. He adopted it as a short-
cut to sudden tax increases. It was therefore protected and extended under the political auspices of the Ch'in state and became
one of the state measures of the new Ch'in, which was strengthening itself through reforms.

Duke Hsiao [361-338 B.C.] of Ch'in employed Shang Yang,
who destroyed the well-field system and erased the paths between fields. Thus the imperial way was lost, and there was
no limit to excesses and discrepancies. Among the people
the property of the rich was counted by the myriads, while
the poor subsisted on chaff...(Han History)

In Ch'in, on the contrary, Shang Yang's laws were used, and
the system of the empire was changed. The well-field was

---

*Attributed to the famous statesman Kuan Chung (died 645 B.C.), a minister
of Duke Huan [685-643 B.C.] of Ch'i, but obviously written after his time.

abolished, and the people were free to trade [in land]. The fields of the rich lay one beyond another, while the poor did not have enough land to stand an awl....(Tung Chung-shu as quoted in Han chih).

//For the time being, of course, this policy of aiding the strong to absorb the small had the effect of "strengthening the state" and "subjugating the neighboring states and assuming the hegemony among the feudal princes." [....]

//Thenceforth the hereditary monarchs of Ch'in found this system highly appetizing, until the time of the First Emperor [221-210 B.C.], when this policy of encouraging unrestricted colonization and occupation by the powerful families was further protected by an order: "In the twenty-first year of the First Emperor [225 B.C.], the people were ordered to report on the true amount of their land." According to Ma Tuan-lin, the reason for ordering the people to report on the true amount of land was that Ch'in "allowed the people to cultivate in unlimited amounts." This explanation is probably correct. In the era of monetary trade, the absorption by local magnates of small people's land through economic pressure was as easy as the maneuverings of a tiger in a flock of sheep, particularly in view of the encouragement given by the government and the emperor. The outcome was that "therefore the poor people are constantly clothed like cattle and horses, and eat the fare of dogs and pigs." This finally led to a fervent examination into the problem of land distribution by those men of all ages who were perceptive and socially awakened. It also led to the first upsurge of the land equalization movement in Chinese history.//

NOTES

吳其昌, "秦以前中國田制史" 社會科學季刊
Wu Ch'i-ch'ang, "Ch'in i-ch'ien Chung-kuo t'ien-chih shih,"
Quarterly Journal of Social Science (Wuhan University), V (1935),
543-583, 833-872.

The author makes extensive use of inscriptions on bronzes; citations are to the name of the bronze vessels. He also relies heavily on the Tso Chronicle, Discourses of the States (Kuo-yü 國語), and the Book of Poetry. Use is also made of the Book of History, Kung-yang Chronicle 公羊傳, Book of Rites, Mencius, Kuan-tzu, and other early works.

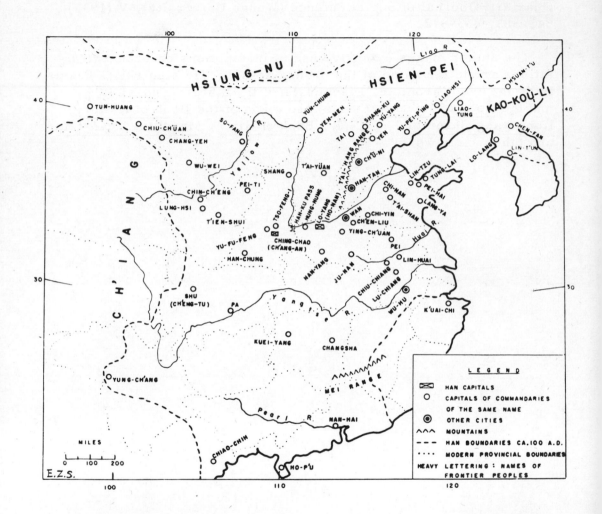

Map 2. China in the Han dynasty

6

POPULATION AND GEOGRAPHY IN THE TWO HAN DYNASTIES

by

LAO KAN

1. Fluctuations in Population Figures

⫽It is indeed not an easy task today to seek a clear picture of the population fluctuations of two thousand years ago. In our estimates we can rely only on the figures in the official histories, but as these were based on the number of tax-paying households rather than on the sum total of individuals, their reliability must be regarded as doubtful. We can see from many examples that at the time of large-scale migrations, which always occurred during great political upheavals, the displaced persons constituted a mobile population and would not all be recorded in the census even though they might be able to find a refuge in some place or other. Consequently population figures would suddenly decrease when actually this was not entirely the case. Furthermore, a comparison of the figures given in different written sources often reveals enormous and unreasonable disparaties. Such difficulties make it hard to begin the investigation, and impossible to reach definitive conclusions. Therefore we can now do no more than make a chronological survey of historical materials that are without contradictions, examine the sources of contradictory data, and then attempt to reach more or less reasonable conclusions.

⫽With the great upheavals and migrations during the transition from Ch'in to Han old metropolises were reduced to desolate areas. The "Life of Ch'en P'ing" in the Han History states:

> Emperor Kao went south through Ch'ü-ni [in Hopei]. On seeing that the houses in this city were very large, he said, "What a magnificent district! In my travels in the empire I have seen only Lo-yang and this city [to be of such size]." He asked an Imperial Secretary for its population. The Imperial Secretary answered. "At the beginning of the Ch'in dynasty there were over 30,000 households; but lately during the

wars most of the people either fled or hid, and at present there
are [only] 5,000-odd households." And so [the Emperor] ordered the Imperial Secretary to invest Ch'en P'ing as the Marquis of Ch'ü-ni, all of which was to be his estate, and to di-
vest him of his former estate at Hu-yung [in Honan].

// Thus at the beginning of Han dynasty the census figures for some
areas were no more than one-sixth of those during Ch'in. Later,
however, as a result of the calling together of displaced persons,
the population in some places in the reigns of Emperors Wen and
Ching [179-141 B.C.] more than doubled that during the reign of
Emperor Kao [202-194 B.C.]. Of course, not all displaced persons returned to their original home districts. For instance, we
see that the bob-haired and tattooed Wu and Yüeh peoples silently
passed from the scene after Yüeh was overthrown during the
Warring States [....] After King Pi of Wu rallied together the
exiles from all parts of the empire, however, K'uai-chi Commandery [in Wu] became known for its celebrities. This was undoubtedly due to the culture that was brought there by the people
from the Central Plain.
// The general trend of population changes during the Western
Han dynasty is discernible from the Preface to "Lives of Upright
Officials" in the Han History:

> With the rise of Han the disintegration of the Ch'in period
> was reversed. The people were given a chance to rest...and
> all was tranquil within the empire. The people engaged in
> agriculture and increased in wealth and numbers. During the
> reigns of Emperors Wen and Ching [179-141 B.C.] the cus-
> toms were changed...and influenced the people to improve.
> During the time of Emperor Wu [140-87 B.C.], externally
> there were campaigns against the barbarians and internally
> the laws and institutions were changed and the people's live-
> lihood declined... During the minority of Emperor Chao [86-
> 74 B.C.], Ho Kuang acted as regent. As a result of the pre-
> vious extravagances and military expeditions, the country
> suffered from heavy expenditures. [Ho] Kuang merely followed
> precedent in carrying out his duties, but made no reforms.
> With the [pacification and] sinification of the Hsiung-nu in
> the same period, however, the people's wealth increased...
> Coming to [the reign of] Emperor Hsüan [73-49 B.C.]...who
> rose from among the general populace...and sedulously ex-
> erted himself in administration,...this was called the
> Restoration.

Thus we know that before Emperor Hsüan the population con-
sistently increased. Although at the time of Emperor Wu "ex-
ternally there were campaigns against the barbarians, and in-
ternally the laws and institutions were changed," this undoubtedly caused a greater increase in migration than in mortality.
Furthermore, the political situation was relatively stable at
that time. Over 2,000,000 migrants were settled along the
northern frontiers, and it was still possible to exploit unoccupied land.//

It was sometimes charged during the reign of Emperor
Hsüan that local magnates fraudulently enlarged the census
reports of their areas so as to increase their own prestige.
This is unfounded. More people meant more taxes. How
would these magnates make up for the taxes that the alleged
increase in population incurred? The over-all doubling of
the population in the fifty-odd years between the time of Emperor Hsüan and the end of Western Han is proved by the
fact that Shan-yang Commandery [in Shantung], an area
where catastrophes both natural and man-made frequently
occurred, was able to effect such an increase. Nor is it prob-
able that Wang Mang [9-25 A.D.] made up the large population figures when he assumed power.

After the disturbances of Wang Mang's time the population again sharply decreased. The following figures for Eastern Han, taken from the Supplementary Han History show the
subsequent fluctuations in population:

Year (A.D.)	Population	Percentage of 57 A.D.
57	21,007,820	
76	34,125,021	163 per cent
89	43,356,367	209 per cent
105	53,256,229	254 per cent
125	48,690,789	232 per cent
142	49,730,550	237 per cent
145	49,524,183	236 per cent
146	47,566,572	227 per cent

// The above figures reached their high point during the reign
of Emperor Ho [89-105]. This fits in with the statement in the
"Chronicles of Emperor Ho" in the Later Han History that
"from the Restoration [25 A.D.] to the Yung-yüan period [89-
104], the situation remained peaceful despite some vicissi-
tudes, with the result that the common people increased in
numbers every year and newly opened land was added with

each generation." The sudden drop in population after Emperor Ho was probably due to the invasions of the Ch'iang people. Migrations naturally greatly increased when the Ch'iang "invaded the Three Supporting Regions [around the former capital in Shensi], reached Chao and Wei in the east and I-chou [in Szechwan] in the south, and killed the Prefect of Han-chung [in southern Shensi]."//

Contemporary edicts mention that people from the northwest were resettled in the interior of the country. The population in those areas must have fled away or been captured by the enemy, thus affecting the total population figures. After the reign of Emperor Shun [126-144] there was a slight increase following the end of the migration. Corruption of officials at that time, however, makes it possible that the figures were under-reported.

Some other sources present higher figures for the period after Emperor Shun. The Supplementary Han History gives 53,869,588 for the period 136-141 and 61,086,224 for the year 146, and the Tsin History gives 56,486,856 for 156. Although the absolute figures may be of questionable accuracy, it is reasonable to suppose that there was quite an increase in population between 140 and 146 A.D. Thereafter the population again decreased as a result of famines and wars.

The effect of famines and wars on migrations can be seen by tabulating the occurrences of these catastrophes during the Eastern Han period. (Material for the Western Han period is not complete enough for tabulation.) The figures were reached by counting each year in which one or more large or small famine or war occurred; invasions were counted as wars, but expeditions were excluded from the reckoning. From these figures it can be seen that famines and wars usually slowed down, or had a negative effect on, the growth of population.

Famines and Wars in the Later Han Dynasty

Emperor	Duration of Reign (Years)	Famines	Wars
Kuang-wu [25-57]	33	6	21
Ming [58-75]	18	1	2
Chang [75-88]	13	2	4
Ho [89-105]	17	8	5
Shang [106]	1	1	1
An [107-125]	19	14	13
Shun [126-144]	19	9	11
Ch'ung [145]	1	1	1

Emperor	Duration of Reign Years	Famines	Wars
Chih [146]	1	1-	1
Hsüan [147-167]	21	15	16
Ling [168-189]	21	11	17
Hsien [190-220]	32	7	18

2. The Kuan-tung Area

Kuan-tung [East of the Pass] by definition should include all
areas east of the Han-ku Pass [in Honan]. But contemporary usage
was otherwise. For our purpose Kuan-tung will be defined as that
area enclosed by the Huai River in the south, the Han-ku Pass and
T'ai-hang Range in the west, and the old territories of Yen and Tai
in the north.

In the main this region consisted of a great plain which did not
exceed 200 [Chinese] feet in elevation, and was best suited to the
development of agriculture and pastoralism. Ancient documents
testify to its economic and political importance during the Shang
and Spring and Autumn periods, as well as to the density of population. For the Han period an example is found in Chi-yin Commandery, which consisted of what are now four districts near
modern Ts'ao-chou in Shantung; it had a reputed population of over
1,300,000. Chi-yin was known as T'ao during the Warring States
period, at which time it was conspicuously rich as a trading center, and the hub of contemporary economic activities.

// After the unification of China by Ch'in the riches of the influential people of the empire were all removed to Kuan-chung [i.e.
"Within the Pass," the modern Shensi where the metropolis of
Ch'in was located] and to Pa and Shu [Szechwan]. This increased
the wealth of the Kuan-chung area. But the sources of such wealth
in Kuan-tung could not be moved to the base area of Ch'in. Consequently during the Han dynasty Kuan-tung still represented the
major wealth of the country. This is seen from the following:

(i) Agriculture

// The economy of Han was undoubtedly mainly agricultural. The
importance of agricultural production can be seen from contemporary opinions that advocated the favoring of agriculture. This was
of course not limited to the Kuan-tung area, but what we want to
look into now is the relative advance of agriculture in Kuan-tung
as compared with other areas, rather than the relative importance of agriculture in Kuan-tung [as against other occupations].

According to our present knowledge, the other areas, except for
Kuan-chung and the region of Pa and Shu, were all inferior to Kuan-
tung in this respect, and even Kuan-chung was dependent on it for
foodstuffs. In the Han History scant attention was paid to famines
in frontier districts, yet those in Kuan-tung were prominently recorded. Actually, the frontier regions must have suffered more
famines than Kuan-tung because of their high terrain, desert soil,
and insufficient rainfall. They were omitted in the records, however, because these areas had only a small population and did not
produce as much food as Kuan-tung. //

There is much evidence in the Han History that not only the metropolitan area of Kuan-chung, but the northwestern frontier area
also found it necessary to import grain from Kuan-tung. The following are some examples from the Han History:

Over 100,000 men were also sent to build defense works in
So-fang [in the Ordos area]. Their provisions were transported from afar, all the areas east of [the T'ai-hang] Range
being affected by the requisitions.

Chang Liang....said: "....Kuan-chung is to be securely defended on three sides. The remaining east side is to be used
to control the feudal lords. When the lords are peaceful,
grain tributes can be transported on the [Yellow] River to
supply the capital; when they are rebellious, the Imperial
forces can easily be sent down the River and the transportation of supplies can also be accommodated."

Ch'in took grain from the seaboard territories and transported
it west of the [Yellow] River.

Yung-yang [near modern Cheng-chou in Honan] served as a trans-
shipment center in this traffic.

// Though agricultural development in Kuan-tung depended on the
vast plains endowed by nature, yet in addition the advancement of
hydraulics was also a significant factor. Judging from the details
in Tribute of Yü, which was completed during the Warring States
period at the latest, we can say that this work was definitely written by a man from Kuan-tung. In it contemporary hydraulics are
reflected in such descriptions as the conservancy of rivers according to the contours of the land, the determining of tribute
payments according to soil fertility and terrain, and the fine
planning and careful investigations. Besides these, there are
many other accounts of hydraulic undertakings such the conservancy work done on the Yeh River by Hsi-men Pao, and the con-

struction of the Hung-kou and Wu-tao canals. The Kuan-tung hydraulic experts had gone through a long period of training. Later
when Ch'in built canals it also depended on hydraulic experts from
Kuan-tung, e.g. those from the state of Cheng. During Ch'in and
Han hydraulics underwent further development. "Rivers and
Canals" in the Historical Records and "Channels and Ditches" in
the Han History deal mainly with the Kuan-tung area, except for
minor parts touching on Kuan-chung and the northern areas of Shu.
The old dammed-up ponds, some drained and others filled with
water, which are mentioned in the Commentaries on the Shui-ching
were also mostly found in Kuan-tung. The combination of natural
resources and artificial irrigation made this the granary of China.

(ii) Industry

//Where the land was well-developed and agriculture flourished
the population was of course denser than in less developed places,
and consequently the production of goods also increased. Hence
in an agricultural region the cities easily became industrial centers for the neighboring areas. In Kuan-tung the products were
plentiful, the population was dense, and there could scarcely be
any question as to raw materials and markets, so that it naturally
had the capacity to become the area with the most highly developed
handicrafts in China. The "Treatise on Geography" in the Han History lists ten commanderies in which there were Supervisors of Industry. These included Ho-nan, Nan-yang, Ho-nei, Ying-ch'uan [all
in Honan], Chi-nan, T'ai-shan [both in Shantung], Shu, and Kuang-
han [both in Szechwan]. According to the Supplementary Han History, "In each commandery and district where handicrafts are numerous there is stationed a Supervisor of Industries to be in charge
of the production and taxation of goods." In other words, Supervisors of Industries were placed in charge of the production and
taxation of goods where there were large numbers of artisans.
The manufactured products were destined for the imperial household; for those goods that were sold [on the market] a tax was
collected by the Supervisor. Thus we can infer that where such officials were stationed, there industries must have flourished. Of
such places, all were located in Kuan-tung, with the exception
of two in Szechwan.//

There were also Supervisors of Weaving during the Han dynasty. Those in Ch'i [in Shantung], whose women were all skilled
in weaving, had the largest number of artisans under their control. The area comprising modern Honan and western Shantung
was a large cloth-producing area in Han.

Salt and iron industries were also most highly developed in Kuan-tung, especially in the present Shantung. From there they were introduced into Shu. The Han History lists forty-six Supervisors of Iron, of whom twenty-six, or more than half of the total, were stationed in Kuan-tung cities. Of the thirty-five Supervisors of Salt, fifteen, or nearly half of the total, were in Kuan-tung; these included five in Tung-lai, three in Lang-ya, and two in Pei-hai [all in Shantung]. Of those not in Kuan-tung, two were in Shang Commandery [in Shensi]; the rest were all scattered one to a city, far below the scale of Tung-lai and Lang-ya. Thus the income from fishing and salt was the highest in the territory of the former state of Ch'i.

Wang Mang later lost Kuan-tung as a result of inappropriate policies regarding salt and iron monopolies, which testifies to the importance of such industries.

(iii) Commerce

The commerce of Kuan-tung was always more advanced than that of the west. For example, the state policies expounded in [the eastern work] Kuan-tzu were often different from those advanced by Shang Yang [minister of the western state of Ch'in]. At the time of Wang Mang, of the five densely populated metropolises--Lo-yang, Lin-tzu, Wan, Han-tan, and Ch'eng-tu--all but the last were situated in Kuan-tung. Close relationships existed between great merchants and famous leaders of Han politics.

//Since Kuan-tung was the greatest producer in all aspects of the economy, the population there was also greater than in other areas. The "Treatise on Geography" in the Han History records the commanderies of Tung [in Hopei-Shantung], Ho-nan, Ch'en-liu, Nan-yang, and Ying-ch'uan [all in Honan] as all having more than 1,500,000 inhabitants, while none of the Three Supporting Regions [in Kuan-chung] had more than 1,000,000. These three commanderies were not small in area, and in addition they had received immigrants and colonists, yet their population still lagged behind the commanderies of Kuan-tung. This shows what an excellent geographic environment the latter area enjoyed.

//The gap between wealth and poverty was also most pronounced in areas where the population was large and industries flourished. There the rich tended to be extravagant and more female entertainers were to be found. The surplus population became wandering professionals, thus promoting the emergence of sophist-politicians and wandering braves.//

Many persons had already been divorced from the land in the

period of the Warring States. The Historical Records quotes one of these, the high official Su Ch'in, as saying, "If I had owned two ch'ing of land in the suburb of Lo-yang, how could I have worn the prime minister's seal from six states?" This means that those who were unable to obtain rents from land became travelling sophist-politicians. Such a phenomenon of course could not have taken place where there was virgin land.

Historical records show that, of the well-known sophist-politicians in early Han up to the time of Emperor Wu, none came from the west. As to the wandering braves, they were the product of a dense population plus the existence of luxurious living. The practice of noble families retaining such braves in their households originated in the Warring States period, for example in the state of Ch'i, and was continued in the Han dynasty. "The Lives of Wandering Braves" in the Historical Records indicates that they were very likely all Kuan-tung men. Finally, Han-tan in the state of Chao was already known for its female entertainers during the Warring States. The tradition continued into the Han period. Besides Chao, other Kuan-tung states like Ch'i and Yen were also known for the musical accomplishments of their people at a time when the music of Ch'in was still in an extremely simple state.

Historical records reveal the contemporary belief that the customs of Ch'i were affected by the high density of its population, which was alleged to have made its people cunning.

Our tentative conclusion is that Kuan-tung had greater economic wealth, a larger population, and a higher level of culture than other areas in China. It continued to be the most densely populated area in the country through the Eastern Han dynasty.

3. Northern and Western Frontier Commanderies

The northern and western frontier commanderies comprised the areas formerly occupied by the Hsiung-nu and by the states of Ch'in, Yen, and Chao. They extended from Tun-huang [in Kansu] in the west to Liao-hsi [southern Manchuria] in the east. The numerous passages in the Han histories describing the frontier areas point to the following conclusions: (a) They covered a vast and sparsely populated area. (b) The character of the people was strong and militant. (c) They had a mixed pastoral-hunting-fishing economy. (d) The population consisted mostly of poor people who had migrated from inner China.

Han followed the Ch'in policy of settling large numbers of people from the interior in the frontier commanderies. The following are a few examples from the Han History for the period of

Emperor Wu: In 127 B.C. 100,000 people were moved to So-fang; in 117 B.C. "cunning and undesirable officials and people" were exiled to the frontiers; in 111 B.C. the commanderies of Chang-yeh and Tun-huang [in Kansu] were created by dividing the terri-tories of Wu-wei and Chiu-ch'üan, and people were moved in to colonize them. In the same reign there were 600,000 frontier gar-rison soldiers, many of whom became inhabitants of the frontier regions. Throughout Western Han the density of frontier popula-tion remained comparatively high; out of these people there emerged a large number of renowned military leaders.

At the time of Wang Mang, however, frontier wars again re-duced the population figures. Early in the reign of Emperor Kuang-wu the inhabitants of the most exposed areas were moved into China proper. Although it was recorded that a revival of frontier commanderies was attempted later in 46 A.D. by the settlement of over 100,000 families in the border regions, and similar efforts were made in subsequent reigns, the frontier commanderies re-mained underpopulated and ill-defended. The invasions of the Ch'iang following those of the Hsiung-nu caused a decrease in the population in all the frontier commanderies. The accompanying table, which is based on data in the Han History and Later Han History, shows the population changes in the northern and western frontiers during the two Han dynasties. (Figures refer to number of persons except in the case of Chiu-ch'üan, for which they repre-sent the number of households.)

Frontier Population Changes

Commandery	Reign of Em-peror P'ing [2 A.D.]	Reign of Em-peror Shun [140 A.D.]	Change
Chin-ch'eng [Kansu]	149,648	18,974	-130,071
T'ien-shui [Kansu]	261,348	13,138	-252,210
Wu-wei [Kansu]	76,419	34,226	-42,193
Chang-yeh [Kansu]	88,731	26,040	-62,691
Chiu-ch'üan [Kansu]	(18,137)	(12,706)	(-5,431)
Tun-huang [Kansu]	38,335	29,170	-9,195
An-ting [Kansu]	143,294	29,060	-114,234
Pei-ti [Kansu]	210,688	18,637	-192,051
Shang [Shensi]	606,658	28,599	-578,059
Wu-tu [Kansu]	235,560	81,728	-135,832
Lung-hsi [Kansu]	236,824	29,637	-207,187
Hsi-ho [Suiyuan]	698,836	20,838	-679,998

Frontier Population Changes, contd.

Commandery	Reign of Emperor P'ing [2 A.D.]	Reign of Emperor Shun [140 A.D.]	Change
So-fang [Suiyuan]	136,628	7,843	-128,785
Wu-yüan [Suiyuan]	231,328	22,957	-208,371
Yün-chung [Suiyuan]	173,270	26,430	-146,840
Ting-hsiang [Suiyuan]	163,144	13,571	-149,573
Yen-men [Shansi]	293,454	249,000	-44,454
Tai [Hopei]	278,754	126,188	-152,566
T'ai-yüan [Shansi]	680,488	200,124	-480,364
Shang-ku [Chahar]	117,762	51,204	-66,588
Yü-yang [Hopei]	264,116	435,740	+171,624
Yu-pei-p'ing [Hopei]	320,780	53,475	-267,305
Liao-hsi [Liaoning]	352,325	81,714	-271,611

In all cases except that of Yü-yang [in northern Hopei], there was a great reduction in population. The reason for the increase in Yü-yang was of course the fact that the people in the areas east of Chü-yung Pass [in northern Hopei] were moved into this commandery.

The question whether or not to abandon the frontier regions became a controversial issue during Eastern Han. By and large the influential officials were Kuan-tung men, who were naturally loath to have their resources taxed for frontier warfare, and so the removal of frontier population into the Kuan-chung area, rather than their defense by armed force, occurred frequently. Han thus gradually neglected the colonization of the frontier territories and came to rely on the policy of "using barbarians to control barbarians" as the only effective way of dealing with border enemies.

One more point of significance is the fact that the four commanderies west of the Yellow River, that is Wu-wei, Chang-yeh, Chiu-ch'üan, and Tun-huang, suffered the least reduction in population throughout Eastern Han. They were situated along the great East-West trade route [in Kansu], and their mixed economy of agriculture and commerce remained stable. Socially they exhibited the highest degree of Sino-barbarian acculturation.

4. Population and Planned Migrations in Kuan-chung

Western Han inherited the Ch'in policy of planned shifts of population. During Ch'in convicts were exiled to the frontier areas, while the wealthy in other parts of the country were moved into the

Kuan-chung region. People were also sent in large numbers--for
example in terms of 30,000 or 50,000 households--to construct
the imperial mausolea.

[The Han official] Ts'ao Ts'o laid down, and [the Han historian] Pan
Ku summed up, the basic principles of population shifts for the
Han dynasties. Convicts, freedmen, and poverty-stricken volun-
teers were to be sent as colonists "to strengthen the frontiers";
those who went were to be accorded favorable treatment. On the
other hand, the movement of people into Kuan-chung was aimed at
"strengthening the main trunk and weakening the branches," that
is at eliminating the danger of insubordination in the empire by
moving all elements of wealth and power to the vicinity of the
capital.

The movement of population into Kuan-chung concentrated on
areas around the imperial mausolea. It appears from the records
that the magnates of distant commanderies faced the danger of
having their property confiscated in the course of the transfer,
while high-ranking officials (those receiving a salary of 2,000
piculs of grain or over) enjoyed priority in grants of good land.
The planned migrations therefore had to be forced through over
the opposition of the magnates. This bred corruption and official
tyranny after the reign of Emperor Hsüan, when the construction
of imperial tombs was itself proving to be a severe drain on the
country.

Planned migrations into Kuan-chung did not take place in Eastern Han. By that time the capital of the empire had been moved
out of this area, and the population sharply decreased. The following table shows the population changes in the Three Supporting Regions of Kuan-chung from Western Han to Eastern Han:

Commandery	Western Han [2 A.D.]	Eastern Han [140 A.D.]	Reduction
Ching-chao-yin [Ch'ang-an]	682,468	285,574	396,894
Tso-feng-hsü	917,822	145,195	772,627
Yu-fu-feng	836,070	93,091	742,979

The wealthy people and sinecure holders of these areas moved
eastward to settle in the commanderies of Ho-nan and Nan-yang.

5. Commanderies and Districts in the Northeast

During the Warring States period the territory of the state of
Yen already included part of the Northeast [i.e. modern Manchuria].

After the subjugation of Yen in 222 B.C. the First Emperor of Ch'in established there the Liao-tung and Liao-hsi commanderies. The Han History records the surrender of 280,000 Eastern Barbarians in 128 B.C. and the establishment of Ts'ang-hai Commandery,* followed by the conquest of Korea in 108 B.C. and the establishment there of the four commanderies of Lo-lang, Hsüan-t'u, Lint'un, and Chen-fan. Chinese sovereignty therefore extended to the present provinces of Liaoning and Kirin and over the major portion of Korea. Fu Meng-chen in his Outline History of the Northeast maintains that during the Chou, Ch'in, and Han periods China's relations with Korea were closer than those with Indochina; in fact, these areas were then as closely affiliated with China as was central China. The Chinese commanderies were maintained in Korea until they were lost to the Hsien-pei and the Kao-kou-li peoples in 145-146 A.D.

The Chinese were already living in the area between the Liao River and Korea during the Chou and Ch'in periods. Later Wei Man [a native of Yen who invaded northern Korea at the end of Ch'in and established himself as the local ruler in the northeast] also brought with him a large number of people from the states of Ch'i and Yen. These people were skilled in navigation. Various works on navigation and the numerous chapters in the Han History on the constellations and astronomical observations at sea were probably done by natives of these states.

The Later Han History records:

> Wang Ching, styled Chung-t'ung, was a native of Nan-tu in
> Lo-lang Commandery [in western Korea]. His eighth-gener-
> ation ancestor [Wang] Chung, a native of Pu-ch'i in Lang-ya
> [in Shantung], delighted in magic and was versed in astronomy.
> During the rebellion of the Lü family...[Wang] Chung...em-
> barked on boats and sailed eastward to Lo-lang, where he
> settled in the mountains.

Several things should be noted in the above passage. First, Wang Chung "delighted in magic and was versed in astronomy," traits which closely resembled those of the "seafaring necromancers"

---

*This short-lived commandery was established on the present Manchurian-Korean border in 128 B.C. and abolished in 126 B.C. Our text corrects Lao Kan's error in dating the setting up of the commandery in 127 B.C. The "Annals of Emperor Wu" (Han shu, chapter 6) notes the establishment under the first year of the Yüan-so period (128-123 B.C.) and the abolition under the third year.

described in the Historical Records. The kind of books mentioned
above, such as the Astronomy at Sea, must have been utilized, and
although the chapters in the Han History were written after Wang
Chung's time, yet the beginnings were undoubtedly emerging long
before then. Secondly, the fact that Wang Chung went straightway
into the mountains of Lo-lang proves that there were already Chinese inhabitants there, for otherwise he would not have been able
to stay isolated in an alien society and yet preserve Chinese culture through eight generations.

Fu Meng-chen's Outline History of the Northeast maintains that
the kingdom of Sin-Han in [southeastern] Korea was actually a
mixed state of Korean and Chinese peoples. The Chinese population there increased with the influx of Ch'in refugees after the fall
of that dynasty. The interesting point here is, how did these Ch'in
people migrate to Korea, so far from their base territory in Shensi? The migration was probably carried out in powerful and organized groups, but the repeated eastward voyages of necromancers during the Ch'in dynasty, sent by the First Emperor in search
of the elixir of immortality, must have aided the settlement of the
Chinese in this part of the empire.

East of the Liao River the territory was comparatively tranquil.
The Later Han History records that during Han it was used as a
refuge by those wanting to escape from the political and military
upheavals of China Proper.

The population of the Northeast has throughout history been
larger than that of the Northwest. Compared with Western Han it
was somewhat reduced during the Eastern Han, but the ratio of reduction was not as high as that for the Northwest. The population
of this area during the two Han dynasties is shown in the following
table (H equals households; P equals population):

Commandery	Western Han [2 A.D.]	Eastern Han [140 A.D.]	Change
Liao-hsi	H 72,654	14,150	-58,504
	P 352,325	81,714	-270,611
Liao-tung	H 55,972	64,158	+ 8,186
	P 272,539	81,714 sic	
Hsüan-t'u	H 45,006	1,594	-43,412
	P 221,845	43,163	-178,682
Lo-lang	H 62,812	61,492	-1,320
	P 406,478	257,050	-149,698

Various factors contributed to the above decreases of population.
Changes in territorial demarcation was one. For example, out of

the eighteen cities in Liao-tung during Western Han, only ten or eleven were left under its jurisdiction in Eastern Han. A similar situation obtained in Liao-hsi, many of whose cities were shifted to other commanderies which were created at a later date, such as the Liao-tung Annex. In the case of Hsüan-t'u, part of its territory was invaded and occupied by the Kou-li [i.e. Kao-kou-li] tribes of southeastern Manchuria.

Another factor was the mobility of population. The slight increase in Liao-tung was probably due to migration from China Proper and also from eastern commanderies like Hsüan-t'u. Conversely, the great decreases in Hsüan-t'u and Lo-lang were probably due to internal disturbances in these commanderies. The invasion of Hsüan-t'u by the Kou-li compelled the commandery to shift its boundaries steadily westward, and the actual population was reduced although the number of cities had increased in number. The policy of creating new territories by dividing old ones, which can be illustrated by the formation of the Eastern Marches of Lo-lang from part of the territory of Lo-lang Commandery, also contributed to an apparent decrease of population in the latter.

6. Population and Territorial Development
South of the Yangtse and Han Rivers

Population in nearly all commanderies and kingdoms south of the Yangtse River increased sharply during Eastern Han. A tabulation of recorded figures for the thirty-odd commanderies in that part of the country shows that the rate of increase covered a wide range, from 9 to 621 per cent. Ch'ang-sha [in Hunan], for instance, reportedly increased from 235,825 in 2 A.D. to 1,059,372 in 140 A.D., or 369 per cent. Pa in Szechuan increased from 708,148 to 1,086,049, or 53 per cent. Nan-hai, in the southern part of modern Kwangtung, increased from 94,253 to 250,282, or 166 per cent. However, the commanderies situated closest to the Central Plain, such as Lu-chiang, Chiu-chiang, Lin-huai [all in Anhwei], and Han-chung [in Shensi], underwent considerable reductions in population.

The increases were probably due to the following factors:

1) The migration of people from the Central Plain to escape from the disturbances.

2) The natural southward movement of people from the Central Plain.

3) The exile of convicts.

4) The activities of famed "Upright Officials," whose reputations were mostly acquired in the south, and whose efforts suc-

ceeded in attracting people from Central China and in assimilating native peoples.

5) The conquest of the native peoples by force.

Because of the strategic advantages of the terrain south of the [Mei] Range and the Yangtse, this region often could be successfully defended when the Central Plain was suffering from military upheavals.

The natural southward movement of population was closely connected with the development of communications. Chang I's proposal in Policies of the Warring States to utilize the upper Yangtse for strategic purposes reveals the advanced state of river transportation in Szechwan at that time. Other materials tend to show the facilities of water transportation south of the Yangtse. Judging from the Han conquest of Nan-yüeh [Kwangtung, Kwangsi, and northern Annam] via Nan-hai [Canton] and the sea, it is evident that communications in the Pearl River area were also highly developed. It was stated on the memorial tablet inscribed in 174 A.D. for Chou Ching, Prefect of Kuei-yang [in northern Kwangtung and southern Hunan], that he promoted the growth of an already existing and flourishing trade in his territory. Economic development of the southern regions therefore was one of the reasons why many people of the Central Plain remained to live in the south, even though they had first moved there for political reasons. Such cases were numerous in the official histories of Han and the succeeding period. It was also during Eastern Han that the grain from the fertile southern fields began to make up for the food deficits of the north.

Another influence on the development of South China was the practice of exiling many convicts to Chiao-chih [in Kwangsi and northern Annam] and having them settle among the aborigines. The Later Han History states that the latter thus came to have some acquaintance with the Chinese language and to undergo gradual improvement in their customs, with the result that the authorities were later able to teach them agriculture, regularize their clothing, acquaint them with marriage, set up schools, and lead them into proper practices. The convicts must have had a considerable influence in the area. Some of them became wealthy and powerful.

During Western Han famous officials came mainly from the Central Plain, but in Eastern Han many of those known for their good administration came from Chiang-nan [i.e. the lower Yangtse area south of the river]. This indicates that great progress was made in opening and developing that region during the latter period. The biography of Li Chung in the Later Han History illustrates this point:

[Li Chung] was appointed Prefect of Tan-yang [in southern Anhwei]. The empire then being recently pacified, there were many who still forcibly occupied coastal territories in the south. When [Li] Chung arrived in the commandery he demanded surrender and killed all those who refused. Suppression was completed within a short time. Seeing that the customs of Tan-yang followed those of Yüeh, that learning was slighted and marriage customs, rites, and justice lagged behind [Central] China, he established schools to teach the people the correct rituals, to conduct the spring and autumn festivals, and to learn from classical writing. The entire commandery admired his work. Cultivated land was increased; in three years over 50,000 immigrants came to occupy and till the land.

The "Lives of Upright Officials" in the same work provides a number of other examples: Wei Sa established postal stations in Kuei-yang Commandery, so that some of the people who had left returned and gradually formed villages and cities. Tz'u Ch'ung while Prefect of Kuei-yang taught the inhabitants sericulture, which benefited even those living as far north as Ch'ang-sha. Jen Yen while Prefect of Chiu-chen [in Annam] taught the people to plough with oxen, to cast metal farming implements, and to open up new farm land, which increased year by year. Wang Ching, Prefect of Lu-chiang [northwestern Anhwei], opened up large areas of land. Others known for outstanding administration included Hsü Ching, Prefect of Kuei-yang, and Meng Ch'ang, Prefect of Ho-p'u [the coastal area comprising present southwestern Kwangtung and southern Kwangsi]. All were active before the time of Emperor Shun, and this undoubtedly was directly related to the increase in population during that reign.

//When the Central Plain people developed the areas along the Yangtse River they did so in north-south and upriver-downriver directions. The most northern upriver commandery of the Yangtse Valley was Shu. It was thus the first to be developed, and became the richest region of the empire and the one in which most of the [southern] Supervisors of Industries were stationed. (According to the "Treatise on Geography" in the Later Han History, the Commanderies of Shu and Pa both had Supervisors of Industries, Supervisors of Tangerines, and Supervisors of Timber. The "Biography of Kung Yü" in the same work remarks that "The main products of Kuang-han [western Szechwan] are gold and silver utensils"; some lacquer ware discovered by the Japanese in the old territory of Lo-lang bears the inscription "Made in Shu Com-

mandery. ") The "Biography of Kung-sun Shu," also in the Later
Han History, states:

> Li Hsiung exhorted [Kung-sun] Shu, saying, "...The land of
> Shu is vast and fertile. Its fruits are sufficient to feed the
> people even without grain; the weaving done by its women is
> enough to clothe the entire empire. There is an endless supply
> of good timber, bamboo, and implements. It is also rich in
> fish, salt, copper, and silver, and has the convenience of
> waterways for the transportation of grain."

⫽The "Ode to the Western Capital" by Pan Ku says, "Bamboo
forests and fruit orchards, fragrant grasses and beautiful tim-
ber--such is the rich countryside of Shu." This passage indicates
the fertility of Shu and the way it attracted everyone's attention.
According to Policies of the Warring States, Ch'in waxed strong
after it sent Ssu-ma Ts'o to conquer Shu, as the wealth of this region exceeded that of all other feudal states and provided the basis
for Ch'in to overrun the empire. Later Emperor Kao-tsu of Han
also relied on it to establish his rule. From then on Pa and Shu
became the source of wealth for Kuan-chung. Successive emperors
therefore paid special attention to this region, which developed
very quickly. Subsequently, under the administration of [the famous
scholar] Wen Weng, to the wealth of Shu was added education and
culture, so that it "abounded in gentle learned scholars."

⫽King Pi of Wu, who ruled for several decades at the beginning
of Western Han, gathered together the displaced persons and errant scholars of the empire. As a result the salt and copper resources of Chiang-nan were successfully developed. Thenceforth
throughout the two Han dynasties K'uai-chi [in Wu] continued to
produce scholars [....]

⫽Although the Eastern Han policy toward the Yangtse Valley was
one of civil pacification, that toward Yunnan and Indochina remained
one of military conquest. The most prominent case in point was
the establishment of Yung-ch'ang Commandery [present western
Yunnan and northern Burma], where the population was reported to
be over 1,000,000. Since this was due neither to the gathering together of displaced persons nor to colonization by people from the
interior, it was obviously the result of military conquest.⫽

Historical records tell of the campaigns against northern Burma
and the setting up of Yung-ch'ang Commandery in 70 A.D. They
also tell of a great rebellion that took place in 67 A.D. in Yung-
ch'ang and other areas and was caused in part by the corruption of
Chinese officials. Over 100,000 local people participated in the

rebellion, and more than 30,000 were killed and 1,500 captured in the course of the suppression campaign.

As to the commanderies in the extreme south, relations with the Han government were on the whole stable, though minor rebellions often occurred. According to somewhat later accounts, Nanhai and Ho-p'u commanderies [southern Kwangtung and Kwangsi] had not yet taken to agriculture, and although they boasted some increases in population their relations with the Central Plain were not yet very vital.

NOTES

勞榦，"兩漢戶籍與地理之關係"，歷史語言研究所集刊

Lao Kan, "Liang-Han hu-chi yü ti-li-chih kuan-hsi," Bulletin of the Institute of History and Philology, V, Part 2 (1935), 179-214.

For a more recent study covering some, but not all, of the ground in the present article and differing with it on some points see Hans Bielenstein, "The Census of China during the Period 2-742 A.D.," Bulletin of the Museum of Far Eastern Antiquities, No. 19 (1947), 125-163.

The detailed figures presented by the author in his tabulation at the beginning of Section 6 have been omitted. We have also omitted two maps showing the population densities of Eastern Han and Western Han respectively.

The major sources for the article are the Han History and the Later Han History, especially the sections on geography, lives of officials, and the imperial chronicles. Population figures are derived chiefly from chapter 28 ("Geography") in the former work and chapters 29-33 ("Commanderies and Principalities") in the latter; these chapters in the two works provide data on the censuses of 2 A.D. and 140 A.D. respectively. Supplementary material includes the Supplementary Han History (Hsü Han shu), Tsin History, the Historical Records (Shih-chi), and some local gazetteers. The author frequently does not give detailed references for sources. Obvious typographical errors in the statistics as given in the article have been corrected after checking the original sources.

The following list of place names mentioned in the article is presented for the convenience of readers desiring to know the Chinese characters for these names:

An-ting 安定
Chang-yeh 張掖
Ch'ang-sha 長沙
Ch'eng-tu 成都
Chi-nan 濟南
Chin-ch'eng 金城
Ching-chao-yin 京兆尹
Chiu-chiang 九江
Chiu-ch'uan 酒泉
Ch'u-ni 曲逆
Chu-yung Pass 居庸關
Han-chung 漢中
Han-ku Pass 函谷關
Han-tan 邯鄲
Ho-nan 河南
Ho-nei 河內
Ho-p'u 合浦
Hsi-ho 西河
Hsuan-t'u 玄菟
Kuang-han 廣漢
Kuei-yang 桂陽
Lang-ya 琅邪
Liao-hsi 遼西
Liao-tung 遼東
Lin-huai 臨淮
Lin-tzu 臨淄
Lo-lang 樂浪
Lo-yang 洛陽
Lu-chiang 廬江
Lung-hsi 隴西
Nan-hai 南海
Nan-yang 南陽

Nan-yueh 南越
Pa 巴
Pei-hai 北海
Pei-ti 北地
Shan-yang 山陽
Shang 上
Shang-ku 上谷
Shu 蜀
So-fang 朔方
Tai 代
T'ai-hang Range 太行山
T'ai-shan 泰山
T'ai-yuan 太原
Tan-yang 丹陽
T'ien-shui 天水
Ting-hsiang 定襄
Ts'ang-hai 蒼海
Tso-feng-hsu 左馮翊
Tun-huang 敦煌
Tung-hai 東海
Wan 宛
Wu-tu 武都
Wu-wei 武威
Wu-yuan 五原
Yen-men 雁門
Ying-ch'uan 潁川
Yu-fu-feng 右扶風
Yu-pei-p'ing 右北平
Yu-yang 漁陽
Yun-chung 雲中
Yung-ch'ang 永昌
Yung-yang 滎陽

7

GREAT FAMILIES OF EASTERN HAN

by

YANG LIEN-SHENG

1. Development of Great Families in Western Han

The two Han dynasties, especially Eastern Han, constituted a long gestation period for the rule of powerful families, a development which came about in the T'sin and Northern and Southern dynasties [265-581 A.D.]. The great families of Han were the forerunners of the powerful families of the later period, whose members filled high government posts, owned tremendous amounts of landed property, possessed vassals, and at the same time were exempt from government taxation. There was no intermarriage between them and the common people; between the two was an unbridgeable social gap.

Liu Pang, founder of the Han dynasty, defeated the last of the Chou-Ch'in aristocrats, Hsiang Yü. This was highly pleasing to the group of non-aristocratic landlords and merchants, who had already emerged during the Warring States as wealthy but socially inferior and politically impotent persons. But now the old social order was overthrown by an emperor of commoner origin. Everyone was equal under him as to obligations; noble rank now held no special privileges.

In the early years of Han, the central government was occupied with several rebellions. The wealthy people utilized these periods of war to expand their industrial, agricultural, and commercial enterprises. There are accounts in the Historical Records, for instance, of high returns on investments, and of private loans to the government. By the time of Emperor Wu [140-86 B.C.], the expansion of the empire in the northwest, coupled with the Yellow River floods, brought the government into financial straits. The moneyed people then began to obtain special privileges, such as exemption from corvée duty, in return for their contributions of money, grain, and slaves to the government.

Pressed by economic difficulties, Emperor Wu began to employ

great salt and iron proprietors like K'ung Chin. These persons,
though rich, had never had official positions before. Once in power
they did not scruple to preserve their own and their friends' fortunes at the expense of the interest of their own class. One by one
such policies as inflation and the monopoly on salt and iron were
put into practice. The worst blow to the rich merchant class was
the property tax on the merchants, based on property reports returned by the owners. Those who evaded reporting, or reported
short, would have their property confiscated. Informers received
one-half of the confiscated amount. Merchants were prohibited
from owning landed estates, on pain of confiscation. As a result,
the government took over enormous amounts of such property, including land, houses, and slaves.

It is reasonable to conclude that at this point many rich people
turned from commerce to invest in agriculture. Land was not subject to the property tax. Moreover, a landlord paid a land tax of
one-thirtieth to the government, but usually took a fifty per cent
rent from the tenant farmers. It is likely that this was the situation throughout all of Western Han, as shown by the writings of
Tung Chung-shu and Wang Mang. From now on the biggest problem of the Han dynasty was that of land, that is of annexations by
the great landlords.

Another Han method of keeping down the wealthy was the moving of their residences, a policy which was inherited from the
Ch'in dynasty. The removals were carried out during the reigns
of the first seven emperors of Han, and especially during the
reign of Emperor Wu, that is in the periods when the central government was strong. Though the first emperor of Han employed
the device of dispersing the descendants of the Chou aristocrats,
by the time of Emperor Wu the removals were directed against
the new great families.

But such temporary restrictions could not prevent the wealthy
from gaining strength. When the government gradually weakened
after emperors Chao and Hsüan [86-48 B.C.], the great landlords
became still more free in their annexations of estates. As a result, in the reign of Emperor Ai [6-2 B.C.], Shih Tan suggested
the need for government limitation of the size of landed property,
remarking as follows:

  Now that for generations the country has enjoyed peace, the
  rich people and the officials have been accumulating fortunes
  amounting to myriads [of cash], while the misery of the poor
  deepens. In the rule of a superior man, there is esteem for
  following past practices together with emphasis on instituting

reforms. The purpose of instituting changes is to remedy a
present emergency. There is no need to be thorough-going,
but merely to provide some general limitations.

The plan drawn up by the ministers as a result of this plea limited estates of the nobility and officials to thirty ch'ing per family;
the number of slaves per household was restricted to 200, 100,
and 30, according to the rank of the owner. Although the limit of
three years in which to achieve the standard does not appear to
be severe, many landlords had exceeded the limits of land ownership and were in a panic to sell, so that the prices of land and
slaves fell precipitously. The plan was vehemently opposed by
many landlords who were at the court. Their influence was shown
in an edict from the emperor which "postponed" indefinitely the
implementation of these restrictions.

Thus, the economic power of the large landlords was already
strongly entrenched. Furthermore, on the basis of this economic
power, the landlords were seeking political ascendancy. Hence
even such a mild reform as Shih Tan had proposed came to nothing. Unexpectedly there appeared a Wang Mang, who "always admired antiquity and knew not the trends of the times," and proceeded to "imperialize" the land. In his edict promulgated after
assuming power, he gave a description of the concentration of
land in the hands of the rich, the plight of the tenantry, and the
iniquities of the distribution of the tax burden. Although nominally
the land tax was one-thirtieth of the yield, actually the landlords
were getting five-tenths from their tenants. Therefore he decreed
that henceforth all land was to become crown land, all slaves
were to be known as "private retainers" [of the emperor], and
both were not to be bought and sold. Persons owning more than
the prescribed amount of land, the area of a "well field" per
family of less than eight males, must distribute the surplus to
their relatives and neighbors, on pain of the death penalty.

Though Wang Mang was able to see the root of the problem, his
government was not strong enough to carry out the reforms,
which were rescinded after three years. Weakness, corruption,
invasion of the Hsiung-nu, and natural calamities threatened the
security of the rich and the existence of the poor. The joint
forces of landlords and peasants ultimately brought about Wang
Mang's downfall.

2. Establishment of the Political Power of
Great Families in Eastern Han

//The activities of the landlord class, to which belonged the successful Kuang-wu emperor, during the revolutionary regime of
Wang Mang, are worth noting.

//The home of Kuang-wu was in the Commandery of Nan-yang
[in Honan]. Wan, one of the great metropolises of Han, was situated in this commandery, and a large number of very wealthy families congregated there. At a time when Nan-yang was suffering
from famine, Kuang-wu's family still had grain to sell in Wan.
According to a commentary on the Later Han History, "At that
time there was a drought and famine in Nan-yang, but His Majesty's
field alone bore a harvest." This indicates that he must have possessed good land, and a great deal of it, so that there could be
surplus grain, since Heaven obviously could not have particularly
sought out the future emperor's fields to rain on. On the other
hand, the account was probably euphemistic, in which case it actually would be that Kuang-wu had hoarded a lot of grain, and
was waiting to sell at a good price. In time of upheaval landlords
were all versed in the art of "robbing during a fire."

//The maternal grandfather of Kuang-wu, of the house of Fan,
was a still greater landlord. The commentary on the Later Han
History records that the family could "close its gates and become
a market in itself."//

A more detailed description of the Fan family is given in the
Later Han History, which shows that it owned more than 300
ch'ing [about 30,000 mou] of land, and was self-sufficient in all
the economic necessities of life. Kuang-wu's sister's husband
Teng Ch'en also came of a wealthy family.

The basic armies of the rebelling landlords were composed of
family members and household followers. The latter were unemployed vagrants, who depended on the great families for a living
in return for services rendered. Their status ordinarily was
probably like that of a first-class butler, though they were
treated with more courtesy by the master when a particular service was required of them, such as, for instance, killing some
adversary in a feud. These followers were usually scornful of
legal authority. For example, as the result of the conduct of his
followers, Liu Hsüan, a cousin of Kuang-wu, once had to pretend
death in order to avoid a bad scrape with the authorities.

The majority of household followers dabbled in crime--rob-
bery and such like--when they were hard up. It so happened that
when the conduct of his followers became too intolerable, Liu

Hsiu, the later Kuang-wu, decided to take them for a trip to Wan. There he met Li T'ung, whose family for generations had been known as great merchants. Li T'ung informed him of an alleged prophecy that "The Liu family shall be restored to the throne with the aid of Li," and the two men decided on an uprising, using their army of family members and followers.

Liu Hsiu's forces were weak at the beginning. He therefore began by cooperating with Liu Hsüan, who headed an army composed mainly of peasants and famine refugees. But the peasant army of Liu Hsüan and the landlord army of Liu Hsiu were uneasy bedfellows, and before long the two forces split. Liu Hsiu obtained a base area on the North China plain, while Liu Hsüan secured his position in Honan and Shensi. Then, without an overall plan and with an army that specialized in plundering, Liu Hsüan was finally defeated by another peasant army, the Red Eyebrows.

The Red Eyebrows had risen in Shantung. According to the Later Han History, they "became bandits under pressure of poverty, and lacked any strategic plans for attacking cities or overcoming fortifications." They apparently had no high political ambitions. Though temporarily able to gain hegemony over Liu Hsüan in Shensi, they were ultimately suppressed by Kuang-wu.

//The peasant armies were not the only ones that were engaged in plundering; their brutality was quite equalled by that of the landlord armies. Kuang-wu's troops were somewhat less predatory than others and so were relatively more popular. After suppressing the Red Eyebrows, Kuang-wu conquered the forces of other local strong men in Shantung and in the Huai River and lower Yangtse regions. Finally he turned his attention to the west, where the territory was divided and separately controlled by the landed magnates Wei Hsiao, Tou Jung, and Kung-sun Shu. It was only after strenuous campaigns in which he employed alternately his tactics of war and diplomacy and allied with Ma Yüan, the great owner of herds and land, that Kuang-wu was able to suppress them. Ma Yüan's economic power in Pei-ti [in Shensi] consisted of several thousand horses, sheep, and cattle, some hundred thousand pecks of grain, and also several hundred vassal families. Here we see that the household followers could become dependent on the great houses in "family" units.

//It is the custom of the dynastic histories to describe the famine refugees and vagabonds as "vagrant bandits," but to refer to the strong and wealthy families as "heroes," a practice which enables us to determine the class origins of the leaders of the rebellions. The famine refugees and vagabonds lacked organization and ambition. By themselves they probably would have been

unable to overthrow Wang Mang. But the strong and wealthy families were also opposed to the Hsin dynasty [of Wang Mang], and
rose together in revolt. When the entire country was torn to
pieces, the landlord army of Liu Hsiu was able to gather the
fragments together and pacify the people, thus easily gaining political power.//

A noticeable feature of the revolts of this time was that the
leaders all claimed descent from the ruling house of Han, and the
name Liu served to rally popular support for many of them. This
was probably an indication of popular longing more for the Han
system than for the Liu family.

Kuang-wu revived the one-thirtieth land tax, which was advan-
tageous for the large landlords. But at the same time he succeeded in keeping the political powers of his enfeoffed officials
and relatives in check. In order to preserve his own prerogatives
he was loath to see other great landlords embark upon unlimited
expansion. He held that "proper administration lies in suppressing the strong and supporting the weak," so that "at Court there
are no officials with overbearing authority, and in the fiefs there
are no powerful heroes." He repeatedly ordered improvement in
the treatment of slaves, and decreed the freeing of some common
people who had been seized and sold into slavery.

In order to rectify landownership, Kuang-wu ordered a general
survey of agricultural land in the country. But the officials returned dishonest measurements, ruthlessly encroaching on the
land of the peasants and causing them to rebel. Kuang-wu was
even willing to punish a few corrupt officials. A story in the Later
Han History tells how the emperor one day found out with the
help of the twelve-year-old heir apparent that his trusted officials
and relatives possessed vast estates near the capital much beyond
the limit set by law, and that the reports of the local officials
were not reliable. Following this revelation many persons were
punished. This story shows that cases of possession of extra-legal properties by powerful officials and imperial relatives were
so flagrant that even the twelve-year-old heir to the throne had
known about it. It also shows that there were certain regulations
regarding the big landlords' property, and that Kuang-wu was de-
sirous of maintaining these regulations. Kuang-wu's whole atti-
tude toward the big landlords was ambivalent, however, and after
the first three reigns of Eastern Han, political power began to
fall into the hands of eunuchs and the families of empresses, thus
bringing about the period of control by the great families.

3. Survey of Great Families in Eastern Han

//What is known as a great family did not consist simply of persons of the same name and lineage. It was rather a group centered around an extended patrilineal family, and included many other families or individuals appended to it through political or economic relations. Such was the unit of a great family.

//Some of the great families first possessed political positions and afterwards established their economic power. Others first possessed economic power and afterward acquired political positions, which in turn helped to develop further their economic power.

//The establishment of the rule of Kuang-wu meant the establishment of the political power of the great landlords, that is, of the great families. Nearly all of his two chancellors and twenty-eight generals came from great families.//

Several typical generals among the twenty-eight are known to have maintained large numbers of followers. Other officials, like Teng Ch'en and Ma Yüan, were also rich individuals, as described above. With the founding of the Eastern Han dynasty these great families received high positions and investitures. The great families had thus succeeded in enhancing their political position through economic power.

There were two major categories of great families in Eastern Han. The first consisted of individuals who suddenly gained importance through connections with the central power; these included members of the imperial family, members of the families of empresses, and eunuchs. The other category consisted of individuals who rose gradually through their own efforts; these included high officials and local magnates.

Members of the imperial family were given the rank of Prince; sons of Princes who were not in the line of inheritance became Princely Marquises. According to one estimate, there were sixty-one known Princes and 344 Princely Marquises in Eastern Han. Though rather numerous, these persons enjoyed no real power. In 52 A.D. Kuang-wu executed several thousand followers of the princely households as the aftermath of a case of vendetta warfare in which these persons were engaged on behalf of their masters. The princes were greatly curbed thereafter in their activities. Few new princes were invested after the reign of Emperor Ming [58-76 A.D.].

Many of the relatives of the empresses belonged already to great families. The system for the choice of "Palace Beauties" in the Eastern Han was the selection by palace officials of girls

from good families around [the capital city of] Lo-yang. However,
it was easy for these officials to be partisan to the great families
either through special connections or bribery. Nine-tenths of the
empresses mentioned in the "Chronicle of Empresses" in the
Later Han History came from great families; some were even
daughters of princesses. For instance, Kuang-wu's wife, Empress
Yin, was a famous beauty who came of an old wealthy family; her
half-brother maintained several thousand followers. Later four
members of the Yin family were enfeoffed. The wife of Emperor
Ming, Empress Ma, was Ma Yüan's daughter. The powerful Tou
and Liang families produced two empresses each. It is known that
there were altogether eighty-nine members of empresses' families
who were invested as marquises. The political influence of such
families far outweighed that of the members of the imperial family.

The growth of eunuchs into great families occurred in the later
part of Eastern Han. The first eunuch to be ennobled was Cheng
Chung in the reign of Emperor Ho [89-105 A.D.]. In 135 A.D.
eunuchs were allowed to have adopted sons inherit their rank. This
was probably the recognition of a fait accompli, since Cheng
Chung's adopted son had already inherited Cheng's rank in 114 A.D.

The power and influence of the eunuchs have been described in
biographical accounts in the Later Han History. For instance, the
eunuchs Ts'ao Chieh and Wang Fu were able to place their relatives in many central government positions; aside from possessing official rank and income they also engaged in business deal-
ings which further increased their wealth. They lived sumptuously,
and lorded it over their home districts, creating resentment among
the people, who, however, dared not remonstrate against them.
During the reign of Emperor Ling [168-190 A.D.] the eunuchs became so oppressive that their activities contributed directly to the
rebellion of the Yellow Turbans. The Ts'ao family that ultimately
usurped the throne was related to the eunuchs Ts'ao T'eng and
Ts'ao Sung. There were altogether seventy-nine members of
eunuch families who were given noble ranks.

It is difficult to distinguish the high officials from local great
families. The twenty-eight generals mentioned above may be taken
as examples of this group of persons. The great families were
scattered over the entire country. T'ao Hsi-sheng has enumerated
a large number of them in the third volume of his History of Chinese Political Thought. Many more can be added. These magnates
were powerful enough to ask the princes to intercede for them
with the emperor.

Some of the great families maintained their status over several
hundred years. For instance, the magnate Lien Fan, who lived

during the reign of Emperor Ming, was a descendant of the famous
general Lien P'o, who lived about 300 years earlier. Another example was the Lu family of Chiang-tung [i.e. the lower Yangtze
region], which began to attain prominence under Kuang-wu and also lasted for about 200 years. Another family, Ts'ui, was active
from the reign of Emperor Chao [86-73 B.C.] to the end of Han,
a period of approximately 300 years; in the time of Emperor Ling
[169-190 A.D.] Ts'ui Lieh was able to purchase with five million
cash the position of one of the three prime ministers in the Han
government.

4. Great Families and the Economy: Misery of the Common People

Those who became dependents of the great families did so for
two reasons, economic and political.

Economic dependency had an early beginning. According to
Huan T'an of early Eastern Han, there were already free men who
served big merchants and money-lenders as dependents, and shared
in the profits. But larger numbers were dependents of great landlords. The case of Ma Yüan's several hundred vassal families is a
good example.

Ts'ui Shih, who was active during the reign of Emperor Huan
[147-168 A.D.], in his Discourses on Politics analyzed with some
care the reasons why free men became dependents. The destruction
of the ancient system by Ch'in, he said, had encouraged the annexation of estates and the accumulation of wealth. Consequently,
the rich amassed enormous property, enjoyed high prestige and
unrestrained power, lived like royalty, and tyrannized the countryside, while the poor could hardly maintain themselves. They therefore bowed their heads and with their families went into the service of the rich. After generations of slavery they were still not
able to provide for their own subsistence. "Alive," says Ts'ui
Shih, "they face a life-time of hard labor; dead, they worry for
lack of a decent burial. When the year is poor, they drift about and
starve in ditches, they marry off their wives and sell their sons."

This hard lot of the free peasant went back to the time of the
Warring States. [A contemporary statesman,] Li K'uei, once drew
up a budget for the small farmer in that period on the basis of 100
mou of land with a total yield of 150 tan 石 of grain per family of
five. After providing for taxes and basic necessities, the farmer
was short 450 cash per year, not counting expenses for illness or
other emergencies. Another budget was drawn up by Ts'ao Ts'o
during the reign of Emperor Wen [179-156 B.C.], also on the basis

of 100 mou for a family. The plight of the peasant worsened with
the increased annexations of estates during the reign of Emperor
Yüan [48-32 B.C.], at which time Censor Kung Yü, in describing
the farmer's life pointed out that many would rather leave the land
to engage in trade or to become bandits.

The small farmer continued to lead a hard life in Eastern Han.
In Ts'ui Yin's On Gamblers, written during the reign of Emperor
Ho [89-106 A.D.], there is a poignant passage describing the
gambler's scorn for the farmers:

> The gambler came upon a farmer clearing away weeds. He
> had a straw hat on his head and a hoe in his hand. His face
> was black, his hands and feet were covered with calluses,
> his skin was as rough as mulberry bark, and his feet re-
> sembled bear's paws. He crouched in the fields, his sweat
> mixing with the mud. The gambler said to him, "You culti-
> vate the fields in oppressive summer heat. Your back is en-
> crusted with salt, your legs look like burnt stumps, your
> skin is like leather that cannot be pierced by an awl. You
> hobble along on misshapen feet and painful legs. Shall I
> call you a plant or a tree? Yet you can move your body and
> limbs. Shall I call you a bird or a beast? Yet you possess
> a human face. What a fate to be born with such base qualities!"

//So the farmer was likened to plants or beasts. But even his
hard labor was not enough for a livelihood, and he was obliged to
make other plans. Of the two alternatives pointed out above by Kung
Yü, the first, selling the land and entering trade, was only a pipe-
dream for the small farmer, for the price of his land would not
even be enough to pay off his debts. The other alternative, becoming a bandit, was quite simple, but there were numerous officials
around, and, once caught, his life would be unbearable. Therefore
the peasant would not choose this alternative unless pressed to
desperation. The small farmers generally took two other alternatives: one was to become dependents of the great families; the
other was to become displaced persons on government relief, that
is, to become a reserve force for bandits.

// Throughout the Han dynasty there were large numbers of displaced persons. These consisted chiefly of peasants who were
victims of famines or warfare and had to leave their villages. The
government had no other alternative but to feed them, which was
known as providing "relief," or to send them back to their home
districts by some means. According to the "Life of Shih Fen" in
the Han History, there were over two million displaced persons in

the Kuan-tung area in the fourth year of the Yüan-feng period of
the reign of Emperor Wu of Western Han [107 B.C.]. In the first
year of the Yung-hsing period of Emperor Huan of Eastern Han
[153 A.D.], there were several hundred thousands of displaced
families.//

A number of edicts of the emperors Chang and Ho indicated that
there were various kinds of corrupt practices connected with the
relief administration, and that the displaced persons had become
a major problem of the state. According to official records, during the seventeen-year reign of Emperor Ho it was necessary to
give relief and loans to people in several prefectures and several
score commanderies, covering nearly all parts of the country.
Despite these government efforts, the number of such persons increased steadily. It was reported in the reign of Emperor An
[107-126 A.D.] that in Lo-yang the number of the "idlers" was a
hundred times that of farmers. Those of the "idlers" who had some
skill were engaged in light handicrafts, such as the making of
toys. But that did not constitute long-range livelihood, as the majority were peasants who had left their villages. They were probably not very different from the displaced persons living on relief,
who played a crucial role in the Yellow Turban uprising.

5. Great Families and the Economy: Wealth and Extravagance of the Magnates

The second way out for the small peasants was to become dependents of great families: Chung-ch'ang T'ung [who lived at the
end of Eastern Han,] described a number of great families in his
work Frank Words:

> The magnate, without being the head of even one platoon,
> commands the services of a thousand families and entire
> townships. He lives more lavishly than a prince, and has
> more power than a district magistrate.... The magnate's
> mansion contains hundreds of rooms. His rich fields extend
> across the land. His slaves are counted by the thousands,
> and his dependents by the tens of thousands. He trades by
> land and by water in all parts of the country. His bulging
> warehouses fill the city, his huge dwellings overflow with
> treasure, his horses, cattle, sheep, and pigs are too numer-
> ous to be contained in the mountain valleys.

//The individual small peasant was unable to produce enough to
meet his own needs. The outcome became different, however, when
land was concentrated under the management of large landlords

and was worked by the dependent small peasant. This was because
with a vast land area and abundant labor supply all sorts of facilities in production and distribution became available. There would
be no lack of ploughing oxen and seeds, and it would also be possible to choose the crop according to the quality of the land. In
the description of the great landlords in Ts'ui Shih's Book of the
Months (fragments collected in Complete Writings of Later Han),
for instance, it is recorded that aside from such crops as glutinous
millet, ordinary millet, rice, and wheat, some scores of other
crops were also planted, including linseed, large and small varieties of onions and garlic, clover, turnips, melons, squash, cele-
ry, mallow, legumes, water-pepper, mustard, indigo plant, chives,
and so forth. Among the trees were bamboo, varnish tree, tung,
catalpa ovata, pine, cedar, and various others. The landlords were
also able to experiment in agricultural methods, such as, among
others, the "rotation" method of Chao Kuo [flourished ca. 140-
86 B.C.], and the "block planting" method of Fan Sheng-chi
[flourished ca. 32-6 B.C.]. Moreover, the water mill has been
very important in agriculture since the time of Wei and Tsin [3rd-
4th centuries A.D.]. This new production tool was perhaps already
invented in Eastern Han, but the records are unfortunately incomplete, so that the details cannot be traced. The only evidence is
found in a passage in [the Sung dynasty encyclopedia] T'ai-ping
yü-lan, chapter 829, quoting Huan T'an's New Discourses:

> An Hsi devised the pestle and mortar, thus benefiting myri-
> ads of people. Later on others added to the design; they de-
> vised a tread mill which utilized the weight of the body to grind
> the grain. The profit became tenfold. Further, a machine was
> installed which employed donkeys, mules, oxen, and horses
> as well as water to grind the grain. The profit became a
> hundredfold.

//Huan T'an lived at the beginning of Eastern Han, so that the
great landlords of that period must certainly have utilized the water-
mill. Further, in chapter 117 of the Later Han History mention is
made of "using canals for irrigation, water-grinding, and grain
transportation." "Water-grinding," according to the commentary
of [Li] Hsien, Prince Chang-huai [of T'ang], is "milling by water."
This seems to be further proof.//
Another advantage of the great landlords was their ability to engage in trade as well as in agriculture. Although the Han government prohibited people from taking part in two professions, actually
the restriction was probably not effective. The great landlords
were not only simultaneously great merchants, but also great

pastoral lords, thus constituting a trinity of economic power. The
Book of the Months also contains accounts of the great landlords'
hoarding of goods, buying cheap and selling dear. From the
second to the eleventh month of the year the landlord was active in
some business transaction in every month except the ninth. His
business activities were concerned with the staple goods of food or
clothing. For instance, cloth was bought during the summer and
sold during the winter, which of course brought in large profits.
Grain was sold in large quantities in the spring, but the [winter]
wheat was purchased immediately on being harvested in the fourth
month of the year [ca. May-June of the solar calendar]. The considerable surplus of cloth produced in the landlord's own household and of foodstuffs from his own fields was probably also sold.

Agricultural work was done chiefly by the male members of the
landlord's family and the dependent small peasants. The majority
of the slaves worked in handicrafts, such as cloth-weaving, but
few took part in agriculture. It is estimated that the proportion between the number of handicraft and domestic slaves and that of
the dependent people was probably one to ten. Slaves were not
free men, and could be bought and sold; the dependents were semi-
free.

With a huge income and the command of the labor of slaves and
dependents, the life of the magnates reached a high state of luxury.
For the wedding of a daughter of the Yüan family in Lo-yang it is
recorded in the Later Han History that the dowry of the bride included one hundred silk-clad slave girls. Funerals also were occasions for an even more lavish display of wealth, from expensive
coffins and burial articles to splendidly constructed mausolea and
family shrines. These phenomena were also described and criticized by Ts'ui Shih in his Discourses on Politics. Excessive sump-
tuousness at funerals occasionally brought forth restrictions from
government authorities.

6. Great Families and Politics:
Disciples and Ex-subordinates

The great families led a luxurious life, but politically they did
not always have influence. Although they were able to purchase for
themselves the status of "exemptees," their slaves and dependents
still could not evade obligations to the government. What the magnates wanted was the total exemption of their dependents from taxation and labor service, that is an increase in the magnates' political power in order to further their own economic interests, as
was done later in the Tsin period. However, while the Han system

still ruled, it was not possible to bring about this radical change. As a first step toward the acquisition of political power, therefore, the great families began to establish connections with the government, and to influence the selection of officials.

To acquire political influence meant the obtaining of official positions. There were three major ways in which one attained the latter in Han.

(a) National Selection: This was done through the recommendation of the authorities in commanderies in accordance with the various government classifications, which consisted of two major categories, the fixed and the non-fixed. For the "Filial and Incorrupt" class in the fixed group, for instance, the general rule was one candidate per 200,000 population. In thinly populated areas, however, the ratio was sometimes changed to one per 100,000, and for some areas with a population of less than 100,000 the recommendation was to be made for one candidate once every three years. Another class, the "Abundant Talents," called for one candidate per year for each commandery, though it is not known whether or not this was made in proportion to the population figure. As for the non-fixed group, the candidates for various classifications were recommended by the local authorities after special decrees were issued by the emperor, at times when men of talent were needed. The selected candidates were often persons who had already had minor official careers, and all were probably given examinations in order to determine their official rank. The examinations were sometimes personally presided over by the emperor. Usually the responsibility for the determination of rank rested with either the Secretary of State or with the three Grand Ministers, between whom there was serious rivalry over this right of patronage. The power rested most of the time with the Secretary of State.

(b) Ministerial Selection: This was done locally to staff the administrative offices of the metropolitan ministers and of the commandery and prefectural governments. In the prefectural governments, for example, there were ten bureaux: Finance, Memorials, Judicature, Police, Criminal Affairs, Criminal Executions, Military Affairs, Coinage, and Public Granaries. Persons selected to posts in the prefectural governments could look forward only to minor local positions. But those selected by the metropolitan ministerial offices could, with the help of the right personal relations with the superiors, hope to advance into high positions in the central government. There were cases in which the same individual was selected simultaneously by a number of Ministeries.

(c) Appointment of Sons: This system resembled inheritance of

rank, and dated from early Western Han. Every official with an
annual salary of 2,000 piculs [i.e. of the rank of Prefect] and up,
and who had had three years' service, was entitled to name one
son or full brother as a lang 郎 , the expectant rank waiting for
appointment to various levels of office. It was very likely that a
large number of persons utilized this special privilege. In Eastern
Han the grandsons of the Grand Minister were sometimes appointed
in a similar fashion. Thus, there were those who entered officialdom on the strength of the influence of their fathers, brothers, or
grandfathers, and were placed on an equal footing with the officially
selected personnel.

The above methods led to the prevalence of the system of "disciples and ex-subordinates." Thus, especially close relations often arose between the selected candidate and the official who selected him. Chou Ching, a well-known Prefect of Eastern Han,
was famous for his specially cordial relations with the official
candidates he selected. Chou usually gave in his own residence
several banquets in honor of each "Filial and Incorrupt" candidate,
and regarded the latter as his son. He often made later selections
from among the candidate's close relatives. On the other extreme,
there was Han Yin, the Prefect of Ho-nei [in Honan], who would
give his candidate only one farewell interview, and did not extend
the favor of selection to members of the candidate's family.

Persons who held positions under a particular superior developed a relationship of specific loyalty to the latter. Even if the
superior were later transferred to another post, the subordinate
still considered himself his "ex-subordinate," and on this basis
the superior-subordinate relationship was continued. At the death
of the superior, the ex-subordinates often erected memorial tab-
lets for him on which were inscribed their own names as testimony
to the relationship. Ex-subordinates often wore mourning for the
superior up to three years. This practice, occurring at a time
when the period of mourning for parents was not yet finally fixed,
demonstrated the importance attached to the relationship with one's
superior official.

Candidates ministerially selected but not yet appointed to sub-
stantive positions were originally not to be considered as ex-subordinates of the selector. But as time went on, the tendency toward
dependency on powerful personages overrode early scruples, so
that by the end of Eastern Han these candidates were also considered as ex-subordinates of their selectors.

Another method of dependency took the form of "disciples."
This did not mean that one actually had to receive instruction from
any person of influence. The word "disciple" was the cover used

for the establishment of a dependent relationship with an influential
person in the hope of receiving appointments. Originally, "disciple"
denoted one who had studied under the direct pupils of a certain
teacher. Ku Yen-wu [1613-1682] holds that, according to Han usage, the "pupils" were people who received instruction, and the
"disciples" were those who attached themselves to a well-known
personage because of his position and influence. For instance,
Great General Tou Hsien, the brother of Empress Tou, and Wang
Fu, a eunuch, were both said to have had disciples; obviously
they could not have had disciples by way of teaching. Chao I [1727-
1814] is of the opinion that, because those who generally followed
the same school of thought were considered "disciples" of a master, as distinguished from "pupils," the practice had grown up
whereby all who became dependents of a person out of consideration not for his knowledge but for his power came also to be known
as disciples. This in later ages developed into the corrupt practice of gathering personal disciples and followers.

//Such great families of Eastern Han as the Yüan of Ju-nan [in
Honan] and the Yang of Hung-nung [in Honan] had attained the rank
of Grand Minister through four successive generations, and their
disciples and ex-subordinates were scattered over the whole country. Take for instance the disciples of the Yang family. When
Yang Chen, due to slandering by others, was dismissed as Grand
Commandant and went back to his home commandery, he was still
followed by a large number of disciples. Before he committed suicide out of extreme chagrin, his disciples heard his will together
with his sons. After his death, two of his disciples "went to prose-
cute his case at the capital, and the people at Court all praised
their loyalty [to Yang Chen]."

//[Yang] Chen probably had four sons. [....] They were Mu,
Jang, Pin, and Feng. Mu's son, T'ung, and Jang's son, Chu,
never became high officials. But Tz'u, the son of Pin, and Piao,
the son of Tz'u, both became Grand Commandants. Later Ts'ao
Ts'ao killed Piao's son, Yang Hsiu, out of jealousy of this great
family. The story that he did it out of personal jealousy of [Yang]
Hsiu's talent probably did not tell the whole truth. Yang T'ung also had disciples, although his official position was low. The
memorial tablet of Yang Chen was erected by [Yang] T'ung's disciples. Thus, the disciples not only served one person, but also
the entire family. Not only did they have to erect a tablet for the
master's grandfather, but also they had to do it for the master's
son. The "Tablet on Fortunate Youth" in the [collection of in-
scriptions] Li shih was erected by disciples. On the memorial tablet of Yang Chu, who had been the magistrate of Kao-yang [in

Hopei], were inscribed these words among the names of the erec-
tors: "disciples of the Second Lord," and "disciples of Sir P'ei."
The Li shih notes: "'Sir P'ei'was Yang T'ung, the Chancellor of
P'ei; 'The Second Lord' was Yang Pin, the Grand Commandant.
The latter was called "Second," because Yang Chen had held that
post before him. [Thus] 'Sir P'ei' was Chu's cousin, and 'the
Second Lord' was his younger paternal uncle."

//It is quite likely that very few of the Yang family in the above-
mentioned generations did not have disciples. That was precisely
one of the major reasons why the Yang became a famous clan of
Eastern Han.//

7. Great Families and Politics:
Selection and Requests for Positions

In order to increase their political power, the wealthy great
families became active in influencing the selection of officials. As
early as the beginning of Eastern Han "dishonest selection" had
become an issue.

Upon his accession to the throne [in 58 A.D.], the second emperor of Eastern Han issued a decree condemning dishonest practices as well as the meddling of powerful families in official selections, and calling for reports on malpractices. This was clear
proof that the great families had already taken root in politics.
It also became obvious that Emperor Ming's desire to correct the
situation did not bear fruit, as was demonstrated by a decree of
his successor, Emperor Chang, one year after the latter's accession [77 A.D.]. Here again irregularities in the selection of
officials were condemned: local officials were said to name the
"Abundant Talent" and "Filial and Incorrupt" classes by the
hundred every year, despite the fact that these were not actually
all men of the right qualifications for official duties. The emperor
invoked as an example the good system of past ages, in which men
of talent, albeit of rustic background and unconnected with the
great families, could expect to be chosen for government careers.

In the fifth year [93 A.D.] of the next reign, Emperor Ho, having killed the members of the dictatorial Tou family, again issued
a decree against current practices. He pointed out that the reforms
were not carried out in the selection of officials, with the result
that "the wrong persons occupy official positions, and the common
people suffer from maladministration." This shows that Emperor
Chang before him had also been unable to effect any reform in the
system.

Another noticeable irregularity was the selection of a large

proportion of young persons, in the hope that they might in the future amply repay the selector. This phenomenon also appeared
early in Eastern Han, for during the reign of Kuang-wu a memorial
from Fan Shu, the son of the great landlord Fan Hung, specifically
mentioned the practice of selecting young candidates at the expense
of men of mature experience and renown.

Thus, the Court was not able to eradicate dishonest practices
in official selection through several reigns. By the time of Emperor Shun [126-145 A.D.], politics had reached such a corrupt
stage that certain literati could not tolerate it further. Tso Hsiung,
for instance, proposed a method of age restrictions, which for a
time resulted in some improvement of the situation. First he described in a memorial the injustices involved in official selections,
and the resultant oppression in government; but the strongly entrenched power of the eunuchs prevented the emperor from taking
effective steps. Then he made the proposal that "those under forty
years of age should not qualify for selection as 'Filial and Incorrupt' candidates," and that there should be exceptions only in
cases of men of extraordinary talent. Opponents of this plan, such
as Hu Kuang, also memorialized the emperor, quoting incidents
in ancient times to prove that age was no determinant of ability.
However, they failed to move Emperor Shun's decision for reform.

Tso Hsiung was then the Grand Secretary of State. He soon successfully disqualified an under-forty candidate who classified himself as one of extraordinary talent, therefore entitled to exemption
from the age regulations. Thenceforth selection practices became
stringent. During the ten-odd years of his Secretaryship the number of candidates drastically decreased, and the system was put
in some order. Among the small number of selected candidates
were persons like Ch'en Fan, Li Ying, and others, who later
figured prominently in the political inquisition owing to their anti-
eunuch stand. Furthermore, Tso Hsiung invited well-known
scholars as instructors, and encouraged advanced studies by am-
bitious and upright young men, so that the number of students in
the capital greatly increased. Tso Hsiung, in fact, was becoming
a leader of the scholars' party.

//The utterly ridiculous practices in official selection before
Emperor Shun's reign can be illustrated by the following story
from the "Life of Chung Sung" in the Later Han History:

At first [Chung Sung] was a minor government clerk in the
district office. At that time Wang Tan, nephew of the Ho-nan
magistrate T'ien Hsin, was known for his ability to judge
personalities. [T'ien] Hsin said to him, "It is now time to

recommend six 'Filial and Incorrupt' candidates. I have already received written requests from powerful personages for most of the quota, and it is better that I do not reject them. But I want to select one scholar of my own choice, in order to repay our country. Do help me to find such a man." The next day, as [Wang] Tan was seeing some guests off at Ta-yang Gate, he saw [Chung] Sung from a distance, and was powerfully impressed. Upon his return he told [T'ien] Hsin, "I have found the candidate for you. He is right at hand, a minor government clerk in Lo-yang."

It was evidently unusual even to have one candidate out of six chosen without special requests. This testifies to the political influence enjoyed by the great families. Moreover, such influence could not be stemmed by temporary corrective measures, such as that initiated by Tso Hsiung.

//The great families made requests not only to the local authorities, but also to the central government. After Tso Hsiung's time the authority of the central government rested with either the empresses' families or with the eunuchs, both of which groups themselves comprised great families. Local great families began to establish connections with them, and the selection of officials worsened. The situation at the end of Han was described by [a contemporary] Wang Fu, in his Discourses of a Hermit, as follows: "[....] Name corresponded not with actuality, desire matched not the recommendations. The rich relied on their wealth, the powerful brandished their weight and influence. The possession of much money constituted virtue, and unyielding hardness became a superior quality." A contemporary doggerel quoted in the "Book on Examination of Officials" in [the fourth century work] Pao-p'u-tzu ran:

> The "Chosen Scholar" thinks learning's a bother,
> The "Filial and Incorrupt" lives apart from his father,
> Poverty and purity are considered not smart,
> Grandees and generals are like chickens at heart.

//With such selection, and such officials, it is not difficult to imagine the degree of corruption in politics. The common people of course were the victims of such government, but the more law-abiding great families--usually the relatively less wealthy--and the scholars who aspired to government positions were also frustrated in their objectives. Thereupon they united their forces, and took action against the corrupt government before the common people had begun to stir.

8. Political Control by Families of
Empresses and Eunuchs

//Political authority in late Eastern Han rested in the hands of
the eunuchs and families of the empresses. These comprised two
sorts of great families; their influence had a particularly close relation with the central government. In general, the empresses'
families were already great families, but suddenly underwent particular expansion after obtaining power in the central government.
The eunuchs were originally not great families, but with their ascendancy to power large numbers of people began to gather under
them as dependents, and with further development the eunuchs too
became especially great families.

//The empresses' families and eunuchs were know as "lucky
risers." This was especially true of the eunuchs, whose rise was
a sudden over-night phenomenon. The two groups were for the most
part untrained in letters. Their elders, "riding on dragons and
flying with phoenixes," did not need to study; those of the younger
generation were pampered from infancy and did not know how to
study. They lacked political insight, not to mention political experience. They were ignorant of the principle "keep by right
methods that which was first obtained by wrong," and thought only
of even more rapid expansion of their suddenly acquired power.
Therefore, aside from exploiting the common people, they had
to strike at other great families and rob the latter of their property and rank. As the large fish finds that eating small fish is
more nourishing than eating shrimp, so did the empresses' families and eunuchs find the above a very convenient method of expansion.

//The sudden rise to power of empresses' families and eunuchs
roused dissatisfaction on the part of the conservative group of
great families. Many persons among these were high officials and
leaders of the intelligentsia. They knew their Classics, and understood the axiom of Mencius: "If close-meshed nets are not allowed in pools and ponds, the supply of fish and turtles will be
inexhaustible." Therefore in addition to their feelings of insecuri-
ty resulting from the selfish attitudes of the newly risen great
families, they also were opposed to the latter's policy of "drying
the lake to get the fish." They realized that, if the newly risen
were given a free hand, the rule of the Han dynasty would be
threatened. Thereupon a sense of loyalty and righteousness suddenly asserted itself. Motivated by a combination of public spirit
and self-interest, they started to resist the newly risen families.

//There was no very clear-cut distinction between the newly

risen and conservative groups, nor did the distinction appear suddenly. That they were each able to form a separate group was due to the fact that owing to their connections with relatives, household followers, disciples, and ex-subordinates, they had already evolved into great-family units. Because of common interest, great families began to unite themselves for the struggle; the more fierce the struggle, the greater the unity.

//It has been argued that the struggle between the newly risen and the conservatives represented one between metropolitan and local great families. This is partly true, but it does not tell the whole story. For, although the empresses' families and eunuchs were the metropolitan great families, they could not have swallowed all local magnates at one gulp. With some of the local magnates they had established friendly connections, and the natural tendency was for them to ally themselves with similar great families and overrun others that were antagonistic.

//The empresses' families and eunuchs were "wealthy but quite ignorant," while the intelligentsia were "learned but not very wealthy." Polarization gradually developed between these two groups. However, not all empresses' families were "wealthy but quite ignorant"; occasionally they also united with the intelligentsia. Hence we cannot call the struggle between the two groups one of empresses' families and eunuchs against the intelligentsia. The intelligentsia often considered themselves the "pure ones." Therefore let us call the "learned and not very wealthy" (i.e. the conservatives) the "Pure Group," and the "wealthy but quite ignorant" ones (i.e. the newly risen) the "Turbid Group." Political struggle intensified with the widening of the gulf between the Pures and the Turbids.

//The influence of the Turbids was due to their control of the sovereign. And the authority of the sovereign resulted from the centralization of power from the time of Emperor Kuang-wu on. Actually the centralization of power did not begin with Kuang-wu, but went back to Emperor Wu of Western Han. However, Kuang-wu made the system more definite. Chung-ch'ang T'ung has given the following clear account of the causes and effects of Kuang-wu's centralization:

> Emperor Kuang-wu, angry at the loss of [imperial] power
> during the preceding reigns, and incensed by the usurpation
> of the [Heavenly] mandate by strong officials, went to the
> other extreme and never delegated administrative authority
> to subordinates. Although the three Grand Ministers were
> installed, matters were actually entrusted to the Grand Sec-
> retary of State. Henceforth, the function of the Grand Ministers

consisted of no more than the staffing of their own offices....
Power then shifted to the empresses' families, and imperial
favor was granted to personal attendants.

The centralization of power was indeed a double-edged sword. Under
an able emperor it could be used to curb the great families; but under an incompetent emperor it could be grasped by the great families and used by them to control the emperor.//

In looking for a reliable force to wield this sword for him, an
ignorant and weak ruler naturally thought his relatives would be
the most trustworthy. During Eastern Han many an emperor died
young and, like as not, left no heir. His widow, fearful of the future,
often chose to supervise the rule of the heir, who was generally
adopted from a feudatory house, thus placing real authority in the
hands of her own relatives. In this way power was transferred to
the empresses' families.

As a result of imperial grants, these empresses' families were
already extremely wealthy, but with the assumption of power they
became even more acquisitive. For example Tou Hsien, as the
Empress Dowager's relative, controlled the government during
the reign of Emperor Ho [89-106 A.D.]. The Tou family had been
magnates for many generations, first achieving prominence as an
empress' family in the time of Emperor Wen [179-156 B.C.] in
Western Han. Their tremendous wealth and power at the beginning
of Eastern Han is described in the Later Han History. Tou Hsien's
sister was the wife of Emperor Chang. On the strength of the sister's position Tou Hsien once even tried to seize an estate belonging to a princess, but was temporarily curbed by Emperor Chang,
who called him a stinking rat. After the death of the emperor, Empress Dowager Tou supervised the reign of Emperor Ho, whereupon Tou Hsien had the control of the government in his hands.
After his successful campaign against the Hsiung-nu he was invested with the title of Great General, ranking above the Grand
Ministers, and his followers filled official posts in all parts of
the country. Ultimately he overreached himself. He was killed
and his party suppressed by the careful planning of the emperor,
who allied himself with eunuchs in the venture. This was the first
instance of the eunuchs' interference in politics.. Thereafter their
influence steadily increased and they constantly plotted to usurp
power. They did so sometimes in alliance with the empresses'
families, sometimes in opposition to them.

Another case of the empress' family assuming power occurred
in the reign of Emperor Huan [147-168 A.D.]. The Empress Dowager Liang came of a magnate's family that dated back to Western

Han. Her brother Liang Chi was also invested as Great General, with 30,000 dependent families to his fief; in addition, other members of the family also received large grants. But the Liangs and their followers were not satisfied, and frequently used various methods to augment their wealth. For instance Liang Chi himself confiscated, on the basis of trumped-up charges, the entire property of some 170,000,000 [cash] that belonged to a miserly magnate, T'u-sun Fen. Many of Liang Chi's own men were also placed at Court, and he became so overbearing in his conduct that the emperor, like Emperor Ho before him, again sought the aid of the eunuchs and suppressed the Liang group in a coup in which thousands lost their lives. Liang's property was auctioned and brought in over 3,000,000,000 [cash] to the government treasury. Again the fortunes of the empress' family were ruined by the eunuchs.

All five eunuchs who helped to organize the coup were ennobled on the same day, and henceforth were known as the "Five Lords." Their fiefs ranged from 20,000 to 13,000 families each, and money grants from 15,000,000 to 13,000,000 cash each. The leading person, Tan Ch'ao, died soon after, but the other four lorded it over the country unchecked. Contemporary epithets described them individually as follows: "Tso [Kuan] can turn heaven upside down; Chü [Yüan] sits on peerless heights; Hsü [Huang] is like a recumbent tiger; T'ang [Heng] rains evil upon us." Sons were adopted to inherit their ranks, and relatives were given official posts. Thus, though without lineal heirs, the eunuchs still succeeded in founding great families with their dependents. These were an utterly unlettered group, very turbid indeed. The Pures could not tolerate them and directly attacked them with the Pures' own dependent groups. The frontal clash between the Pures and the Turbids constituted the two "political inquisitions" of Eastern Han.

9. Rise of Great Families of the Intellectuals

Though economically not as strong as the Turbids, the Pures nevertheless had large numbers of dependents who followed them for the fame that could be derived from such connections and the moderately well-to-do intellectuals, such as the Fellows of the National Academy, originated what was known as "public opinion" in Eastern Han. The interpretation of Chang Ping-lin [1868-1936] that they were "representatives" of public opinion who aided the administration of local governments, is probably far-fetched. Nevertheless, according to some extant stone inscriptions dating to Eastern Han, the term i-jen 議人 or i-min 議民 referred to corvée-exempt privileged persons, and presumably denoted those who expressed opinions on public affairs and also occupied positions of prestige in society.

Many persons resorted to deceitful devices in order to create favorable local opinion of themselves and facilitate selection to officialdom. Some succeeded, as for instance Hsü Wu and his two younger brothers, all of whom displayed the proper fraternal behavior under conditions of stress and succeeded in winning candidacies. Others failed, as in the case of Chao Hsüan, who first won a reputation as a filial son who lived for twenty years at his mother's tomb, but later was punished when it was found out that five sons were born to him during his period of mourning [which should have been a period of continence].

In response to the demand for local evaluation of personality, "censurers" appeared. For example, Hsü Shao at the end of Eastern Han was director of official selection at Ju-nan. He and his cousin Hsü Ching were both fond of censuring the local people, and published their comments once every month. Once, pressed for an opinion by Ts'ao Ts'ao before the latter had gained power, Hsü Shao had commented " You are a villain in times of peace and a hero in times of trouble," which despite the obvious barbs greatly pleased Ts'ao Ts'ao. Relations were not friendly between Hsü Shao and Hsü Ching; other censures had a low estimate of the former, owing, very likely, to unfavorable comments on him from Hsü Ching.

Another famous censurer and contemporary of Hsü Shao was Kuo T'ai [127-169], leader of the National Academy Fellows. At that time the Academy Fellows were restless, and spent their time in criticizing current affairs or political personages. Kuo's policy was never to speak against others, but always to confine himself to favorable comments when he did express his opinion. His fame was prodigious. On one occasion when he left Lo-yang for his home district the scholars who came to bid farewell arrived in several thousand chariots. When among all these multitudes Li Ying, the Pure magistrate of Ho-nan, alone was allowed to cross the river with him, the others envied Li for such immortal honor.

The Grand Ministers often solicited advice from censurers before reaching decisions on the selection of officials. This opened the way for opportunists and imposters, such as the two self-styled censurers Chin Wen-ching and Huang Tzu-ai. They began by striking an impressive pose, thus winning the admiration of many high officials at Court, but they were exposed as frauds by Fu Jang, disciple of the afore-mentioned Li Ying. Chin and Huang fled Lo-yang sans honor and sans fame. Since his delineation of their character had turned out to be correct, Fu Jang was able to reap further honors out of this episode as a censurer.

The National Academy was actually an avenue to officialdom. At first fifty fellowships were created by Emperor Wu of Western Han. The Fellows were selected by the Minister of Rites, or recommended by local officials, and all were exempt from labor service. Examinations were held once a year, out of which a number of Fellows were sent to fill official posts. Gradually the number of Fellows was increased, until it reached three thousand in the time of Emperor Yüan [48-32 B.C.]. Extra quotas were added in the reign of Emperor P'ing [1-6 A.D.] for sons of officials of the yüan-shih 元 士 rank. Placements through examination thenceforth were divided into three classes, with a total of one hundred per year.

In the early years of Eastern Han the scholarly traditions of the former period were maintained in the Academy, but the spirit of learning declined sharply after the reign of Emperor An. The professors neglected their teaching, the Fellows neglected their studies, and the Academy premises were turned into a vegetable garden. Later Emperor Shun, following the advice of high officials, restored and expanded the physical plant of the Academy, which now possessed 240 buildings with a total of 1,850 rooms. The Fellows at this time numbered some 30,000, ten times that of Western Han.

//Most of the Fellows probably came not to learn the Classics but to seek entrance into officialdom. Actually contemporary scholarship in the Classics was probably not very interesting. It merely involved extremely detailed textual commentaries; sometimes a ten-thousand word study was made to explain one word. Therefore the Academy Fellows paid scant attention to the Classical texts, but concentrated on frivolities, political discussions, and the making of social connections. They can be considered as a kind of public opinion makers, who often voiced their criticism of political affairs and personalities. Some high officials, fearing their unfavorable comments, personnaly sought them out for friendship. The Fellows were glad of this opportunity to establish connections with those in high places, and called themselves the latter's friends or disciples. Such persons as Kuo T'ai and Chia Piao, for instance, became leaders of the 30,000 Academy Fellows, and together with people like Li Ying mutually sang each other's praises. The fellows coined seven-word slogans for every person whom they esteemed. [.....]

//Thus, the Academy Fellows became united with the Pure ministers into a clique, and later were banned from official employment due to their strife with the eunuchs. However, the political
inquisitions did not originate in the Eastern Han period. On the
contrary, they had made their initial appearance, at the latest,
during the reign of Wang Mang. It is recorded in the "Biography
of Yün Ch'ang" in the Early Han History:

> Yün Ch'ang, styled Yu-ju, was a native of P'ing-lin [in Hopei].
> He studied under Wu Chang of the same district, who was a
> specialist on The Book of History and an Academy professor...
> Being a famous scholar of the time, [Wu] Chang was exceed-
> ingly popular as a teacher, having under him over one thou-
> sand pupils. [Wang] Mang considered them a villainous clique
> deserving to be banned entirely from official employment.
> Thereupon his pupils named others as their teachers.

> ([Yen] Shih-ku comments: The pupils changed to other teach-
> ers, and avoided mention of [Wu] Chang as their teacher.)

The eunuchs of Eastern Han probably were merely following the
example of Wang Mang.
//The formation of the Northern and Southern factions in Kan-
ling Commandery [in Shantung] probably marked the beginning of
political cliques in Eastern Han. Chou Fu, a native of Kan-ling,
had tutored Emperor Huan when the latter was still a prince. Upon the latter's accession Chou Fu was raised to the office of Secretary of State. At that time Fan Chih, the magistrate of Ho-nan
who also came from Kan-ling, was a man of renown in the government. The friends and relatives of Fang Chih then began to circulate the saying: "Fang Po-wu [i.e. Fang Chih] sets an example
of good for the country; Chou Chung-chin [i.e. Chou Fu] is appointed for his connections as tutor," which was somewhat dis-
respectful toward Chou Fu. Thereupon the followers of these two
families began to jeer at and attack each other, each rounding up
its own group, and a feud gradually developed. Kan-ling was thus
divided into the opposing Northern and Southern factions. "Faction"
meant "clique," which shows the importance of the role played by
the followers and disciples in the ranks of each camp.//
   The keeping of household followers prevailed in Eastern Han.
These persons still maintained a degree of the sense of personal
loyalty that had marked their counterparts during the Warring
States. Like the disciples and ex-subordinates, they were often
willing to risk their lives for their masters, as several episodes
show. The episodes involving Li Ku's disciple Kuo Liang and Tu

Ch'iao's ex-subordinate Yang K'uang during the time of Liang Chi's
control of government is a case in point. The Pures, then, encouraged by the prospects of fame and supported by loyal followers,
charged into the field and gave battle to the overwhelmingly powerful Turbids, thereby touching off the earth-shaking political contest that followed.

10. Internal Strife among Great Families:
The First Political Inquisition

The eunuchs ennobled by Emperor Huan after his coup against
Liang Chi brought the tyranny and rapacity of their conduct to a
new height. Some of their followers actually practised highway
robbery, not to speak of the more refined methods of extortion and
oppression. Their first major setback was suffered in 165 A.D.,
when Grand Commandant Ch'en Fan, who succeeded Yang Chen,
was able to force the suicide of two of the eunuch leaders and
bring about the demotion or dismissal of many of their relatives
and followers from official posts. A few years before, however,
three Pure officials--Li Ying, magistrate of Ho-nan; Feng K'un,
Governor of a jail; and Liu Yu, Minister of Agriculture--had been
sentenced to hard labor because of their actions against the interests of influential eunuchs. They were only pardoned upon the
vigorous intercession of Garrison Commander Ying Feng.

In 166 A.D. Li Ying was appointed a Garrison Commander.
Within ten days of his taking office he tried and executed Chang
So, a tyrannous magistrate who happened also to be the brother
of the eunuch Chang Jang. Thereafter the eunuchs conducted
themselves with extreme caution, and upon the emperor's query
tearfully answered that they "feared Commander Li."

Meantime, other Pure officials also were exerting themselves
in the suppression of eunuch agents within their jurisdictions.
For instance, Fan Pang, personnel director at Ju-nan, had the
support of his superior Tsung Tzu, the Prefect of Ju-nan, in his
stand against pressure from eunuchs. Ch'ing Chih, personnel
director at Nan-yang, also was trusted completely by Ch'eng
Chin, the Prefect of Nan-yang. Both Ch'ing Chih and Liu Chih,
Prefect of T'ai-yüan, resorted to confiscation of property and execution of eunuchs or their followers, after the latter had already
received formal pardons. Chang Chien, a famous scholar who
was Post Inspector of Shan-yang [in Shantung], once impeached
the eunuch Hou Lan because "He forcibly seized others' property
to the amount of 381 houses and 118 ch'ing of land. He built sixteen mansions....and robbed graves..." Failing to receive orders

for action, Chang Chien proceeded on his own, confiscating Hou's property and destroying his home. Many other cases involving prominent eunuchs also occurred in the years 165 and 166. In the latter year, as a result of pressure brought to bear on Emperor Huan by the eunuchs, the first political inquisition took place against outstanding anti-eunuch officials who were members of the Pure Clique. In the autumn of 166, Ch'eng Chin and Liu Chih both died in prison. In the winter of the same year, Li Ying and some two hundred others were imprisoned on grounds of being Pure men. Emperor Huan initiated this mass imprisonment on charges lodged against them in 165 by Lao Hsiu, disciple of the charlatan Chang Ch'eng, who bore a grudge against Li Ying. In his charge Lao Hsiu said Li Ying and others "maintained Academy Fellows and errant scholars....and formed themselves into factions and cliques. They criticized the government and disturbed the public morals."

Arrests were carried out, and a man-hunt was begun for those who escaped. Grand Commandant Ch'en Fan, however, refused to put his signature to the order for imprisonment, saying: "All those who are about to be investigated are persons highly regarded throughout the country as loyal and public-spirited officials; they deserve to be pardoned even if their descendants should be criminals for ten generations to come. How can we round them up in prison before their offense has been defined?" This further incensed the emperor, who summarily jailed Li Ying and others. Ch'en Fan advised against it, but to no avail. Instead, he himself was dismissed by the emperor on the grounds that he had proved himself incompetent in the selection of officials.

Among those imprisoned was Fan Pang, who proved to be an outspoken leader of the jailed scholars. Asked at their trial why they had organized into a clique, Fan Pang replied, "To bring good persons together so as to magnify their goodness and bring about a united effort to eliminate evil persons." On another occasion he said, "In olden times people were good so as to increase their own fortune. Nowadays people who are good invite catastrophe [....] I have a clean record and a clear conscience...."

There were some among the Pure clique who were more cautious. Seeing that the inquisition was calamitous and involved large numbers of persons, they began to appeal for help from the Empress Tou's relatives and other high officials. Moreover, Li Ying and others also named some of the eunuchs' followers as members of the Pure Clique, which intimidated the eunuchs. Prompted by the latter's importunities, the emperor decreed a general amnesty in 167 A.D. The members of the clique were banished to their home districts and were forbidden to have official employment as long as they lived. Thus ended the first political inquisition.

11. Internal Strife among the Great Families: The Second Political Inquisition

The first political inquisition was but a prologue to the serious frontal clash that was to occur later.

Emperor Huan died without heir in 167 A.D. Ch'en Fan, Tou Wu, and others placed a minor on the throne as Emperor Ling, and the Empress Dowager Tou supervised the reign. The Tou family had retained a good deal of power. Tou Wu, the brother of the Empress Dowager, had already established good relations with the Academy Fellows and the Pure party. For instance, the Academy Fellows had chosen as the Three Esteemed ones Tou Wu, Ch'en Fan, and Liu Shu, the last-named being a member of the imperial house. With the accession of Emperor Ling, Tou Wu became invested as Great General, and Ch'en Fan became Assistant Grand Tutor. Under them people like Li Ying, Wang Ch'ang, and many other Pures received official appointments. Besides the Three Esteemed Ones, the Academy Fellows also had a series of four gradations of eight persons each, denoting succeeding levels of esteem for each person. Among these figured Fan Pang, Chang Chien, Ch'ing Chih, and others, all of whom, with only minor exceptions, were officials.

There was thus a total of thirty-five Pure leaders who had the support of the Academy Fellows and were in a position to eradicate the Turbids. However, though the political views of the Pures differed from those of the Turbids, they were none the less also out to seek political power for themselves. Now that this had been largely achieved, especially for Tou Wu and his family, the urge to act became dulled. Despite repeated promptings by Ch'en Fan for action against the eunuchs, Tou Wu and the Empress Dowager continued to procrastinate.

Then in 168 the news leaked out that Ch'en and Tou were determined to kill the eunuchs. The latter forestalled them with a coup d'état, took the imperial seal from the Empress Dowager, and placed it in the hands of the twelve-year old Emperor Ling. On hearing of this Ch'en Fan rushed to the palace with a group of eighty-odd armed disciples, but they were overpowered and Ch'en was murdered in prison that night. In the meantime, Tou Wu succeeded in rallying a few thousand metropolitan Guards to fight an equivalent force commanded by Wang Fu and other eunuchs.

But the Guards, used to fearing the authority of the eunuchs, failed Tou Wu, who thereupon committed suicide. The Ch'en and Tou families, together with their followers, were convicted and sentenced. The families were sent into exile and the disciples and ex-subordinates were barred from official employment. This was the beginning of the second political inquisition, which was marked by the destruction of the Ch'en and Tou families.

In 169, in an attempt to curry favor with the eunuch Hou Lan, someone informed the emperor against Chang Chien and twenty-four others on grounds of "plotting against the state." Emperor Ling thereupon ordered the imprisonment of over one hundred scholars, including Li Ying and Fan Pang. Li died of torture in prison. Fan Pang, on hearing that the government agent assigned to arrest him was instead closeting himself at home with the warrant and weeping, went and delivered himself to the local magistrate. The latter advised him to flee, but Fan Pang refused; later he too died in prison together with some hundred others.

Chang Chien, on the contrary, fled from the authorities and went beyond the Great Wall. All along his route of escape entire families were exterminated by the eunuchs' agents for giving him aid and comfort. Altogether a large number of families were directly or indirectly involved in this inquisition, and six or seven hundred persons were permanently barred from further employment.

However, there were some cautious elements among the Pures who were able to escape the upheaval. For instance, Kuo T'ai secretly lamented the deaths of the scholars, but did not openly express any opinion on the subject. He had been listed in one of the categories of esteemed persons by the Academy Fellows, but had been careful not to offend any quarters in his daily utterances.

Now the Academy Fellows were the only remaining force of the Pure group. The Fellows had had a long history of participating in political affairs; their first intercession went back to the end of Western Han, and several others occurred previous to the first political inquisition. On each occasion, as when they interceded for the Prefect of I-chou in 153, their efforts were met with some success. It did not appear that the Fellows themselves had suffered great losses in the two inquisitions just described. Yet the eunuchs were aware that the Fellows were seething with unrest. In 170 the Empress Dowager Tou, who had lived under surveillance of the eunuchs since the coup of 168, died. Shortly afterward someone scrawled various accusations on the Palace gate, charging the eunuchs with murdering the Empress Dowager, the high officials with accepting sinecures and being disloyal, and Hou Lan

with killing Pure men. After this incident over one thousand Fellows were thrown into prison by imperial order. Thereafter misfortune became the lot of whoever spoke in favor of the Pures.
The eunuchs and their Turbid faction lorded it over the entire country, staffed the government at all levels with their own men, and
wantonly killed off all opponents. It was not until 184 A.D. that
a slightly more enlightened eunuch, Lü Ch'iang, advised Emperor
Ling to rescind the order banning the Pures from government employ, so as to prevent them from collaborating with the Yellow
Turbans. By that time the revolt of the Yellow Turbans was already a year old.

To sum up the political contest of the two decades: Despite the
fact that the actual conditions were quite complex, this was nothing but an unrelenting struggle for power between the Pures and
the Turbids. Both were supported by family members, household
followers, disciples, and ex-subordinates. The martyrs showed
to a high degree a sense of loyalty and righteousness, but the object of such loyalty was not so much the country and sovereign as
their own superiors and teachers. Nevertheless, the fact that
they were able to fight showed that they could unite in one purpose;
it also showed that the political influence of great families was already strong. Such unity of great families was further evidenced
during the upheavals of the Three Kingdoms period, as described
in the Records of the Three Kingdoms and the Tsin History. With
the granting of legal recognition to the special privileges of the
great families, the rule of powerful families during the two Tsin
and Northern and Southern dynasties was initiated.

NOTES

楊聯陞, "東漢的豪族," 清華學報

Yang Lien-sheng, "Tung-Han-ti hao-tsu," The Tsing Hua Journal, XI, 4 (1936), 1007-1063.

This article is distinguished by the fact that the author displays
a considerable feeling for literary style. In addition to being
forcefully written it is also well documented. Main reliance was
placed on the Later Han History, supplemented by such contemporary sources as the Book of the Months.

While it is true, as the author holds, that the importance of the
great families of Eastern Han lies in their being the forerunners
of the "powerful families" that in effect ruled the country in the
two Tsin and Northern and Southern dynasties, the present study

also is significant in that it throws much light on the power structure of Eastern Han itself--that is, the latter part of China's
first period of centralized empire. It should be further noted that
the author is primarily not so much concerned with the actual
mode of life of the great families, material for which is also
available, as with the social and political implications of their
special position and economic power.

A good complement to this article is the study by Etienne
Balázs, "La crise sociale et la philosophie politique à la fin des
Han, T'oung Pao 39 (1950), 83-131. Balázs here views the social
crisis in the light of the political philosophy of three contemporaries, namely Wang Fu 王符, Ts'ui Shih 崔寔, and Chung-
ch'ang T'ung 仲長統.

II

THE MIDDLE PERIOD

(220-1368)

8

EARLY DEVELOPMENT OF MANORIAL ECONOMY
IN WEI AND TSIN

by

HO TZU-CH'UAN

1. Growth of Great Families

Since the Ch'in and Han dynasties the great families had steadily developed their power. By the end of Eastern Han the land had
become concentrated in their hands and the common people had become their servitors. Their wealth and their command over vast
manpower are clearly described in the contemporary works of
Chung-ch'ang T'ung.

When the rebellions of Tung Cho [died 192] and of the Yellow
Turbans broke out, the government was already so weak that it
was unable to render protection to the landlords and great families.
These therefore began to act in their own defence. The way in
which the great families of the Kuan-tung region, the eastern part
of North China, rose against Tung Cho is described as follows in
the Records of the Three Kingdoms:

> Thereupon they raised a great righteous army; famed mag-
> nates and great heroes, wealthy families and powerful clans,
> all came together from afar like clouds rushing toward a
> vortex...And so [Tung] Cho moved the emperor west to
> Ch'ang-an [in Shensi]. Of the Kuan-tung forces, the large
> ones united whole commanderies and kingdoms, the medium
> defended cities and estates, and the small gathered in the
> fields and hamlets.

The various biographies in the Records of the Three Kingdoms further reveal that the great landlord families sometimes could establish armed camps of their own which included as many as several thousand or tens of thousands of families. For instance, Hsü
Chu "at the end of Han gathered several thousand youths and family units and strengthened the defence works to repel the bandits."
Again, when Yüan Shao was the all-powerful magnate in Ju-nan

[in southern Honan], his followers were strongly entrenched in
that territory. An account of Ts'ao Ts'ao's warfare against them
indicates that they possessed at least twenty-odd fortresses;
20,000 families and 2,000 troops were taken by Ts'ao Ts'ao's men.
Other accounts in Records of the Three Kingdoms also testify to
the strength of local militarists, who submitted to no authority in
the country.

With the Hsiung-nu invasion and the establishment of the Tsin
capital in the south [316 A.D.], the situation reached a state of
anarchy. The country became studded with the fortified manors
of powerful families. Biographies of eminent persons in the Tsin
History mention their possession of thousands of families and record the warfare and alliances conducted among those who held
fortified manors in North China. One such magnate, Tsu Ti, who
held the post of the Governor of Yü-chou [in Honan], using his own
army of "Dependents" [pu-ch'ü 部曲] as the nucleus was able to
rally the militarists on the south bank of the Yellow River, won
their allegiance for Tsin, and added that territory to the dynasty.

During the fighting much agricultural land was abandoned by
the small peasants, and ownership became confused. In the time
of Ts'ao Ts'ao, for instance, Ssu-ma Lang proposed the restoration of the well-field system since "the people are scattered, the
fields are ownerless, and therefore all is public land." Such conditions in North China must have been further accentuated after
the fall of the capital to the Hsiung-nu. The common people, unable to defend themselves in a military upheaval, were compelled
to leave their land. The great families with armed forces, on the
other hand, took this opportunity to work the abandoned land with
the labor of "Dependents." They sometimes also took over the
fields of the small peasants by force. Thus, the small free peasant declined and land became concentrated in the hands of the
great families.

2. Transition from Free Peasants to Serfs

By the end of Eastern Han there had emerged a new and numerous social class consisting of the "Dependents," followers, and
household troops of the great families. These made up the majority of the population. A great landlord could possess tens of
thousands of these "Dependents." For instance, Li Tien "moved
over 12,000 persons, consisting of his family members and 'Dependents,' to live in Yeh [in Honan]." Again, "[Sun] Ch'üan attacked [Li] Shu at Wan-ch'eng [in Anhwei],....beheaded him,
and moved away his 30,000-odd 'Dependents'." Many similar

examples can be found in other biographies in the Records of the
Three Kingdoms.

These "Dependents," followers, and household troops were
semi-free in status and were vassals of the great families. They
were obliged to till the master's land in peaceful times, fight for
him in war, and give him unqualified loyalty. The exact origin of
the "Dependents" is not yet clear. It seems that during the upheavals of the Three Kingdoms there were many destitute refugees
who upon returning to their home districts were recruited into the
services of the local magnates as "Dependents." In addition to
these "Dependents" there were others, known as auxiliaries and
tenants, who had also lost their original status as free men, had
become vassals of great families, and were exempt from government taxation and labor service. Hsiung-nu also became tenants
in groups numbering as many as several thousands.

With North China overrun by the Hsiung-nu, the small free
peasants were unable to fend for themselves, and therefore placed
themselves under the armed protection of the great families. The
Tsin History abounds in records of the formation of groups headed
by magnates. For example, after the fall of Lo-yang, Hsi Chien
took refuge on Mount I [in Shantung] together with over one thous-
and families; in three years his following increased to several
tens of thousands. In a period when fields lay waste and the magnates often fought for the possession of farm laborers, such
voluntary dependency was greatly welcomed by the landlords. The
free peasants who attached themselves to the great families as
dependents could, of course, derive the benefits of protection in
times of disturbance and tax and corvée exemption in times of
peace as a result of their relation to the great families. However,
with that dependence came regulations and restrictions on their
life and work, which gradually lowered their status to that of
serfs.

3. The New Society of Manorial Villages

Urban economy was greatly developed during the two Han dynasties, and wealth was concentrated in cities. Large numbers of
dispossessed peasants went into the cities to seek their livelihood.
As Wang Fu said in his Discourses of a Hermit, there were in Lo-
yang ten times as many tradespeople as there were farmers, and
ten times as many idlers as there were tradespeople, so that each
farmer had to produce food for one hundred consumers, and each
farm wife had to weave cloth for a hundred persons. The concentration of population was not only evident in Lo-yang, but also in

all other urban centers. However, such urban growth was arrested in the Three Kingdoms period. Lo-yang and Ch'ang-an together with many other cities were destroyed by warfare, and urban commercial economy suffered a sharp decline.

Another indication of such decline was the currency situation.
The wu-chu 五銖cash of Han was temporarily abolished by Tung
Cho in 191 A.D., and in the succeeding years of warfare money
continued to decrease in value, so that its circulation was practically stopped. Exchange had begun to be conducted on a barter basis.

The new organs of production were the above-mentioned manors
and estates, which were not only military defense units but production organizations as well. The territory around each manor
or estate was included in a self-supporting unit. Production was
carried out by the "Dependents" and tenants under the direction
of the lord of the manor or estate. Such production methods reflected, on the one hand, a natural tendency under given circumstances, and indicated, on the other hand, the existence of official recognition of manorial economy. The latter was embodied
in formal grants in the Three Kingdoms period. The Records of
the Three Kingdoms states, for example, that "[Sun] Ch'üan gave
the wife and sons of [Chiang] Ch'in two hundred families and two
hundred ch'ing of land at Wu-hu [in Anhwei]." "In addition," reports the same source, "[Lü Meng] was given 600 colonist families at Hsün-yang [in Kiangsi]." After the unification of China by
the Tsin dynasty, regulations were officially drawn up as to the
amount of land and number of tenant farmers to be controlled by
officials of various ranks. The section on "Food and Money" in
the Tsin History gives the gradations as follows: First class officials, fifty ch'ing of land and not over fifty tenant families;
second class, forty-five ch'ing and not over fifty families; third
class, forty ch'ing and ten families; and so on to the lowest
(ninth) class official, who was allowed to own ten ch'ing of land
and one tenant family. These regulations did not represent the
initiation of a new system, but rather the recognition of an already
existing one. This is effect legalized the manorial production of
great families and officials.

The population declined sharply in the Wei and Tsin periods.
According to accounts in the Records of the Three Kingdoms and
the Tsin History, the population of the Three Kingdoms period
amounted to only one-fifth or one-tenth of that of Han, and the
figures for Tsin were still only three-tenths of Han. In 156 A.D.
at the end of Eastern Han 10,677,960 households (56,486,856 persons) were recorded, while the figures for Tsin were 2,459,840

households and 16,163,863 persons. Such a drastic reduction of
population figures could not have been caused by war alone. It
seems that the answer lies in the vast number of free peasants
who had become serfs and were split up among the manorial units
of the big landlords. Since the population census covered only
those who paid taxes to the government, the dependents of the manors, paying no taxes, were not included in the census. The fall
in population in the government records proves precisely the
expansion and proliferation of the manors.

4. Conclusions

The following tendencies were manifest in the social and economic development of China during the Wei and Tsin periods:
(1) Great families emerged and the land became concentrated in
their hands. (2) Free peasants declined as they lost their land
and became "Dependents," tenants, and semi-free serfs. (3) The
economy of exchange was destroyed, and natural economy predominated. Manorial production gradually took shape.

This production organization was later adopted by the alien
house of To-pa, who systematized it by distributing the conquered
territories and population in North China among the princes and
military leaders, thus founding the manorial system of the Northern Dynasties.

NOTES

何 兹 全, "魏晋時期莊園經濟的雛形", 食貨
Ho Tzu-ch'üan, "Wei Chin shih-ch'i chuang-yüan ching-chi-
ti ch'u-hsing," Shih-huo, I, 1 (Dec. 1, 1934), 6-10.

The chief sources for this article are the Records of the Three
Kingdoms (San-kuo chih 三國志) and the Tsin History (Chin Shu)
About a quarter of the quotations cited by the author from various
sources have been translated.

9

EVOLUTION OF THE STATUS OF "DEPENDENTS"

by

YANG CHUNG-I

1. Introduction

In Chinese historical records one frequently encounters the expression pu-ch'ü 部曲. The typical gloss on this term is illustrated by the notation of the Later Han History that Generals and Commanders* all had pu-ch'ü, that a Great General controlled five pu, each of which was headed by a Marshall, and that the pu possessed ch'ü, each of which was headed by a Constable. It goes without saying that this explanation cannot encompass the meaning of pu-ch'ü.

Let us proceed next to the study made by Ho Shih-chi on this term. His conclusions are: 1) The original meaning of the compound expression pu-ch'ü was "detachment of soldiers." 2) In the T'ang dynasty the term referred to servants. But these interpretations also fail to enlighten us on the evolution of the term. The best explanation I have seen is the following from T'ao Hsi-sheng's History of Chinese Political Thought:

> At the end of the Later Han dynasty and during the Three
> Kingdoms period there existed the status called pu-ch'ü.
> This had evolved from the status of household servants in
> Later Han. In the T'ang legal system pu-ch'ü entailed a semi-
> independent status. In Later Han and the Three Kingdoms it
> most likely merely comprised the petty military leaders of
> private families..... The large private estates of Eastern
> Han became manors after the Tsin dynasty, and the servi-
> tors and military leaders of private individuals became pu-
> ch'ü.

---

*These were officers who controlled the imperial bodyguard and were equal in rank to Generals.

This brief explanation is good as far as it goes, but it is still inadequate for a detailed understanding of the evolution of the term. The present study, while not definitive, is intended to advance the study of the term a bit further.

2. Origin of pu-ch'ü

The pu-ch'ü originated in Western Han as a systerm of military organization of an army on the march. The Later Han History states:

> Generals were not established on a permanent basis. The original commentary [by Yen Shih-ku] says: "They commanded expeditions and campaigns against rebellions....
> When these were ended, then [the positions] were abolished"
> ..... The Commanders all had pu-ch'ü. A Great General controlled five pu, each of which had one Marshal, whose stipend was 2,000 piculs [of grain], and one Colonel, whose stipend was 1,000 piculs. Under the pu were the ch'ü, each of which had one Constable, whose stipend was 600 piculs. Under the ch'ü were the "camps," each of which had one Camp Leader, whose stipend was 200 piculs.... The other [ranks of] generals, though lacking a regular staff owing to their being set up for military expeditions, also possessed pu ch'ü, Colonels, and Constables to lead the troops.

Similar evidence can be cited from the Han History, which has the following passage in the biography of Li Kuang:

> In going out to attack the barbarians [Li] Kuang's forces were without pu-ch'ü. (The Historical Records has wu 伍 [in place of pu-ch'ü]; this is also a part of military organization.) The formations on the march camped wherever there was water and grass. Every man took care of his own needs and maintained his own guard without any beating of the alarms. Encampments and official documents were economized....when on the march they ignored formal pu-ch'ü, ranks, and camp formations.

Yen Shih-ku in his commentary on this says: "[Li] Kuang esteemed simplicity. Hence when on the road he did not set up pu-ch'ü."

From these and other early sources we can see that pu and ch'ü were both military entities. They were comparable to modern military formations like armies, divisions, and brigades.

3. Change in the Meaning of pu-ch'ü

//It is likely that because the words pu and ch'ü were always
linked together until people became accustomed to the pair, therefore what was originally the designation of a military formation
changed into a synonym for a military force. This extension of
meaning must have taken place during the Wang Mang upheaval
[9-24 A.D.], a time when military affairs were all-pervading and
the expression pu-ch'ü must have been constantly on people's lips,
so that it was probably for this reason that pu-ch'ü acquired the
meaning of "detachment of soldiers." At the beginning of Eastern
Han the term was chiefly used in the meaning of "detachment of
soldiers," the detachment under such-and-such a person being
called so-and-so's pu-ch'ü.//

That pu-ch'ü had now become a general term for "armed
force" is indicated by passages in the Later Han History. The
"Chronicle of Emperor Kuang-Wu" states: "There were also
those known as Brigands, Bronze Horses, [.....] and others
who commanded pu-ch'ü totalling altogether several million men,
and plundered everywhere they went." The "Biography of Teng
Yü" in the same work records that Teng executed an official, Li
Pao, for the latter's insolence, whereupon "[Li] Pao's younger
brother gathered together Pao's pu-ch'ü and attacked [Teng] Yü."

4. Evolution of pu-ch'ü into Private Soldiers

The change in the status of pu-ch'ü occurred during the period
which encompassed the end of Han and the Three Kingdoms. As
we know, the Three Kingdoms was a time of great change--a
time when the slave system was changing into serfdom. It was
quite similar to the Roman Empire of two centuries laters. During this period the meaning of pu-ch'ü changed from soldiers in
general to private soldiers. There were four reasons for the
change:

(a) The rank of general changed into a permanent post. During
Western Han, when this position was on a temporary basis, it
was not easy for close relations to develop between the commanding officers and the pu-ch'ü. During the reign of Emperor Ming
[58-75 A.D.] of Eastern Han the position of General was set up
on a permanent basis, whereupon the opportunity arose for the
development of a special relationship. Hence the commanding officers and the pu-ch'ü not only possessed a superior-subordinate
relationship, but also developed the statuses of masters and subjects.

(b) The heads of commanderies and principalities were permitted to set up their own officials. In Eastern Han the subordinates of the prefect looked upon him as master. The historical data show that the subordinate officials not only acquired the status of subjects relative to their superiors, in which capacity they had even to die for their masters, but also that they come to develop something approaching a consanguinal relationship, as indicated by their observing for their masters the three year period of mourning [which was due at the demise of one's parents]. This relationship was extended still further when the local authorities increased in strength following the disturbances of the Yellow Turbans.

(c) The system of garrison colonization, though not originating in the Three Kingdoms period, was considerably extended at that time. An example of such colonization is the case of Teng Ai, a military leader who brought together some 50,000 people and settled them over a distance of 400 li in the Huai River region; at intervals of five li he set up a camp, each with sixty men, who cultivated the land as well as defending it. Teng Ai's minor officers in the garrison fields which he had set up were also called pu-ch'ü. Records show that a very close relationship had developed between higher and lower officers in the garrison colonization.

(d) Great families arose in large numbers following the annexations of land. This was particularly true after the disturbance of the Yellow Turbans. The situation can be illustrated with the incident in which Yüan Shao, a magnate who together with his followers was all-powerful in several commanderies, was defeated on the orders of Ts'ao Ts'ao [155-220] by another magnate, Man Ch'ung, who was appointed governor of Ju-nan [in Honan] and mobilized 500 men for this purpose. Man Ch'ung captured more than twenty fortresses, 20,000 families, and 2,000 soldiers, who were then made to till the land. Here then is a case of a great family maintaining private soldiers for its own defense. These great families could not be separated from the bureaucrats.

From the above points we can trace the evolution of pu-ch'ü in the direction of private soldiers. The pu-ch'ü and the leading officials, owing to long contacts with each other, developed a specially close relationship. Gradually changing into personal subordinates, the pu-ch'ü subsequently acquired the responsibility of providing protection and thus became private soldiers similar to the knights of the West.

5. Obligation of pu-ch'ü to the Lord

// The medieval knight of the West had the duty of performing
military service for his lord at all times.* At the time of attach-
ing himself to a lord the knight had to swear an oath of fealty. The
pu-ch'ü also had to swear an oath to his commanding general. The
Rites of Chou says:

> The commandery officials led forth their people with ban-
> ners and bells. At break of day they lowered the flags, and
> down to the lowest.....the assembled officials pledged an
> oath.

In a comment following this [the T'ang scholar] Chia Kung-yen has
the following notation:

> It has been stated (by [the Han scholar] Cheng K'ang-ch'eng)
> that "After the assembled officials had pledged the oath they
> all returned to their pu-ch'ü." All the military officials were
> at the head of their categories of pu and ch'ü: The Corporal
> headed five men, the Lieutenant headed twenty-five men, the
> Captain headed a hundred men, etc. All these were pu-ch'ü.
> At the time of the pledging of the oath, [the leaders] went out
> in front of the assembled throng. When the oath was finished,
> each returned to the original place of their pu-ch'ü. This ex-
> plains the phrase "returned to their pu-ch'ü."

// In my opinion the Rites of Chou was a Han forgery; Cheng
K'ang-ch'eng too was born at the end of the Han dynasty. Hence
the statements "the assembled officials pledged an oath" and "returned to their pu-ch'ü" must be a reflection of the Han system. In

---

*Dr. Sylvia L. Thrupp in commenting on this article states that the Western
knight did not have the duty of performing military service "at all times," except
perhaps in the early days when he was literally a household retainer; when he had
a fief he gave only forty days service free and wanted pay as well as expenses for
service in excess of that time. Another medievalist, Dr. Robert S. Lopez, likewise questions some of the comparisons with Western institutions by remarking
that although the basic differences between China on the one hand and England or
France on the other make the comparative study all the more interesting and valuable, care needs to be exercised not to transplant technical terms when they do
not fit the picture. Pointing out that the pu-ch'ü of China appears originally to
have been a blending of vassals and serf, whereas these groups were quite distinct
in the West, he adds that for this reason the expression "feudal serfdom" used
below on p. 153 by Yang Chung-i would sound to a Western scholar like a "mon-
strosity."

the course of time the [military] oath of the pu-ch'ū became an oath pledged by them to their lord. //

The pu-ch'ū had the duty of performing military service for their lord at all times. The biography of Wei Yen in the Records of the Three Kingdoms, for example, states that "He followed our late lord into Shu [Szechwan] with pu-ch'ū, and achieved military success on several occasions."

// Apart from military service, the pu-ch'ū also had the obligation of providing their lord with rent and labor service. The Tsin History states, "In the first year of T'ai-shih [265 A.D.] a decree ordered the restoration of labor service. The chih-jen 質任 was abolished from the chief officers of the pu-ch'ū on down." The same work says, "In the third year of Hsien-ning [277 A.D.] there was a general amnesty. The chih-jen was alleviated from the pu-ch'ū supervisors on down." Liang Ch'i-ch'ao [1873-1929] in his Lectures on the History of Chinese Civilization explains chih-jen as follows: "Chih is what is called a 'pledge' in the Rites of Chou, and jen is a 'guarantee.' The chih-jen therefore is similar to the deeds of later time covering the surrender or sale of one's person."

// Liang's interpretation is of doubtful accuracy. The terms "to abolish" and "to alleviate" do not properly relate to deeds, for since there was earlier mention of "abolishing," there was no point in speaking later of "alleviating." Moreover, "to alleviate" has the meaning of "to reduce," and how is it possible to "reduce" a deed? I suggest, therefore, that the chih-jen was the service owed by pu-ch'ū to their lords. Only thus is it possible to understand the terms "to abolish" and "to alleviate." This interpretation is not fabricated out of thin air but is supported by the following points: //

(i) The character chih is synonymous with tzu 貲 , which denotes the presents given by an inferior when visiting his master. In ancient times, as the Chou dynasty texts show, inferiors had to pay certain tributes to their master, and in the Han period princes also had to make contributions toward the imperial sacrificial offerings. These were forerunners of the services which the pu-ch'ū owed to their lords. Such duties were therefore called chih-jen [i.e. the chih duty].

(ii) A parallel to the duty of the Western medieval knight to present tribute to his lord is suggested by the fact that the Tsin History records the abolishing of chih-jen after "the restoration of labor service."

(iii) The pu-ch'ū had to pay taxes to their lord. The Tsin History records how Li Hsiung, who was assigned to lead a military campaign, was rewarded: "His pu-ch'ŭ were restored, military expeditions were not required, and all taxes reverted to his house."

∥Thus it would seem that chih-jen should be explained as tribute and labor service.* The pu-ch'ŭ then had not only to pledge an oath of fealty and perform military service for the lord, but also to offer tribute and labor service.

6. Responsibilities of the Lord toward the pu-ch'ŭ

∥In view of the duties owed by the pu-ch'ŭ to the lord, did the latter have any responsibilities toward the pu-ch'ŭ? There are two aspects to this question: 1) protection of the pu-ch'ŭ, and 2) provision of land to the pu-ch'ŭ for cultivation.

∥As to the pu-ch'ŭ receiving protection from the lord, this was just empty talk. The lord himself needed the protection of the pu-ch'ŭ, so how could he give protection to them? To be sure, the lord and his pu-ch'ŭ formed a bloc which was better able to ward off trouble from soldiers and brigands than a solitary individual would be. The so-called protecting of the pu-ch'ŭ was actually a matter of their protecting themselves, therefore, with the lord merely having the responsibility of providing leadership. The pu-ch'ŭ were very happy to accept this nominal protection from their lord. At times they would present their advice to the lord, since their own safety depended on that of the latter.∥

This is illustrated in a passage in the Records of Wei which describes how "the relatives and pu-ch'ŭ" of Li T'ung tearfully gave advice to their lord in a time of great crisis.

Politically, when the authorities wished to extend their control over the magnates it was the latter's pu-ch'ŭ that first had to be taken care of. There was therefore a relationship of mutual protection between the lord and his pu-ch'ŭ.

As to the pu-ch'ŭ's cultivating the lord's land, evidence of this can be found for the Wei and Tsin periods, although it was most highly developed during the Northern and Southern Dynasties [386-589]. The "Biography of Liang Hsi" in the Records of Wei relates the following:

[Liang] Hsi was [....] the Commissioner of Ping-chou [northern Shansi-Shensi]. At that time the disturbance of Kao Kan was just over; the barbarians were at the border

---

*Prof. L. S. Yang, who has made a special study of hostages in Chinese history, is in agreement with Ho Tzu-ch'üan's contention that chih-jen refers to hostages, not "tribute and labor service" as interpreted here.

and Chang Hsiung was lording it over the countryside, receiving people and petty officials, fugitives and rebels into
his group [....Later] the Khan became submissive, the renowned princes bowed their heads, and their pu-ch'u were
expected to render the same specific services as the registered civilian households.

The previously cited example from the Tsin History mentions that
"all taxes reverted to his [i.e. Li Hsiung's] house." These facts--
the similarity of the pu-ch'u's duties and those of registered civilian households, and the reverting of taxes to a lord's house--in-
dicate that the pu-ch'u had to till the lord's land. Hence the relation between pu-ch'u and the lord became still closer, for the
former depended on the latter's land for livelihood.

7. Relations between the pu-ch'u and the Lord

// We have mentioned before that the pu-ch'u were evolving in
the direction of private troops. This development reduced the relationship between the pu-ch'u and the government to the barest
minimum, while the pu-ch'u's dependence on the lord was intensified. The pu-ch'u under a provincial governor were actually his
private troops, although nominally they belonged to the government, as indicated in the following passage from the Records of
Shu:

> As to extending an invitation now to the Deputy General [Liu
> Pei], who has a reputation as a headstrong person, if he
> were treated as your pu-ch'u, he would surely feel dissatis-
> fied; on the other hand, as to treating him as a guest, it is
> impossible to tolerate two rulers in one state.*

This shows that a governor was in effect the ruler at the frontiers, and his subordinates had only the slightest connection with
the government. The pu-ch'u at this time were actually household
troops under a different name. The distinction between pu-ch'u
and household troops lay not in any difference that might exist in
their relationship with the lord, but in whether or not they had

---

*This passage consists of advice given to Liu Chang, Governor of an area in
what is now Szechwan, who sought to have his kinsman Liu Pei come and help him
against Ts'ao Ts'ao, a powerful military leader who shortly before had been appointed Minister of State in the crumbling central government. The fears indicated
by this advice were well justified, as Liu Chang was eventually squeezed out by
Liu Pei.

been registered (that is, had been recognized by the government).
Those that had been recognized by the government were called pu-
ch'ü; those that had not were known as household troops.

⫽A sentence in the Wei lüeh 魏略 says: "The various generals
. . . .also competed in publicly inducting their camp followers as
pu-ch'ü." That is to say, when the households troops had been publicly inducted, they became pu-ch'ü.

⫽With the increased private nature of pu-ch'ü, the distinction
between them and household troops gradually diminished. By the
time of the Ch'en dynasty [557-589] the two had become indistinguishable. The following passage from the "Biography of Hsün
Lang" in the Ch'en History illustrates this point:

> At that time [toward the end of the Liang dynasty, ca. 556]
> when there was a serious famine in the capital [at Nanking]
> and the people left to beg for a living north of the [Yangtse]
> River, [Hsün] Lang gathered pu-ch'ü and maintained them
> with food and clothing, so that the group came to number
> several tens of thousands of people. . . .He led over ten thous-
> and pu-ch'ü households, crossed the river, and established
> a camp within the territory of Hsüan-ch'eng Commandery
> [south of Nanking]. . . .When the emperor died, [the empress
> dowager]. . . . .kept it secret and did not announce the death.
> [Hsün] Lang's younger brother, Hsiao-wei, learned of this
> . . . .and planned an attack on T'ai [i.e. the capital] with his
> household troops.

Thus the terms "pu-ch'ü" and "household troops" were used inter-
changeably, which shows that they referred to the same thing.

⫽The pu-ch'ü had now become private troops (that is, household troops). They depended entirely on the cultivation of the
lord's land for a living, while the lord also relied on the tributes
and services paid by the pu-ch'ü as his source of income. The relationship between pu-ch'ü and the lord became still closer. The
more pu-ch'ü a lord possessed, the greater became his power and
the more elegant his way of life. Most of the lords therefore
sought to gather more pu-ch'ü. As stated in the "Biography of
Wei Ch'i" in the Records of Wei:

> At that time there were good harvests all over the country.
> [The people] returned to Kuan-chung and were recruited by
> the various generals as pu-ch'ü [. . . .] The commandery and
> district government were impoverished and could not com-
> pete [with the militarists].⫽

When a lord had acquired large numbers of pu-ch'ŭ and could not personally control all of them, officers were appointed to lead them. Such a leader of pu-ch'ŭ was called "pu-ch'ŭ chief" or "pu-ch'ŭ supervisor." The historical records for the Wei period contain many references to such officers.

In order to preserve his own strength a lord would do his best to prevent the loss of his pu-ch'ŭ. The Records of Wei contains a vivid account of Ts'ao Jen's personal rescue in the thick of battle of his pu-ch'ŭ personnel from encircling enemies. Such close relations between the lord and the pu-ch'ŭ led to the emergence of similar relations between the pu-ch'ŭ and the family and kin of the lord. Records show that at times thousands of pu-ch'ŭ moved to other places with the families of their lords. The pu-ch'ŭ chiefs and supervisors became hereditary positions. Our conclusion, therefore, is that the pu-ch'ŭ were becoming private troops during the Wei-Tsin period.

8. Decline in the Status of pu-ch'ŭ

The increasingly private nature of pu-ch'ŭ had the effect of lowering their status. In ancient times soldiering was pursued by aristocrats, but now it was lowered to [the census category of] "military households," whose status was below that of the civilian population, though still above that of slaves. Historical records for the Southern Dynasties indicate that those who were dependent on others for protection were assigned to military status, and that this was inferior to civilian status. The Records of Wei narrates with regard to two captured soldiers who died unflinchingly at the enemy's hands that they were both posthumously awarded the title of marquis, which could be passed on to their sons, and were to be relieved of their soldier's status and accorded the burial rites of a pu-ch'ŭ chief. The "soldier's status" was probably that of pu-ch'ŭ. The steady debasement in the connotation of pu-ch'ŭ led to the discontinuance of its use as a term in military organization during the Sung period [420-478] of the Southern Dynasties. There still were officers in charge of pu-ch'ŭ during the Northern dynasties, however, and in the Sui period official regulations still existed as to the costumes of pu-ch'ŭ chiefs and supervisors.

// At first pu-ch'ŭ was a designation for a military formation of an army on the march; subsequently it changed to signify "army." Its emergence as the designation for a class began with the system of military colonization, as the major responsibility of the pu-ch'ŭ during Wei and Tsin was to serve as tenant-soldiers, partly farming as tenants and partly defending the land. From

tenant-soldiers the pu-ch'ù gradually evolved into private retainers
of the commanding generals, and their affiliations changed from
governmental to private. By the T'ang dynasty they had become
similar to serfs with a semi-free status.//

9. The pu-ch'ù during the Southern Dynasties

From the Sung period on during the Southern Dynasties the pu-
ch'ù became completely subordinate to private individuals. A passage in the Liang History reads, "[Yang] K'an refused to accept
(the rewards of the Court). He had over one thousand pu-ch'ù, to
whom he privately gave rewards." This shows that the relation
of pu-ch'ù with the government was slight indeed, since their
master could refuse Court rewards but could himself give prizes.
Since the pu-ch'ù had now completely become private retainers
they are often mentioned in the records together with their families. References to "pu-ch'ù and their wives and children" and
"pu-ch'ù and their families" are to be found in the Ch'en History.
The same work also contains the expression "pu-ch'ù whom my
family has owned for generations." This of course denotes the
completely private nature of the pu-ch'ù. The latter thus became
the basis of the lord's power: no pu-ch'ù, no power. A person
"without pu-ch'ù" was described by the History of the Southern
Dynasties as "lacking the means to stand on his own feet."
　//Owing to the importance of pu-ch'ù to the lord, the latter began to embark on large-scale enlistments of these "Dependents."
The story of Su Chün aptly illustrates the enlistment and formation of private pu-ch'ù. His biography in the Tsin History says:

> During the upheavals of the Yung-chia period [307-312] the
> people fled their homes....[Su] Chün gathered several thous-
> and families...who elected him as their leader....[Su]
> Chün was afraid and moved south via the sea with several
> hundred families....At that time he possessed some 10,000
> crack troops....Fugitives and convicts were taken in by him,
> and desperadoes were given asylum, so that his forces were
> steadily strengthened....As a result a conciliatory decree
> was issued which appointed him to the post of Minister of
> Agriculture....His brother [Su] I then headed the pu-ch'ù
> in his place.

　//The above account reveals the true picture of the origin and
formation of the pu-ch'ù of a lord. Such large numbers of "Dependents" were used by the lord for defense or military expeditions

in times of war. Thus the "Biography of Li An-min" in the South ern Ch'i History says: "There were constant disturbances and war-fare from the time of the T'ai-shih reign [465-471] of Sung. From Generals on down [the military leaders] all recruited pu-ch'ü and stationed them in the capital."//

In times of peace the pu-ch'ü were employed to cultivate the land. For instance, the Liang History in its biography of Chang Hsiao-hsiu says, "He thereupon resigned from his post, returned to the mountains, and lived in Tung-lin Temple. He had a few dozen ch'ing of land and several hundred pu-ch'ü who devoted their energies to tilling the soil. [The proceeds] were given to these mountain people. Large numbers thereupon came to him from far and near, so that his followers became as multitudinous as a market throng." The fact that Chang won numerous followers because of his giving the proceeds of the land to the mountain people [that is, the local inhabitants who worked on his land as pu-ch'ü] very likely indicates that the usual practice of a lord was to exact heavy rents from his pu-ch'ü. The details on this point, however, have unfortunately not yet been investigated.

The cultivation of the soil by the pu-ch'ü led to their attach-ment to land and to their evolution toward the status of serfs.

10. The pu-ch'ü during the Northern Dynasties

Like the Germanic people who conquered the Roman Empire and established the medieval feudal system, the Northern Wei dy-nasty conquered North China and established feudal serfdom in China. As plainly indicated by Ch'en Teng-yüan in his Land Sys-tem of China, the policy of equalization of land could only be emp-ty talk under a feudal system, as vast amounts of land would in-evitably come under the control of the aristocrats. The policy of allotting land to each slave, for instance, only served to increase the holdings of slave-owners. What this amounted to was that the so-called "equalization" policy which was carried out at the time did not eliminate the annexation of land during the Northern Dy-nasties. The components of the landlord class, however, had shifted from merchants to aristocrats.

The landed aristocrats naturally needed people to cultivate their vast estates, and the pu-ch'ü answered this need. Hence during the Northern Dynasties "Rural Dependents" emerged on the scene; these were people who worked the aristocrats' land in the country. The fact that these people had now become a major factor in production led to many instances of aristocrats subjuga-ting ordinary civilians by violence and forcing them into pu-ch'ü status. This was similar to the Han practice of seizing civilians and turning them into slaves.

The pu-ch'ü not only became serf-like because of their cultivation of the soil, but they also came to resemble slaves. A number of examples of their being given away as presents can be found in the History of the Northern Dynasties. The "Biography of Tou Chih," for instance, states that he "was granted 300 horses and 8,000 pu-ch'ü families." Similarly, at the freeing of slaves the latter were liable to be retained by the lord as pu-ch'ü and "Female Dependents,"* as indicated by a decree recorded in the Chou History.

The enserfed pu-ch'ü cultivators of the land had the obligation, like the slaves of Han times, of paying taxes to the government. This requirement was not abolished until the time of Emperor Yang [605-617] of Sui. By the T'ang dynasty the pu-ch'ü had become serfs of private families and were no longer required to pay taxes to the government.

11. The pu-ch'ü during the T'ang Dynasty

During the T'ang period the status of pu-ch'ü fell still lower. According to the Explanation of the T'ang Code, "The person of a slave or pu-ch'ü belongs to the master." Pu-ch'ü had no separate census status of their own, but were appended to the census registration of their masters. They did not pay taxes. They were "maintained by their masters as slaves" and "had to serve their masters respectfully and carefully." A master found guilty of raping his own Female Dependent or the wife of his own or another's pu-ch'ü was by law exempt from punishment. Thus, pu-ch'ü were in fact not much different from slaves. There was, however, one point of distinction between the two in that pu-ch'ü were generally permitted to change to the service of another master. Their status therefore was somewhat better than that of the slaves, who could be freely disposed of by their masters.

According to the recent study on pu-ch'ü made by Ho Shih-chi, there were four census statuses in T'ang; these ranged between full civilians and slaves in the following descending order: (1) full civilians, (2) descendants of convicts, (3) convict families owing labor service by rotation, (4) slaves. Pu-ch'ü belonged to the same category as the persons owing labor service by rotation; in other words, they belonged to the third category, the one above

---

*This term excludes the wives of pu-ch'ü, but includes their daughters and other females.

the slaves. However, this distinction should not be over-empha-
sized, since both pu-ch'ü and slaves constituted the major productive forces, and both were the subjects of the lord's exploitation
and commands. So far as the general relationship of dependence
was concerned, the two were of equal importance.

Judging from the fact that pu-ch'ü were allowed to change masters, and that they were relatively freer than slaves, it would
seem that they correspond exactly to the position of serfs. Though
our data are still incomplete, we can at least conclude for the
time being that pu-ch'ü approximated serfs in status. Our conclusion is supported by two considerations: (1) Before T'ang it was
possible for the rural dependents, who cultivated the land, to drift
into serfdom. (2) After T'ang there emerged a category of people
known as "pu-ch'ü householders," such as mentioned in the Sung
History, who were similar to serfs. I believe therefore that it is
reasonable to suggest that pu-ch'ü were close to serfs in status
during the T'ang dynasty.

12. Another Usage for the Term pu-ch'ü

It should also be noted that the term pu-ch'ü was often used in
different senses even in the same historical period. Take the following example from Old T'ang History: "The officers and men
under [P'u-ku] Huai-en were all former pu-ch'ü of (Kuo) Tzu-i."
In the T'ang Code, on the other hand, it is stated: "Pu-ch'ü are
household servitors, and must serve their masters respectfully
and carefully." The pu-ch'ü in these two passages have entirely
different meanings.

What is the reason for this? It seems to me that, with the increasingly private nature of pu-ch'ü, specialization took place,
so that some pu-ch'ü still had to fulfil military duty, while others
became separated from soldiering and engaged solely in agricultural work as "rural dependents," thus closely resembling serfs.
The original designation, however, still applied to both groups,
so that private troops and serf-like tillers of the soil were both
known as pu-ch'ü.

The use of the term pu-ch'ü gradually decreased after T'ang.
This probably came about because the pu-ch'ü had by now become
tenants, and so the designation was superseded by "tenant households." But pu-ch'ü as an expression for the military rank and
file continued to be used down to the Ming dynasty. At this time,
as many passages in the Ming History show, the expression had
reverted to its original meaning. It is to be noted, nevertheless,
that the term was used in connection either with unsuccessful

rebels, or with enemy forces. It was not used to describe the regular troops belonging to the government.

13. Conclusions

//(a) The term pu-ch'ü originated in Western Han and was at first a military designation. This use of the term continued until the Sung period in the Southern Dynasties.

(b) At the beginning of Eastern Han, pu-ch'ü came to mean a detachment of soldiers.

(c) Eastern Han and the Three Kingdoms periods saw the evolution of pu-ch'ü in the direction of private troops.

(d) During the Wei and Tsin periods, pu-ch'ü became private troops. Some also worked on the land. They constituted the officially recognized household troops.

(e) During the Southern Dynasties pu-ch'ü had all become privately owned household troops, most of whom engaged in agricultural work. In the Northern Dynasties, owing to the emergence of manors, the pu-ch'ü became "Rural Dependents" and gradually became attached to the land.

(f) In the T'ang dynasty pu-ch'ü who did agricultural work occupied the status of serfs. Some people, however, still used the term as a designation for armies.

(g) After T'ang the term pu-ch'ü referred mostly to military detachments, that is, there was a return to the earlier usage. For the most part, however, it was not applied to the regular forces.//

NOTES

楊中一，"部曲沿革略考"，食貨

Yang Chung-i, "Pu-ch'ü yen-ko lüeh-k'ao," Shih-huo, I, 3 (Jan. 1, 1935), 97-107.

The main sources for this article are the dynastic histories of the various periods covered in the study, from the Han History to the Ming History. The most useful items from these works are the biographies of individuals. In addition, such official compilations as Explanation of the T'ang Code (T'ang-lü shu-i 唐律疏議) and T'ang hui-yao 唐會要 are also used. Reference is made to a few modern studies that touch on the subject.

10

THE SYSTEM OF EQUAL LAND ALLOTMENTS
IN MEDIEVAL TIMES

by

WAN KUO-TING

1. Introduction

What we now know of the Chinese land system prior to the Shang period is only unreliable legend. The Shang dynasty was a period of village communes, a system that later underwent changes under the conquering Chou people, who divided the land into feudal fiefs. The system of fiefs in turn gave way to private ownership, which began to flourish during the Warring States. In the Ch'in and Han periods the evils of this system became apparent and led to the equalization movements of the two Han dynasties, but these failed to bring any results.

The system of "occupation" or "holding" was initiated during the short-lived Western Tsin dynasty [265-316], under which land was allotted to the people according to a fixed scale. During the period of the Northern and Southern Dynasties [386-589], the Western Tsin legacy of land allotments was taken over by the northern kingdoms, which practised the policy of equal allotments; in the kingdoms south of the Yangtse River, on the other hand, annexations prevailed. The equal allotments policy was continued by the Sui [589-618] and T'ang [618-906] dynasties down to the reign of the T'ang emperor Hsüan-tsung [713-755], when it was completely destroyed. Thenceforth the system of private land ownership became deeply rooted in China. The period from the fifth century to the eighth therefore constituted a unique era in the history of Chinese land systems in that it saw the application of the policy of equal allotments [in between periods of private ownership].

Yet we must not come too quickly to a conclusion. To be sure, the system of equal allotments was there, and the terminology was there. But was the system actually carried out in fact as well as in name? Was it true that "for three hundred years between the T'ai-ho [477-499] and K'ai-yüan [713-741] reigns the people were very fortunate......Before the K'ai-yüan period the population was numerous, and everyone possessed land," as [the Sung writer] Cheng Ch'iao has declared? Were traditional historians correct in painting a scene of equal landownership and equal taxes for this period? These are rather difficult questions to answer.

2. Equal Allotments in Later Wei

During the Three Kingdoms and Western Tsin periods [220-316] China was torn by internal strife, visited by droughts and locusts, and invaded by border peoples. The population decreased, and many people migrated southward. Out of this situation two factors emerged that led to the instituting of equal allotments. One was the scanty population and the deserted state of land at the start of the Wei dynasty [386-535]; with most of the land ownerless it was possible for the government to introduce the policy of allotments. The other factor was the necessity to adjudicate land disputes arising out of conflicting claims of persons who had been absent for long periods of time during the upheavals, and the need to deal with the situation where strong persons had forcibly occupied more land than they could work, while weaker individuals lacked land to maintain themselves in one place; the policy of allotments was intended to eliminate the disputes and the unequal holdings. Moreover, despite their barbarian origins the Wei rulers, especially Emperor Hsiao-wen [471-499] exerted themselves in assimilating Chinese culture. In them the Confucianist idea of the "well-field" found ready proponents. These rulers also had the Western Tsin policy of land allotments as precedent. Given impetus by the actual importance of the land problem, therefore, the policy of equal allotments was soon implemented.

According to a passage in the Wei History, planning for equal allotments began with a memorial presented by Li An-shih to Emperor Hsiao-wen. In it Li described the general disrupted state of agriculture and confusion of ownership, and proposed the system of allotments in order to benefit the common people. The suggestion was heartily approved by the emperor.

The first order for the equal allotment of land was issued in 477. The immediate cause of this order was a cattle epidemic of the previous year which had greatly reduced the agricultural work force. In view of this situation the decree ordered that when supervising the farmers the officials should urge the latter to exert themselves, and added the following: "Let each adult man cultivate

forty mou of land, and each secondary adult* twenty mou. Let
there be no unexpended energy among men, and no unexploited profits in the soil."

A decree dated 485, noting that the people's wealth was evidently very unequal and that the poor were suffering from want, proclaimed the following:

> Commissioners have now been dispatched to travel through-
> out the provinces and prefectures. They and the governors
> and prefects are jointly to undertake the equal distribution
> of land in the empire. The land should be held on a lifetime
> basis and should be returned at the time of death. Let agri-
> culture and sericulture be promoted and supervised, so that
> the foundations may be laid for the enrichment of the people.

In order to allot land on a per capita basis it was necessary first
to make a complete record of the population. In 486, primarily as
a measure to counter the prevalence of dependent households attached to great families, which deprived the government of taxes,
the system of "three local heads" was instituted, and the census
statuses of the people were determined. The system of three local heads included the following arrangement: (a) five families
constituted a lin 鄰 , which was headed by a lin-chang 鄰長 ; (b)
five lin constituted a li 里 , which was headed by a li-chang 里長 ;
(c) five li constituted a tang 黨, which was headed by a tang-
chang 黨長 . All these headships were to be filled by powerful
and responsible persons in the respective units. The obligations
of the people for taxes and corvée were scheduled according to an
individual's age and marital and census status. . With the clarifi-
cation of the census records it was possible to distribute the land
systematically.

Here we must pause to point out that, although the text of the
Wei History gives the date of the decree on equal allotments as
485, and the establishment of the three local heads as 486, this
is nevertheless contradicted by a sentence in Li An-shih's [earli-
er] memorial, mentioned above, which states, "Now that the three
local heads have been established, the people are beginning to return to the towns and villages." Li's biography further reports
that "This [memorial] marked the start of the policy of equal allotments." This shows that the three local heads were instituted
before there was any talk of equal allotments.

The working of the system of equal allotments is described below.

---

*For these categories see the table on page 164.

(i) Distinction between "Open Fields" and "Mulberry Fields"

∥ Land was divided into these two categories. The Open Fields
consisted of land which was used ordinarily to raise the staple
crops. These fields belonged to the category of land which was received from and returned to [the government]. The Mulberry
Fields did not have to be planted exclusively with mulberry trees,
but could also be used to raise elms, dates, and other fruit trees.
They were hereditary holdings, not returnable at the person's
death and were therefore basically different from the Open Fields.
∥ It should be noted that, judging from extant records, the
owner of Mulberry Fields was apparently free to plant any fruit
or vegetables that he wished. The term "Mulberry Fields" was in
fact the equivalent of the "permanent holding" of the Sui and T'ang
periods, and was used solely to distinguish such land from "Open
Fields." This was an outgrowth of the fact that private ownership
existed along with the system of government ownership of land.
∥ There was another category known as "Flax Fields," which
like the Open Fields were subject to the law of receipt and return.
On the landholdings designated as Mulberry Fields it was permitted to plant large numbers of mulberry or other trees. On the
land that had to be returned to the government, however, no trees
were to be planted. Anyone who planted trees there was judged
guilty of disobedience, and his land was confiscated. ∥

(ii) The Amounts Allotted

Male adults fifteen years or older received 40 mou of Open
Fields, and women 20 mou. Those receiving land for the first
time were [also] given 20 mou of Mulberry Fields per male adult;
this was to be planted with 50 mulberry trees, 5 date trees, and
3 elms. Where the soil was not suited to mulberry each man was
to receive one mou of land (I suspect that this figure, which should
not be so small, is erroneous*), on which he was to plant elms
and date trees according to the regulations. All planting had to
be completed within three years, [after which] any unplanted land
would be taken back [by the government]. As to land for the raising of flax, when a man reached the taxable age he was given 10
mou of Flax Fields and a woman 5 mou.
The above figures for Open Fields, Mulberry Fields, and Flax
Fields were the amounts allotted to ordinary civilians. Slaves received the same allotments. A man possessing cattle was entitled

---

*Prof. L.S. Yang suggests that the "one" be emended to "ten."

to 30 mou of Open Fields per head of working cattle, to a maximum
of 4 heads. If there were households in which all the members
were either too young or too old or were disabled or infirm, and
had not received land, they were to be given half of the adult male's
portion for every person who was over eleven years of age or who
was infirm; those over seventy years were not required to return
their allotments to the government. Widows who did not remarry
were also given the women's [regular] allotment, although they
were exempt from taxation. Such was the usual practice of the system.

(iii) Adjustment of Population to Available Land

One of the most difficult problems faced by the administrators
of the equal allotments system was how to adjust the size of allotments to the available land, a problem that was created by the
disparate population densities. Thus, where the population was
sparse and the land plentiful, there would be wasted land if the
allotments were not increased; conversely, where the population
was dense and land insufficient, some measures would have to be
adopted to remedy the shortage of land. The Wei authorities
adopted various devices to meet this problem. In places where
there was an oversupply of land, the Open Fields allotment was
often doubled; this was called "Double Fields." If the land was
poor and could be cultivated only once every four years, then the
amount would be quadrupled (i.e. those entitled to 40 mou would
now receive 160 mou per person). The hereditary Mulberry Fields
were not to be returned to the government. When a father died,
therefore, his Mulberry Fields would accrue to the holding of his
son, who might then possess a surplus amount, which he was allowed to sell. No one was permitted to sell so much as to reduce
his own holding of Mulberry Fields below 20 mou, however, and
no one was permitted to buy so much as to make his total over 20
mou. Often the amount of Mulberry Fields beyond the basic 20 mou
was computed as part of the 40-mou Double Fields; the amount
thus computed would then be supplemented with the necessary
amount of Open Fields to make up the 40-mou allotment of Double
Fields. When the Open Fields and Double Fields were returned
to the government at the holder's death, however, the section
that had originally been Mulberry Fields was not to be returned
with the rest.

In places of sparse population and plentiful land the government
helped the people to work on the land as far as possible; those
who were already living in the locality were also given allotments

according to the regulations. In places of dense population and
scanty supply of land, if a man who was due to receive an allotment of land upon coming to adulthood did not wish to move, the
Mulberry Fields of his family were made into his regular allotment [of Open Fields]; if this was still not enough, then he would
not receive the Double Fields; if the land was still insufficient,
then the allotments of the members of the household would be reduced. Persons who were willing to move [from areas of land
shortage] were allowed to work on unoccupied land wherever they
might settle. Where land was locally sufficient for the allotments
the people were forbidden to move without cause. To those setting
up a new household one mou was given to every three persons as
a site for the house, and one [additional] mou was given for every
five slaves. Each man or woman over fifteen was required to
plant one-fifth mou of vegetables per person on his own allotments.

(iv) Method of Receiving and Returning Land

All the people were to receive the land allotments when they
came of age, and return them upon retirement in old age, or at
death. In the case of slaves and cattle the receipt or return of
land depended on the actual ownership of them. The land was always given out or returned in the first month of the year. If soon
after receiving his allotment a person died or sold his slaves or
cattle, the land could not be returned until the first month of the
next year. The regular and double allotments of each person were
kept separate from each other, and were not to overlap. Adults
receiving land were given allotments close to their homes. Of
those who came up for allotment at the same time, the poor were
given their allotments first, the wealthy later. The same procedure was followed in the case of the quadruple allotments. The
houses and trees belonging to exiled or heirless persons were
taken over by the government for use in making allotments; what
remained after the allotments had been made was given to the persons' relatives, who also could use the property on loan before
the final awards were made.

All the above information is available in the text of the decree
of 485 on equal allotments, as recorded in the section on "Food
and Money" in the Wei History.

3. Equal Allotments in Northern Ch'i,
Northern Chou, Sui, and T'ang

The systems of equal allotments in the Northern Ch'i, Northern Chou, Sui, and T'ang dynasties were based primarily on that of Wei, with modifications in detail.

(i) Age Categories

The receipt and return of Open Fields as well as the corvée obligations of an individual were determined by age and sex. Through the different dynasties, therefore, the population was divided into a number of age categories. The periodic changes can be tabulated as shown on page 164.

In Northern Ch'i, people were allotted land and began to pay taxes when they became adults (age 18); at twenty the men began to do military service; at sixty corvée labor stopped; and at sixty-six the land was returned to the government. Data are lacking on Northern Chou, except for a sentence in the Sui History which states: "Taxes were levied on all men between the ages of eighteen and sixty-four, including those who were slightly infirm." The system was probably on the whole similar to that of Northern Ch'i.

The age limits of the categories during Later Wei are not directly obtainable from historical records. From the Wei regulations and land allotment we may infer, however, that probably a person aged ten or less was classified as a "child," and one over seventy as an "old person."

(ii) Lifetime and Permanent Holdings

//During the Later Wei land was classified into Open Fields and Mulberry Fields, of which the latter constituted hereditary holdings. The same method of classification was adopted by Northern Ch'i, which initiated the practice of referring to the Mulberry Fields as "permanent holdings." Written records for the system in Northern Chou are lacking. Sui followed the Northern Ch'i system. In T'ang the Open Fields became known as "lifetime holdings," while the Mulberry Fields continued to be called permanent holdings. The latter was the hereditary portion [of a man's allotments], but the lifetime holdings were owned by the government and were subject to return and reassignment.

//During Northern Ch'i an adult man was allotted 80 mou of Open Fields, and an adult woman, 40 mou. In addition every adult man was given 20 mou of Mulberry Fields as a permanent holding,

Age Category \ Period	Western Tsin	Eastern Tsin	Northern Ch'i	Northern Chou	Sui	Early T'ang	705 A.D.	738 A.D.	744 A.D.	763 A.D.
Infant					Under 3	Under 3		Under 3		
Child	Under 12		Under 15		4-10	4-15		4-15		
Secondary Adult	13-15, 61-65		16-17		11-17	16-20		16-20	18-22	
Adult	16-60	16-60; women were adults when married, or at 20	18-65	18-64	18-59 (later 21 and 22-59)	21-59	22-57		Over 23	23-57
Old person	66 and over		66 and over		60 and over	60 and over	58 and over			58 and over

in which were to be planted 50 mulberry trees, 3 elms, and 5 date
trees. Where the soil was unsuitable for mulberry, the man was
given Flax Fields on the same basis as the Mulberry Fields. In
Northern Chou a married man was allotted 140 mou of land, and
a single adult man, 100 mou. Some observers hold that this was
a larger allotment than that of Northern Ch'i. This seems to be
so at first glance, but actually it was not the case. [.....] In
Northern Ch'i an adult man received an allotment of 80 mou of
Open Fields and his wife received 40 mou; added to the man's
permanent holding of 20 mou this made a total of 140 mou. An un-
married man would receive a total of 100 mou. These figures
were identical with those for the [Northern] Chou period.//

Again, it appears on the surface that the allotments of Northern Ch'i were twice the size of those of Later Wei, whereas in
fact there was no difference, since during Wei the allotments
were often made in the form of Double Fields, which brought the
amount of land up to the higher figures shown by the Northern
Ch'i regulations. Little actual change took place through Sui and
T'ang, so that throughout all these periods the per capita allotment of land remained essentially the same.

Sui followed the system of Northern Ch'i as regards age limits
and apportionment of land. In 624, during the reign of Emperor
Kao-tsu of T'ang, new regulations were issued which provided
that "All adult men are each to be given one ch'ing [100 mou] of
land, of which two-tenths comprises the permanent holding and
the rest the lifetime holding." An order of 737 stated:

> An adult man is to be allotted 20 mou of permanent holding,
> and 80 mou of lifetime holding. Secondary adults over eighteen
> years of age shall receive the adult's allotment. Old men,
> the chronically ill, and the disabled are each to receive a 40-
> mou lifetime holding, and widows are to receive a 30-mou
> lifetime holding. Land [belonging to these persons] that was
> previously a permanent holding is to be made into a lifetime
> holding. Infants, children, youths, and old men, the ill and
> disabled, and widows who were heads of families are each to
> be given 20 mou as a permanent allotment and 20 mou as a
> lifetime allotment.

The order further stated that in areas where land was plentiful
the allotments were to be made according to the stipulated amount;
where land was insufficient, however, the lifetime portions were
to be reduced by half; where the land could be planted only every
other year, on the other hand, the lifetime portions were to be
doubled.

All who made their living by handicraft or trade were to receive
half of both the permanent and lifetime portions, and those living
in areas with insufficient land were to receive no allotment at all.
In every mou of the permanent portion there should be planted at
least 50 mulberry trees, and at least 10 each of elms and dates.

The plantings had to be completed within three years. If the
local soil was not suited to these trees, some suitable ones were
to be planted instead. (In the Wei and Northern Ch'i decrees the
statement that "50 mulberry trees were to be planted" referred
to the 20 mou of Mulberry Fields as a whole, but here the reference
is to each mou. This is a huge difference. One of the two versions
must be in error.)

Aside from the permanent and lifetime portions there were also allotments for residences, the amount varying from time to
time.

The amounts of the various categories of land allotted throughout the four dynasties can be tabulated as shown on page 167.

(iii) Permanent Holdings of the Nobility and High Officials

The above-mentioned allotments of 20 mou of permanent holdings concerned only the common people. The nobility and high officials were governed by another set of regulations which provided
them with much more generous portions. According to a decree
of Emperor Wen of Sui, "Permanent holdings are to be given to
all from the princes down to the commanders in accordance to a
scale in which the maximum is 100 ch'ing and the minimum 40
mou." Emperor Kao-tsu of T'ang fixed the scale in 618 for the
permanent holdings from princes on down between 100 ch'ing and
60 mou, a scale that was reinforced in general by another decree
in 737. An order of 782 went about reducing the permanent holdings of princes and persons lower down, but from the actual amount
granted it appears that the reduction did not take place, probably
owing to the fact that previously there had been extra-legal increases in the amounts allotted.

In the T'ang system those who, having both government positions and noble ranks, were entitled to receive land grants on both
counts, were allowed the larger allotment but not both. In the
case of any person in this category who originally possessed land
(other than the lifetime holdings) not located in areas where land
was scarce, if the original holding was equal to the official allotment due him through his office or title he was not to receive any
more; if the original holding exceeded the official amount, the excess was to be taken by the government; if it was less than the

	Man		Woman	Total allotment Man and wife	Residence Allotment	Remarks
	Open Fields	Mulberry Fields	Open Fields			
Later Wei	40 mou; usually double, i.e. 80 mou.	20 mou	20 mou; usually double i.e. 40 mou	140 mou	1 mou every 3 persons. Slaves 1 mou to every 5 persons.	Other provisions for aged, disabled, etc. See text above.
Northern Ch'i	80 mou	20 mou, called Permanent Portion.	40 mou	140 mou		
Northern Chou	100 mou single 140 mou married			140 mou	5 mou for 10 persons and over. 4 mou for 9 or less. 2 mou under 5.	
Sui	80 mou	20 mou	40 mou	140 mou	1 mou every 3 persons. Slaves 1 mou to every 5 persons.	
T'ang	80 mou, called Lifetime Portion.	20 mou	Widows each 30 mou	100 mou	1 mou to 3 persons or less; 1 additional mou every 3 persons. Lower castes 1 mou to 5 persons; 1 additional mou to every 5 persons.	Persons living on handicrafts or trade received 1/2 of life-time portion; nothing in areas of land scarcity.

official amount, then the difference was to be made up to him. These permanent holdings were hereditary and not returnable to the government. Ownership lay with the grantee's descendants even though the latter might become divested of the title.

If, after having received a permanent allotment, a person was demoted or dismissed during his term of office, his land was to be taken back by the government to the extent of his demotion. A person who was divested of his title [during his own lifetime] would be given the regular lifetime allotment of land, but land owned in excess of this amount as well as other grants were to be retaken by the government. If in a household the lifetime allot- ment of a person holding an official position or noble rank was less than that which he was entitled to, the difference was to be given him; if it was in excess, the surplus was to be returned to the government.

If those in official positions who were entitled to permanent allotments did not apply for them, or died before the grants were completed, their sons and descendants were not allowed to apply for the allotments in their place. Those who inherited noble ranks could only take over the permanent portions of their forefathers' allotments, and were not to request more. If their forefathers had not applied for the permanent allotments, or had died before the grants were completed, the inheritors were to receive half the grant. Landless persons on receiving the grants were also given grain to the amount of 0.2 picul per mou.

(iv) Allotments for Slaves and Cattle

//The system of Northern Ch'i followed that of Wei, which al- lotted 60 mou of land per ox to a maximum of four oxen [per fami- ly]. There are no clear data for the [Northern] Chou period, and the whole thing was abolished in Sui and T'ang.

//Slaves were allotted land on the same basis as full civilians. During Later Wei there were no restrictions as to the number of slaves owned by a family. In Northern Ch'i, however, the num- bers were limited, according to the Sui History, as follows:

> An Imperial Prince should not own more than 300 slaves
> eligible to receive land; a Hereditary Prince 200 slaves; a
> Hereditary Prince of the Second Grade and below, and Princes
> of Common Surnames, 150 slaves; [officials] of the third
> grade and above, and Princes of the Blood, 100 slaves; those
> of the seventh official grade and above, 80 slaves; those of
> the eighth official grade and below, down to the ordinary

civilians, 60 slaves. Slaves who are outside the above limits
and do not receive land are exempt from taxation.

// There were no regulations as to land allotments for slaves during Sui and T'ang. However, the Sui system of levying half-taxes
on slaves and servants, a system inherited from Wei and Ch'i,
probably indicate that those people also were given land grants.//

(v) Adjustments to Areas with Plentiful or Insufficient Land

Landless people were shifted in 557 during Northern Ch'i to
areas where land was plentiful. During the Sui dynasty the unequal
distribution of land was realized to be a grave problem. In 592 it
was discussed at Court, though no solution was suggested. A survey at that time showed that in land-scarce regions the allotment
was only 20 mou per adult man; that of old and young persons was
still less.

There were detailed regulations during T'ang with regard to the
quantity of land available. Allotments in regions where land was
scarce were half the size of those in places with plenty of land;
when there was not enough, allotments would be made in the latter instead. Those living by handicraft industry or trade were given
half allotments in plentiful regions, and no allotments in scarce
regions. Members of lower census categories, such as Dependents, Female Dependents, and Freedmen, were to be assigned
land in plentiful regions. Officials of the fifth grade and up had to
take their permanent allotments from ownerless land in plentiful
regions; those of the sixth grade and below could either have their
permanent portions in the scarce regions in which they resided,
taking them out of government land, or in plentiful regions. Any
surplus land within an administrative unit was to be transferred
to the neighboring unit; thus, surplus land of a sub-district was
to be transferred to the jurisdiction of the adjacent sub-district;
that of a district to an adjacent district; and that of a prefecture to
a neighboring prefecture.

(vi) Restrictions on Sale, Exchange, and Renting of Land

The sale and private exchange of land were prohibited during
Northern Ch'i. The T'ang system, on the other hand, permitted
a certain amount of transfer or sale of land within specific limits.
For instance, the sale of the permanent allotment was permissible
in cases where the people needed the proceeds to cover funeral
expenses. Again, when a family wanted to move to a plentiful

region, the lifetime allotment also became saleable. As to the purchasers, the amount bought was not to exceed the limit set by allotment regulations, but those in scarce regions were allowed to
follow the proportions of plentiful regions. The renting out and
mortgaging of land was prohibited, except in cases where the persons involved were away on corvée duty or in official posts. None
of the prohibitions applied, however, to the permanent allotments
and land grants of officials.

(vii) Regulations for Receiving and Returning Land

The system in Northern Ch'i provided that "in the tenth month
of every year a general allotment is to be made. A man receives
land upon coming of age, and returns the land at old age."

The allotments were also made in the tenth month during the
T'ang dynasty, with the poor people and those paying taxes and
corvée having priority. Lifetime portions had to be assigned in
the [recipient's] neighborhood and not in distant areas. In case of
shifts in administrative areas, so that a person's land became demarcated into another prefecture or district, his original allotment would continue to stand. City dwellers were to be assigned
allotments in a neighboring district if their own district lacked
land. In the case of those long absent on the frontiers in line of
official duty, if their families were living with them the lifetime
allotments could be retained for six years before reverting back
to the government. Upon their return home, if accompanied [by
their families] they were to be given land immediately. The descendants of those who died in line of duty were allowed to keep the
latter's lifetime allotments, even if they had not yet come of age.
Persons disabled by war or disease also could retain their [life-
time] allotments so long as they lived.

4. Equal Allotments and Equalization of Wealth

Such was the system of equal allotments during the Northern
Dynasties, Sui, and T'ang. Now let us see if it really was a system under which land holdings and tax burdens were equal among
all.

(i) Inequality of the "Equal Allotments"

//Looking at the system itself, we find that during Wei and Ch'i
an adult man received 80 mou of Open Fields, while each ox was
entitled to 60 mou of land, to a limit of four oxen [per family].

Thus, a person who was richer and owned four oxen could receive 320 mou of Open Fields, or four times the amount received by a person who was poorer and had no oxen.

// Slaves were entitled to the same allotments as full civilians, but were bought and sold like horses and cattle. A rich man, having bought 100 slaves, would then receive 8,000 mou of land. There was no limitation in Later Wei on the number of slaves owned by a household. It follows, therefore, that the rich would buy slaves--the more slaves they owned, the more land they would receive; the more profits they obtained from land, the more slaves they could buy. The rich therefore became richer all the time. Although [the number of slaves] was restricted during Northern Ch'i, an Imperial Prince could nonetheless own 300 slaves, bringing the amount of his land allotments to 24,000 mou. Even ordinary civilians were allowed to own 60 slaves, which, together with the allotments the master himself was entitled to, meant the receipt of 4,880 mou of Open Fields. Such an amount was far above that received by the poor peasants, who were too poor to own either oxen or slaves.

// During Sui and T'ang the permanent allotments of the aristocracy and high officials reached a maximum of 100 ch'ing [10,000 mou] per person; even an official of the ninth grade was granted two ch'ing. The difference between these figures and the ordinary civilian's 20 mou of permanent allotment is striking.

// Furthermore, such devices as "Salary Fields" and "Office-Expense Fields" were also instituted. Who worked these fields? During Later Wei one-tenth of the population of the prefectures and districts were assigned this work as garrison colonists. T'ang also recruited the people to cultivate the garrison fields. This indicates that large numbers of people were unable to possess their own land. Who can say, then, that the system of equal allotments meant the equal allotting of land to all the people?

// During the reign of Emperor Wen [581-604] of Sui the population had increased and land was insufficient for distribution among the people. Someone thereupon suggested that the land grants to officials should be pared down in order that the people might be given allotments, but the proposal was rejected as a result of the objections of Wang I. The rulers treated the officials generously so as to enlist their support. How could the common people share in such favors? Thus, it is obvious that the officials were favored and the people were discriminated against. //

Moreover, the actual application of a system was an entirely different matter from the system itself. We need not go into the details of the forceful occupation by the rich and the destitution

and misery of the dispossessed before the establishment of equal
allotments in Later Wei. Even after this the sale of land was not
prohibited, so that the more tyrannous among the rich even went
so far as to evict the common people from their land and compel
them to sell it.

Nominally the sale of land was forbidden in Northern Ch'i, but
actually sales frequently took place. The rich held unlimited
amounts of land while the poor "did not have enough land to stand
an awl." Powerful individuals took over other people's land by
force; disputes sometimes lasted some thirty years without being resolved. Cases of litigations over land abounded also in
Northern Chou.

The administration of the Chen-kuan period [627-649] was considered the best in T'ang. But even at that time the magnates
were already occupying more land that the regulations permitted.
The New T'ang History relates, for instance, that while Chia
Tun-i was serving as governor of Lo-chou (in Honan) immediately
following the Chen-kuan period, he found that the local magnates
owned large amounts of extra-legal land. Chia confiscated over
3,000 ch'ing of such land and distributed it among the poor. After
this period, however, the sale and annexation of land became even
more widespread. The instituting of Salary Fields and Garrison
Fields also frequently resulted in encroachment on the common
people's property or in the exchange of poor land for the people's
good land. It seems, therefore, that the equal allotments system
gave rise to malpractices soon after its establishment, and that
it had neither a widespread nor a prolonged implementation.

(ii) Land Grants and Provision Estates

Even the ruler himself did not obey his own regulations. Aside
from giving the large allotments to wealthy and powerful persons,
the ruler also arbitrarily presented them with grants of land. During Northern Ch'i the fertile land was all owned by influential
people, none being left for the common people. Emperor T'ai-tsu
of T'ang granted P'ei Chi, [who had helped him overthrow Sui],
1,000 ch'ing of land, a mansion, and an estate of three hundred
households, besides other gifts and titles. Numerous other persons received grants of five, ten, or several dozen ch'ing of land
as well as mansions and manorial estates.

In addition to grants of land there were also gifts of provision
estates. At the beginning of T'ang the royal princes were awarded
estates of 1,000 households each. The officials who had helped in
the founding of the dynasty were also rewarded with grants of
households as follows:

No. of Grants	No. of Households
1	1,500
5	1,300
4	1,200
3	1,000
2	900
4	700
8	600
10	400
6	300

The grantees could collect taxes in their estates, and were more strict in exacting payments than was the government. According to the New T'ang History, during the reign of Emperor Chung-tsung [705-709] provision estates existed in fifty-four prefectures, where they occupied the most fertile land. The imbalance between the wealth of these landowners and the common people, and between the vast incomes of the magnates and the limited means of the government, was a source of anxiety for many officials, some of whom proposed the ending of the practice of letting the estate holders levy taxes in their own domains. In any event, the wealth of the magnates was far above the level of that of the ordinary people.

(iii) Unequal Taxation

Since slaves were entitled to the same amount of land as full civilians, but were assessed only half the tax [in Later Wei the assessment was less than half], and since the tax rate on oxen was still lower, rich persons thus received more land but paid lighter taxes. In addition there existed the system of tax exemption for families of old lineage, so that those in high places often possessed vast amounts of land but paid incommensurate taxes.

Actually the inequalities in taxation were still more pronounced, for under the aegis of corrupt officials the wealthy and influential were allowed to get off easily, while the poor and unresourceful were pressed hard. This situation elicited a petition from Su Cho in 544 for the equalization of taxes and corvée. During the upheavals at the end of Wei, government was tyrannous and inefficient, while taxes and corvée multiplied. The more resourceful people often abandoned their original homes, and many attached themselves as tenants to powerful families in order to evade tax

payments. The result was a decrease in government revenue. This
in turn forced the weaker individuals who had not fled to assume an
even heavier tax burden than before while powerful families were
able to derive benefits for themselves in the name of protecting
others. It is recorded in the Wei History that some 600,000 refugees were collected by the authorities in 544; the account in the
Sui History adds that these people were ordered to return to their
own districts, after which government revenues became augmented.
At the height of tax evasion and confusion during the reign of Emperor Wen-hsüan [550-559] of Northern Ch'i a local official instituted an investigation of the situation, but was himself reprimanded by the emperor as "making trouble." Malpractices thereafter
became even more rife. According to the Sui History, some 60
to 70 per cent of revenue was lost to the government during this
period.

Such evils were not reformed until the Sui government instituted
the system of tax payments according to a rectified census record.
The census investigation was carried out in 583, when Emperor
Kao-tsu of Sui ordered the prefectural and district authorities to
compare the census entries with the people's likenesses, and, if
discrepancies were found, to exile the local officials responsible
for these households. Furthermore, remote relatives subject to
less than the nine-month mourning obligations were ordered to establish their own households, so as to prevent concealment of tax-
owing individuals. As a result of these measures the able-bodied
men entered in government books were increased by 443,000, in
addition to 1,641,500 persons newly incorporated into the census.
On the fifth day of the first month of every year the local officials
made the rounds of their territories to check on the population and
their tax assessments. The confusions consequently abated considerably.

Under T'ang, however, the old abuses soon reappeared. Although there were legal regulations governing taxation as time
went on, they ceased to be observed by unscrupulous officials, so
that tax evasion again became an issue. According to a contemporary work,

> Cunning individuals evaded their obligations by either enter-
> ing officialdom on some pretext, or assuming clerical garb,
> or getting recruited into the army, or becoming dependents
> of powerful families, so that they were exempted from all
> corvée payments. As a result the unresourceful were sub-
> ject to onerous corvée assignments and tax payments, and
> their lot became increasingly worse.

(iv) Buddhist and Taoist Clergy and Livelihood of the People

From the Wei and Tsin periods on, Buddhism began to flourish in China, reaching its apex during the Northern and Southern, Sui, and T'ang dynasties. We are here concerned only with the economic effects of the large number of religious adherents on Chinese society.

In Later Wei the number of priesthood licenses was initially limited by law to 50 for each large prefecture, 40 for each small prefecture, and 10 for each border prefecture or garrison area. Later the numbers were raised to 100 per large prefecture, 50 per medium prefecture, and 10 per small prefecture. The limits were subsequently again raised to 300, 200, and 100 respectively. By the Cheng-kuang reign [519-524] of Later Wei the number of Buddhist monks and nuns had reached a total of 2,000,000, scattered in more than 30,000 monasteries.

Northern Chou adopted an anti-Buddhist policy leading to the confiscation of some 40,000 monastic establishments, which were given to the aristocrats as manors, and the secularization of some 3,000,000 Buddhists, who were returned to the census statuses of military or civilian categories. Again in the fifth year of the Hui-ch'ang reign [845] during T'ang another persecution took place which ended with the destruction of over 4,600 temples and more than 40,000 shrines and the secularization of 260,500 monks and nuns, who then became semi-annual taxpayers. Hundreds of thousands of ch'ing of top-grade land were confiscated, as were also some 150,000 slaves, who also were assigned the status of semi-annual taxpayers.

Taoism likewise flourished at the same time. It too had a considerable number of priests and nuns, although these were not as numerous as the Buddhists.

Did this vast number of Buddhist and Taoist priests and nuns all join the church out of religious conviction? The answer for ninety per cent of the cases is in the negative. The reason for their flocking to the church lay in the fact that clerics were exempt from taxation and corvée; many took the orders so as to escape from the oppressive exactions. The practice went so far that one out of three able-bodied men in a household joined the priesthood, to serve as grounds for evasion of corvée and as protection for the family property. Some people were willing to purchase priesthood licenses at a high price. Li Te-yü, a seventh-century T'ang official who at one time served as the Imperial Supervisory Commissioner of Western Chekiang, once observed that priesthood licenses were being issued at the rate of over 100 a day, and that

if this were not checked the government would lose the services
of some 600,000 able-bodied men within a year. The license fees
obtained by the government were small indeed compared with the
amount of taxes and labor services lost to it through the large
number of tax-exempt clerics.

The more people evading the tax obligations, the heavier the
burden became on the ordinary civilians. Furthermore, the monks
and priests were not all of the same character, and many did not
live according to religious precepts. An account in the Wei History of a campaign of Emperor Shih-tsu [424-451] relates that
when the emperor's entourage stopped at a Buddhist temple, wheat
was found planted in the temple yards, the monks drank wine with
the aides, and the temple was discovered to have a large store of
weapons. The incensed emperor, fearing that the weapons were
destined for his opponent, ordered that they be seized. In the
process a number of the temple's illegal possessions also came
to light, including a wine distillery, treasures worth tens of thousands [of cash] held in custody by the temple for local magnates,
and secret apartments for the carrying on of illicit love affairs
with ladies of rank. The clerics also widely encroached on the
property of the common people and occupied their land and houses.
These abuses could not be eradicated despite the repeated government efforts at their elimination.

The Six Institutes of T'ang provided that "each Taoist priest
is to receive 30 mou and a Taoist nun 20 mou. The same is true
for Buddhist monks and nuns." There were other ways of adding
to the holdings of a monastic establishment, however, such as by
gift or purchase. By the Hui-ch'ang period (841-846) the land
owned by Buddhist institutions totalled several hundred thousand
ch'ing, while the number of clerics was 260,000 and their slaves
150,000, making a total of 410,000 persons. Thus the average
amount of land owned by those in the religious orders was approximately one ch'ing per person. The monks and nuns probably did
not work this land themselves, but gave it to others to cultivate
while sitting back and enjoying the proceeds. Consequently a category known as "Temple Households" prevailed throughout the
country during Later Wei. In the T'ang dynasty 150,000 slaves
were owned by monasteries. These people had the duty of working
the temple lands and sending in their crops for the provisioning
of the temples. By and large, therefore, the huge number of clerics
during this period deeply affected the livelihood of the peasants.

(v) A Fair Appraisal of the System of Equal Allotments

Since the system of equal allotments was imperfectly egalitari-
an both in the system itself and in its application, we must inquire
whether it had any merit at all. The answer is yes.

In discussing the system we must take into consideration the
historical background. In the days of absolute monarchy the only
way to found a new dynasty was by force of arms. Once a dynasty
had been successfully established, it was natural for the ruler to
award land and mansions to those who had fought in his military
group, or to the nobility that had followed him. Then, in order to
maintain his hold in the country, the ruler also needed to enlist
the support of the officials and magnates by granting them rich
gifts. Therefore, notwithstanding the existence of the equal allotments system, the officials and aristocrats were accorded favored
treatment, and received land far above the amount allotted to the
common people.

Furthermore, since it was human nature to strive for gain, the
magnates were wont to utilize their power to encroach on others
for their own aggrandizement. It was no easy matter to bring about
a division of property in order to aid the poor. The fact that in the
two Han dynasties the equalization movement and the "imperiali-
zation of land" had both failed of implementation was also due to
the entrenched strength of the magnates. The actual state of affairs made it necessary [for the ruler] to temporize with the magnates and give them special treatment so as to reduce their opposition.

In sum, the motive behind the establishment of the equal allotments system was commendable, and some success was achieved
in the attempt to equalize land distribution. Its weakness lay in
the compromises made with those of power or wealth. Although
the system had many drawbacks and seldom achieved its aim, it
still would seem to have been better than nothing.

(vi) Equal Allotments and Displaced Persons

There is another aspect of the problem that merits attention,
namely, that the number of households of displaced persons
reached a high point during the Northern, Sui, and T'ang dynasties,
when the equal allotments system was in operation. Was this due
to the people's unwillingness to receive land allotments? Not at
all. Rather, it was due to the fact that, while the common people's
tax burdens per household were greatly increased with the institution of the allotments system, the land allotments were granted

to them only in limited periods, when the administration was good
and land was plentiful. For the most part, however, the wealthy
carried on annexations and the poor lost their land. What the people
fled from, therefore, was the heavy taxation, not the land allotments. Thus, the poor actually suffered as a result of the nominal
system of allotments. One could of course contend that this was a
weakness of the times, not of the system itself. Yet if a system
merely existed in theory but could not be applied, and if evils
were perpetrated under the name of this system, then the system
itself is also to be blamed. In this light, then, there is some question as to the validity of the contention that the existence of the
system was better than nothing.

5. Instability of the System of Equal Allotments

From its initiation in Later Wei through the successive dynasties to T'ang the system of equal allotments was repeatedly abolished and reestablished, and hence was never able to persist over
any prolonged period. Ultimately, after the reign of Empress Wu
[685-704] it was completely destroyed. These phenomena can be
attributed to four major causes: (i) the growth of population; (ii)
the unreliability of the census returns owing to heavy taxation;
(iii) the intrinsic defects of the system; and (iv) the natural tendencies in human psychology and socio-economic development.
Let us now examine each of these points separately.

(i) Growth of Population

The systems of "occupation" and "equal allotment" of land could
be practised only during post-upheaval periods, when the decline
in population and the abundance of ownerless land enabled the government to distribute the land by allotment. According to the census figures, the population of China stood at over ten million
households at the height of Han power, declined sharply after the
fall of the dynasty, and rose to only 6,000,000 households in the
country as a whole during the period of the Northern and Southern
Dynasties. In the early Chen-kuan period [627- 649] of T'ang the
population was [recorded as] less than 3,000,000 households but
by 755 it had risen to 8,914,709, comprising 52,919,309 persons.
The actual number was even greater than this.

The census figures for Han, according to the T'ung-k'ao 通考,
were reliable because taxes were light, whereas those from Wei
and Tsin on became increasingly distorted owing to the rise in
the tax rates; this was especially true during the Northern and

Southern Dynasties, when various means were used by the people
to conceal their household identity. Sometimes as many as thirty
or fifty households banded together and were reported as one household to escape corvée and taxation. Even during the period of prosperity in early T'ang the census figures remained low. As to the
8,914,709 households recorded for 755, no less than 3,565,500
were tax-exempt; these comprised widows, widowers, the disabled and infirm, slaves, and officials. Since these could not
have amounted to one-third of the total population, however, the
existence of fraud is obvious. Indeed, concludes the T'ung-k'ao,
the population figures always were unreliable after great upheavals.

It can be seen that after a period of dynastic wars the population
often declined, thereby facilitating the carrying out of the policy
of equal distribution, whereas with the return of prolonged peace
the population would increase by three or four times while the
land could not be increased to twice as much as the original amount.
With unused land gone, and all land in individual possession, it became difficult to implement the policy of equal allotments. The
question of insufficient land had begun to plague the government
even during the time of Emperor Wen of Sui, but no solution was
found. The population of T'ang exceeded that of Sui, thereby ag-
gravating the problem of land allotments. No wonder that the system of allotments could not be practised on a permanent basis.

(ii) Unreliability of Census Registration

The operation of the system of equal allotments was based on
the census returns. The T'ang administration, apparently following a practice inherited from Sui, instituted the system of "checking likeness," by which the age and likeness of the individual were
entered into the census records, in order to determine his tax
obligations and to prevent fraud. The term "checking likeness"
applied both to the entering of the likenesses in the records, and
to the records themselves. The checking was usually done once a
year. T'ang hui-yao records the periodic decrees issued through
the Kuang-te reign [763-764] which dealt with "checking likeness"
and which indicated its importance in determining the age status
of the individual at particular times--whether he was a child,
secondary adult, adult, or old person. In 741 a decree ordered
that the annual checking be stopped in order to reduce red-tape
and that it be replaced with a general checking once every three
years together with the making of the triennial census accounts.
In 763, however, the annual checking was restored; changes in
age status were ordered to be noted down, and males were excused

from the checking procedure after reaching the age of 59.

The local census records were made by the Hamlet Head. With regard to the administrative divisions of the population, the <u>Six Institutes of T'ang</u> informs us that

> 40,000 or more households constitute a Large Prefecture;
> over 30,000, a Medium Prefecture; and less than 30,000, a
> Small Prefecture. 6,000 or more households constitute a
> Large District; over 2,000, a Medium District; more than
> 1,000, a Medium-Small District; and less than 1,000, a
> Small District. 100 households constitute a hamlet, and 5
> hamlets are a sub-district. The area inside the city walls
> of the two capitals, prefectures, and districts is divided in-
> to wards; and that outside the walls into villages. Each ham-
> let, ward, and village has a head [cheng 正] who supervises
> the unit. Four families make a <u>lin</u> 鄰 , and 5 <u>lin</u> make a <u>pao</u> 保.
> For each <u>pao</u> there is a chief to control it.

At the end of the year the Hamlet Head recorded the people's ages and the size of their land holdings; this information constituted the "sub-district accounts." These accounts were transmitted to the district, which passed them on to the prefecture, which in turn sent them to the Board of Finance. Once every three years in the period from the first to the third month, a [more detailed] census was compiled and the status of each household was noted. These records were sent from the district to the prefecture and thence to the Department of State Affairs.

The Board of Finance had over-all supervision of all these rec-ords. The "sub-district accounts" and census records were com-monly known as "Census-Accounts." Regulations concerning "Census-Accounts" can be found in a section bearing that title in <u>T'ang hui-yao</u>. The <u>New T'ang History</u> also informs us

> In addition there are "Estimate-Accounts," which are esti-
> mates of the taxes and labor service of the following year
> presented to the Imperial Commissioners of Finance. The
> government needs are first memorialized, and then the
> levies are made. The amounts to be levied are published at
> the district city gates, in the villages and the wards, so that
> everyone will known of them.

Such were the comprehensive and orderly procedures, which, however, could be carried out only during periods of good govern-

ment. When the administration deteriorated and the people began
to flee the heavy tax burdens, fraud became rampant, and the officials neglected the census. This meant that the foundations were
destroyed for the system of equal allotments, thus leading naturally
to the latter's destruction.

(iii) Intrinsic Defects of the System

The seeds of its own destruction were contained in the system
of equal allotments at its very beginning. The nobility and officials
received as permanent allotments land in amounts ranging from
several ch'ing to as much as a hundred. Since the official personnel
was constantly changing, this meant the allotting of limited land to
unlimited numbers of officials. Therefore land steadily became
more and more scarce. We have seen that even at the beginning of
Sui there was a shortage of land, but that the emperor let the allotment to each able-bodied man be pared down to 20 mou rather than
reduce the land grants to his followers. We may gather that after
a prolonged period of peace in T'ang, the number of old and new
officials must have become tremendous, and the encroachment of
their permanent allotments on the common people's land must also
have far exceeded that in the Sui period.

Under the T'ang system, moreover, poor people were allowed
to sell their permanent portions to defray funeral expenses, and
those moving to other areas were further allowed to sell their lifetime portions. Though the regulations enjoined the buyer to purchase within the limits of his own legal allotments, the permission
to buy and sell in itself nevertheless marked the beginning of annexations. Gradually the extremes of wealth and poverty emerged.
The officials no longer implemented the controls but instead came
to regard land sales as matters of course, while the magnates one
after another went beyond the limits of the law. Annexations then
became no less rampant than before the establishment of the equal
allotments system.

(iv) Natural Tendencies

In his Historical Records Ssu-ma Ch'ien once remarked: "Hust-
ling and bustling, after gain the world is rushing. The king of a
thousand chariots, the prince of ten thousand vassals, and the lord
of a hundred households even complain of their poverty. How much
more is this true of ordinary individuals and common taxpayers!"
Since it is human nature to seek profit and amass treasures, and
since land was the source of wealth, few indeed there were who did

not desire it. Consequently the wealthy and the powerful began to
annex and encroach on other people's land, despite the severe legal restrictions. The fluctuations of wealth and poverty were also always present. When the poor sold their land to tide over
their difficulties, the land would fall into the hands of the rich.
When peace was restored after upheavals and the population began
to increase, it became increasingly difficult for them to make a
living. This, together with the heavy tax burdens and the government policy of favoring the magnates and discriminating against
the poor, led to the sale of land and abandonment of their homes
by the common people. The natural tendency, therefore, was toward the concentration of land in the hands of a few and the impov-
erishment of an increasingly large number of people. This process could not be entirely checked even at the initiation of the
equal allotments system, when the laws were strict, and went completely out of control later when the laws became lax.

6. Disintegration of the System of Equal Allotments

Owing to the above-mentioned causes, the system of equal allotments could only be carried out intermittently from Late Wei
through the early reigns of T'ang. Matters took a drastic turn for
the worse during the time of Empress Wu, when heavy taxation
and official corruption led to numerous cases of land sales and
abandonment of their home districts by the poor. The magnitude
of the problem is indicated by a memorial submitted in 695 by
Li Ch'iao, who in the course of a discussion of the question of
census records proposed that fugitives be allowed to be registered
at the place to which they had fled.

When the people left their home areas, their land was annexed
by the powerful. The prefectural and district authorities were unable to prevent this. In 721, therefore, the concealed households
and surplus land [i.e. land owned beyond the legally permitted
amount] were ordered to be confiscated by the [central] government. According to the New T'ang History, this measure yielded
some 800,000 tenant households and a corresponding amount of
land, from which the government realized several million strings
of cash by the end of the year. In 730 a decree was issued forbidding the wealthy families to ask to be registered as small
households by the local officials; violators of this rule were to
be punished.

A decree of 735 prohibited the sale, purchase, or mortgage of
the common people's lifetime and permanent allotments; buyers
of such land were to return the land and receive punishment besides.

In 737 the equal allotments system was promulgated again. A decree of 752 repeated the prohibition against the sale of lifetime
and permanent allotments, and also against petitions for allotment
of pasture land without cause [i.e. without actual possession of ani-
mals], the keeping of tenant households, and the clandestine en-
gagement in agriculture by certain officials.

But as the census reports had become unreliable ever since the
reign of Empress Wu, and had worsened during the K'ai-yüan
period, such regulations concerning the equal allotments system
could of course amount to nothing more than paper plans. The actual contemporary scene was instead reflected in such facts as
these: The estates of Princess T'ai-p'ing were spread over all the
land near the capital, and consisted entirely of top-grade land.
Eunuchs like Kao Li-shih owned some sixty per cent of the mansions, estates, and good land in the capital. The gentry also
amassed vast estates to leave to their descendants, so much so
that the refusal of Chang Chia-chen, the Prime Minister, to engage in the founding of manors and estates was singled out as an
example of meritorious conduct.

In fact, the repetition of prohibitive decrees during T'ang was
itself an indication of the decline of the system of equal allotments.
Things had come to such a pass that it was beyond the power of
Emperor Hsüan-tsung to effect a remedy, however much in earnest he might have been. The system had utterly disintegrated within one hundred years of the founding of the T'ang dynasty.

NOTES

萬國鼎, "北朝隋唐之均田制度", 金陵學報
Wan Kuo-ting, "Pei-ch'ao Sui T'ang chih chün-t'ien chih-tu,"
Nanking Journal, I, 2 (Nov. 1931), 269-300.

The material in this article was incorporated by the author in
his History of the Chinese Land System (Chung-kuo t'ien-chih shih
中國田制史), Nanking, 1934. The latter version contains additional material on the effects of the tax systems and of the Salary
Fields and Office Expense Fields on the equal allotments system
of the period under consideration.

There is an extensive literature in Japanese on the equalization
movement. For the orthodox Confucian interpretation of some of
the data contained in the present article see Chen Huan-chang,
The Economic Principles of Confucius and His School, 2 vols.
(New York, 1911). Mabel Ping-hua Lee in her Economic History

of China appears to have followed Chen's material closely. A more critical evaluation is presented in Henri Maspero's " Les régimes fonciers en Chine des origines aux temps modernes," in his Mélanges posthumes sur les religions et l'histoire de la Chine (Paris, 1950), p. 165 ff., an article reprinted from Recueil de la Société Jean Bodin (Brussels), II (1937), 765-314.

The major sources used by the author are the dynastic histories of the periods covered, as well as other compilations like the T'ang hui-yao 唐會要, Six Institutes of T'ang (T'ang liu-tien 唐六典), Ts'e-fu yüan-kuei 冊府元龜, and T'ung-tien 通典. Some secondary authorities are also consulted.

11

LOWER CASTES IN THE T'ANG DYNASTY

by

YANG CHUNG-I

// The lower castes* in the T'ang dynasty included such diverse census categories as Slaves, Government Householders, Descendants of Convicts, Musicians at the Court of Ceremonies, Skilled Artisans, Ordinary Musicians, Dependents, Female Dependents, and so on. The statuses of these persons differed widely and comprised many gradations.

// In his History of Chinese Political Thought T'ao Hsi-sheng [1898-   ] holds that the gradations in the T'ang population were in descending order as follows: (1) Full Civilians, (2) "Dependents" and Musicians at the Court of Ceremonies, (3) Government Householders and Descendants of Convicts, and (4) Slaves. Chü Ch'ing-yüan, on the other hand, states in his Government and Private Industries of T'ang and Sung that "There were three gradations within the category of Government Householders; these were the government slaves, the persons owing service by rotation, and the descendants of convicts." Of these two divergent views, which then is correct? Or is it that both are reasonably valid?

---

*We have rendered the term chien-min 賤民 as "lower castes," although we are aware of the fact that "caste" as such is considered by Western sinologists as never to have existed in China. However, the characteristics of these segments of the population--the specific, legally assigned duties, obligations and rights of these people, the hereditary nature of their statuses, the prohibition of inter-status marriage, and the lack of inter-group mobility except by special government "pardons"--delineate a rigid stratification of a large segment of society that falls into the descriptions of caste system given by modern social scientists. Thus W. Lloyd Warner defines either class or caste as "a theoretical arrangement of the people of the given group in an order in which the privileges, duties, obligations, opportunities, etc., are unequally distributed between groups that are considered higher or lower." In addition, caste does not allow marriage between groups, and there is no opportunity for lower group member to rise into upper group, or vice versa. (See Warner's "American Class and Caste," American Journal of Sociology, XLII, 2 [September, 1936], 234.) On the basis of such criteria we believe that the rendering of chien-min as "caste" is warranted. We trust that our handling of the matter will at least provoke a fuller discussion of the problem.

The answer cannot be obtained in the views themselves, but must be sought from contemporary records. [....]

// For the sake of convenience, let us first look into the Government Householders. What sort of persons constituted this category? On this point the Explanation of the T'ang Code states: "Government Householders refer to those born of forebears exiled in previous reigns, or to those convicted and exiled in the present reign; they are not registered with the prefectural or district authorities but are subject to the control of particular official agencies." This source adds: "Government Householders are subordinate to the Department of Agriculture, and are not registered with the prefectural or district authorities." Thus those known as Government Householders were legally convicted persons who had lost their independent status, and who "are subordinate to the Department of Agriculture, and are not registered with the prefectural or district authorities."

// However, Government Householders who had been legally convicted and lost their independent status were still entitled to receive land allotments from the government. The Six Institutes of T'ang states: "The allotment of a Government Householder shall be half the lifetime holding of the common people." Under the T'ang system of land allotment, of the one ch'ing [100 mou] of land allotted to the common households, 20 mou was known as the permanent holding, and 80 mou the lifetime holding. A Government Householder, receiving half of the temporary portion of the common people's allotment, would thus be allotted only 40 mou. The land used for these allotments was probably government land, of which each government department possessed a certain amount. //

The Government Householders were also known as Government-land Householders, because of the fact that they received allotments from government land. It is not clear whether or not they were obliged to pay taxes to the government. The Six Institutes of T'ang informs us, however, that they had to give three months' labor service each year to the office which controlled them.

// During their terms of service the Government Householders were given food rations. According to the Six Institutes of T'ang, "All Government Slaves are to be given rations. The same is true for Government Householders on labor duty." For those who were on long-term service the government provided clothing, the amount of which is indicated by the same source as follows:

A new suit of spring garments is to be provided every year, and a new suit of winter garments every two years...A male slave is to receive one spring cap, one hemp shirt, one pair

of hemp trousers, one pair of leather shoes, and a felt blanket. A female slave is to receive in the spring a blouse and
a skirt, one unlined silk garment, and two pairs of shoes.
In the winter each [slave] is to receive one [lined] jacket and
one pair of lined trousers, one pair of cowhide shoes, and a
blanket. For those under ten years of age, each boy is to
receive in the spring one hemp shirt and one pair of shoes;
and each girl, one hemp blouse, one hemp skirt, and one
pair of shoes. In winter boys and girls are to receive one
hemp jacket, and one pair each of shoes and socks. Government Householders who are on long-term service are to be
provided for in the same way.

Government Householders received more food rations per capita
while on long-term service than did the Government Slaves. As to
the rations of the latter: "An able-bodied man is given a daily
ration of 2 pints of rice per day; a youth [aged 16-21], 1.3 pints;
a child [aged 4-16], 0.6 pint." The Government Householders,
however, were given "3.5 pints of rice per day for each able-
bodied man, and 2 pints per day for each youth." The larger ration
probably stems from the fact that the Government Householders received the combined portions of the equivalent of Government Slaves
plus the rations due them while on duty.
  // The Government Householders had to "marry within their status." The Explanation of the T'ang Code states that, "In accordance
with the order, Skilled Workers, Ordinary Musicians, Descendants
of Convicts, and Government Householders are to marry [each]
within his own status." Again, "The Government Householders are
subordinate to the various departments, do not belong to the prefecture and districts, and should marry [each] within his own status." It further informs us that "When young Government Householders and Slaves, both male and female, come of age, they shall
be married off first of all to persons of their own status."
  // Government Householders constituted a separate category,
different from the Descendants of Convicts. A passage in the Explanation of the T'ang Code says, "[....] Descendants of Convicts and Government Householders must each marry within his
own status; in accordance with this they therefore comprise
distinct categories and should not raise each other's children."
We can infer from this that Government Householders, Skilled
Workers, and Ordinary Musicians also each belonged to a distinct
category. Since "each is to marry within his own status," it follows that a Government Householder could marry only another

Government Householder. This is expressed in the Six Institutes of T'ang as follows: "When boys and girls come of age, each is married according to his or her kind."

⫽This much is clear from the above: The Government House-holders comprised people who had been convicted by law, who were controlled by the Department of Agriculture, and who were not registered with the prefectural or district authorities. They could each receive forty mou of land, and had to give three months' labor service every year to the controlling office. Those giving long-term service were provided with food and clothing by the government on the same basis as were the Government Slaves (except that they received a larger food ration than the Slaves). They were required to "marry within their own status"; marriage with persons of other statuses was forbidden.

⫽Having thus ascertained the characteristics of the Government Householders, we can then compare them with the other castes, and get a picture of the gradations of the categories. Let us first compare the Government Householders with the Slaves.

⫽Slaves were regarded as property; they were compared to livestock and considered as not having personalities. In the Explanation of the T'ang Code are the sentences "Slaves are of the same nature as property"; "Slaves and low-caste persons are comparable to livestock under the law"; and "Of those that multiply themselves, there are, for example, slave women giving birth to sons, and mares giving birth to colts." Slaves were property, on a level with livestock, and government slaves were therefore the property and livestock of the government, and were kept as horses and oxen by the latter. The chapter on slaves in the Institutes of T'ang states:

> The following procedure has been approved: In the first month of every year the offices in charge of Government Slaves are to make a report in duplicate, of which one copy is to be sent to the head of the department, and the other is to be retained in the original office. Every year a roll [of the slaves] is to be called and their likenesses checked against the record, after which they shall be given clothing and food rations.

⫽In return for being thus kept by the government, the slaves were to render unconditional permanent service to the latter. As noted by the Six Institutes of T'ang, "Government Slaves are to render permanent service without rotation." Since the Government

Householders had only three terms of service [of one month each]
per year, and could receive forty mou of land, they plainly occupied a higher status than the slaves. Furthermore since the "Dependents" were higher than slaves, and since, according to the
Explanation of the T'ang Code, "Government Householders have
the same status as Dependents," it follows also that Government
Householders were higher than slaves. This source also informs
us that "The daughters of 'Dependents' (that is, Female Dependents) are also considered as convicts, on a level with Government Householders and 'Dependents'." This indicates that the legal status of Dependents and Government Householders was the
same, the only distinction between them being that the former
were appended to the census registration of their masters, and the
latter were controlled by the Department of Agriculture. In other
words, one group was privately owned and the other was government-owned. According to the T'ang code, "Dependents" are not
property....Slaves are property, and hence are specially mentioned here." Again, "'Dependents' are allowed to change masters, while slaves are equivalent to property." "Dependents" therefore were ranked higher than slaves. Consequently it becomes
quite clear that Government Householders were one grade above
slaves.

⫽Next, let us compare Government Householders and Descendants of Convicts. It has been indicated above that these two were
separate census categories. What then was the difference in rank
between them? The Explanation of the T'ang Code states that "Descendants of Convicts are those whose forebears were exiled and
assigned by the government. They are subject to control by the
various government agencies and have tax and labor obligations
different from those of the common people. They are exempted
by decree from obligations in old age. Land is to be given to them
when they come of age on the same basis as the common people;
it is to be registered with the office in charge." Another passage
in the same work explains: "Descendants of Convicts are those
whose forebears were convicted of crimes and had been taken over
by the government. They are assigned to various government
agencies for service. They are registered with the prefectural
and district authorities, but pay taxes and labor dues different
from those of the ordinary people."⫽

These therefore were the differences between the Government
Householders and Descendants of Convicts: The latter possessed
their own census registration with the local authorities, and received the same land allotment as the common people, while the
former had no registration with the local authorities, and could

receive only half of the lifetime portion of the common people's
land allotment. Furthermore, the Government Householders had
to give labor service three months out of each year, but the Descendants of Convicts were only due for service five months out
of every two years, that is, for an annual term of seventy-five
days. The law provided, moreover, that such labor dues could be
commuted to 1,500 [cash] per year, after payment of which the
Descendants of Convicts would not be required to give labor service. Thus we see that the status of Descendants of Convicts was
much higher than that of Government Householders.

All the above points to the conclusion that the gradation among
the lower castes in the T'ang dynasty was as follows in descending order: Descendants of Convicts, Government Householders,
and Slaves. This is borne out by a passage in the Six Institutes of
T'ang, which records: "Those convicted of rebellion shall have
their families taken by the authorities and become Government
Slaves. [In the case of pardon] the first pardon shall raise their
status to persons owing labor service in rotation, a second pardon shall raise it to Descendants of Convicts, and a third pardon
shall raise it to that of a Full Civilian."

Thus, the theses of both Chü Ch'ing-yüan and T'ao Hsi-sheng
seem to be incorrect.

As to the Musicians at the Court of Ceremonies, they occupied
a higher position than Government Householders, and were of the
same status as the Descendants of Convicts. The laws show that
these Musicians, like the Descendants of Convicts, were registered with the prefectural and district authorities; like them, too,
the Musicians received land allotments on the same basis as the
common people, and were exempt from obligations in old age.

The Skilled Artisans and Ordinary Musicians had the same
status as the Government Householders. The Skilled Workers
were administered by the Imperial Workshop Administration; the
Ordinary Musicians were administered by the Court of Ceremonies.
Judging from the penalties provided in case of their infringing the
law or killing their controlling officials, it is seen that these persons occupied the same position as the Government Householders.

//Why, then, did these groups among the lower castes--Musi-
cians at the Court of Ceremonies, Descendants of Convicts,
Skilled Artisans, Ordinary Musicians, and Government House-
holders--belong to different census categories? This was probably caused by the differences in their respective functions and
in the offices controlling them. According to the Six Institutes of
T'ang, "When first convicted and taken by the government, those
skilled in some art are to be assigned to a government agency in

accordance with [the nature of] their skill. Skilled women are to
be assigned to work in the Palace Annex. All unskilled persons
are to be administrated by the Department of Agriculture." Those
assigned to the Court of Ceremonies were called Ordinary Musicians, and those to the Imperial Workshop Administration, Skilled Artisans. Because of their special skills they were placed one
grade above the Government Slaves, and were equal to the status
of Government Householders, who stood "one pardon" above the
slaves. Thanks to their specially high skill, or to tradition, the
Musicians at the Court of Ceremonies, on the other hand, were
placed on the same level as the Descendants of Convicts, who were
"two pardons" above the Slaves. Although the members of these
groups, on the basis of their functions or affiliations, fell into
distinct groups, they nevertheless all belonged to the general
category of people who had been "taken over, exiled, or assigned
by the government."

From the above we can conclude that the lower castes of the
T'ang dynasty were ranked, in descending order, as follows:

1. Descendants of Convicts, Musicians at the Court of Ceremonies.

2. Government Householders, Skilled Artisans, Ordinary
Musicians, "Dependents" (privately owned, like serfs), Female
Dependents.

3. Government Slaves.

NOTES

楊中一，"唐代的賤民，" 食貨

Yang Chung-i, "T'ang-tai-ti chien-min," Shih-huo I, No. 4
(Jan. 16, 1935), 124-127.

As indicated in the text of this article, the author has drawn
most heavily on the T'ang dynasty works, Explanation of the T'ang
Code (T'ang-lü shu-i 唐律疏議), Six Institutes of T'ang (T'ang
liu-tien 唐六典), and T'ang hui-yao 唐會要 . The New T'ang
History (Hsin T'ang shu 新唐書) is also referred to in the
footnotes.

12

OFFICIAL SALARIES AS REVEALED IN T'ANG POETRY

by

CH'EN YIN-K'O

In one of the three In Memoriam poems of Yüan Chen [779-831] for his first wife is the sentence, "Now my salary exceeds a hundred thousand cash." This opens up the question of T'ang official salaries, the scale of which varied locally and from time to time, so that it is difficult to ascertain the exact rate of official pay for that period. I have suggested elsewhere that Yüan Chen wrote these poems while he was the Superior Administrator of T'ung-chou [in Szechuan] in charge of prefectural administration, because any person lower than a prefectural administrator could not have received a monthly salary of one hundred thousand cash. Let us use this as the starting point of our investigation.

A comparison of Yüan's poems with those of his friend, Po Chü-i [772-846], and with the writings of Han Yü, indicates that Yüan's wife had died in 809 A.D., and that the In Memoriam poems were very likely written in 810. But at that date Yüan had been demoted from an Imperial Censor at the capital to a post at Chiang-ling [in Hupei]. It would not be reasonable to suppose that such a demotion actually entailed an increase in salary, and yet the monthly sum of one hundred thousand cash was well in excess of the statutory provisions as recorded in the New T'ang History, T'ang hui-yao, and Ts'e-fu yüan-kuei [completed 1013]. These sources, however, do not contain full information on official salaries. The best we can do is to compare the government regulations for the period between 785 and 846 with the references to salary rates in the poems of Yüan Chen and Po Chü-i which fall within this time-span. Po Chü-i in particular has been known for the frequent mention of salaries in his poetry.

According to a remark by Po Chü-i, when he was an Imperial Collator his monthly salary was 16,000 cash, more than sufficient for his needs. The statutory scale for a Collator was sixteen strings of cash, which tallies with Po's statement. Again, while he was a member of the censorate Po recorded his annual salary as 300,000 cash, [close to, though not precisely] the same as the statutory scale of 30,000 cash per month. However, the sum recorded by Po for the post of Financial Administrator of Ching-chao Prefecture [Ch'ang-an], "40,000 or 50,000" each month, is above the rate set by the official regulations for the period between 766 and 788 A.D., which provided for a monthly pay of only 35,000 cash.

It appears that an Advisor to the Heir Apparent and a Director of the Imperial Library received the same salary of 80,000 cash per month, a sum referred to by both Po Chü-i and the statutes. A Tutor to the Heir Apparent, on the other hand, was an official of the second grade, and therefore had a monthly income of 100,000 cash. Po Chü-i wrote on the occasion of his own accession to that position: "At second rank and a hundred thousand cash, the Court hires me with nought to do." T'ang hui-yao and Ts'e-fu yüan-kuei bear this out in their citations of the regulations. The New T'ang History text has "one million cash," but this can be explained as a typographical error.

At seventy-five Po had retired as an official of the second grade with a pension of 50,000 cash per month, that is at half-salary, his last rank being that of the President of the Board of Punishments. According to the regulations, Board presidents, like Tutors to the Heir Apparent, also received a monthly salary of 100,000 cash, and in 789 were given the privilege of retiring at half-pay. All this tallies with the information presented in Po's poems. Before 789 the retirement pay consisted only of a half portion of the regular grain payment, together with a gift of cloth from the Court.

In a send-off poem to a friend leaving for the post of Superior Administrator at Shan-chou [in Honan], Po Chü-i wrote, "Your income equals that of a Board President"--that is, 100,000 cash per month. According to the official regulations, however, between 763 and 904 A.D., in which period Po's poem fell, the holder of such a position received only 55,000 cash each month. There is thus a considerable discrepancy between Po's statement and the statutory scale.

Moreover, Po wrote to a friend in 815 that as the Superior Administrator of Chiang-chou [modern Kiukiang in Kiangsi] he was an official of the fifth rank, with a monthly income of 40,000 or 50,000 cash. In 818, however, when he composed his Account of Chiang-chou Sub-prefecture, he stated that his monthly salary amounted to some 60,000 or 70,000 cash. An examination of the statutory provision shows that the Superior Administrator of a large prefecture received 50,000 cash per month, a sum that tallies with Po's figure in the 815 letter, but not with his later piece of writing. Therefore there was a difference of some 20,000 to 30,000 cash in the two accounts by Po Chü-i, even though he was holding the same post and presumably receiving the same salary.

In sum, whenever the question was one of salaries of central government officials, the statutory provisions and Po Chü-i's statements coincided. If, however, the question was one of salaries of local officials (including those in Ching-chao Prefecture at Ch'ang-an), the statutes and Po invariably differed. Furthermore, the figures quoted in Po's poems and essays were always higher than those given in the official regulations. This leads to the conclusion that in the last part of the T'ang dynasty local officials could receive extra-quota pay that was also recognized as a part of their normal income, thus making the latter considerably higher than the salary scale of central government officials. Moreover, salaries also varied for the same kind of position in the same period. The student of history, therefore, should not take the statutory provisions as representing the actual salaries of local officials.

Take again the case of Po Chü-i as Superior Administrator in Chiang-chou. It seems that when he wrote his friend in 815, shortly after his appointment, he was only aware of the statutory regulation for his salary; after three years at the post, however, he became fully conscious of the actual higher amount that he could receive, and recorded the figure in his later composition. Knowing this, we shall then not be surprised by the discrepancy in Po's writings, nor by the differences between his figures and those in the legal provisions.

Now let us turn to the last of Yüan Chen's In Memoriam poems, in which occurs the sentence, "Now my salary exceeds a hundred thousand cash." Let us suppose that it was written during the poet's demotion to a minor position in Chiang-ling. The official salary rate for vice-prefects in Chiang-ling and other prefectures, according to T'ang hui-yao and Ts'e-fu yüan-kuei, was 50,000 cash; that for the secretaries, etc. was 45,000. The New T'ang History, however, records the rates as 65,000 and 45,000 respectively. This difference might be due to the difference in time when these rates were supposed to have prevailed. In any case, it is enough to reveal to us that the salary of local officials in the latter part of T'ang was never quite conformant to the regulations on paper.

For instance, although a Superior Administrator of Shan-chou nominally was paid only 55,000 cash a month, his actual income was the "equivalent of a Board President's," that is 100,000 cash,

which was a difference of 45,000 per month between the statutory
and the actual pay. The official salary rate for the vice-prefect
of Chiang-ling was already 65,000 cash per month, according to
the New T'ang History; it is therefore not difficult to conceive of
the actual monthly pay as 100,000 cash. Even though the secretaries and section directors of Chiang-ling received a statutory
stipend of only 45,000 cash, yet together with local differences
and additional grain payments the salary could very easily have
been raised to an actual total income of 100,000 cash per month.
However, since it is not yet establishable whether Yüan Chen had
actually been transferred from his post as Director of Personnel
to that of a secretary of the prefecture, or had been placed in
charge of the vice-prefect's office at Chiang-ling, this can be regarded only as a hypothesis and not a definitive conclusion.

Although material on the salaries of local officials is scattered
and fragmentary, so that it is difficult to obtain a systematic,
over-all view of the situation, nevertheless this much seems
clear: The local officials of T'ang could properly receive payments
much above the statutory provision, whereas the central government officials were the only ones whose actual incomes approximated the statutory scale.

Tu Mu once wrote: "When one becomes a prefect, one's whole
family can live in ease, but a hard life in all respects awaits the
family of a metropolitan official." This was not a sentiment
unique with Tu Mu, but was rather a universal feeling among officials of late T'ang. It serves to illustrate the differences in the
salaries of metropolitan and local officials during that period.

NOTES

陳寅恪，"元白詩中俸料錢問題," 清華學報
Ch'en Yin-k'o, "Yüan Po shih-chung feng-liao-ch'ien wen-t'i,"
The Tsing Hua Journal X (1935), 877-886.

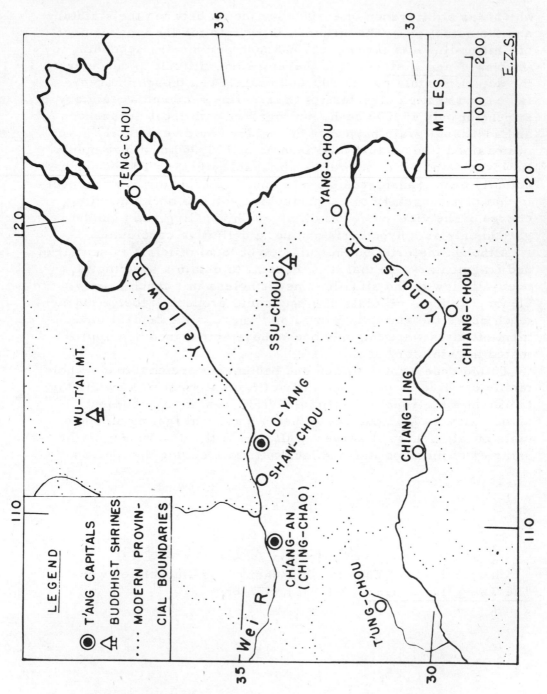

Map 3. North China in the T'ang dynasty

13

THE CHURCH-STATE CONFLICT IN THE T'ANG DYNASTY

by

CHIA CHUNG-YAO

Introduction

The suppression of the Buddhist clergy by the T'ang emperor Wu-tsung [841-846] is a subject about which not enough has been known owing to lack of material. Historians usually refer to the suppression edict of 845 A.D. but say very little about the whole story. Buddhists always place the blame on the Taoist priest Chao Kuei-chen. However, two points have come to light from an examination of the source materials. In the first place, Emperor Wu-tsung probably was prompted by the desire to continue the T'ang policy of suppressing corrupt practices in the Buddhist church. In the second place, the estates, money, and slaves owned by the monasteries were a major incentive of his action.

While the campaign was in progress the Japanese monk Ennin [794-864] happened to be in China. Events touching on the clergy during 843-845 were carefully recorded in his Journal, which can be considered a reliable source. The following sections contain excerpts from the Journal, supplemented by other material, and present the suppression of the Buddhist clergy in chronological order.*

1. Chronology of the Suppression

(i) Second Year of Hui-ch'ang [842 A.D.]

//It was decreed as follows on the ninth day of the tenth month: "All monks and nuns in the empire who practise alchemy, incantation, and stoppage of the breath, who have deserted from the army,

---

*This article consists almost entirely of excerpts from various sources. These are indicated in the present summary by a number at the end of each paragraph, and are listed in the Notes at the end of this article.

who bear on their bodies the scars of flagellation and tattoo marks
[for former offenses, who have been condemned to] various forms
of labor, who infringe the rule of continence and maintain wives,
and who have been careless of spiritual discipline, are ordered to
become secularized. If the monks and nuns own money, goods,
grain, and landed estates, these are to be taken over by the government. Those who desire to become secularized in order to protect their property should be allowed to do so; they shall be included in the semi-annual taxes and labor service."// (1)

The Supervisors of Buddhist establishments in the Left Streets
and the Right Streets [i.e. the eastern and western sections of
Ch'ang-an] notified the monasteries, closed their gates, and did
not allow the monks and nuns to pass through. [Previously] the
monk Hsüan-hsüan had memorialized that he himself could make
a "sword wheel" and that he himself would lead the troops on a
campaign against the Uighurs, but upon being ordered to make the
"sword wheel" he was unable to produce it. The Supervisor of the
Left Streets memorialized for permission to be granted to 1,232
monks and nuns who desired secularization out of consideration
for their property; those who remained were either too old in age
or were found to be living in strict accordance with religious precepts. The Supervisor of the Right Streets memorialized for permission to be granted to 2,259 monks and nuns who desired secularization. (1)

//Of the slaves owned [by monasteries], each monk is allowed
to retain one male slave, and each nun two female slaves; the
others will be returned to the care of their own families. The government will sell those who are homeless. The remaining wealth
of the clerics is to be stored by the government pending further
orders for its disposal. If among the slaves retained by the monks
and nuns there are those who are versed in military tactics or in
various arts such as that of medicine, they may not be kept, nor
may they be shaved and clandestinely ordained. Infraction of this
rule should be reported in writing to the authorities by the monastery administrators. As to the other property, money, etc.,
they should be turned over to Supervisors, who will themselves
make a report to the throne.// (1)

(ii) Third Year of Hui-ch'ang [843 A.D.]

In the first month, the secularization of 1,232 monks and nuns
from the Left Streets and 2,259 from the Right Streets was reported. (1)

In the second month, secularized monks and nuns were forbidden
to stop or tarry at monasteries. (1)

In the second month, an edict ordered that the Uighurs who were training for religion around the capital should wear civilian clothes and should be placed under the jurisdiction of the appropriate offi-cials. The Manichaean temples, estates, money, and other prop-erties of the Uighurs were to be inventoried by the metropolitan offi-cials. No one could presume to take these over on pain of death and confiscation of property. (2)

In this year all Manichaean temples were dissolved and their property confiscated. All seventy-two Manichaean nuns in the capi-tal died. Moreover the Uighur Manichaeists in this country were exiled to various places, and the majority of them died. (3)

On the twenty-ninth of the seventh month* a hay-storage depot outside Ch'ang-lo Gate was destroyed by fire following a decree that the Buddhist sutras in the palace were to be burned; in addi-tion the images of Buddha and other deities were buried.** This fire was followed by several others in other parts of the capital. (1)

On the thirteenth of the ninth month, it was ordered that all un-registered monks in the capital as well as other parts of the coun-try must leave the priesthood and return to their homes. In Ch'ang-an the monks who could not account for themselves were arrested by the metropolitan government. Some three hundred persons were put to death, and the fugitives dared not show themselves in the streets. (1)

(iii) Fourth year of Hui-ch'ang [844 A.D.]

Third month. On the emperor's birthday Buddhist and Taoist priests are customarily invited into the palace to expound their re-spective doctrines. But this year only the Taoists were invited; it seems that henceforth Buddhists are to be permanently barred from such functions. This was caused by the talk of the Taoists, who said that Confucius had prophesied that the Buddhists would usurp power in the eighteenth reign of the Li family [the present reign]. Supervisors of monasteries have prohibited monks and nuns to go about the streets after the ringing of the temple bells; nor are they allowed to spend the night in other than their own temples. (1)

It has been decreed that in famous pilgrimage centers, such as Wu-t'ai Mountain, no more sacrifices or pilgrimages are to be al-lowed. If in the various provinces, prefectures, and sub-prefec-

---

*Prof. E.O. Reischauer notes that this date is an error for the sixth month.
**Presumably the sutras were taken to the depot for destruction by fire.

tures anyone is found giving money or making offerings in kind, he
is to be punished with twenty lashes on the back. Any monk or nun
found accepting even one cash is also to be given twenty lashes.(1)

In the seventh month, all Buddhist monasteries, halls of wor-
ship, and "charity wells"* were ordered destroyed. In institutions
that do not qualify as temples the monks and nuns are to become
secularized and to be included in the corvée. In Ch'ang-an there
are over three hundred magnificent Buddhist shrines, each the
equivalent of a large temple in the provinces. Over the entire
country numerous shrines have been destroyed, as is true also of
Buddhist monuments and tombs of monks. (1)

This year the Taoist and Buddhist priests have been asked to
pray for rain, but when it came only the Taoists were rewarded by
the emperor. (1)

Offerings of flowers, candles, etc. presented in the temples by
Buddhists to celebrate the fifteenth of the seventh month are especially abundant this year. But on the emperor's order they have
been removed to the Taoists' Hsing-T'ang Temple as a sacrifice
to the Taoist God. (1)

Ninth month. The emperor is fond of making excursions, for
each of which the Buddhist temples have been ordered to provide
seating mats, blankets, flower bunting and arches, dishes, trays,
chairs, and so forth, which cost each temple at least four or five
hundred strings of cash. The smaller temples in the country have
been ordered to be demolished. Their Buddhist literature is being
removed to large temples, and their bronze instruments are being given to Taoist temples. Monks of irregular conduct are forced
to leave the priesthood and are assigned various kinds of corvée.
Young monks, even though of good conduct, must also leave the
priesthood. Thirty-three small temples have been abolished in
the capital. (1)

(iv) Fifth Year of Hui-ch'ang [845 A.D.]

//(On the third day of the third month,) it was decreed that no
monastery in the country should be allowed to acquire estates. Further, an inventory was ordered to be made of the slaves, money,
goods, grain, and textiles owned by all monasteries in the land;
these are to be memorialized in an itemized report. The inventory
of the temples in the capital is to be handled by the chiefs of the
two [metropolitan] armies, and that of the monasteries in the prov-

---

*Wells opened for public use as a means of winning merit.

inces by the Imperial Grand Secretariat and the Imperial Chancellery. The slaves of the metropolitan monasteries comprise three
classes: those without* skills or professions are to be assigned
to the army; those who are young and strong but have no profession are to be sold; and the old and weak are to be sent to the
palace. And so at present fathers and sons are being scattered
hither and yon, and the slaves are weeping with grief. The Supervisors of Buddhist establishments have notified the temples that
every five slaves are to make up one pao 保 , and that the penalty
for each person missing from a pao is 2,000 strings of cash. The
government is to assume the money and goods of the temples, together with the proceeds from the sale of slaves, and these are to
be used to pay official salaries. Moreover, it was ordered that all
monks and nuns in the empire under forty years of age must become secularized and return to their own homes. // (1)

A few days later, it was ordered that all those under fifty years
of age should leave the priesthood; this was followed by the order
that the same applied to all those over fifty who had no license
from the Bureau of Religious Affairs. Those who had licenses were
to submit them to the local authorities for inspection. The Supervisors are very strict in carrying out these orders. All details in
the licenses are noted, and the slightest discrepancy entails ex-
pulsion from the priesthood. Those licenses showing no discrepancy are to be kept indefinitely on file, so that the monks and nuns
are deprived of their proper papers. People have concluded that
the keeping of the licenses foreshadows the total abolition of the
clergy, and that the confiscation of monastic property presages
the destruction of monasteries. Ennin petitioned for his own abandonment of the priesthood and return to Japan; the Supervisors
accepted his petition but handed down no decision. All clerics
have been confined within the monasteries, and those who venture
out of the premises are to be executed immediately. (1)

In the fourth month it was decreed that any monk or nun who
resisted secularization was to be judged guilty of insubordination
to imperial commands and hence subject to immediate execution.(1)

From the first of the fourth month on, all monks and nuns under
forty years of age were secularized; three hundred persons were
processed each day, the task not being finished until the fifteenth
of the month. From the sixteenth of the fourth month to the tenth
of the fifth month, those under fifty were processed; from the
eleventh on, it was the turn of those over fifty without a license.
In the previous year those who failed to live according to religious
discipline had been made to abandon the priesthood, but now the

---

*Prof. Reischauer suggests that the text should read "with" rather than "without."

axe fell without regard to the cleric's conduct. Foreign monks who
do not have the Bureau licenses have also been classified with
those who should withdraw from the priesthood and return to their
native lands. Ennin is one of these. (1)

In the fourth month, according to the Bureau of Religious Affairs, there were in the entire country a total of 4,600 Buddhist
temples, 40,000 shrines, and 260,500 monks and nuns. (2)

In the fourth month the Imperial Grand Secretariat and the Imperial Chancellery memorialized that they feared that local officials, magnates, gentry, merchants, and the common people
might hide or purchase minors among the slaves freed in the abolition of monasteries. If such cases were found, the minors were
to be sent back to their parents. Those who persisted in hiding
such slaves would, upon conviction through information, be given
the extreme penalty. Each informer was to be rewarded with one
hundred thousand cash out of the public treasury. (4)

// (In the fifth month,) on the morning of the sixteenth, I said
farewell [in Ch'ang-an] and started on my way, together with nineteen Chinese monks. Stopped for the night at Chao-ying District.
In the group is a twenty-year-old monk, a native of Ch'ang-an,
whose parents, sisters, and brothers are all living. He was committed to Buddhism at an early age, and became a disciple of a
Hsin-lo [Korean] monk at Ta-chien-fu Temple. Upon the death of
the monk he assumed the latter's name and stayed in the temple.
When the government came to inspect the monks, he was ordered
to go back to Hsin-lo. He tried every means to argue with the prefectural government, but failed to stop his expatriation. His relatives saw him off in the street with tears. And so he too had been
sent to spend the night at Chao-ying District. When we resumed
our journey at the fifth watch [about 4 a.m.], this monk slipped
away without others realizing it. His escape was discovered when
it became light.* Two of the three servants were sent to search
for him on separate trails, but could not find him after spending
a whole day at it. He probably had already gotten home and was
hiding there. The authorities have requested the prefectural government to institute a search for him. // (1)

On the twenty-second of the sixth month, we arrived at Ssu-
chou [in Anhwei]. The P'u-kuang-wang Temple here has been a
famous spot in the country. But now it is completely deserted, its
estates, property, and slaves taken over by the metropolitan government. (1)

_____

*The context suggests that <u>tao hsien ming</u> 到縣明 should be emended to read
<u>tao t'ien ming</u> 到天明 "when it became light."

Met a former Hanlin scholar on the way to Yang-chou. He said that when he departed from Ch'ang-an, on the twenty-ninth of the fifth month, all the monks and nuns in the capital had become secularized. Every monastery was to keep three monks as caretakers pending the inventory of the property and its acquisition by the government; then they too were to be secularized. The monasteries were being demolished; three of them had been turned into palace grounds. (1)

In the seventh month, a general investigation of the Buddhist monasteries was ordered. Later it was ordered that in each large prefecture one monastery should be kept intact if the buildings were well built; otherwise they were to be demolished. On festivals the officials were to repair to the Taoist temples. In the capital four monasteries were to be retained, with thirty monks to each monastery. Of the metals acquired from Buddhist images and bells, etc., the copper was to be used for the mint, the iron for the making of agricultural tools, and the gold, silver, and jade was to be given to the government treasury. (2)

In the eighth month, arrived at Teng-chou [Shantung]. This is the northeastern extremity of the T'ang Empire, but even here the destruction of Buddhist institutions was carried out as fully as in the capital.

It was ordered that all pigs,* black dogs, and black donkeys and oxen should be killed. Is this because the Taoists took yellow as their own color, and feared that black might dominate it? Recently it was ordered that all the black robes of the monks and nuns who had left the priesthood should be burned. (1)

Eleventh month. During the past three or four years, all monks and nuns throughout the empire have been made to abandon the priesthood. All shrines and monasteries have been destroyed. All Buddhist sutras, images, and robes have been burned. All gold-leaf as well as copper and iron obtained from the images has been taken over by the government. The prefectural and district authorities have taken over all properties and estates, all dependents and slaves of the monasteries. All this has occurred throughout the entire country, except in four marches north of the Yellow River, where Buddhism has always been honored. (1)

---

*Chu 猪 "pig" is commonly associated with the color black in China, as in the popular maxim Lao-kua chan-tsai chu-shen-shang, k'an-pu-chien tzu-chi-ti hei. "The crow alights on the pig's back and cannot see his own blackness [i.e. can only see the blackness of others]."

(v) Sixth Year of Hui-ch'ang [846 A.D.]

In the fifth month, the new emperor, surnamed Li, granted a general amnesty. It was also decreed that each sub-prefecture could build two monasteries, and each march three monasteries, each with 50 monks. The monks over fifty years of age who were secularized last year were permitted to return to the priesthood. Those approaching eighty years of age were awarded five strings of cash by government. (1)

2. Results of the Suppression

//Edict of the eighth month, fifth year of Hui-ch'ang [845 A.D.]:
//"To Our knowledge there was no talk of Buddha before the time of Hsia, Shang, and Chou. It is since Han and Wei that the idolatrous religion has gradually flourished. Of late the propagation of this alien belief has become so pervasive and proliferating that it has imperceptibly corrupted the morals of Our country, seduced the will of the people, and placed the masses increasingly under its spell. From the remotest corners of the provinces to the royal palaces of the two capitals, the Buddhist monks are daily increasing in number and the Buddhist monasteries are daily becoming more imposing. They are exhausting the people's labor to construct their buildings and are taking away the people's resources to bejewel their images. They spurn ruler and kin to become acolytes and abandon their mates to become celibates. Never has there been anything more harmful to the law or injurious to the people than this religion.
//"Furthermore, when one man does not till the fields, others will lack food; when one woman does not weave, others will suffer cold. Now the countless monks and nuns in the country all look to the farmer for food and to the silk-raiser for clothes. The monasteries and temples, incalculable in number, are all lofty in structure and lavish in decoration, rivalling the imperial palaces. It was none other than these things which caused the material poverty and moral decadence of the Tsin, Sung, Ch'i, and Liang dynasties [265-556 A.D.]. Furthermore, Our Kao-tsu and T'ai-tsung [618-649] were able to pacify the country with military might and to rule it with cultivated accomplishments. These two devices suffice for the administration of the country. How can this trifling religion from the west obtrude upon Our authority?
//"During the Chen-kuan [627-649 A.D.] and K'ai-yüan [713-741 A.D.] periods some attempt was made to remedy matters, but the evil was not eradicated and continues to proliferate. We

have looked widely into the precepts of the past and sought advice from those about Us. The extirpation of an evil is dependent upon resolution [.....] Hence We order the destruction of over 4,600 temples and the secularization of over 260,000 (another source has 265,000) monks and nuns who shall henceforth pay the semi-annual taxes. The 3,000-odd monks and nuns subject to the control of the bureau of state guests, being propagators of foreign religions, such as Nestorianism and Zoroastrianism, are to be secularized lest they contaminate any longer the customs of China.

// "Alas! that this was not done before but seems to have been deferred. Now that there has been a complete extirpation how can it be said to be inopportune? We are rid of hundreds of thousands of vagrant idlers and billions worth of useless ornamental buildings..... Let everyone submit to the imperial way." // (4)

With regard to the number of clerics who were secularized, a comparison of several sources reveals that there were three versions, of which 260,500 seems to be the most likely figure. [Author's note].

More than 4,600 temples were demolished and altogether over 410,000 monks, nuns, and their slaves were returned to the world and designated as payers of semi-annual taxes. Fugitives have now become common people, and the best land is now subject to imperial taxation. (5)

According to the Collected Essays of Tu Mu [803-852], when Emperor Wu-tsung ascended the throne he declared angrily, "It is the Buddhists who are reducing Our empire to poverty," and he ordered the destruction of thousands of temples. Four Censors were sent to travel over the entire country and see to the execution of the orders. The clerics who were made to wear civilian clothes numbered 260,500. The slaves taken from the temples numbered 150,000, and the "attached persons" [under the authority of the monasteries] were as numerous as the clerics. Of the several tens of million ch'ing of confiscated land, each slave was given one hundred mou. These holdings were assigned to the category of agricultural land; the rest was sold cheaply, the proceeds being placed in charge of the authorities. (6)

According to Tu Mu's figures, the monasteries also had large numbers of "attached persons." There were 260,500 monks and nuns, 150,000 slaves, and 260,000 "attached persons," making a total of over 650,000 people. This was a tremendous number in view of the fact that the tax-paying households numbered only 2,800,000 at that time. [Author's note].

Many clerics after leaving the priesthood found that they "had nothing to eat and nothing to wear," and became robbers. (1)

// The best land was sold, the proceeds being kept by the Board of Finance. Land of medium and poor grades was given to able-bodied temple slaves, who were now designated as semi-annual tax payers and received ten mou per person. Since there were no longer monks and nuns [to take care of charity work], the public cemeteries and charity hospitals in the two capitals were given ten ch'ing of land each; the provinces were given thirty-seven ch'ing for the care of the old. // (2)

Note the difference between Tu Mu and the Old T'ang History on the amount of land given to each slave. Other records do not deal with this point. [Author's note].

When Emperor Wu-tsung suppressed Buddhism the monk Jih-chao went deep into the mountains and eked out a bare existence on millet and spring water. With the restoration of Buddhism by the next emperor, Jih-chao was able to return to Ang-t'ou Mountain [in Hunan] with some sixty disciples and rebuild his home on the old site. (7)

The Great Monks of Sung gives further illustration of the way the clergy was affected by the suppression. Some tried vainly to petition the Court against assuming civilian costume; others hid themselves in the mountains and evaded the decrees.

NOTES

賈鍾堯, 唐會昌政教衝突史料, 食貨
Chia Chung-yao, "T'ang Hui-ch'ang cheng-chiao ch'ung-t'u shih-liao," Shih-huo, IV, 1 (July 1, 1936), 18-27.

The sources used in this article, and the numbers added at the end of each paragraph of the summary to refer to the sources, are as follows:

1. Yüan-jen, Ju-T'ang ch'iu-fa hsün-li hsing-chi 圓仁, 入唐求法 巡禮行記(Ennin, Journal of My Travels to China in Search of Buddhist Doctrine)
2. Chiu T'ang shu 舊唐書 (Old T'ang History)
3. Seng-shih lüeh 僧史略 (Brief History of Priesthood)
4. T'ang hui-yao 唐會要
5. Li Wen-jao ch'üan-chi 李文饒全集 (Complete Works of Li Wen-jao)
6. Fan-ch'uan wen-chi 樊川文集 (Collected Essays of Tu Mu)
7. Sung kao-seng chuan 宋高僧傳 (Great Monks of Sung)

14

SOCIAL RELIEF DURING THE SUNG DYNASTY

by

HSÜ I-T'ANG

1. Introduction

There were two kinds of relief administration during the Sung dynasty, the emergency relief and the normal relief. The former usually was of a temporary nature. Whenever there was a catastrophe, be it a flood, drought, fire, or warfare, which resulted in displaced persons suffering from lack of food and shelter, the local authorities would obtain the permission of the government to distribute grain and cash from the Ever Normal Granary or the Charity Granary to the victims. The amount distributed differed according to the seriousness of the emergency. This kind of relief involved no complex or permanent administrative organs, and stopped when the emergency was over.

Normal relief, on the other hand, operated among the general mass of poor people. These consisted of indigents who were unable to maintain themselves--aged widowers, widows, orphans, and the childless old. For this kind of relief there were regular dwellings and definite periods of operation, special officials in charge of the administration, and laws regulating the procedures. This was in fact along the general lines of the social relief measures of today.

In this paper, we are concerned only with normal relief.

2. Categories of Normal Relief Agencies

The indigent were made the object of the normal relief because, according to the guiding principle of Sung relief administration, "since ancient times aged widowers, widows, orphans, and the childless old have been unfortunates, and it is the responsibility [of the government] to see to it that the living are given sustenance, the sick, medical care, and the dead, interment."

The T'ang system of Charity Homes was taken over by the early

Sung emperors, who began by first establishing a Benevolence
Home in K'ai-feng, the capital. There were twenty-four relief recipients in the first days of the home, which handled all relief matters concerning the living, the sick, and the dead. By the reign of
Emperor Ying-tsung [1064-1067] the number of recipients had increased to 300 per day, and the Home was operating on an annual
budget that reached 8,000,000 [strings of cash] at its peak.

It was not until 1098, however, that an edict was issued calling for the general establishment of relief homes all over the empire. The edict of the tenth month of that year, later known [from
the reign-title] as the "Yüan-fu edict," set out the procedures as
follows: the sub-prefects and district magistrates, upon learning
of the existence of persons who could not support themselves,
were to check on the veracity of the cases. After verification of
the cases, the needy were to be supplied by the government with
the means of subsistence; the sick among the poor were likewise to be attended to. These people were to be checked by inspectors sent by the government. The ones who needed shelter were
to be lodged in the homes of those who had died without heir, though
if such dwellings were not available they could be lodged in government buildings, and were to have their expenses paid out of the
property of the heirless, with no limitations as to the length of
time when payments were to be made. The relief recipients were
to be given rice and beans as in the case of beggars. Deficits were
to be made up from interest earnings of the Ever Normal Granary.
Those who had gone on relief but later were able to support themselves were to be taken off the rolls.

The above served as the basic framework for all relief homes
set up in the years that followed. Sung hui-yao records that in
1106 they were formally named Relief Lodging Homes.

In addition, medical relief institutions were established by imperial decree in 1102, and two years later public cemeteries were
also ordered set up to take care of those who could not pay for
their own burials, or who had died in the course of travel away
from home.

Henceforth relief homes, medical clinics, and public cemeteries
each functioned in its respective field. This system was first initiated in the provinces, however, and it was not until 1105 that it
was applied in K'ai-feng prefecture, when relief lodging homes
and relief clinics were established there by decree.

When the Sung capital was moved to the south by Emperor Kao-
tsung [1127-1162], large numbers of people also migrated southward. Among these uprooted people the toll of death was high, and
relief in its above three aspects was carried out continuously in
answer to the needs.

3. Relief Lodging Homes

As an edict of January 10, 1070 indicates, the system of relief
homes was not definitely established until that time. This document ordered the systematic rounding up by prefectural authorities in K'ai-feng of "all the aged, the infirm, the orphaned, and
the young who are helpless and go about begging in this cold snowy
weather," and further commanded that they be lodged in the Benevolence Home. Funds were to be appropriated for their care, even
though they were beyond the regular quota of relief recipients at
the Home. This was to continue until after the coming of warm
weather at the Spring Equinox, when the Imperial Grand Secretariat was to be informed to stop appropriations.

Since there were considerable climatic variations in different
parts of China, the dates of the relief lodging periods also varied.
At T'ai-yüan prefecture, for example, cold weather set in early,
and the period of relief lodging started, initially, on the first of
the tenth month [in November] and lasted until the end of the second
month [late March to early April] of the following year; if there
were surplus rice and beans from the winter's use, the period
might be extended to the end of the third month [around late April].
After the issuance of the "Yüan-fu edict," these lodging homes
came to be supported with the property of the heirless dead, and
no time limit was imposed. Later, however, with vast increase
in the number of recipients, the cost became too high, so that a
time limit was again placed on the operation of these homes, with
the period usually ending in the third or fourth month of each
year. The name "Relief Lodging Homes" was given to these institutions by approval of the emperor in 1106.

No permanent officials were in charge of the Relief Lodging
Homes, but the custom was, in the capital, to let the Board of
Civil Service appoint minor functionaries who were awaiting va-
cancies to make periodic inspections [of the needy among the
people] and send them to the Charity Home or Relief Lodging Home.
In the provinces the sub-prefect or district magistrate was to
check the needy cases, and send the persons to the Relief Lodging
Homes in his area. The management of the homes was left in the
hands of clerks until 1105, when a chün-tien 軍典 was especially
appointed to the job of handling the distribution of government relief material and making reports. In the provinces one shou-fen
手分 from among the functionaries of each district was given the
special task of managing the income and distribution of relief materials in the locality. This job was rotated annually.

In 1107 the relief clinics, as well as the Relief Lodging Homes,

were placed under the charge of the chün-tien , but later, for the
sake of greater efficiency, the Relief Lodging Home and the clinic
were each placed under the charge of an officer of its own. The
special duties of the chün-tien thus fluctuated from time to time.

From the Cheng-ho reign [1111-1117] on, corruption in the relief administration became increasingly pronounced. Some officials, for example, failed to procure the materials needed for
clothing and quilts; others discriminated against qualified recipients in favor of their own relatives. After the removal of the dynasty to the south, the relief rolls expanded to vast proportions,
and the amounts dispensed were greatly increased. The sub-prefects and district magistrates, unable personally to check the
cases, entrusted the task to their underlings and clerks. The latter were thus given an opportunity to maneuvre for their own benefit, such as by padding the rolls of relief recipients, by engaging
in graft and favoritism, and by embezzling articles due sick recipients who were unable to come for the dole. The government's
relief expenditures were inflated while the people received little
real benefit therefrom. Although some reforms were later instituted, among which were included the use of precinct heads in the
cities and neighborhood heads in the villages as dispensing officers, the malpractices could not be entirely eradicated.

Food and money were distributed once every five days to the
relief lodgers. Each adult was given one pint of rice and beans
plus ten cash per day. Children received half this amount. Those
above eighty years of age were by regulation allowed to have new
white [i.e. finely hulled] rice and extra money for fuel wood.
Those above ninety were given an additional daily sum of twenty
cash for preserved vegetables and received cotton garments in
the summer and quilted clothing and coverlets in the winter. Those
above one hundred years were given money for meat as well as
thirty cash per day for preserved vegetables; in addition they
were given quilted clothing and coverlets lined with silk gauze in
the winter, and garments of unlined silk gauze in summer. In 1107
it was ruled that only persons fifty years of age or above could be
admitted as "aged" relief lodgers.

A spell of great extravagance occurred in the dispensation of
relief after 1102, as illustrated by the provision of such items as
banquets, mosquito nets, and burial sacrifices and the hiring of
wet-nurses and maid-servants. The cost was so great that the expenditures could not be met even when the normal funds were supplemented by the interest earnings of the Ever Normal Granary.
As a result the government subsequently ordered a reduction in
the daily rations, which for a time consisted only of one pint of

grain per adult, and half of that amount per child. Owing to the difficult times, which called for urgent military preparations and endless relief expenditures, while savings were limited and the treasury was depleted, the government was forced to give titles to the rich in exchange for financial assistance.

The system of relief homes was, however, of a negative character, devoid of any significance in educational or social reform. With few exceptions, such as the sending of children to school in Ch'eng-tu, the recipients of relief were merely expected to subsist on their rations in idleness.

4. Relief Clinics

When the medical relief clinics were first established in 1102 they were called Nursing Homes; later in the year the term "Relief Clinic" was used. The plan called for setting up these homes in the provinces under the supervision of special government agents. Each home was to include separate wards for the critical and the light cases and was also to be equipped with a kitchen. In the following year it was ordered that the clinics were to be financed in the same way as were the relief homes according to the Yüan-fu edict. Following the example of the institution set up by Su Shih at Hangchow, the clinics were placed under the management of monks.

Aside from the monk-managers the clinics were supervised, at the capital, by a chün-tien. At first a clinic was administered seperately by a chün-tien, later it was administered by the same chün-tien jointly with a Relief Lodging Home, and still later it was separated again from the latter. In the provinces each clinic was supervised by a shou-fen. In each clinic were stationed one or more official physicians, whose services were watched over by the Superintendent of Ever Normal Granaries in the provinces and by the Superintendent of Criminal Courts at the capital. Careless performance on the part of a physician was a matter calling for disciplinary action.

Each of the official physicians was given a case book in which he entered the cases treated and the results, and at the end of each year he would be either rewarded or reprimanded according to his accomplishments. The regulations can be summarized as follows:

Any neighborhood head who sent to the clinic healthy persons as sick was to be given 100 lashes. As for the physicians, if 1,000 or more sick persons had been sent to the clinic during the year and less than 20 per cent died, the physician was rewarded with a certificate of merit; if 500 or more patients had been treated during the year and less than 20 per cent died, he was given fifty strings of cash; if 200 or more patients had been treated during the year and less than 20 per cent had died, he was given twenty strings of cash; and if 1,000 or more patients had been treated during the year and less than 10 per cent died, the physician was specially recommended to the government.

The patients were of two kinds. The resident patients lived at the clinic and were supplied with food by the authorities and with medicine by the Medicine Office of the Office of Palace Physicians. The out-patients lived at home and were treated by the official physicians on circuit; they procured their medicine from the Medicine Sales Office.

As early as 1083 the Office of Palace Physicians had begun to select official physicians to take charge of the sick in the vicinity of the capital who were either paupers or travellers. In 1097 the cost of the medicine began to be defrayed out of the surplus revenue that was stored at the palace treasury. Soon afterward each official physician was given a regular salary according to his rank.

After the removal to the south, Emperor Kao-tsung in 1136 increased the number of Medicine Offices under the Office of Palace Physicians to four, one of which was designated as the Medicine Sales Office. At the same time regulations for the operation of these agencies also were promulgated. The Medicine Sales Office was placed under the direction of two officials, one civil and the other military, while the Medicine Offices were each headed by a minor functionary. All these persons received regular salaries. The proceeds from the sale of medicine were delivered once every five days to the Pharmaceutical Bureau for payment of the medical supplies; whatever cash remained after these payments was used for miscellaneous expenditures and purchases. Each of the Medicine Offices took its turn in opening for business, and the officials in charge rotated the task of being on duty. Any person on duty who was found to have refused to sell immediately to people who came for medicine at night for emergencies was punishable with 100 lashes.

In 1148 the name of the Medicine Offices [in Hangchow] was changed to Offices of Peaceful Benefits; three years later this was extended for the whole country. Still later in the Yüan dynasty the task of providing the poor with medicine devolved on the Office of Medical Benefits.

5. Public Cemeteries

Burials for the unclaimed dead were temporarily carried out by the government in the vicinity of the Sung capital during the years 1017-1021, but the formal establishment of a public cemetery was not ordered until 1078, when some non-arable land near K'ai-feng was purchased for the interment of travellers who had died on the way and for those who were too poor to afford funerals. A monk was placed in charge of this task. It was ruled that [as a reward], after 3,000 persons had been buried, an additional monk was to be granted his priesthood license. After serving three years a monk was to be given a purple robe and a Buddhist honorific title and was eligible for the directorship of the public cemetery for three years, a term that was renewable if so desired.

In 1104 the emperor approved a memorial submitted by the Imperial Grand Secretariat on the establishment of public cemeteries in all the provinces. This document included rather detailed plans for the management of the cemeteries. Among other things, the relatives and descendants of one buried by the government could claim him later if they wished and remove him for private reinterment. On the other hand, relatives of either soldiers or poor people who wanted to bury their dead in the public cemetery could request permission from the authorities and were allowed to pick out their plots. Pasturing was prohibited on cemetery land, and a building was erected in each cemetery for the carrying out of sacrifices by the relatives of the deceased. The actual administration of the public cemeteries was, however, of an uneven nature, fluctuating between carelessness and extravagance and waste.

The dynasty's removal to the south brought with it high population pressure on land in the lower Yangtse region, and in many cases the public cemetery land fell into the hands of local influential and unscrupulous persons who wanted to put it under cultivation. This created such a serious situation that in 1144 it was ordered that all public cemetery lands should be restored for burial purposes. This order was first carried out in Hangchow and later in other places as well. Monks remained the designated managers of these cemeteries, serving for a fixed salary.

As a result of warfare and natural calamities, the need for public burials exceeded the government's ability to take care of all cases. The authorities therefore encouraged the wealthy families to take part in this service, for which they were rewarded with government posts or ranks. During the drought and epidemics in the period 1174-1190, however, the interment facilities were greatly expanded by the government in Hangchow prefecture.

6. Conclusion

As the Sung History has aptly stated, "A guiding principle of
Sung administration was benevolence. Its endeavors toward reliev-
ing the sufferings of the poor and helping the unfortunate excelled
those of previous dynasties...." In addition to the relief measures
described above, there were others which were carried out throughout the Sung period. In a year of bad harvest, for example, the government would first distribute grain from the Ever Normal Granaries, and at times these would be supplemented by the provincial
granaries or the rice tribute of other provinces. The wealthy were
sometimes asked to contribute money or grain in return for official posts or ranks, and if this was still insufficient to meet the
needs, gold and cloth from the palace storehouses would then be
contributed to the emergency, or money might be raised by the sale
of priesthood licenses. As to the displaced persons, those who
were able to return to their professions were sent back by the authorities; those who had nothing to return to were either admitted
into the army or given unoccupied land to work for their own living, or, in the case of the young and able-bodied, were recruited
into work gangs for the construction of public works; the old, the
sick, the weak, and the minors who had no way of supporting themselves were given sustenance by the government. Again, when the
winter weather in the capital became too severe or the commodity
prices rose too high, the government would pour its stocks of rice
or fuel into the market and sell them to the people at low prices.

In the Sung History and some contemporary accounts many instances have been recorded of the particularly notable relief measures adopted by specific officials. One such measure was the instituting of maternity clinics for needy women. Another was the
organizing of various means to cope with the problem of abandoned
children; one district magistrate, for example, initiated a legal
adoption system for children abandoned by their parents during a
flood. Still another measure was the purchase of rice at high
prices in a famine area to attract the presence of grain merchants,
thereby lowering the market price of grain. Work-relief was a
measure often resorted to. The famous writer Ou-yang Hsiu [1007-
1072], for instance, while serving as prefect of Ying-chou [in
Anhwei] employed the famine victims there to work on dykes, so
that the workers profited from wages and the area profited from
irrigation.

In short, the social relief measures of the Sung government
highly deserve our admiration.

NOTES

徐益棠， 宋代平時的社會救濟行政， 中國文化研究彙刊
Hsü I-t'ang, "Sung-tai p'ing-shih-ti she-hui chiu-chi hsing-
cheng," <u>Bulletin of Chinese Studies</u>, V (September 1945), 33-47.

The chief sources for this article are <u>Sung hui-yao</u> 宋會要
and the treatise on "Food and Money" and biographical chapters in
the <u>Sung History</u>. In addition, <u>Wen-hsien t'ung-k'ao</u> 文獻通考 ，
<u>Hsü Wen-hsien t'ung-k'ao</u> 續文獻通考 and a few contemporary
treatises on relief work, such as Yang Chin-hsing's 楊景行
<u>Ch'ou-chi pien</u> 籌濟篇 , have also been drawn upon.

LEGEND
⊚ SOUTHERN SUNG CAPITAL
▱ LAKE T'AI
╫ CANAL
▬ ▬ SUNG BOUNDARIES
x x x BOUNDARY BETWEEN CHIN
AND SOUTHERN SUNG
· · · MODERN PROVINCIAL
BOUNDARIES

HUNG-CHOU
PAO-CHOU
T'AI-YÜAN
Yellow R.
PIEN-LIANG
(NAN-CHING, K'AI-FENG)
YING-CHOU
Hua R.
YANG-CHOU
CHINKIANG
CH'ANG-CHOU
SOOCHOW
CHIA-HSING
CHIEN-K'ANG
NING-KUO
HU-CHOU
MING-CHOU
HANGCHOW
T'AI-CHOU
CH'ENG-TU
MEI-SHAN
CH'ING-SHEN
Yangtse R.
NAN-K'ANG CHÜN
Hsiang R.
Kan R.
JAO-CHOU
WEN-CHOU
YING-CHOU
CH'ÜAN-CHOU
CHANG-CHOU
Pearl R.
CANTON
TUNG-KUAN
HUI-CHOU
CH'AO-CHOU
CH'IN-CHOU
NING-YÜEH
CH'IUNG-CHOU
Hainan Island

MILES
0   100   200

E. Z. S.

Map 4. China in the Sung period

15

PERIODIC FAIRS OF SOUTH CHINA IN THE SUNG DYNASTY

by

CH'ÜAN HAN-SHENG

1. Periodic Fairs before Sung

Trading marts had a very early beginning in China. Legend has it that the Divine Cultivator initiated the setting up of market places where people traded at mid-day. As for periodic fairs, their history can be traced back to the Tsin period [265-420], and during the T'ang dynasty they were further greatly developed.

2. Dates of Fairs

The South China term for periodic fair, hsü-shih 虛市 ["empty market"], was derived from the fact that the market place was filled only on the days when the fair met, but was empty when the fair was over; most of the time the market place was empty, as the fair met only on a limited number of days. The expression hsü-shih describes the same pattern of commerce as the North China term chi 集 ["to gather"]. They are each concerned with a different aspect of the periodic fair.

Sung hui-yao records that "in the countryside there are periodic fairs which meet only once every three days or so." The dates for the fairs varied. In his account of Hainan Island [the twelfth century writer] Chao Ju-kua records that the native Li people traded with the Chinese on every yin 寅 and yu 酉 day [that is, at alternate intervals of four and six days]. Other sources record fairs that took place once every three days, and another passage in Sung hui-yao mentions village fairs in South China that occurred once every other day.

Even when they took place the fairs were not day-long affairs, most of the business being transacted in the morning. That is why "village fairs" and "morning" were often associated together by Fan Ch'eng-ta [1126-1193], as in his poems Leaving Ku-ch'eng-shan at Dawn, Ch'ing-i River, and others. There were, however,

some fairs where people traded all day. An example was the fairs
in Ch'iung-chou (Hainan), where the Li people came to do business
until late in the day, as described by Chou Ch'ü-fei in his Ling-
wai tai-ta [1178].

What accounted for the periodic nature of the fairs and their
short business hours was the small volume of trade. For business
the fairs depended on the farmers who lived in the surrounding
areas; these farmers were few in number, and their purchasing
power was low. Furthermore, those who had goods to sell at the
fairs were also local producers, whose products were quantitatively small owing to backward methods of production. There was
therefore no need for prolonged trading periods. Consequently the
fairs took place only once every three days or so.

A certain amount of trading was of course also done at the fair
sites outside the scheduled time of the fairs. Contemporary descriptions show that there were permanent stores at these places,
such as rice shops and wine shops. However, it is safe to conclude that the volume of business on days of the fair was larger
than that on non-fair days.

3. Geographic Distribution of Fairs

The periodic fairs known as hsü-shih occurred only in South
China, as the term in use in North China was chi. They were most
numerous in the provinces of Kwangtung and Kwangsi. The Sung
History mentions abolishing the taxes on eighty-one periodic fairs
in Kwangtung in 1205. The fairs in Ch'in-chou [in Kwangtung] were
the most widely written about, while mention of Kwangsi fairs was
also made in contemporary works. Next were fairs in Kiangsi, mention of which appeared often in literary works, such as
the writings of Fan Ch'eng-ta and Hung Mai [1124-1203]. There
were periodic fairs also in Chekiang, Anhwei, and Hunan. Some
fairs in South China traded primarily with the minority peoples of
the regions, such as the Li on Hainan Island and the Miao in
Hunan.

A characteristic of the periodic fairs was that they occurred
in the villages. The reasons for this were: First, it was a more
economical form of business exchange for the rural population in
that it eliminated many trips to the cities. Secondly, there was a
need for local exchange in the countryside, as no farmer was actually self-sufficient with his own products. The appearance of
periodic village fairs, therefore, answered the needs of rural consumers and producers.

4. Commodities Exchanged at the Fairs

From a poem written by a Sung monk we learn that at the village fairs there was much bustling activity, with crowds gathering
at the village hostelry. Someone would act as a middle-man in supervising the business transactions; his judgments were accepted
by everyone. The merchandise included foodstuffs like chickens
and pigs, and handicraft products like cloth, paper, and brooms.
Other sources also mention fish, beans, pigs, and jelly-fish. The
sale of butchered pork was apparently a sizable business at some
fairs, with many persons engaging in it. Firewood, vegetables,
and tea were also sold. Contemporary writings mention tea merchants and rice and wine shops.

In sum, the following conclusions can be drawn from available
data: First, the commodities bought and sold at the periodic fairs
were chiefly goods for daily consumption, such as foodstuffs and
handicraft goods. Secondly, most of the sellers were the producers
themselves, and the business was done without merchant intermediaries. Lastly, the purchasers were predominantly ultimate
consumers, who bought the goods for their own use and not for resale.

Thus, the periodic fairs were small in scope and highly local
in nature. They took place once in several days, and when they
were over the market place would become utterly deserted.

How small in scope was the business transacted at the fairs
can be deduced from the amount of business taxes paid by them
each year. For instance, Sung hui-yao records that the amount of
taxes paid in 1077 by the twelve periodic fairs in Ying-chou,
Kwangtung, ranged between 194 strings, 794 cash and 928 strings,
76 cash. Tax records for Kwangsi fairs in the same year were
equally small. Compared with trade in the big cities of the time,
such as Pien-liang and Hangchow [i.e. the capitals of Northern
and Southern Sung respectively], where business was carried on
day and night, and where "each transaction usually involved thousands (of cash)," the trade at the periodic fairs was indeed pitifully small.

However, the existence of hostelries and inns at the fairs shows
that certain transactions were carried on there which went beyond
the limit of local exchange. The hostelries in Sung cities served
both as resting places for travelling merchants and as storage
depots for their goods. The same would be true of the ones located in the villages, since many of the fairs were also gathering
places of travelling merchants. Some fairs were said to contain
several hundred establishments, and to be thoroughfares for merchants and salesmen.

The outside merchants were breaking down the local character of the village fairs owing to their dual capacity as sellers and buyers of goods. Salt was a major item of import into the villages, as indicated by a report in Sung hui-yao of a proposed regulation for the sale of salt in periodic fairs in Hunan. Since salt was produced only in such places as along the sea coast, in southern Shensi, and in Szechwan, but was consumed universally, the volume of its traffic into the villages must have been considerable. Such things as cloth, paper, etc., mentioned in the contemporary accounts, though largely produced locally in the villages, were also partly imported from the cities, where they were manufactured by handicraft artisans. Therefore, as sellers of goods at the fairs, the outside merchants were a factor disturbing their local nature.

Again, as purchasers of village goods the outside merchants, especially itinerant traders, also disturbed the local nature of the fairs, particularly since they bought not for their own consumption but for resale elsewhere. Although no direct evidence is available to prove this point, enough can be gathered indirectly from contemporary accounts of city merchants and butchers going to buy pigs from the villages both in small amounts and on a large scale. Apparently these persons from the cities bought the foodstuffs from the fairs and then resold them in their own retail shops.

5. Fairs and the Rise of Cities and Towns

One of the origins of the towns in Europe was the fairs that were held around castles and monasteries. What was the relation, then, between the periodic fairs of the Sung dynasty and the rise of cities and towns?

A passage in a work by Hung Mai states: "Outside Ning-shan District in Ning-yüeh [in Kwangtung....] there used to be a periodic fair. The population continuously increased there, merchants and travellers gathered together, and eventually it became a town." Other records also indicate that sites of periodic fairs could gradually develop into cities and towns. This was due to the following two reasons:

(a) These fair sites were conveniently located, drawing merchants and travellers from elsewhere.

(b) The growth of local population created a greater demand for business, so that a village where fairs were held once every few days became a town where business was carried on every day.

6. Conclusion

To sum up: The periodic fairs of Sung were a pattern of commodity exchange that occurred in an economy of rural self-sufficiency. For the most part the merchandise consisted of things of daily use that were produced in the near-by villages, and the traders were largely local producers and consumers. The characteristics of such trade were its local nature and the small scope of the transactions owing to limited purchasing power.

However, the local nature of the fairs was sometimes broken by merchants from other places who both sold and bought at the fairs. Nevertheless, their importance must not be overemphasized, as fairs remained predominantly a form of local exchange. Some fairs developed into cities and towns owing to their convenient locality and the increase in the volume of business.

NOTES

全漢昇，宋代南方的虛市，歷史語言研究所集刊

Ch'üan Han-sheng, "Sung-tai nan-fang-ti hsü-shih," Bulletin of the Institute of History and Philology, IX (1947), 265-274.

This volume of the Bulletin of the Institute of History and Philology was originally to have been published in 1941 by the Commercial Press in Shanghai, but the printing was interrupted by the Pacific War. The volume was finally published in 1947.

The chief sources used in this study are Sung works. Sung hui-yao 宋會要 , though compiled in the Ch'ing period, is made up of material drawn from various Sung compilations covering the period from 1041 on.

16

PRODUCTION AND DISTRIBUTION OF RICE IN SOUTHERN SUNG

by

CH'ÜAN HAN-SHENG

1. Introduction

Rice occupies second place among the staple foods of the world's population. Its production is concentrated in the southeastern part of Asia. The geographic location of Southern Sung made rice the predominant food for most of its population, hence a product of great importance.

2. Production of Rice in Southern Sung

The foremost rice-producing area in Southern Sung was undoubtedly the Yangtse Delta, comprising modern Kiangsu and western Chekiang. This area had been the granary of China since the T'ang dynasty. From its fields large quantities of rice were sent north via the Grand Canal. By the time of Southern Sung the amount of rice produced here was further increased. The section on "Geography" in the Sung History contains passages that testify to the rich products of this region; these included fish, salt, silk, tea, and gold, in addition to rice.

The foremost rice-producing places in this region were the prefectures of Soochow, Hu-chou, Ch'ang-chou, Chia-hsing, and others, then known as Western Chekiang. Contemporary records abound in descriptions of these as places where "rice is concentrated" and "the land is the most fertile." "When Soochow and Ch'ang-chou have harvested," went one saying, "the empire will have enough food."

There were two reasons for the rich productivity of the Yangtse Delta. The first was the favorable natural environment, and the second was the large amount of human effort spent on improvement. As regards the first, the level terrain contributed to the formation of vast expanses of arable land, and Lake T'ai insured an even supply of water. It was recorded that here "each year there are two harvests of rice and eight cultures of silkworms."

As regards the second reason, the effort spent on improvements had two aspects. The first was the industriousness of the Yangtse Delta farmers. It was often recorded that the farmers here, wasting no land, put new areas under cultivation and planted vegetables, wheat, hemp, and beans in addition to rice. Furthermore, the government at the beginning of Southern Sung also employed the refugees from the north to improve and cultivate the marshy land near Soochow. An account in Sung hui-yao tells how in 1133 a member of the Ministry of Public Works proposed using refugees to reclaim large amounts of land that had become submerged in water; these people were then to be given seeds for cultivation and were to be exempted from the payment of rent for three years, after which they were to be charged a special low rent. This proposal was adopted by the government. An eye-witness account of the careful methods by which Chekiang farmers worked their land reports that as a result of the painstaking efforts the rice yield per mou might run as high as five or six tan 石 on the best land.

The second aspect of effort toward improvements was the attention paid to the selection of seed rice. During the reign of Chentsung [998-1022] in the Northern Sung dynasty twenty tan of drought-resistant rice were imported by the government from Southern Annam for seed. The poems of Fan Ch'eng-ta [1126-1193] suggest that during Southern Sung this drought-resistant Annamese rice became particularly widespread in the Yangtse Delta.

The second-largest rice-producing area in Southern Sung was up-river from the Delta, in Kiangsi Province, that is in the Kan River valley. The high level of rice production in Kiangsi can be gathered from descriptions of water control in that province and the repairing of dykes for irrigation, such as given in the Sung History and contemporary works. The rice produced here was predominantly the Annamese variety.

West of Kiangsi up the Yangtse was Hunan, that is the Hsiang River valley, the third important rice-producing area. Here the production of rice was aided by the favorable soil and by the immigration of Kiangsi farmers, who took up plots of land, cultivated them with care, and achieved in general a high level of prosperity. In Hunan the local farmers also used bamboo waterwheels for irrigation, which effectively increased the yield of rice. Consequently large amounts of rice were exported from Hunan to other parts of the country each year. In Hunan, according to a contemporary writer,

Rice is the chief product, yet families of moderate wealth have no store of grain. The reason for this is that owing to the excellent boat transportation on the network of rivers and lakes the people calculate what they need for food and seed each year and sell the rest. Big merchants collect what the small families have. Small boats accompany the large junks so that the trade can be carried on jointly. Big profits are earned in the many processes of selling.

West of Hunan was Szechwan, the fourth large rice-producing region. The combination of fertile soil and an industrious farming population had earned for this region the nickname of "Paradise on Earth." In Kao Ssu-te's contemporary account of agriculture in Szechwan the following description is given:

In the spring, when farm work is to be started, the village elders gather the younger people and admonish them: "We are beginning our farm work. Our life for a year to come depends on this time. Do not drink or gamble, nor quarrel with one another, nor indulge in frivolities, nor fight one another, but concentrate on ploughing." [....] Everyone exerts himself in sowing the fields. When weeds appear along in the fourth month, all those with adjoining land co-operate wholeheartedly in cultivating. The shifts are timed with hour-glasses, the changes being marked by the beating of drums. There are penalties for the indolent and rewards for the fast workers. In mid-summer the blazing sun is like fire and the water in the fields is boiling hot, making culti-vation doubly difficult, but the farmers also redouble their efforts.

At the same time irrigation was also highly developed in Szechwan. There are many references to various irrigation canals and resevoirs and to the repairing of dikes in the areas surround-ing Ch'eng-tu, Mei-shan, and Ch'ing-shen. The land under irri-gation in some of these districts was said to range between 72,400 and 340,000 and sometimes up to 1,000,000 mou.

As a result of the above causes Szechwan became a rich rice-producing area with "three or four harvests per year." This of course does not refer to harvests of rice alone but also to har-vests of several different crops before and after the planting of rice.

Aside from these rice-producing areas along the Yangtse River,

the Pearl River valley in South China was also a great producer
of rice. The warm climate there enabled the people to reap two
harvests a year. There was a good deal of fertile land, though,
as indicated by a passage in the section on "Food and Money" in
the Sung hui-yao, it was largely owned by great landlords. In addition to meeting the needs of local consumers, the rice produced
in this region was largely sent down the Pearl River to Canton,
to be transported thence by sea-going ships for sale elsewhere.
[The twelfth century writer] Chou Ch'ü-fei reports that, owing to
the small population of Kwangsi, the price of rice in that province
reached a low of 50 cash per peck. Wealthy merchants bought
large quantities of the cheap surplus rice and resold it in Canton
at high profits.

There were several regions in Southern Sung where rice production was deficient. In Hupei and in the Huai River area, where
the land was often ravaged by war owing to its proximity to the
Chin Empire, rice production suffered the greatest setback as a
result of the desertion of the population. The Sung hui-yao and the
Sung History in numerous passages referring to the Shao-hsing
[1131-1162] and Chia-ting [1208-1224] periods contain such statements as "The people went off, and the land in Hupei and Huai-
nan was mostly uncultivated" and "The uncultivated and waste
land could not be counted by the mou."

With regard to Hupei, the records indicate that the people
there had largely changed to crafts and trade as their occupation,
and were losing interest in agriculture. The section on "Geography" in the Sung History, for instance, observes that "agriculture was neglected" in Hupei. "Food and Money" in the Sung hui-
yao contains the passage: "In Hupei province...the farmers
have largely turned to inferior occupations [i.e., crafts and
trade]...."

Another effect of the wars on Hupei was the destruction of irrigation facilities. Ditches and dykes sank into a state of neglect,
retarding the development of agriculture. Despite the effort of the
government to resettle some of the abandoned land, the general
picture in Hupei remained one of desolation throughout the sixty-
three year period [1127-1189] of the reigns of emperors Kao-
tsung and Hsiao-tsung. Hence rice production in Hupei was very
limited.

The Huai River region, a frequent battle ground for the repeated wars between Sung and Chin, was unable to recover from
the devastations, and throughout the twelfth century official
records as well as contemporary private writings abound in descriptions of the Huai River region as deserted and ruined by the

wars. According to the Sung History, the situation remained bleak
down to the Chia-ting period in the first quarter of the thirteenth
century.

Along the seaboard in Chekiang and Fukien rice production was
also low. But here the causes were natural rather than military.
The terrain in Eastern Chekiang being primarily hilly, the prospect of famine loomed large whenever there was a lack of rainfall,
as the writings of Chu Hsi [1130-1200] and passages in Sung hui-
yao plainly indicate. The cultivated area along the Eastern
Chekiang coast also suffered periodically from wind storms and
floods, which greatly reduced the harvests. The great storms of
the eighth month in 1173 at Wen-chou, which flooded the fields,
destroyed the crops, wrought havoc among the population, and
spoiled the land with sea water that came in tidal waves, are a
case in point.

Like Eastern Chekiang, Fukien also had a hilly terrain. However, much of the hilly areas had been terraced and put under cultivation by the local farmers. Whenever available, mountain
streams were utilized for irrigation, and where there were no
rivers or streams, wells were dug. Even marginal land was
turned into rice fields. Despite such diligence, the poor soil and
high population density still resulted in food deficits for this province, so that "even in years of good harvests it still depended on
rice imported from Kwangtung, Kwangsi, and Western Chekiang."
Contemporary observers, such as Chen Te-hsiu [1178-1235],
were of the opinion that a good harvest in Fukien was equal only
to about half a harvest elsewhere, and Sung hui-yao holds that in
the event of a bad harvest Fukien would immediately experience
starvation.

In sum, the general picture of rice production in Southern Sung
was as follows:

(a) As far as climate is concerned, the country as a whole was
suited to the growing of rice. There were differences, however,
in the productivity of the various regions. As a result there were
areas where rice was produced in great abundance, and there were
also areas where the amounts produced fell short of what was
needed.

(b) There were four important rice-producing areas along the
Yangtse River, namely the Yangtse Delta, Kiangsi, Hunan, and
Szechwan. There was also a great rice-producing area in the
Pearl River valley.

(c) There were several areas along the Yangtse River and the
eastern seaboard which were characterized by deficits in the production of rice. These comprised Hupei and the Huai River region
along the Yangtse, and Eastern Chekiang and Fukien along the
seacoast.

3. Distribution of Rice in Southern Sung

The distribution of rice was closely linked to the regional production pattern. The amount produced by each area in the country
determined whether it was an exporter or an importer of rice.
The following pages will investigate the scope and actual methods
of rice distribution in the various parts of the country.

(i) The Yangtse Valley Distribution Area

Rice traffic in the Yangtse Valley generally took an eastward
direction, that is, from the Upper to the Lower Yangtse. The surplus rice from Szechwan was sent down-river and sold in Hupei.
Hunan had enough rice for export even in bad years, with the exports in good years presumably reaching considerable amounts.
Together with the rice of Kiangsi the exported amounts were sent
by boat down the Yangtse. The first gathering point along the way
was Nan-k'ang-chün in [northern] Kiangsi. According to Chu Hsi,
who was for some time the Prefect there, Nan-k'ang-chün depended on imports from up-river to meet the needs of the local
population. Much large-scale buying of rice was involved here.
In bad years Chu repeatedly urged his official colleagues to lift
the local restrictions on rice sales in other parts of the province.
At one time agents sent out by him from Nan-k'ang-chün with
50,000-odd strings of cash from the official treasury proceeded
to other localities that had good harvests that year and bought
23,522 pecks of rice for relief and military provisions.

Aside from meeting local demands, the rice imports at Nan-
k'ang-chün were also designated for redistribution and sale further down the river. There are references in the Institutes of
Sung, for instance, to encouraging the sale of rice of Hunan, Kiangsi, and other areas in Chekiang in 1164 and 1187, when the latter
province was suffering from drought. Under such circumstances
the sale of Hunan and Kiangsi rice in Chekiang was usually stimu-
lated by the temporary suspension of the rice sales tax.

The densely populated metropolises of Southern Sung, such as
Chien-k'ang [Nanking], Chinkiang [Chen-chiang, in Kiangsu], and
Hangchow, the capital city, also imported rice from Kiangsi and
Hunan. Accounts of the flow of rice into these cities are especially
numerous for times of famine. In one of his works Chu Hsi re-
counts a proposal by a colleague that the government buy enough
rice from Kiangsi and Hunan so that Hangchow, whose monthly
consumption of rice was 145,000 piculs but whose provincial reserve was never enough to cover more than two month's need,

would always have an annual reserve of some 2,000,000 piculs. Though the proposal was not adopted, the importance of imported rice from Hunan and Kiangsi is evident.

The Huai River region was another outlet for mid-Yangtse rice, since the land there was often devastated by war and hence produced insufficient rice. Sung hui-yao contains reports for the years 1128, 1175, and 1210 of illegal tax exactions on the rice merchants who were bringing their commodity to sell in the Huai region. Although during the Southern Sung dynasty the Huai River region was an occasional exporter of rice, the area was by and large a heavy importer rather than exporter.

Finally, large amounts of rice were also exported from the fertile Yangtse Delta. Their destination was primarily Hangchow, where the large urban population depended on rice imports. Yangchou in the Huai River region was another large receiver of Delta rice. In addition, considerable amounts were also shipped elsewhere by sea.

(ii) The Coastal Sea Route

The coastal trade of China underwent great development during Southern Sung, partly because Hangchow, the capital, was located on the coast, and partly because commerce was encouraged by the government as a means of augmenting the national revenue. Since sea transportation could now handle large volumes at low cost, the goods came to include not only the luxury articles of small bulk and high value characteristic of earlier periods, but also items which, like rice, occupied much space but had relatively low value.

Both the Yangtse and Pearl River deltas were seaboard areas that exported large amounts of rice. At the same time, Eastern Chekiang and Fukien, also coastal areas, were importers.

Much of the rice that was imported by Eastern Chekiang came from Western Chekiang, a region belonging geographically to the Yangtse Delta. Some of this rice was shipped by inland waters, but some was also sent via the coastal route. The coastal route was also used for rice imports from Kwangtung, Kwangsi, and Fukien. The rice from Fukien, a deficit area, probably originated in the Pearl River area but was transshipped at Fukien en route.

Rice from Western Chekiang was also exported to Fukien. It was necessary for the latter province to import from Kwangtung, Kwangsi, and Western Chekiang even in good years; in years of poor harvest the need for Chekiang rice was still more pressing.

On one occasion Chu Hsi wrote in regard to rice imports into Fukien:

> I hear that quite large amounts have arrived [in Fukien] from
> Western Chekiang, so that the market price has come down
> precipitantly. The local people are very happy about it, but
> the more far-sighted are afraid that they [the Chekiang rice
> merchants] will not come again. [.....] We should use all
> available means to encourage their coming, such as by
> slightly raising the market price and instituting government
> buying.

The Yangtse Delta also exported rice to foreign countries* via
the sea route, in ships that could carry at least one or two thous-
and hu 斛 [one hu equals five "pecks"] per trip. A petition from
officials in 1217 complained to the emperor that merchants in various districts in the Delta area were engaged in exporting rice in
large ships and selling it to the barbarians for profit, causing high
prices and food shortages at home. A proposal was adopted whereby each ship was allowed to carry only the amount of rice needed
by the ship's crew during the voyage, and no one was permitted
to export or sell rice to other countries. In the same year a report on the smuggling trade included rice as one of the items being sold to "barbarian countries." The Chin Empire was one of
the importers of Yangtse rice. Once when there was famine in
[Chin-controlled] Shantung, some Southern Sung functionaries sold
considerable amounts of rice there, exporting it from Soochow,
Hu-chou, and neighboring areas. This was condemned by some
Southern Sung officials as emptying the resources of Sung for profit
from the enemy.

Below the Yangtse Delta on the seacoast was Eastern Chekiang,
which, as mentioned above, was a regular importer of rice. Its
imports were first gathered at the ports of Ming-chou and Wen-
chou and were redistributed from there to other places. These

---

*The sources cited by the author for this section refer for the most part in gen-
eral terms to the rice trade with "foreign countries" of the North and South, and
the only specific references here cited concern places in North China then under
the control of the Chin Empire. Although the existence of political borders, trade
controls, and currency differences, etc., placed this area outside the main Sung
economic pattern of the time, the area was culturally Chinese and the economic
ties with the rest of China were not easily broken. While it is understandable how
the majority of the contemporaries might have regarded the area as foreign or
"barbarian," it is questionable for a modern author to take these accounts at their
face value instead of analysing them from a non-Sung approach.

two places are mentioned, for instance, as the assembly centers for relief grain in years of famine.

The next rice importing region down the coast was Fukien, where the poor soil and natural calamities had made it "constantly dependent on neighboring areas for provisions." Besides importing from Western Chekiang, Fukien also took rice from the Pearl River valley.

To the south of Fukien lay the Pearl River provinces of Kwangtung and Kwangsi, both great rice-producing regions. The rice from these areas was first gathered at Canton, and was then sent out via the coastal routes, either northward for sale in Fukien and Chekiang, or southward to the markets in Ch'iung-chou [Hainan]. For instance, one memorialist wrote: "I have learned that when there is a food shortage in Ch'iung-chou and [Tung-] Kuan [in Kwangtung], they depend on imports from [the Pearl River valley in] Kwangtung for relief. Fukien and Chekiang also import rice from Kwangtung. These shipments are made mostly by sea."

There are many indications that the rice produced in the Pearl River valley was sold in Fukien. Furthermore, large amounts of rice from eastern Kwangtung were also sold in nearby Fukien, the ports of Ch'ao-chou and Hui-chou in Kwangtung being used as redistribution centers. Chu Hsi once wrote regarding relief needs in the prefectural city of Chien-ning in Fukien: " When the above-mentioned rice arrives at the prefectural city from Kwangtung, then the inhabitants of the city of course will not lack food." In the writings of another contemporary is also to be found mention of the coming of "rice merchants from Ch'ao-chou and Hui-chou" to Fukien.

There are many accounts of the sale of Kwangtung and Kwangsi rice in Eastern Chekiang. These cargoes first arrived by sea at the main ports of Ming-chou, Wen-chou, and T'ai-chou, and then were redistributed thence to other places. Large amounts of rice were also imported into Hangchow from the Pearl River valley to meet the demands of its urban consumers. It is recorded for the year 1130 that 150,000 hu of rice was purchased from Kwangtung by imperial order. Another 150,000 hu was bought for Hangchow in 1135, the shipment first arriving in Fukien by sea from Kwangtung, and then being transshipped to Hangchow.

There were also occasional proposals to transport Pearl River rice to the Huai River region for relief purposes. This shows how widely the Pearl River rice had spread across the country.

In a word, coastal transportation of rice was highly developed during Southern Sung. The general pattern was the movement of

rice from the exporting areas, that is the Yangtse and Pearl River
deltas, toward the importing areas in between, that is Fukien and
Eastern Chekiang. Evidence points to the fact that large amounts
of Yangtse Delta rice were also transported along the coast for sale
in foreign countries, thus making the Delta the granary of Eastern
Asia at that time.

4. Conclusion

The above sections present a general outline of the production
and distribution of rice during Southern Sung. The following are
points of significance which merit our attention.

In the first place, this highly developed circulation of rice between the different parts of the country was of significance in respect to Chinese economic history in that it marked the growth of
an exchange economy and the decline of the economy of local self-
sufficiency. As to how the people in the rice-importing areas
found the money to pay for the imports, the answer is that they
were engaged in many kinds of non-agricultural activities, such
as industry, trade, and transportation. For instance, the people
of agriculturally backward Hupei were known for their activities
in "inferior occupations," that is as artisans or traders. The
Sung History and Sung hui-yao record that the people of the Huai
River region depended largely on tea, salt, silk weaving, trade,
and transportation for their livelihood; those of Eastern Chekiang
depended on fishing, salt, mining, and other industries, and also on sea trade; and the people of Fukien depended on the handicraft, mining, tea, and salt industries, as well as on fishing and
sea trade. Such places as Ch'üan-chou, Foochow, and Chang-
chou in Fukien were highly developed as overseas trade marts,
of which Ch'üan-chou was the most advanced during Southern
Sung.

In brief, most of the population of the rice-importing areas
were engaged in non-agricultural occupations to provide themselves with the means of paying for imported foodstuffs. On the
other hand the population of the rice-exporting areas, engaging
primarily in agricultural production, needed to purchase industrial products from the rice-importing areas. Thus during Southern
Sung there had already become strongly established an exchange
economy in which the slightest happenings in one part of the country would have repercussions in other parts. At the same time
the economy of local self-sufficiency steadily declined.

Such large-scale circulation of rice during Southern Sung naturally had considerable effects on the economic life of the people.

One of the major effects was the transfer of surplus rice from the fertile areas to famine-stricken places for relief, thus avoiding much starvation. Another effect was that, with the establishment of the economy of local specialization in Southern Sung, people in the agriculturally backward areas could devote their energies to the production of non-agricultural goods as a means of exchange for food imports, instead of wresting a bare existence from the reluctant soil, as they had to do in an economy of self-sufficiency.

Furthermore, the growth of sea transportation for rice indicates the advance of coastal transport during Southern Sung, for the large-scale shipping of rice by the sea route could take place only when the vessels were capable of handling large bulk cargoes at low cost. Hence rice became a major item of merchandise transported by sea. This meant that sea transportation was now no longer the servant of the aristocrats, bringing them luxuries, but a means of transportation supplying goods for the common people.

Finally, to compare the picture of rice circulation in Southern Sung with that of today, there were very many points of similarity with the present, including the great productive power of the Yangtse River region. There are, however, several points of difference. The first is that Southern Sung was able to export to other countries, whereas nowadays China has to import grains in large amounts from abroad. Secondly, such ports as Canton, Ch'ao-chou, and Hui-chou were rice export centers then, whereas now they are marts for importing rice from other parts of China as well as from Annam, Siam, and other countries. And lastly, Wu-hu [in Anhwei], the greatest rice mart in China today, was still undeveloped and unknown in Southern Sung.

NOTES

全漢昇, 南宋稻米的生產與運銷, 歷史語言研究所集刊
Ch'üan Han-sheng, "Nan-Sung tao-mi-ti sheng-ch'an yü yün-hsiao," Bulletin of the Institute of History and Philology, X (1938), 403-432.

Two of the author's major sources of information are the Sung History and Sung hui-yao. Besides these he has drawn on many contemporary works, including Chu Hsi, Collected Works and Additional Works; Chou Ch'ü-fei, Ling-wai tai-ta 嶺外代答 ; Yeh Shih, Shui-hsin wen-chi 水心文集 ; Chen Te-hsiu, Collected

Works; Li Tao, Hsü tzu-chih t'ung-chien ch'ang pien 續資治通
鑑長編. Also used are the poems and essays of Lu Yu, Kao Ssu-
te, Fan Ch'eng-ta, Wei Liao-weng, and others, which shows the
possibility of literary works as source material for social history.
It is to be recalled, however, that in addition to literary pieces
a good number of memorials and official correspondence are to
be found in some of the collected works. Those of Chu Hsi are a
case in point, Chu having served in various magisterial capacities
in the Sung government. A further source that deserves mention
is Li Hsin-ch'uan 李心傳 , Chien-yen i-lai hsi-nien yao-lu 建
炎以來繫年要錄, the chronology-encyclopedia covering the
reignal periods of the first emperor of Southern Sung. This work
is of the same genre as the Hsü Tzu-chih t'ung-chien ch'ang-pien,
which deals with events and institutions of Northern Sung.

17

GOVERNMENT ARTISANS OF THE YÜAN DYNASTY

by

CHÜ CH'ING-YÜAN

1. Distinction between Government Artisans, Military Artisans, and Civilian Artisans

The census status of "artisans" in the Yüan dynasty included three categories of people: First, the government artisans, who worked in government factories and were supplied by the government either with the raw material or with money for its purchase. Second, the military artisans, whose census status was placed under the army; in wartime they constituted the work battalions, and in times of peace they probably made weapons in factories. Third, the civilian artisans, who could freely carry on their own manufacturing and trade, though on occasion the government might requisition certain amounts of their products or assign tasks to them for which they would be compensated with food rations and wages. The difference between civilian artisans and government artisans was that the latter received long-term rations from the government, whereas the former received only temporary wages while on government jobs.

The distinction among the three categories of artisans was clearly set forth in the Institutes of Yüan in an entry for the year 1317 on the manufacturing of weapons. For the weapons needed by the armies in the south, the government was to provide the necessary iron for manufacture into weapons by government artisans and military artisans. In places where there were no government factories the military artisans were to have priority in the work; they were to be supplemented by civilian artisans assigned to the job by local officials. The civilian artisans were to be paid food rations and wages and could be adjudged guilty of infraction of the law for shoddy work on their part.

Sometimes the government artisans were termed "destined artisans" in contrast to the "undestined artisans," as indicated by contemporary writings.

The Institutes of Yüan also contains passages that reveal the relationship between the government and the civilian artisans. In
1292 a Mongol official reported that, as a measure against popular
uprisings, blacksmiths in Ning-kuo and Jao-chou [in modern
Anhwei and Kiangsi respectively] should be forbidden to make arms.
Another passage reveals that in 1285 requisitions were imposed on
the vinegar and wine merchants as well as on various kinds of artisans.

2. Organization of Government Artisans

While nomad conquerors of agrarian peoples usually massacred
the peasantry, they often made captives of artisans and treated
them with leniency so that the latter might work for them. This
was the policy adopted by the Mongols in their conquest of Southern
Sung. The status of artisans, therefore, became the sole means
by which the Chinese could save themselves in a period of "city-
wide massacres." A Chinese who survived in this way has left the
following account:

> During the city-wide massacre at Pao-chou [modern Pao-
> ting in Hopei], only the artisans were spared. I joined their
> group, pretending that I was an artisan, and there were many
> others who did likewise. There were some [artisans] who
> wanted to screen us as to our abilities, but they were stopped
> by one who said "Everyone who can pull a saw is an artisan.
> It is your choice whether to allow these people to live, or
> whether to leave them to their deaths." All who pretended to
> be artisans were thus enabled to survive.

Thus, the Mongol conquerors often reported that they had captured so-and-so many artisans. On occasion the government ordered that these either be assembled together and placed under official control locally, or that they be removed to the capital. Many
such cases were recorded in the Yüan History, Institutes of Yüan,
and Selected Yüan Essays. In 1279, for instance, some six hundred
mangonel-makers in the Huai River region, together with all
others who could make mangonels, whether Mongols, Moslems,
or Chinese, were rounded up and sent to the capital. Again, after
a government factory was established at Hung-chou [in Hopei],
several hundred captured weavers of silk and woolen cloth were
sent there to work under the supervision of a Mongol official.
Many writers on the Yüan social system hold that the artisans
who were captured were gathered together and administered by

the Yüan forces as slaves. Actually that was not the case. The
contemporary records refer to "restoring to them their census
status" and "paying them rations" so that the artisans could engage in their own trade, which proves that these artisans were not
slaves. As to the fact that the artisans were "captured," it seems
that the use of such a word was merely a stylistic habit of the historians which by no means indicates that these persons actually
were "captives" or "captured slaves." For example, in the account of the fall of Nan-ching [modern K'ai-feng] to Mongol forces,
it is recorded that thousands of artisans flocked to the local administrator, who had surrendered to the invading forces and been
ordered by the latter to collect local artisans. Many thus were
able to escape death. The administrator fed them with his own provisions, and took them north to T'ai-yüan [in Shansi]. It was found
that many of these did not know any crafts. The administrator let
them stay, however, and after a period they all learned to be good
artisans.

Another method of recruiting government artisans was the sifting of the various population status groups through a number of
procedures called registration, assignment, allotment, recruit-
ment, and enlistment. It is recorded that when the Lower Yangtse
and Huai River regions were first conquered, some households
were "allotted" to the artisan profession, with the government
providing paper currency as capital for their undertakings. In 1280
the authorities of the above regions were ordered to "recruit" artisans. Later, in 1282, a Mongol official reported that of the
300,000 artisan households formerly "assigned" to that status, only a small proportion knew the crafts; after the persons skilled
in the various crafts had been selected, the rest, some 190,900
households, were returned to civilian status. There are also mentions of those who "enlisted" in the artisan status, and of the reassignment of people from the military or communications statuses to the artisan status. Now there were four general status
groups during the Yüan period: military, civilian, communications, and artisan. All of the above-mentioned changes were
changes in the census status of the people and were without any
reference to slavery. The return of artisans to civilian status,
for instance, was not the same as the freeing of slaves. Evidence
points to the fact that the position of artisans was somewhat better
than that of slaves.

Three other categories of people were sometimes also recruited into government factories to learn the crafts. They were
called "split households," "returners to good status," and "former monks and priests." The Yüan History contains references

to many instances of the government's gathering these people into factories, as in 1271, when 285 members of these categories
were recruited. It is to be noted, however, that the three terms
are merely designations of census statuses. They do not mean
"brothers living apart," "slaves restored to good status," and
"monks and priests who abandoned religious life," as they have
been erroneously interpreted by the Japanese author Aritaka
Iwao in his Slavery in the Yüan Dynasty.

There were occasional instances of the government's assign-
ing civilians to pan gold, work in iron and silver works, etc., but
there does not seem to have been any systematic application of
this practice. Fugitive slaves and convicts also were often sent
to pan gold or perform other labor services; this, however, was
not the normal practice, and did not affect the composition of
"destined" artisans. Neither can we consider the fugitive slaves
as slave labor when thus employed by the government factories,
for most of them probably received employment by pretending to
be free men.

There were in addition chained convicts who were sent to work
in mines and kilns, on road and bridge construction, and on the
repairing of local temples, officials' stables, and so on. These
chain gangs were probably the "laborers" who were described by
Ibn-Batuta, and who were also taken by Aritaka Iwao to be slave
laborers. However, we can find no other instances of permanently
chained workers among ordinary artisans.

3. Status and Treatment of Government Artisans

It has been the opinion of many scholars that the Yüan government possessed some 300,000 slave laborers. These scholars,
however, have not investigated the actual treatment of the artisans
as revealed in Chinese source materials. It is the purpose of the
present section to show that in status and treatment the government artisans of Yüan were not slaves, but were closely similar
to the "corvée troops" or "military artisans" of the Sung dynasty.

To begin with, the Yüan History plainly states that artisans
wore the same kind of clothes as "the common people"; the latter were of course not slaves. Furthermore, the artisans had to
pay land tax when engaged in agriculture. The records further indicate that artisans could also possess land and had the right of
disposal. For example, twenty per cent of those who donated land
to the Academy of Tan-yang [in Kiangsu] were of artisan status.

The Yüan History and Institutes of Yüan also show that there
were law courts specially set up for artisans; these offices were

under the jurisdiction of officials in charge of artisans. There
were in addition courts of appeal to handle artisan cases, and offices that could enter litigation on behalf of artisans. Legal disputes
between artisans and civilians were adjudicated jointly by the civilian authorities and the officials in charge of artisans. Cases involving artisans also were handled by the Regional Financial Commissioner's Office after its establishment.

Government artisans were exempt from corvée, and were paid
food rations, clothing, paper currency, and salt. The Institutes
of Yüan and contemporary writings contain several passages which
show that artisans, whether working in government factories or
manufacturing at home with material provided by themselves,
were to be exempt from corvée and the silk levy. It is clear that
the chief distinction between the status of civilians and artisans
was that the latter were free from corvée. The "corvée" from
which they were so exempted probably consisted only of the "miscellaneous services," to which there are frequent references in
the Institutes of Yüan, and did not extend to service as "archers"
and "neighborhood heads." Exemption of the artisans from the latter duty, which was possible before 1303, was apparently ended
in that year by a decree stating that "the military, communications,
artisan [.....] groups shall all be held responsible for miscellaneous services." This point cannot yet be conclusively proved,
however, since not enough positive evidence is available. What is
clear is the fact that before 1303 so many people had enlisted in
the artisan status to escape from corvée and silk levies that the
government had to prohibit the recruiting of artisans by officials,
and the census registrations were sometimes rectified.

References to the artisans' rations and wages occur in many
contemporary works and official documents. The following scale
seems to have been the standard of pay: The maximum grain
allowance per month was 4 pecks and the minimum 2.5 pecks, the
average being one pint per day [i.e. 3 pecks per month]. Sometimes the artisans were also given monthly rations of half a catty
of salt, 15 catties of white flour, and 1.5 taels of silver in paper
currency, and they also received summer and winter clothes. The
rations and wages were paid on either a semi-annual or quarterly
basis. The exact amounts of monthly and quarterly pay of some
of the artisans have been recorded in the documents of the Grand
Secretariat. The Institutes of Yüan also contains the account of
official deliberations in 1304 which resulted in the payment of
rations and wages in semi-annual instalments in advance on condition that the assigned work be finished by the year's end. In
contrast to such provisions, the lot of artisans was very hard at

the beginning of the Yüan dynasty, when no regular system yet existed. There were reports of the starvation of artisans during
Chingis Khan's reign [1206-1227].

The rate of pay of temporarily employed artisans is not known.
We may reasonably assume that it could not have been lower than
that for corvée labor, which was somewhat higher than the wages
of government artisans. The Yüan History mentions daily payments of three pints of grain and one tael in paper currency. These
figures probably do not portray the general situation, however,
since the exchange rate of paper money and the quality of grain
are factors that must be taken into consideration. Actually, the
government artisans had sufficient extra-factory time for them to
engage in private work, so that their income was probably much
better than that of artisans and laborers temporarily employed by
the government.

It might be more helpful to compare the rations and wages of
the government artisans and of the military troops, the latter presumably not considered as slaves by those scholars who hold that
government artisans were slaves. Now we know that persons of
military status were especially well-treated by the Yüan authorities. At the beginning of the dynasty the military rations were indeed a little higher than those for artisans. In the 1280's, for
instance, the Newly Incorporated troops were paid a monthly sub-
sidy of 6 pecks of rice, 1 catty of salt, and 4 pecks of rice for
each member of the family. However, during the Ta-te period
[1297-1307] the military pay had been lowered to 1 pint of rice per
day, which was no higher than that of artisans. Moreover, deduc-
tion was made in military pay in short months [28 days], while the
same appears not to have been done in the case of artisans. In
years of famine, however, as indicated by a decree of 1287, the
"vegetable money" of the artisans was sometimes abolished together with that of the troops.

The rewards given to artisans consisted mostly of money and
goods; occasionally land and farming implements or oxen were included so that they might engage in agricultural work. When artisans were moved to other places by the government the latter
sometimes paid their travelling expenses. If out of extreme poverty the artisans had sold their wives or children, the government
occasionally ransomed the latter for them. Those who fell sick
on the job received special money, and those who died were accorded funeral fees. The children of artisans were entitled to receive monthly grain rations from government granaries. Moreover, artisans who were reinstated in their profession after leaving their home districts were exempt from government work for

three years. This surely shows that they were not slaves.

The artisan status of Yüan was hereditary. The Yüan History states that, "Of the children of artisans, the boys should be taught crafts and the girls sewing and embroidery. Deviations are prohibited." Sometimes the inheritance of artisanship was restricted because of the superfluity in numbers. In 1320, for instance, a decree ordered that the children of physicians, mediums, and artisans were not to inherit their respective professions; only those who already had acquired good skills should be given work in these occupations.

Since sometimes "whole families of artisans" worked in the factories, there were presumably large numbers of child artisans in government institutions. The Yüan History contains several passages that refer to "girl embroiderers," who were probably the daughters of artisans. The statements that "Embroiderers were gathered from among the common people" and "Embroiderers were allowed to marry as they pleased" indicate that they were not slaves. There is also mention of the paying of money to child artisans who were poor. It would seem, then, that even if the children were treated somewhat like slaves when young, the treatment was changed to conform with that of adults as they grew older, and so even the early tinge of slavery disappeared.

In a word, the status and treatment of artisans in the Yüan dynasty were relatively good. So far as concerns their rations, wages, clothing allotments, etc., there was even plenty of room for waste and graft by the artisans in the early phase of Mongol power owing to the lack of fixed rules. Not until the time of Yeh-lü Ch'u-ts'ai [died 1244] were regulations instituted to remedy the situation. Chances for graft still existed, however, so that rules were promulgated requiring the return of all surplus material to the government, and an office was set up in the capital to estimate the amount of material needed for work.

Aside from the above-mentioned advantages enjoyed by the artisans, their families were also favored by exemption from corvée. As a result, large numbers of people, including some who were wealthy and powerful fraudulently began to join the artisan category. Artisans so swamped the government factories that it was necessary for the authorities to examine their abilities, and return to civilian status all those "whose skill was mediocre." The Yüan History records several instances of this process of elimination, such as in 1280, 1290, and 1308. Sometimes the expelled artisans were given farming equipment so that they could join agricultural colonies, or were sent to other areas to seek their livelihood.

4. Working Procedure of Government Artisans

Most of the government artisans worked in government factories with material provided by the latter, though sometimes the government provided only the money with which the foreman or artisans purchased the material.

There were two kinds of government factories: those having division of labor, which were actually handicraft factories; and those without division of labor, which were merely collections of small producing units. The factories in the capital were extremely diversified in character, so that for any given task, such as the decoration of a portrait of the emperor or the making of a Buddhist image, inter-factory cooperation was necessary. In the provinces there also seem to have been factories with division of labor. The available data concern only the silk weaving industry; here the division of labor was generally the same as that which existed during the Sung dynasty. Satin-weaving, according to a document dated 1301, involved such processes as spinning, dyeing, and weaving in the same plant.

Officials in charge of government factories were called, in order of their ranks, Superintendent, Associate Superintendent, Deputy Superintendent, Supervisor, Inspector, Deputy Inspector, and Factory Manager in accordance with the number of artisans under their respective control. Most of the Inspectors and Factory Managers had gradually risen from the rank and file of artisans. Under them were the Foremen or Chiefs, who received higher stipends than the artisans. For example, Tung Chi, a Chief under the jurisdiction of the Grand Secretariat, was paid a monthly salary of six taels while he was a Foreman, and after his promotion to the position of Chief his salary was increased to ten taels per month and 0.5 picul of rice; the money payment was subsequently raised to fifteen taels. As a sculpture foreman Tung Chi usually had under his jurisdiction thirty-nine sculptors and sixteen seal carvers. The relationship between such persons as foremen and artisans is vividly described in the following passage from Selected Yüan Essays:

> There is a small woodworking factory in the capital with a
> few hundred artisans, who were divided by the government
> into small units, each headed by a foreman. One of the arti-
> sans quarreled with his foreman. The latter was in the wrong
> but would not admit it, whereupon the artisan refused to be
> on speaking terms with him. After some six months of this
> the other artisans, holding that a big thing ought not to be

made out of a little argument, bought meat and wine, compelled the artisan to go to the foreman's home, and there
mediated the dispute. The relations thereafter became as
happy as they had been at first.

The government artisans worked under the supervision of the
above-mentioned officials. Their failure to meet the official quotas
and time schedules was punishable by the law unless caused by illness or incapacity due to bad weather. Surplus supplies were to be
returned to the government, while waste materials were mostly
sold for cash to meet the factory's incidental expenses.

There were differences in procedure in factories of different
crafts. The bow factories, for instance, operated on a basis of
contract work, the government setting the price at so much per bow,
which varied between 1,400 and 2,000 cash. In the armor factories
each artisan was assigned a certain quota; instances are recorded
in which corrupt supervising officials dismissed some artisans,
distributed their work among the others, and pocketed the wages
due the dismissed workers. In the making of suits of leather armor,
the material was sometimes bought by the government and distributed to the factories, but in most cases it was bought by the factories themselves for the sake of convenience, as indicated by an
entry for 1303 in the Institutes of Yüan. This easily led to graft
and corruption on the part of the supervising officials. Together
with other forms of corruption, such as clandestinely dismissing
artisans and pocketing their pay, these malpractices were repeatedly prohibited by law. The corrupt practice whereby supervising officers had their artisans manufacture things for themselves or for others was also forbidden by a special decree in 1282.
The situation became such, however, that any supervisor who did
not impose his private tasks on the artisans was considered a virtuous man.

As for the artisans who were dependents of noble estates, they
worked either in factories or at home, and delivered their products to the estate administration. The government sometimes
also assigned work to these dependent artisans.

Finally, it must be made clear that artisans in government factories did not work all year long. Their annual quota of work could
be fulfilled in less that a year, leaving them with time for private
work. At the same time, however, the government could also
order them to work on emergency calls. Let us take the armor
industry as an example. Data are lacking as to the exact time
needed by Yüan artisans to fulfill their yearly quota, but from the

records of the Sung dynasty we may conclude that each artisan in
the armor factories had to work no more than 294 days out of the
year. Since the Sung armor was made of iron and the Yüan armor
of leather, the time required of the Yüan artisans was probably
still less.

Now after meeting the quota in the factory, the artisan was
likely to leave and engage in private production. Under such circumstances, when a government emergency call came, the only
way to obtain artisans was for the supervising official to recruit
them at his own discretion. This led eventually to such corrupt
practices as issuing calls at random or over-reporting the number of artisans recruited. There were proposals to institute the
system of rotation of artisans for emergency work, but it is not
known whether these proposals were adopted. Moreover, the texts
of these proposals are ambiguous, so that it is difficult to judge
today whether the system of rotation so proposed was the same
as that which existed during the Sung dynasty. In any case, it
differed from the "rotation artisans" of both T'ang and Ming, in
that the latter involved corvée duty, while the rotation proposed
in the Yüan documents concerned only wage hiring.

In sum, when we consider only the regular work quota of the
Yüan government artisans, excluding emergency work, it becomes
clear that the artisans did not need to work all year long in the
government factories, but had a good deal of free time to themselves.

5. An Estimate of the Number of Government Artisans

Owing to the lack of data it is very difficult to make a thorough
study of the number of government artisans. It is dangerous to
draw conclusions for the whole country on the basis of information
concerning one local factory, as Aritaka Iwao has done. A more
reliable method, it would seem, is to compare all the references
to factories, supervising officials, and artisans in the Yüan History and the Institutes of Yüan, and then to derive our answer on
the basis of the grade of supervising officials and the corresponding number of artisans under their control.

A tabulation of the government factories of the Yüan dynasty
reveals that there are 169 factories and supervisory offices of
which the grade of the official in charge can be ascertained. The
grades of these officers and the numbers of persons in each grade
are as follows:

Official Grade	Number of Persons
Complementary 3rd	1
Complementary 4th	1
Regular 5th	15
Complementary 5th	54
Regular 6th	14
Complementary 6th	5
Regular 7th	23
Complementary 7th	34
Regular 8th	7
Complementary 8th	10
Complementary 9th	5
	169

The grades of officials in charge of 72 factories and 5 Superintendencies are not known. There are 19 establishments of which
the number of artisans is known to have totalled 9,377.

Now let us examine the relation between the grade of the official supervisor and the number of artisans under his control. The
Institutes of Yüan gives two somewhat different sets of figures,
one for 1272 and the other for 1277, of which the second seems
to be more complete. On the basis of this second set of figures
it is possible to draw up the following table of official grades and
number of artisan households controlled by each.

Official Grade	Households
Complementary 3rd	3,000
Complementary 4th	2,000
Regular 5th	2,000
Complementary 5th	1,500
Regular 6th	750
Complementary 6th	600
Regular 7th	400
Complementary 7th	200
Regular 8th	150
Complementary 8th	100
Complementary 9th	100

For those cases where the grade is not known, the officials in
charge of Superintendencies will be counted as belonging to the
complementary 5th grade, and those in charge of factories, the
regular 7th grade. Now, multiplying the number of officials of
each grade by the number of artisan households under each grade,

we get a total of 148,050 households for those institutions for which the rank of the official in charge is known, and 36,300 households for those where this information is lacking. Adding to these the 9,377 mentioned earlier as recorded in the official accounts, we get a total of 193,727 artisan households. Assuming that about one-fourth of the artisans entered the factories with their families, and that each family averaged two men, and further assuming that one-fourth of the artisans brought with them one apprentice each, then there should be an additional 100,000 artisans in the total figure. In addition, there were other Yüan government offices which controlled factories of their own. Assuming, on the basis of information contained in the Institutes of Yüan, that these factories had a total of 100,000 artisans, then the grand total of government artisans would not be over 400,000. In terms of households this would probably amount to some 300,000 families. Because of the lack of data we are not including here the military artisans, with the exception of 10,000 mangonel-makers.

At this point the question may arise as to whether this estimate of 200,000-400,000 artisans is not too low. However, considering the fact that many artisans were "returned to civilian status," as noted above, and that the large figures appearing in some contemporary accounts involved some double counting of Southern artisans who were moved to the capital and later dispersed in various factories, it would seem that our estimate is correct. Indeed, if we remember that in the nineteen establishments where the number of artisans is definitely known the total was under 10,000, then our estimate may even be too high. On the other hand, since the government artisans did not need to work in the factories throughout the year, and since there was probably a system of rotation among the artisans, the number of persons regularly employed in the factories was probably not very large. It would seem likely that the 400,000 artisans were employed in the factories according to some scheme of rotation.

6. Conclusions

(a) The government artisans of the Yüan dynasty were definitely not slaves, although occasionally slaves and convicts worked in government factories.

(b) The government artisans had the special privilege of exemption from miscellaneous corvée duties; this was not a privilege enjoyed by persons of civilian status.

(c) The status of government artisans was comparable to that of the "corvée troops" or "military artisans" of Sung in that they worked in government factories on a wage basis.

(d) The pay of the government artisans was slightly higher than that of workers temporarily employed by the government, but was lower than that of persons of military status.

(e) Government artisans generally worked in factories on a quota system. In addition, emergency tasks were assigned to them occasionally. However, they also had enough spare time to engage in private business.

(f) There seems to have been a system of rotation among the artisans, but it was different from the systems that existed in T'ang and Ming.

(g) The artisan households of the Yüan government totalled approximately 200,000-300,000, making a working force of probably 400,000 persons. The idea that there were 300,000 slave artisans in the Yüan dynasty is entirely fallacious.

NOTES

鞠清遠, 元代係官匠戶研究, 食貨

Chü Ch'ing-yüan, "Yüan-tai hsi-kuan chiang-hu yen-chiu," Shih-huo, I, No. 9 (April 1, 1935), 367-401.

The major sources of the article are the Yüan History and the Institutes of Yüan (Yüan tien chang 元典章), supplemented by the accounts of various Yüan industries and crafts in Kuang-ts'ang hsüeh-ping ts'ung-shu 廣倉學賓叢書　and other contemporary accounts in a number of essay collections.

III

THE LAST DYNASTIES

(1368 - 1911)

18

LOCAL TAX COLLECTORS IN THE MING DYNASTY

by

LIANG FANG-CHUNG

The system of "Tax Collectors" was a notable feature in the history of the land tax in the Ming dynasty. Apart from its bearing on various questions concerning the collection of land taxes, the system also had social and political significance. A study of the system will shed considerable light on local political organization. It will also shed much light on the power of the gentry in Chinese society.

The office of Tax Collector was instituted in the autumn of 1371 by Emperor T'ai-tsu with a view to alleviating the oppression of local officials on the taxpayers. The method of appointment was as follows: First the Board of Finance was ordered to have the local authorities make a clear survey of the people's land. Then the land was demarcated into areas each of which paid an annual tax of approximately 10,000 tan 石 [of grain]. In each of these areas [the head of] the household owning the largest amount of land was then appointed Tax Collector of the area. This person had the duty of managing the collection of the taxes in his area, and seeing to their transportation to the government.

The Veritable Records of Ming quotes Emperor T'ai-tsu as remarking thus on the device: "This is to use good people to rule good people. The evils of graft and corruption will now certainly disappear."

1. Objectives in Establishing Tax Collectors

The establishment of the Tax Collectors was motivated by political considerations as well as by those of financial administration. There were four objectives, namely to eliminate graft by minor functionaries, to abolish "tax middlemen," to simplify the procedures in tax payments, and to establish good relations with the magnates. Further discussion of these four objectives is given below.

(i) Elimination of Graft by Minor Functionaries

// This point, which we mentioned above, was discussed in the emperor's Great Ordinance of 1385, the year in which local Tax Collectors were restored after having been temporarily abolished in 1382, in the following terms:

> That Tax Collectors heretofore were an inconvenience to the people was due to the fact that the officials in charge were not kind to the people, but collaborated with cunning persons to create trouble and demand payments. The people had no way of presenting their case to higher authorities. Now We are instructing all of you as Tax Collectors.

[The early Ming writer] Sung Lien gives us a more detailed description of the situation.

> When the present dynasty first acquired the empire, [the emperor] was disturbed by the officials' oppression of the common people. The high ministers then suggested that, since the [local] officials were all natives of other provinces, were ignorant of local conditions, and were surrounded by unscrupulous clerks and entrenched magnates, it was no wonder that the people were misgoverned. It would therefore be better to appoint as Collectors those magnates who were trusted by the people and to make them responsible for the land taxes of the common people and for their delivery to the government. Thereupon the magnates were appointed Tax Collectors. The major ones oversaw the collection of ten thousand piculs of tax grain, and the minor ones of several thousand piculs. Malpractices again emerged, however, and could not be stopped even with legal measures. The observation of the "rule of avoidance" for local officials was extremely strict. Since he was not a native of the territory under his jurisdiction, the local official was unfamiliar with the conditions of the locality and could be easily hoodwinked by unscrupulous clerks and cunning gentry. This was what prompted the ministers at Court to propose the appointment of magnates as local Tax Collectors.

(ii) Abolition of "Tax Middlemen"

// To be a middleman was to contract for the collection and delivery of the taxes of other households so as to reap a profit in the transactions. As early as the Southern Sung dynasty there were persons known as "tax middlemen." Court officials had commented at the accession of the [Southern Sung] emperor Li-tsung [1225-1264], for instance, that the remission of taxes benefited only the tax officials and middlemen but did not touch the common people, and suggested the instituting of reforms in the method of remission. Yet middlemen continued to flourish through Yüan to Ming. Emperor T'ai-tsu of Ming was aware of this and set up the following regulation for the punishment of offenders: "Those who act as tax middlemen shall be given sixty lashes and be made to pay up the deficits [i.e. short deliveries] at the proper granary. An additional half [of the deficit amount] shall be confiscated from the criminal's property." Exempted from confiscation, however, were the odd amounts of grain due from small households, which appended their tax payments to other households [i.e. tax middlemen] for the sake of convenience.//

The evils of middlemen were clearly described in the Great Ordinance. The common people paid their tax dues indiscriminately to the middlemen, without inquiring into the latter's property qualifications, so that when the middlemen pocketed the tax collections there would be no way of making them reimburse the government if they owned no property; for such persons the only penalty was death. The second reason for the instituting of Tax Collectors, therefore, was to eliminate losses to the government by having large, substantial landowners of the locality act as collectors of revenue.

In addition to these primarily negative reasons, there were also positive reasons for the setting up of Tax Collectors.

(iii) Expediting Tax Payments

According to the Great Ordinance, the establishment of local Tax Collectors saved the local officials the trouble of attending to the actual collection of taxes, while it also enabled the taxpayers to pay on the spot. As to the first point, there is no doubt that the officials were saved a great amount of leg work; they now merely had to receive the amounts delivered by the Tax Collectors. According to the Ming system the tax rates could not be altered except with imperial approval; theoretically, therefore, no corruption could emerge from the system of Tax Collectors. As to its effect on the common people, the system of Tax Collectors did eliminate the need for personal deliveries to the authorities. This was especially helpful to the very small householders, who previously were required to undertake lengthy trips in order to deliver their small amounts of taxes to the government, but now could pay the dues locally. But corrupt practices naturally emerged out of the practice of having the Tax Collector keep the collected amounts in trust. During the Hsüan-te reign [1426-1435], for example, many cases of tax arrears were reported from the Chiang-nan region, those of Soochow alone amounting to some 800,000 piculs. After conducting an investigation of the situation the governor concluded that it was caused by the lack of a central collecting office, and by the Tax Collectors' keeping the grain in their own homes.

(iv) Establishment of Good Relations with the Magnates

Toward wealthy households Emperor T'ai-tsu employed two contrasting policies. The first was that of exerting pressure and taking preventive measures aimed at curbing the magnates' power so as to eliminate the potential threat to the imperial family. This policy is exemplified by his moving, exiling, or killing the rich people of Soochow, a stubbornly defended city, after taking it in 1367. The second policy was that of conciliating the magnates by awarding them official ranks and positions. Thus in 1385 the emperor had the Board of Civil Service select the sons of rich families and send them to the capital for appointments to office; some 1,460 persons competed for selection.

The instituting of local Tax Collectors can be regarded as a forerunner of this policy. During the reign of T'ai-tsu it was the system for the Tax Collectors and Deputy Collectors to go to the capital in the seventh month of every year, obtain personal instructions from the emperor, receive "tally sheets" for the collection of taxes, and then return to their own areas to collect the tax grain. Those who delivered the taxes to the capital on schedule were likely to be given audiences, and often were promoted to higher positions. Contemporary writings reveal that Tax Collectors often filled official positions in early Ming.

2. Duties and Special Rights of Tax Collectors

The responsibilities of the Tax Collectors consisted of three things: collecting, receiving, and delivering the taxes. The first detailed account of the organization of this system is to be found in a decree dated the ninth month of 1373, which stated that "Under each of the Tax Collectors previously established in such prefectures as Sung-chiang and Soochow [both in Kiangsi] there should be placed an Accountant, twenty Measurers, and one thousand transportation laborers, so that the transportation and delivery [of tax grain] every year will not be a burden to the people."

//As delineated in the <u>Supplement to the Great Ordinance</u> of 1386,
the procedure followed by Tax Collectors in carrying out their
duties was as follows. When collection was being made the small
taxpayers were to elect a few representatives from units comprising three, five, or up to a hundred households; these representatives, with funds and in boats or carts provided by the taxpayers'
families, were to accompany the Tax Collector to the proper government granary and deliver the taxes. A regulation of 1393 ordered the local authorities in areas that had Tax Collectors to appoint an official to lead all the Tax Collectors in a delegation to
the capital to be received by the emperor [. . . .] and to be given
tally sheets for the collection of taxes in their home areas.

//When the taxes had been collected the tax-payers, supervised
by the Tithing Head, who was supervised by the Neighborhood
Head, who in turn was supervised by the Tax Collector, loaded
the grain for transportation. After checking the load the Tax Collector then led the Neighborhood Heads and transportation laborers
in delivering the grain. The amount classified "transfer" was
transported to a specified garrison office and delivered according
to a bill of lading. The amount classified "retain" was sent to be
stored in various granaries in the locality. The amount classified "transport," which was sometimes commuted to payment in
kind, was sent to various granaries. It was imperative that the
deliveries be made according to schedule. At the end of the process the Tax Collector filled in the amount delivered in the tally
sheet and affixed his seal. The document was then personally presented [to the authorities] and was subsequently cancelled at the
Board of Finance, which obtained the tally sheet from the Bureau
of Finance of the Treasury, kept it on file, and used it as a basis
for checking. In case short payments were discovered [the Tax
Collectors] would be called for an accounting.//

Two noteworthy points emerge from the above. First, the procedure indicates careful planning and strict control of the whole
process. Second, the Tax Collector was responsible for all three
steps, the collection, receiving, and delivery of taxes, which
made him a more important personage during this early period
than his counterpart of a later date.

As to the obtaining of tally sheets, when the capital was
moved to Péking in 1421 the Tax Collectors were still ordered to
obtain them from the Board of Finance at Nanking. In 1522, however, the Board of Finance was ordered to send the tally sheets
to the local authorities, so that the Tax Collectors would not need
to undertake the long journeys but instead could get the sheets

from the local government. In brief, after the removal of the capital to Peking the Tax Collectors no longer had the opportunity for
audiences with the emperor, and hence became increasingly remote from the Court.

From source materials of a later period it appears that different persons were assigned to the specific tasks of collection
and delivery. This is indicated by a descriptive prefix which was
added to the title of Tax Collector for the sake of distinction. The
Wan-li [1573-1619] edition of the Gazetteer of Shanghai states:

> It has been the established system of the present dynasty....
> to have a Tax Collector supervise the tax matters of an area
> ....Within this [Shanghai] district...there used to be 92
> areas, of which 56 remain; in each area there is a post of
> the Tax Collector, which is filled by persons serving three
> purposes respectively: The one in charge of the collection
> of the grain is called the Expediter, recently re-named the
> General Expediter; the one in charge of receiving the grain
> is called the Receiver; and the one in charge of the sending
> of the grain is called the Delivery Chief. They rotate once
> every five years. In the poorer areas each of these posts is
> filled jointly by several persons....

According to some local gazetteers, in addition to these three posts
there were also officers known as "Southern Transporter" and
"Northern Transporter" to oversee the delivery of grain to the
northern and southern capitals. The Ch'ung-chen [1628-1644] edition of the Gazetteer of Sung-chiang, for example, contains such
titles as "Expediter Tax Collector," "Receiver Tax Collector,"
"Southern Transporter," "Northern Transporter," and so on. The
truth is that the duties of Tax Collectors varied from time to time,
but that in the long run the functions continuously increased, so
that there was a rather widespread tendency toward division of
labor.

In addition to the above three functions, Tax Collectors were
also ordered by decrees promulgated in 1385 and 1386 to fulfil the
following four tasks in their own areas: (1) In their leisure time
they were to gather the people in their neighborhood, exhort them
to engage in agriculture, and explain to them the purposes of the
religious altars set up by the prefectural and district authorities.
(2) They were to persuade the rich householders who had evaded
tax payments to forsake their improper ways and meet the tax
and corvée obligations in the same way as did the common people.
(3) They were to report on the areas stricken by famine, the

amount of land involved, and the amount of taxes that should be remitted. (4) They were personally to report willful tax evaders.

Here we must pause to point out the self-contradictory nature
of the second task, that of reporting on rich households, which,
according to an entry in the Great Ordinance, "own hundreds,
thousands, or tens of thousands of mou of land [....] but often form
a relationship with the officials and [so] do not fulfil their obligations [to the government...]" The Tax Collectors were exhorted
to persuade such persons to behave properly and stop encroaching
on the common people. But were not the Tax Collectors themselves recruited from the rich families? Such an order was like
"asking a tiger about obtaining his skin."

In some localities the Tax Collectors were empowered to de-
cide legal disputes. In 1446, in answer to a complaint from the
Governor of Hukuang [Hunan and Hupei], Tax Collectors were forbidden to engage in such activities, in order to stop their oppression and corruption. Later information shows, however, that the
restrictions were not effective.

During the earlier days of their office Tax Collectors enjoyed
the special privilege of redeeming themselves from penalties with
money. According to the Veritable Records of Ming, Emperor
T'ai-tsu ordered in 1375 that Tax Collectors sentenced to death
or exile were merely to be beaten instead and retained as Collectors. A suggestion by the Censorate that they be allowed to buy
off punishment with money was approved. This was probably not
a widespread practice, however, as there are many records of
Tax Collectors who were sentenced to death during the early and
middle part of the Hung-wu period [1368-1399]; their sentences
were re-examined and reduced only after appeal by members of
their families, and sometimes only after hair-raising experiences.
Punishment for the offense of incomplete payment by Tax Collectors
sometimes continued through two generations, so that, with money
all gone and without hope of release, the son of a guilty Tax Collector could be found languishing in jail for the crime of his father.

Furthermore, the job of being Tax Collector was transferable
[from the appointed person] to other adult men of the family. Local
records show there were many cases in which a son filled the position for his father, or a younger brother for his elder. This
shows that the duty of Tax Collector was a household and not a
personal obligation; in this respect it differed from the corvée
duties of the common people.

In addition to the annual quotas of rice tribute, the five prefectures of Soochow, Sung-chiang, Ch'ang-chou [in Kiangsu], Chia-
hsing, and Hu-chou [both in Chekiang] also had to send over 174,000

tan of white glutinous rice (including over 8,000 tan commuted to payment in money) to the Treasury, and over 40,000 tan of coarse rice (including some 8,800 tan commuted to payment in money) to the various government bureaus every year. The transportation devolved upon the people and was known as White Grain Boats. The persons in charge of the matter were also called Tax Collectors. The burden of these Collectors of the White Grain was extremely heavy. At the accession of Emperor Shih-tsung [1522-1546] it was reported that for the transportation of one tan of White Grain to the Treasury the cost to the Collector was some four or five tan. It had become so unpopular that at the assignment of this position the rich would "dress themselves in rags, pretend to be poor people, and tearfully beg to be excused from the duty." As the White Grain Collectors existed only in five prefectures, however, we shall not discuss them in detail.

3. Evolution of the System

(i) The Number of Tax Collectors

When the system was first instituted in 1371 there was one Collector to every "area." In 1377 a Deputy Collector was added to each area that paid over 10,000 tan of tax grain, and in 1397 the total personnel was increased to three in each area. The wealthy of the area served as Tax Collectors and Deputy Collectors by rotation. In 1463 those areas paying less than 10,000 tan of grain were ordered to have only one Collector, a move caused by the sub-quota payments. On the whole, however, the number of Collectors tended to increase with the passage of time. The trend was particularly obvious after the Cheng-te reign [1436-1449], when the practices of "joint undertaking" and "joint-names" became prevalent. A decree of the 1520's noted that "in recent years there are over ten Collectors to an area." The Gazetteer of Hai-yen [in Chekiang] relates:

> In the early days of the Hung-wu period it was the practice, in each area paying 10,000 tan of grain in the prefectures and districts, to set up one Tax Collector to take charge of collecting and delivering the taxes. Later a Deputy Collector was added, making two persons in each area.... At that time there were only 134 collectors in the entire province of Chekiang [....] Then, because the people were poor and could not qualify for the posts, the number was increased to three or four persons per area. During the reign of Cheng-te

the "joint names" method emerged. In the Chia-ching reign
[1522-1566] the normal number of collectors in the five
districts [around Hai-yen] was forty-two persons, among
whom the work was usually divided [. . . .] Compared with
early Ming the number of Collectors now was several times
that of the early period.

The Wan-li edition of the Gazetteer of Shang-yüan District [in
Kiangsu] states that in each of the seven areas within the district
there were "one General Tax Collector, five Deputy Collectors,
and a minor collector to each neighborhood." That adds up to at
least seven collectors to an area.

(ii) The Tax Collector's Term of Office

This was closely related to the question of the number of personnel. When the system was first set up in the early part of the
Hung-wu period, the collectors probably were appointed on a permanent basis. As mentioned above, the rotation scheme was introduced in 1397, when the personnel was increased to three or four
persons per area. In the Hsüan-te period the permanent appointment was revived. The latter, however, proved to be a source of
oppression for the people. The evil effects of the permanently appointed Tax Collectors were described in a petition dated 1430
submitted by the elders in the districts of Lu-ling and Chi-shui
in Kiangsi. The abuses included arbitrary levy by the Collectors
of cotton cloth from Tithing Heads, or extra-quota levies of grain,
or arbitrary assessments of money on the tax-payers on the pre-
text of meeting government expenses. On the strength of their
permanent positions some Collectors even unjustly seized irrigation ponds and dykes, obstructed irrigation, and caused distress
among the people.

There were two reasons for the change from permanent appointment to rotation. One was to combat the tyranny, such as described
above, of permanent local collectors, and the other was to recruit
enough personnel. As time passed and tax matters became increasingly complex, the government's demands on the Tax Collectors also increased, so that many rich persons who had served
as Collectors became bankrupt, or fled the district. The authorities then began to recruit for the post from among the lower-up-
per or middle brackets of wealth. Finding that those of moderate
means were unable to bear this responsibility for prolonged periods, the government then resorted to the rotation system. This
latter evolved into the "joint undertaking" method, which arose

out of the fact that, because persons of medium wealth also had
fled the areas, the government was compelled to recruit from
among the families of small means. As these persons were unable
to bear the responsibilities singly, a method was devised whereby three, four, or even a dozen families would be in charge of the
Collector's post together; this was known in the districts of Hai-
ning, Yung-k'ang [both in Chekiang], and Chiang-yin [in Kiangsu]
as the "joint names" method. The burden created by the collectorship on the people was so oppressive that it became the subject
of ditties composed during the Chia-ching period [1522-1566].

At Wu district in Soochow Prefecture the "joint undertaking"
method was carried out as follows: The tax dues of an area were
divided into ten portions, of which a certain percentage was assigned to each individual Tax Collector as his quota. A Chief Collector (i.e. wealthy household), for example, would be responsible for the collection of 10, 20, or up to 50 per cent of the total,
while a Small Collector would be responsible for something like
7 or 8 per cent. At Ch'ü-chou Prefecture in Chekiang there were
thirty collectors to a district; among these the wealthy and large
households were assigned their portions outright, while the poorer
families participated through the "joint undertaking" method. In
sum, the direction of evolution was toward greater numbers of
Tax Collectors and shorter periods of service.

At first, when the Collectorship constituted a permanent post,
it could be a highly profitable position for the incumbent. With the
introduction of the rotation system the lucrativeness of the position
diminished, and after the instituting of the joint undertaking
method it became an unprofitable and burdensome post, so that
the people's only thought was the avoidance of the duty. The
Gazetteer of Wu District [Soochow] contains an account of the im-
positions on those who acted as Tax Collectors after the introduction of rotation of persons of medium wealth and the decline of
Tax Collectors as an effective system of taxation. Such manifesta-
tions of decline and distress were probably not confined to Soochow
alone, but must have been a general trend in places where Tax
Collectors were installed.

(iii) Relation between Tax Collectors and Neighborhood Heads

There was a close relationship between the two, and a tendency
for the functions of the former to be performed by the latter.

According to Ming documents, the system of Tithings and Neighborhoods was established in 1381. It operated as follows: 110 adjacent households constituted a Neighborhood. The ten largest and

wealthiest of these families were chosen to be the Neighborhood
Heads, and the remaining 100 families were then divided into ten
Tithings, each of which was headed by a Tithing Head. Each year
one Neighborhood Head and the head of one Tithing led the members of that Tithing to render labor services and pay taxes. These
duties were taken up by the next Tithing in the following year. In
this operation of the ten-year rotation system each Tithing thus
came up for its turn of service and taxation once in a decade. The
Neighborhood Heads were in charge of labor service and taxes,
the government courier service, and so forth.

The Tax Collectors and Neighborhood Heads were similar in
that they were both responsible for tax payments within their own
territories, and that they were both chosen from among the well-
to-do households. They differed, however, in two other aspects.
One was that the work of Neighborhood Heads belonged to the category of Regular Corvée, while that of Tax Collectors belonged to
Miscellaneous Corvée. Further, the collection of tax grain was
the major--at first it was the only--task of a Tax Collector, but it
constituted only one of the many functions of the Neighborhood
Head. Again, in terms of the scope of jurisdiction, the Tax Collector was supervisor of an "area," a larger territorial unit than
the Neighborhood, which was the responsibility of the Neighborhood Head. At the same time, the latter was in charge of labor
services as well as tax payments, so that from his viewpoint the
scope of his jurisdiction can be regarded as more extensive than
the Tax Collector's. Moreover, the Neighborhood Head had a fixed
term of duty, which was one out of every ten years, while the Tax
Collector's term of office was indefinite. Finally, the Tax Collector, supervising a wider area than did the Neighborhood Head,
did not have to be resident of each place under his control; therefore the post could be shifted and reassigned. The Neighborhood
Head, on the other hand, had to be a resident of the place in his
charge; therefore the personnel could not be easily changed.

The most notable point, however, is the inter-relation between
these two groups. The following are some examples to show that
through the years the Neighborhood Head tended to assume the
functions of the Tax Collector:

//In the fourth month of 1382 Tax Collectors were abolished.
The persons [in charge] of Neighborhoods and Tithings were ordered to see to the collection of the tax grain in accordance with
the Yellow [Census] Books.

//In 1386 the Tax Collectors of Ch'ang-shu District [in Kiangsu]
were abolished. The Neighborhood Heads were placed in charge
of tax collection.

//In 1454 the Tax Collectors in the various districts in Hukuang were abolished; the collection of taxes was placed in charge of the Neighborhood Heads. [....]

//In 1553 Chao Chou, Magistrate of Jen-ho District [under Hangchow, Chekiang], replaced Tax Collectors in that district with Neighborhood Heads. [....]

//In 1583 Chu T'ing-i, Magistrate of Chia-ting [in Kiangsu], introduced the method of having Neighborhood Heads serve as Tax Collectors by annual rotation.//

The above are cases wherein Neighborhood Heads acted as Tax Collectors. In other cases the two posts were merged into one, and became known as "Collector-Neighborhood Head." In still other cases the two functions were performed by the same person in different years. Such was the case in the system that prevailed in Chinkiang [Chen-chiang, in Kiangsu], where a person on finishing his duties as Neighborhood Head would serve in the succeeding year as the Tax Collector [of the Neighborhood]; the post of the supra-neighborhood Tax Collector was never created here. The same procedure was followed before the introduction of the single-whip taxation in 1575 in Ch'ang-shan District, Ch'ü-chou Prefecture, Chekiang, as indicated by a passage in the local gazetteer.

Three causes had led to the substitution of Tax Collectors by Neighborhood Heads: (a) The size of the Tax Collectors' area and the complexity of procedures involved were more than the Collector could bear. The Neighborhood Head, on the other hand, had only a limited area to look after, and was under lighter financial burdens. (b) Sometimes the Tax Collector was not a native of the area under his jurisdiction; this made it difficult for him to discharge his duties. The Neighborhood Head, however, was a resident of his Neighborhood, and in addition was in charge of the other families therein, so that it was easier for him to make the tax collections. (c) With the tax grain paid to the Neighborhood Head, administrative costs were reduced. The following examples illustrate the above points:

A passage on official corruption in the third edition of the Great Ordinance (1386) explains the abolition of Tax Collectors of Ch'ang-shu District [in Kiangsu] as follows:

Originally Tax Collectors were appointed from among the great households to take charge of the Summer and Autumn taxes paid by the village people in their own districts. Then the officials, seeing that the laws were regular and pure and that their opportunities for corruption were slim, initiated

a scheme for the confusion of the system. The scheme worked
as follows: The Tax Collectors were forbidden to take charge
of tax collection in the villages of their own districts, but
were transferred to places 70, 80, or 100 li away to serve
as Collectors. [The officials] have sought by all means to
confuse the accounts to such an extent that they would be enabled to engage in malpractices. In view of this trouble and
injury to the common people, We hereby abolish the thirty-
odd Tax Collectors who had previously been instituted. . . .
The Collection [of taxes] shall now be placed in charge of the
600-odd Neighborhood Heads.

Thus, the abolition of Tax Collectors in Ch'ang-shu was attributed to official corruption. There was an intrinsic difficulty
in the very system of the Tax Collectors, however, in that the
appointment was based entirely on property qualifications, so that
an absentee landowner could be appointed to the Tax Collectorship
of an area to which he was a total stranger. This in itself tended
to make the operation of the system difficult. The difficulty was
plainly pointed out by Magistrate Chao Chou of Jen-ho District
when he enumerated the reasons for the employment of Neighborhood Heads in place of Collectors for the collection of tax grain.
Under the previous system not only did the rich persons try to
avoid taking on the duties of the Collectors, he declared, but once
the appointments were made the Collectors were plagued with the
difficult task of tracking down unknown taxpayers who lived far
apart. The Collectors nevertheless were charged with delivering
the tax quotas, and often had to pay the amount out of their own
pockets. Now the Neighborhood Head lived right in his precinct,
the territorial unit was smaller and easier to manage, the families and Tithing Heads were under his control, and there were
fewer opportunities for arrears to develop. The Neighborhood
Heads should therefore serve as collectors on an annual rotation
basis, a plan, Chao held, that had already worked satisfactorily.
Further descriptions of the undesirability of the system of Tax
Collectors are to be found in the memorial of Liu Kuang-chi, Governor of Kiangsi, when he urged the adoption of the single-whip
system of taxation in 1568. After relating the heavy burden of
Tax Collectorship on the local population, he concluded that each
Neighborhood should be allowed to pay its own taxes under the supervision of its Head. In the making of payments to the authorities,
grain was to be received by officials at the granary, and money
was to be received by officials at the treasury. By this plan Tax
Collectorships would be eliminated from the scene.

With the spread of the single-whip system during the Lung-
ch'ing and Wan-li periods [1567-1619] there occurred certain
changes in the Tax Collector system. First, the functions of Tax
Collectors were gradually assumed by the Neighborhood Heads.
Second, with the growth of commutation into money payment under
the single-whip system and delivery by government personnel,
the responsibilities of the Tax Collectors became relatively fewer.
This development is observable in a number of districts over a
wide area, as indicated by accounts in the gazetteers of P'ing-hu
and K'uai-chi [both in Chekiang] and of the districts in Ch'ang-
chou Prefecture [in Kiangsu].

4. Some Problems of Organization

(i) Grain Quota per Tax Collector

// Was there one Tax Collector for every 10,000 tan of tax grain?
According to the Veritable Records of Ming, the Institutes of Ming,
and other sources, the decree of the ninth month of 1371 had
plainly stated that "Tax Collectors are to be established at the
rate of 10,000 tan of tax grain." This is rather questionable and
is conducive to misinterpretations, for the rate of one Collector
for 10,000 tan was actually the theoretical scale, and the facts generally proved to be otherwise. Thus in the twelfth month of the
fourth year of Hung-wu [January-February, 1372], only three
months after the promulgation of the decree establishing the Tax
Collectors, a memorial from the Board of Finance was approved
which mentioned that in Chekiang Province an annual tax of
933,268 tan was levied and 134 Tax Collectors were set up. This
shows that there was a Tax Collector to less than 10,000 tan of
grain. Again, the third edition of the Great Ordinance of 1386
states that "The Autumn tax of Ch'ang-shu District amounts to
over 400,000 tan and is handled by 30-odd Tax Collectors." Here
then each collector was responsible for more than 10,000 tan.
In sum, the amount of 10,000 tan was used merely as the general
standard even at the beginning of the system of Tax Collectors,
the actual situation being that each person could be in charge of
an area which paid either more or less than 10,000 tan. Furthermore, only the regular Tax Collectors' quotas are considered
here. That of the Deputy Collectors, who were set up in 1377 and
1397, is not included. //
Another aspect of this problem was the unequal distribution of
tax grain quotas in different areas. This is evident from material
presented in the preceding section. Here we shall cite one more

piece of evidence. The Wan-li edition of the <u>Gazetteer of Chi-ch'i</u>
<u>District</u> [in Anhwei] contains the following account:

> The towns and countryside [of the district] are divided into
> seven areas. Previously one Collector and two Deputy Col-
> lectors were assigned to each area regardless of the amount
> of tax grain due from the area, so that the weight [of the
> Collector's burden] varied. (Between 1562 and 1565) Gover-
> nor Chou Ju-tou suggested assigning the post as a part of
> equalized corvée, but failed to get approval. [Then] Ho Tung-
> hsü, the prefect, notified [the authorities of] this district of
> a plan whereby the Tax Collectorship was to be assigned on
> the basis of the amount of tax grain instead of the number of
> households, so that the arrangement could be more flexible.
> If an area was short on grain, it could be aided by neighbor-
> ing households possessing more grain.

Apparently previous to Ho Tung-hsü's reform the area under a Tax
Collector was defined in terms of the Tithings and Neighborhoods
in it, which resulted in unequal burdens for the Collectors. Ho
changed the basis of definition to the amount to be collected, and
introduced a more flexible method.

(ii) Criteria for the Appointment of Tax Collectors

The only criterion used at the initiation of this system was the
amount of taxes paid by the individual. It would seem that when the
system was restored in 1385 the number of able-bodied men in a
household also had become a factor. Generally speaking, the criterion for appointment as Tax Collector was the amount of property,
but owing to various local factors--such as the overall lack of
wealthy households in a region, or evasion of the duty by the rich
--not all who became Tax Collectors were wealthy persons.
Records of the fifteenth and sixteenth centuries show that in
many districts the population as a rule was of the "common people"
category, and that when such persons were assigned to the post
of Tax Collector they were "unable to control the masses." As a
result different methods were adopted to cope with the situation.
In some places, such as Ch'ang-chou, wealthy persons from
other localities were assigned to fill the position. In other cases,
such as reported in 1540 from Chia-hsing District, the authorities
allotted certain amounts of land to the Tax Collector on duty so as
to help him meet his obligations.
Avoidance of the post by the wealthy led to the burden of Tax

Collectorships falling on other than the rich households. In 1597 the Magistrate of I-hsing District [Kiangsu] maintained that of the approximately 11,000 ch'ing of land in that district, 30 per cent belonged to absentee owners who were not registered with the local authorities and 10 per cent belonged to famous old families which enjoyed special privileges, so that the common people, who owned about 50 per cent of the land, had therefore both to shoulder the taxes for the entire district and to meet the "obligation of the wealthy" [i.e. serve as Tax Collectors]. Such a situation, he felt, could hardly be considered equitable.

On the other hand, every year the rich households were often subjected to blackmail by unscrupulous officials in charge of assignments. These officials went the rounds of the wealthy families with threats to announce them as the next Tax Collector unless bought off with bribes. When this was done the family whose turn it properly was to serve as Tax Collector would be announced.

The evidence cited above shows that the criterion for appointment to a Tax Collector's post initially comprised the individual's tax assessment. Later it was extended to include all his property. After the introduction of the single-whip system the qualification again tended to include only the tax assessment. The Gazetteer of K'uai-chi reveals, however, that those who belonged to the census category of "Paupers"* were barred from the posts of Tax Collector and Neighborhood Head and from receiving literary education, even if they were property owners. This was probably a phenomenon not unique to K'uai-chi.

(iii) Distribution of Tax Collectors

Were Tax Collectors established over the entire country? The answer is no. They were not instituted in Shantung and Szechuan, and the term Tax Collector is absent also from available historical material dealing with the provinces of Fukien, Kwangtung, Kwangsi, Yunnan, and Kweichow. In Shantung, Shensi, and Honan there prevailed a kind of corvée known as "Great Households" which resembled the position of the Tax Collectors, but was actually different in that it did not involve the definition of specific territorial units.

The date of the Tax Collectors' establishment in various places

---

*A socially inferior group which originated in the Sung dynasty, either from convicts or, according to another source, from followers of a general who had surrendered to the Jurchen invaders. The term kai-hu 丐戶 "Paupers," which was adopted at the time of the first Ming emperor as the designation of the census category of these people, refers to a group delimited by social, not financial criteria.

can be gathered from the Veritable Records of Ming and local
sources between 1371 and 1386. The system began with the appointment of 134 Tax Collectors in Chekiang, and was then extended to
prefectures in Kiangsu, Kiangsi, Hupei, and Anhwei. In the course
of development Deputy Collectors were added to the roster. It is
plain that the Collectors were concentrated in the southeastern
part of the country, and that the number fluctuated from time to
time according to the economic abilities of the locality. The total
number of chief Collectors in each district in Chia-hsing Prefecture during the Chia-ching period, for instance, was only 34. In
Hua-t'ing District [in Chekiang] during the Wan-li reign, on the
other hand, there were 117 Tax Collectors.

As to the ratio between Tax Collectors and Neighborhood Heads,
the Gazetteer of An-ch'ing Prefecture [Anhwei] shows the following figures for the six districts under its jurisdiction:

District	(A) Neighborhood Heads	(B) Tax Collectors	(C) Ratio between A and B
Huai-ning	42	7	6
T'ung-ch'eng	52	9	5.7
Ch'ien-shan	51	7	7.2
T'ai-hu	60	10	6
Su-sung	43	8	5.3
Wang-chiang	17	-	-

Tax Collectors were not established in Wang-chiang District, which
shows that even in the same prefecture the system was not universally applied.

The above figures indicate that the ratio between Tax Collectors
and Neighborhood Heads was not fixed and that the area under the
control of individual Tax Collectors also varied. Assuming that
the tax quota of each Tax Collector's area in a district was more
or less equal, then column B indicates in general the relative
amounts of taxes paid by the districts--that is, the more Tax Collectors, the greater the amount of taxes assessed; and column C
indicates the relative tax assessment of each Neighborhood--that
is, the more Neighborhoods controlled by a single Tax Collector,
the smaller the assessment of each Neighborhood. Thus column
B indicates that on the basis of amount of taxes paid the districts
are to be ranked, in descending order, as follows: T'ai-hu, T'ung-
ch'eng, Su-sung, Ch'ien-shan, and Huai-ning. Column C indicates,
however, that on the basis of the quota for each neighborhood the
districts are to be ranked, in ascending order, as follows: Ch'ien-
shan, Huai-ning and T'ai-hu, T'ung-ch'eng, and Su-sung.

The distribution of Tax Collectors in the eight districts in Chin-hua Prefecture, Chekiang, where there were [statutorily] one Tax Collector and two Deputy Collectors to each area, was as follows:

District	Collector's Areas	Collectors
Chin-hua	22	66
Lan-hsi	20	54
Tung-yang	18	30
I-wu	10	30
Yung-k'ang	10	21
Wu-i	7	21
P'u-chiang	6	18
T'ang-hsi	12	36

The system of Tax Collectors seems to have spread to Japan. It also was continued in China down to the Yung-cheng period [1723-1735] in the Ch'ing dynasty, when complaints against the Collectors' burdens were still being voiced.

5. Rise and Decline of Tax Collectors

The golden age of the Tax Collectors occurred in the reign of Emperor T'ai-tsu of Ming, when numerous such persons were elevated to high official position after their audience with the emperor in the course of delivering their charges to the capital. Historical records abound in accounts of such rises, such as, for example, that of Yen Chen, who was appointed a Secretary of the Board of Civil Service in 1394. Other records relate the meritorious conduct of Tax Collectors whose suggestions were adopted by the government. These were the better elements among the Tax Collectors.

On the other hand, there were many rapacious characters among them. In the Hung-wu period, for instance, three Tax Collectors in Chia-ting District invented eighteen categories of tax dues with which to exact payments from the taxpayers. Other methods of corruption included the exaction of additional amounts on grain payment; the compulsory forfeiture of the taxpayer's house, clothing, livestock, and farming implements in payment of assessments; the false reporting of famines in order to obtain government remission of taxes; the retention of tax payments in the Collector's own coffers and deliberate delaying in remittance to the authorities; and so forth. Instances of such malpractices were numerous, and continued throughout the Ming dynasty.

The decline of the Tax Collector's station began with the removal of the capital to Peking [in 1421]. By the time of the Cheng-te
and Chia-ching reigns the material losses suffered by Tax Collectors had become a serious problem. The losses were the outcome of the excessive tax assessments, the making up of other
people's deficits, and the heavy extra-legal exactions of the government. The last included both the extortionate demands of "cunning fellows" at the point of delivery, and such incidents as the
following, reported by the Ming writer Huang-fu Lu:

> Emperor Hsüan-tsung [1462-1435] was fond of cricketfights,
> and sent emissaries to procure the insects in Chiang-nan,
> whereupon their price shot up to the sum of dozens of taels
> of silver apiece. A Tax Collector of [the market town of]
> Feng-ch'iao [in Chu-chi District, Chekiang], who had been
> ordered by the district authorities to obtain crickets, found
> a superb one for which he paid with his own good riding
> horse. His wife and concubine thought it must be an extra-
> ordinary insect to warrant its exchange for a riding horse.
> While they were stealing a look at it the insect jumped away.
> The Tax Collector's wife, fearful of the consequences,
> hanged herself, whereupon her husband, driven by grief
> over his wife and fear of the law, also committed suicide.

Thus two lives were lost on account of one cricket.

Some Tax Collectors became rebels under the unbearable oppression. Thus Huang Hao, who became a Tax Collector in Yung-
hsin District, Kiangsi, in 1511, was so pressed by the government when unable to make full delivery that he and others similarly situated turned outlaw. The government was hard put to suppress his group. The official Ming History does not record this
particular episode, but judging from its references to many serious uprisings between 1509 and 1513 in Kiangsi and other provinces, it would seem that Huang Hao's rebellion had constituted
one wave in this tidal onrush.

The plight of the Tax Collectors is amply testified in contemporary writings. A bit of doggerel entitled "Ridicule of the Rich,"
composed by Sang Min-i of Ch'ang-shu, went as follows:

> Gather vast landholdings while you may
> For Collecting and Delivering are due your way,
> And the day will come, in three or four years,
> When your pleas for buyers will fall on deaf ears.

A later commentary on these lines explains that many property owners, ruined by their heavy obligations as Tax Collectors, were eager to sell their lands, but found it difficult to get buyers even at depressed prices. Such a state of affairs certainly constituted a serious problem.

In addition, officials occasionally appointed persons to the post of Tax Collector for purposes of personal vengeance. Thus there was one gentry family in Ch'ang-chou District [in Kiangsu] which was assigned seven Collectorships simultaneously by the Magistrate, who bore it a grudge, with the result that the family was broken up and ruined.

A decree of 1527 describing the evils of the Tax Collector system reveals that the malpractices included the evasion of this job by wealthy and powerful families, the foisting of the job on law-abiding persons, and the demands by local officials that the Tax Collector provide all their material needs, including such things as local products, silks and brocades, and other items used as presents for the influential personages with whom the officials had to deal. In addition, the Tax Collectors had to pay the fees demanded by the functionaries in charge of tax grain, and were also expected to make up the deficits when the local magnates refused to pay their share of the taxes. Other detailed accounts of the ruinous effects of Tax Collectorship on those serving in that post abound in contemporary writings.

It was mentioned above that the idea had been advanced of instituting public land to assist the Tax Collector in meeting his obligations. In 1561 the Board of Finance rejected one such proposal, however, so that the idea could not be implemented. Even if the scheme for public land had been set up in the districts it probably would not have been of real help, but instead might have led to additional abuses and corruption.

Another aspect of the problem was the graft committed by the Tax Collectors; this was closely connected with the question of their heavy burden and losses. Local records indicate that many were the individuals who took advantage of their position as Tax Collectors and exacted large sums from the common people, which they used for the aggrandizement of their own estates while fraudulently reporting to the government that the tax payments were in arrears. A vivid contemporary characterization of such people stated: "The Tax Collectors acted as man-eaters toward the common people in order to be able to fawn upon the district authorities." The wealthy often used bribes to avoid assignment to the Collectorships and its attendant responsibilities; the sufferers from the system were the poor people and small households.

//Late in the Ming period Ting Yüan-chien of Ch'ang-hsing [in Chekiang] expressed the following views:

> The majority of the great gentry families in the Wu region [i.e. Lower Yangtse] have risen from the Tax Collectors, whose descendants are continuing to prosper. My own family, for example, and that of the Chus, the Suns, and the Lis, had all laid the foundations of their fortunes while serving as Tax Collectors.... Nowadays the wealthy can only think of evasion [of Collectorship].... When they deliver the grain they invariably mix it with husks and chaff or privately keep a portion. This is rather ridiculous.

We are not convinced, however, that the Tax Collector's morals were any better in early Ming than they were in later times. On the contrary, we feel that the rise of Tax Collectors into great gentry families during the earlier period was due to causes not mentioned in the quoted passage.//

NOTES

梁方仲, 明代粮長制度, 中國社會經濟史集刊

Liang Fang-chung, "Ming-tai liang-chang chih-tu," Chinese Social and Economic History Review, VII, 2 (July, 1946), 107-133.

The chief sources for this article are the Ming History (Ming shih), the Veritable Records of Ming (Ming shih-lu), the three editions of the Great Ordinance (Ta-kao 大誥) issued by the first emperor of Ming, and a number of local gazetteers. Also extensively used are essay collections of contemporary writers, and such material on institutional history as the collected statutes (hui-tien 會典) of various reigns.

The term liang-chang 粮長 has been rendered as "Tax Collectors" since this best expresses the function of such persons. It is therefore a technical term denoting the title of a specific office, and is to be distinguished from collectors of taxes in general.

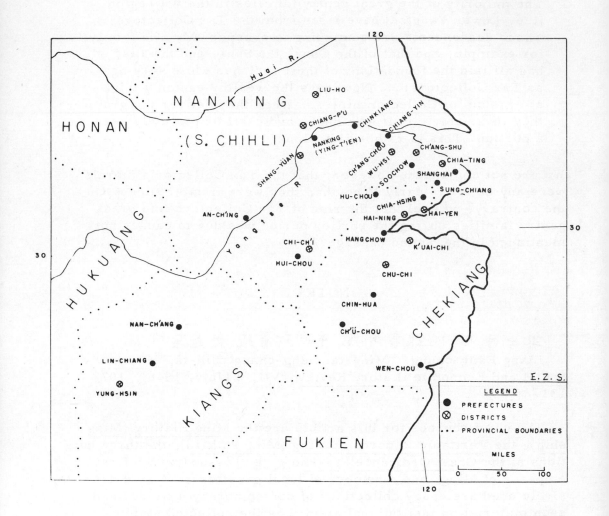

Map 5. The lower Yangtse region during Ming

19

THE "TEN-PARTS" TAX SYSTEM OF MING

by

LIANG FANG-CHUNG

1. Nomenclature and Contents of the "Ten-Parts" System

The "ten-parts" system is a general term applied to one of the many changes in the Ming tax system that occurred in the middle of the Chia-ching period [1522-1567]. This system prevailed for a time in South Chihli [i.e. Nanking Province, approximately modern Anhwei and Kiangsu], Chekiang, and Fukien provinces, and was known under various names. Its full name was "the system of the ten-parts account book." Of its variants, some referred to the objects and procedure of the tax, such as "ten-parts land account," "ten-parts corvée," and "ten-parts rice tribute." Some referred to its scope and method, such as "additional corvée levy." Some referred to its aim, such as "equalized levy." The term "ten-parts system" does not appear in the section on "Food and Money" in the Ming History, but an examination of the contents of the "advanced levy" mentioned therein shows that it was but another name for the ten-parts system. Furthermore, we should also correct the confusion, found in many books, between the "ten-parts" system and such other taxation systems as the "single whip." The present study will analyze the characteristics and trace the development of the ten-parts system.

The ten-parts system first appeared in the 1510's in Ch'ang-chou Prefecture, in South Chihli. Originally it was intended as a means to revamp the tax system; but later, with the Mongol and Japanese incursions following one upon another, the system was employed in some southern provinces for the raising of revenue. However, by the Wan-li period [1573-1620] it was largely superseded by the "single-whip" system. Although its history was short, the ten-parts system nevertheless enables us to see the general trends of change in tax systems, and the financial conditions of the time.

The first aim of the ten-parts system was to reform the corvée system, and also to straighten out the land tax. Both of these had hitherto been based on population: the exactions were assigned to neighborhood units of ten tithings each on a rotating basis, with each tithing due for service and taxation once in every ten years. With the passing of time and changes in population, injustices began to appear. Moreover, owing to differences in the corvée requirements each year and to the different number of exemptions carried by each tithing, the distribution of the burden of taxation and corvée became highly uneven. Official corruption and manipulation managed to defeat the "equal corvée" regulations that sought to establish a balanced distribution.

Officials and the gentry were legally entitled to exemptions on certain amounts of property, and on this basis many devices were employed by the unscrupulous to evade taxation. Some of the most serious were: (1) The methods of division, false custody, and transference, in which, for example, an official who was entitled to exemptions on 1,000 mou of land in a tithing but owned 10,000 mou might divide his land into ten sections, place each one in a different tithing, and thus obtain a total exemption on his property. He might also do the same as a favor for others, acting as a custodian of such land. (2) The method of temporary transference, which involved transferring the title of one's property to someone in the next tithing when one's own tithing was due for taxation and corvée, and then having it transferred back to the already taxed tithing when the turn came for the next tithing to pay. (3) The method of absentee ownership, in which estates were acquired in other prefectures and districts; since local authorities could not check with each other, a person could often obtain a different exemption in each locality, with a total much beyond the limits set by law.

All the above offenses were particularly flagrant in the lower Yangtse region. For instance, Governor Tung Yao-feng of [South] Chihli memorialized in 1567 that in the four prefectures of Soochow, Sun-chiang, Ch'ang-chou, and Chinkiang there were as many as 1,995,470 mou of land in false custody, and 3,315,560 mou of estates divided among different tithings. He therefore proposed the ten-parts system as a remedial measure to even out the tax burden.

The ten-parts system varied according to time and place, but in general it involved two methods. The first was the "ten-parts land tax." In this method all the land in a district was divided into ten approximately equal "parts," and each year one of the "parts" was subject to taxation and corvée. The government first

subtracted the number of exemptions from the total amount of land
and labor in the "part," and then divided the annual quota of taxation and labor service by the remainder, thus giving the amount
due from each man and each mou for that year. In order to simplify the payments, sometimes the corvée was commuted at a certain rate into land tax, and vice versa, and each was payable according to fixed rates. Two things are noticeable in this method:
(1) The taxes were computed on the basis of land, not production,
and therefore were not affected by fluctuations in the crops. (2)
The commutability of labor service into money payment eliminated much of the bother of personal service, and, because income
was budgetted according to expenditures, made it possible to fix
the rates of payment beforehand.

The second method in the ten-parts system was that of the "advanced levy." This was a method of alleviating the rigidity of the
ten-parts tax stemming from the fact that one of the ten parts
was solely responsible for the whole tax once in ten years. According to the Institutes of Wan-li,

> In the 44th year of Chia-ching (1565) permission was granted
> to introduce the system of the ten-parts account book in the
> Chiang-nan area [modern Kiangsu and Anhwei]. The tax and
> corvée dues were calculated for each year, the rates being
> fixed on the basis of the total amount of land in ten tithings.
> If there was a surplus from the first tithing,* it was to be
> retained for the use of the second and third tithings [in sub-
> sequent years]. If there was a deficit, additional sums could
> be taken [in the same year] from the second tithing to supple-
> ment it. The gentry and officials were allowed only one
> exemption in every ten years, and that was to be limited to
> the main estate. Land owned elsewhere, whether in the same
> prefecture or not, could not qualify for exemption once the
> exemption had been obtained in the original district.

Two points are notable in the above. One is that the tax for each
year was not necessarily restricted to one tithing. If there was a
surplus from the land of one tithing, it was retained and used in
the second or third year following. It there was a deficit, it was

---

*The use of the word "tithing" here and below indicates that the term was car-
ried over into the "ten parts" system. Presumably after the division of land into
ten parts the population in each part constituted the "tithing."

made up by the second or third tithing. From this stems the name
"advanced levy." Actually, the likelihood of reserving the surplus
of one tithing for later payment by another was probably less frequent than the chance of requesting one tithing to make up the
other's deficit. The other point to be noted is the restrictions
placed on the exemptions of gentry and officials, who were allowed
only one exemption in ten years and only within an individual's
own district in any one year.

We may conclude that the advanced levy method was a revised
version of the ten-parts land tax system. The result was that the
way of meeting the quota was made more flexible.

There was a new trend evident in both the ten-parts land tax
and the advanced levy methods, namely that the object of taxation
had changed from people to property, that is from a personal to
a territorial basis. Since the taxes were levied on property and
locally assessed and collected, it was easier to prevent corrupt
practices in connection with exemptions. This is another difference from the old tax system.

After the advanced levy, the next step in the development of the
tax system was naturally the single annual tax, levied universally
every year. This was the form taken subsequently by the "single
whip" and similar systems. The introduction of a unified annual
tax was not accomplished without controversy. The advocates of
the annual tax argued that when the ten-year rotation system was
abolished, corruption and evasion could more easily be prevented,
and that an annual system under which the tax burden would be
divided among ten years instead of being payable all in one year,
as had been the case, would be less burdensome. However, the
opponents of a unified annual tax held that the ten-parts system
was better. Their chief contentions are embodied in a letter
written by T'ang Shun-chih to Wang I, Prefect of Soochow.

The corrupt practices and evasions, T'ang maintained, were
not faults of the ten-parts system, but were things that could be
eliminated with better bookkeeping and more vigilant supervision
of the land. A unified annual tax, on the other hand, had many
shortcomings. For instance, all the people would have to be
troubled with tax payments once every year, instead of each taking his turn once in a decade. The authorities also would be bogged
down with ten times as much assessing, commutation of corvée,
and bookkeeping to do, making for inefficiency. The cost in time
and money for the tax-payers in sending payments to the government offices would increase tenfold, as would be true also of
official supervision of the collections. Therefore T'ang advised
Wang to use the ten-parts system in Soochow as the most practical.

But the trend of the times was such that, in spite of the opposition, the unified annual tax system was soon to supersede the ten-parts system of rotation.

2. History of the Ten-parts System

The earliest record of the ten-parts system appeared in the Cheng-te period (1506-1521), when a sub-prefect Ma had the land divided into ten parts, and taxed one part each year. After some initial success, the account continued, the system broke down as a result of evasions by the wealthy, population changes, and changes in property status.

In 1535 magistrate Ma Ju-chang of Wu-chin District [in Kiangsu] discovered the existence of flagrant cases of false custody, division, transference out of tithings, and the like. He therefore instituted some changes whereby government and private land, mountain areas, marshland, and male population were all computed in terms of mou of private land. In the computation one mou of private land was equal to five mou of government land, or ten mou of mountain or marshland, or one able-bodied man. He obtained by this means a total of 1,455,757 mou of land. This was divided into ten parts, and each year one part was taxed in turn. This system was known as the ten-parts tax or ten-parts land tax. It could only be carried out intermittently. A little later a similar device was used by the district magistrate of Wu-hsi [in Kiangsu], and reportedly was welcomed by the local people.

Toward the middle of the Chia-ching period the Fukien provincial authorities also ordered the introduction of the ten-parts system. Subsequently the system was made flexible by a method similar to that of the "advanced levy." In 1537 a plan for the "equalization of corvée" was drawn up by the prefect of Ch'ang-chou, but it involved annual levies and was therefore closer to the single whip system than to the advanced levy. In 1550 the prefect of Soochow also prepared to institute the ten-parts system. Then with the intensification of the Mongol and Japanese incursions after 1550 the ten-parts or advanced levy system became a regular way of raising revenue.

In a memorial dealing with the question of army provisions in the lower Yangtse region, Governor Wen Ju-chang of [South] Chihli suggested in 1565 that in order to check the abuses of the privilege of exemption, the ten-parts system with advanced levy should be introduced. The suggestion received official approval. Contemporary local accounts show that by this time the ten-parts system had become widespread in the lower Yangtse region, and

again assumed the role of a reform measure. Some local authorities disliked the additional levy, but adopted the ten-parts rotation
system, the use of which was recorded in the local histories of
many districts, such as Chiang-p'u and Liu-ho [both in Kiangsu].
The system was also reported to have been adopted in some
districts in Hui-chou [in Anhwei] in 1560.

An outstanding advocate of the ten-parts system was P'ang
Shang-p'eng, Governor of Chekiang from 1561 to 1567. He inaugu-
rated the ten-parts system in order to have vigorous control over
the exemptions. All exemptions were listed and no one was permitted to have exemptions in more than one tithing. The taxable
land and labor was then computed in terms of labor.

The actions of P'ang in this respect have been recorded in the
gazetteers of various districts in Chekiang. The Gazetteer of Wen-
chou described his simplification of the miscellaneous corvée
duties, such as the purchasing duties, courier service, treasury
guards, and many others, in the administration of which local
functionaries found plenty of opportunities for corrupt manipulation. P'ang placed these labor duties in a ten-parts system called
"equalization." All obligations were payable in a "single-whip"
assessment. The heads of the ten-tithing unit now became responsible only for the transmission of orders, while the dues were
paid by the people directly to the government.

The above account presents some ambiguity as to the identity
of the "ten-parts" or "equalization" system on the one hand, and
the "single-whip" payment on the other. A comparison of the accounts in the district gazetteers brings out the fact that P'ang
Shang-p'eng first adopted the "equalization" system in 1561, but
that after a thorough survey he introduced the single annual payment scheme in 1572 and 1573. P'ang is known to have originated
the single-whip system when he found out that the ten-parts system was riddled with malpractices; however, it has been little
realized that his first innovation in the taxation of Ming was the
ten-parts system. His part in bringing about the latter, although
often left out in contemporary accounts, can be proved by checking
the date of its first introduction in Chekiang with his term of office.

There is evidence that the ten-parts system spread into Nan-
ch'ang and Lin-chiang prefectures in Kiangsi Province during the
Chia-ching period.

After 1573 the ten-parts system gradually disappeared while
the single-whip system became prevalent. However, it appears
that the former was still employed in Yunnan province during the
Wan-li period [1573-1620]. The Gazetteer of Yunnan published in
that period mentions the introduction of the ten-parts method in

the "equalized dues" system. All land in a ten-tithing unit was
divided into ten parts, and the taxes were imposed on each tithing
in turn. Some districts, however, adopted a five-year rotation
plan for the payment of taxes.

The ten-parts system was used also in 1590 by I Fang-chih,
Prefect of Ch'ü-chou in Chekiang, as a corrective measure against
the over-charging of tax-payers for the cost of transporting their
tax payments. In this plan the land of an entire district was divided
into ten parts, and one part was made responsible each year for
the payment of the transportation fee. This fee, which was pro-
portional to the amount of taxation, was calculated on the basis of
so much money per picul of tax grain. This differed from the previous ten-parts systems, however, in that it included only land
[i.e. not corvée], and also that it was used solely for the purpose
of allocating transportation charges.

The method was introduced in various districts in the prefecture. Let us take Hsi-an District, where it was first introduced,
as an example. In Hsi-an the gross tax levied on the "part" due
for taxation was 2,450.17 tan   of grain. Subtracting 200 tan for
exemptions, and 100 tan which were set aside for emergencies,
the actual tax [to be transported] amounted to 2,150.17 tan. On
this a transportation fee of 0.22 tael per tan was assessed. The
"Regular Households" (those that possessed more grain) were
given the additional duty of actually transporting the tax grain,
while the "Auxiliary Households" (those that possessed less grain),
were responsible only for their share of the transportation fee.
The Regular Households collected the fees from the Auxiliaries;
they were not allowed to ask for more than the fixed amount, nor
were the Auxiliary Households allowed to delay payment.

The same system functioned in the other districts, with some
variations in the rate of the transportation fee. With the passage
of time, however, the regulations grew lax, and the fee increased
in amount. In 1622 a new element cropped up: The transportation
fee was fixed at 0.0048 tael for each tael of the single-whip tax.
This was an indication of the general transition from the ten-parts
to the single-whip system.

3. Relation between the Ten-parts System
and the Levying of Extra Land Taxes

The Ming government found itself in deepening financial straits
from the Cheng-te [1506-1521] and Chia-ching [1522-1566] periods
on, as clearly proved by the extra levies of land taxes. In the
Cheng-te period 1,000,000 taels were levied as extra taxes for the

construction of the Ch'ien-ch'ing Palace. This sum was to be paid up over a five-year period. However, at that time the term "advanced levy" was not used, so it did not concern the ten-parts system.

It was during the Chia-ching period that the drain on the government, resulting from such things as Taoist sacrifices and increased palace expenditures, became obvious. After the middle of the reign the difficulties were accentuated by increased military expenditures. The annual revenue of the Ming central government was some 2,000,000 taels, of which sum 70 per cent was ordinarily spent on administration and 30 per cent was set aside for emergencies. Before 1550 the total annual expenditure ranged between 700,000 and 2,000,000 taels. From 1551 on, however, with Mongol invasions in the north and Japanese incursions along the eastern coast, the military expenditures sky-rocketed. The sums spent by the central government on military matters ranged from 5,950,000 taels in 1552 to 3,020,000 taels in 1558, tremendously in excess of the annual income of 2,000,000 taels. In order to meet the deficits the government had to resort to various means of obtaining more revenue, including such devices as redemption of stolen goods, imposition of stamp taxes, commutation of service, sale of monastery land, etc. The extra land taxes and the ten-parts system were also outcomes of this situation.

Extra land taxes were first levied in 1550 after the invasion of the Mongol prince Anda in the north. The entire country, with the exception of the northern prefectures and Kweichow, had to pay an additional 1,150,000 taels, of which Soochow alone was responsible for 85,000 taels. In 1551 the Board of Finance and the Board of Works reported that for the three-month period ending in the second month of 1551, the total revenue, including regular and extra levies as well as the salt gabelle, amounted to over 9,000,-000 taels. In the expenditures, the regular army appropriations took 2,800,000 taels; war relief and defense construction raised the total to over 8,000,000 taels. A further 345,000 taels were paid out through the Board of Works for wages, food, materials, and so forth. Sensing corruption in these huge expenses, the emperor ordered an investigation by the Imperial Censors. Just the regular army expenses of 2,800,000 taels were themselves nearly six times the total army appropriation at the beginning of Ming.

With the intensification of border warfare and coastal attacks by the Japanese it was necessary to make "advanced levies" on the land in South Chihli, Chekiang, and Fukien Provinces. "Advanced levies" is another term for "extra levies," and is also to be included in the ten-parts system. The flexibility of payment

resulting from one "part" having to make up the deficit of another
"part" was a great boon to the administration. This was probably
a major reason for the prevalence of the ten-parts system.

As to the amount of the additional levies, it varied from time
to time. South Chihli, which at one time was assessed over 400,000
taels, had its quota reduced to 291,892 in 1563. Chekiang had to
fill a quota of 475,900 taels. From 1555 to 1561 Fukien varied between the annual sums of 280,000 and 600,000 taels, according to
the financial policies of the incumbent governor. But the details
are not known.

It appears that the practice of the extra levies spread to the entire country. An account in the Veritable Records of Ming records
that in 1555 the emperor approved a suggestion of the Board of
Finance whereby all provinces were ordered to send additional
levies to specific military areas to meet the costs of the campaigns.
The administrative areas exempted from this additional levy were
Kweichow Province, probably owing to its poor resources, and the
prefectures of Shun-t'ien [Peking], Ying-t'ien [Nanking], Soochow,
Sung-chiang, Ch'ang-chou, and Chinkiang, probably because they
had already been assessed previously for additional levies. However, since the funds thus raised seem to have been in the nature
of an advance drawing on the tax, we cannot therefore conclude
that it proved the adoption of the ten-parts system on a national scale.

As soon as the system of advanced levies was put into practice
it was attacked from all sides. The Board of War held in 1556 that
of all funds designated for military use this was the most difficult
to handle. A Censor memorialized in 1557 that the extra levies
were administered by unfit officials who sometimes exacted twice
the legal amount; he asked that they be discontinued. There were
others, however, who held opposite views. Documentary evidence
shows that the system continued in force, but it is also evident
that the advanced levies were collected only with great difficulty.

NOTES

梁方仲, 明代十段錦法, 中國社會經濟史集刊
Liang Fang-chung, "Ming-tai shih-tuan-chin fa," Chinese Social and Economic History Review, VII, 1 (1944), 120-137.

The chief sources used by the author are Ming shih, Ming
shih-lu, T'ien-hsia chün-kuo li-ping shu 天下郡國利病書
by Ku Yen-wu, as well as the gazetteers of K'uai-chi District,

Ch'ang-chou Prefecture, Wu-hsien, and the other localities mentioned in the article.

This is one of a number of articles written by the same author on the Ming system of taxation. Not included in the present volume are two accounts of the "Single-whip" system, another major tax measure adopted by the Ming government; regarding this measure, however, our knowledge is not yet complete, and scholars differ in their reconstructions of its operation. As indicated by the present article, any study of the Ming tax system would necessitate consideration not only of the technicalities of government finance, but also such aspects of economic life as landownership and tenure; the traditions of local administration, and magisterial interpretation of the tax laws; the extent of money--as against the remnants of natural--economy; the government's immediate needs projected against the country's total production capacity and the people's ability to pay; and so on. The sixteenth century being a period of dynastic decline and political and economic disturbances in China, the significance of the ten-parts system would seem to lie in its reflection of contemporary social conditions as well as in its function as a government fiscal measure.

20

PRICE CONTROL AND PAPER CURRENCY IN MING

by

LI CHIEN-NUNG

Prefatory Note

While reading Asai Torao's History of Chinese Laws and Institutions (1903), in the section on the civil laws of the Ming dynasty
I came across the statement that "Commodity prices were fixed
by the government and could not be changed at will." This statement was followed by a table listing the official prices. I was
struck by two things in the table: (a) Gold was exceedingly low in
value, its ratio to silver being only 5:1. (b) The unit kuan 貫 , or
string of copper cash, which was used throughout the table as the
standard calculating unit, did not actually refer to copper cash but
stood for units of paper currency. Since the material in the table
is of vital importance to the study of Chinese economic history, I
have sought to determine the dates covered by the table, and the
relationship between the fixed prices and the paper currency of
Ming. Unfortunately the source of the price list was not given by
Asai Torao, and I have been unable to locate it in either the section on "Food and Money" in the Ming History or in the supplements
to the San-t'ung 三 通 . The Institutes of Ming may be the answer,
but it is not available to me at present, nor are other works which
might be consulted. I therefore have to leave the table as presented
in Asai's work.*

---

*Asai Torao's price list is to be found in the Institutes of Ming (Ta-ming hui-
tien), edition of 1587, chüan 201, pp. 2-13; this is the section on "Current prices
on confiscated goods" in the volumes entitled "Board of Punishments." The prices
follow an order by the Emperor T'ai-tsu that "the value of all confiscated goods
should be computed at current prices of the locality where the crime is committed."
Some of the items in the Hui-tien list are excluded from that of Asai. A comparison of the three versions has revealed a few errors in Li's list, which will be corrected in the table on pages 285 and 286 of this article.

1. Paper Currency before and during Ming

The credit system had an early history in China, its first appearance being the "flying money" which was introduced during the reign of Emperor Hsien-tsung (806-820 A.D.) of T'ang. The method of its operation was similar to that of the drafts of today: A merchant going to trade in a distant place who found it inconvenient to carry large amounts of cash with him could deposit the cash and exchange it for a paper voucher at the offices which were maintained in the capital by the various provinces, armies, imperial commissioners, and wealthy households, thus entitling him to draw cash in any region of the empire. The same system was continued through the reign of Emperor T'ai-tsu (960-975) of Sung, except that during the latter period it was known as "credit cash."* During the reign of the Sung Emperor Chen-tsung (998-1022) a system known as the "exchange medium" was initiated in Shu [Szechuan] by Chang Yung, governor of Shu, to replace the clumsy iron coins then in use. One chiao 交 of this paper currency was worth one min 緡 , that is, 1,000 cash. Three years constituted a "period of circulation" at the end of which the old notes were recalled and new ones issued. At first the issuing of the notes was undertaken by sixteen wealthy families, but in the T'ien-sheng reign (1023-1031) a Bureau of Exchange Medium was established by the government, and private issuance was prohibited. The maximum quota for a "period of circulation" was 1,256,340 min, which was to be backed by 360,000 min of cash as the basis for redemption.

From then on paper currency was continuously in use. In different periods the currency was known under various names, such as "check mediums," "communicating medium," and "communicating check" in Southern Sung, "exchange vouchers" in Chin, and "precious notes" in the Yüan dynasty. Regardless of the name by which they were known, however, the paper currencies of Sung, Chin, and Yüan were all redeemable. The Bureau of Exchange Medium of Sung, for example, was in charge of exchanging the notes for cash as well as of issuing the notes. The Treasuries for

---

*The pien wu ch'ien 便務錢 of our text is apparently a slip. Other sources cite the name of the money as pien ch'ien 便錢 "credit cash" and mention the establishment of a pien ch'ien wu 便錢務 "bureau of credit cash." (Cf. Liensheng Yang, Money and Credit in China [Cambridge, Mass., 1952], paragraph 6.5).

Professor Yang's work cited here contains a very useful index to the special terminology of his subject. For the sake of uniformity we have sought to make our renderings of Chinese technical terms conform as closely as possible to those advanced by him.

Price Stabilization and Paper Currency in the Yüan dynasty were offices that maintained stores of bullion in the various provinces and handled the conversion of paper currency there. The difference between the Sung, Chin, and Yüan dynasties was that Sung and Chin based their currencies on the copper cash, whereas Yüan first used silk as the basis and then changed to silver. Toward the end of Yüan copper money was designated as the supplementary currency, that is, the currency system was shifted to a paper standard, which led to unlimited issuance of the paper currency and hence to inflation. Such inflationary developments had also previously occurred at the end of Sung and Chin, but in all three periods, or at least in the early stages, the paper money was adequately backed, limited in the amounts that could be issued, and was able to circulate widely on good credit. The Ming government, however, adopted from the beginning the bad monetary policy of late Yüan.

In 1368 the Board of Finance was ordered to mint copper coins in five denominations:

$$
\begin{array}{ll}
1.0 \text{ ounce} & (10 \text{ cash}) \\
0.5 \text{ ounce} & (5 \text{ cash}) \\
0.3 \text{ ounce} & (3 \text{ cash}) \\
0.2 \text{ ounce} & (2 \text{ cash}) \\
0.1 \text{ ounce} & (1 \text{ cash})
\end{array}
$$

The real value and face value of the coins were identical. But in 1375, owing to the scarcity of copper and for the sake of convenience, paper money was introduced. Paper notes were issued in six denominations: 1 "string," 500 cash, 400 cash, 300 cash, 200 cash, and 100 cash. The notes were made of mulberry paper, measured 1 [Chinese] foot by 6 [Chinese] inches, and were printed with a border design of dragons and the likeness of a string of cash in the center. The legend across the top of the note read "Precious Note Circulating throughout Great Ming." One string in paper currency was worth 1,000 copper cash, or 1 tael of silver; 4 strings were equal to 1 ounce* of gold. People were forbidden to use gold, silver, or goods as the media of exchange, but the exchange of gold or silver for paper notes was allowed. In the collection of commercial taxes both copper and paper currencies were used; they were paid 30 per cent in copper cash and 70 per cent in paper notes. For amounts less than 100 cash, however, copper was used exclusively. Such in brief was the Ming paper currency system.

---

*We render liang 兩 as "tael" when it refers to silver and as "[Chinese] ounce" when it refers to other things.

2. Confusion Resulting from Government Price
Regulations and Depreciation of Paper Money

// According to the paper money regulations established in 1375, the Ming currency system was shifted from a copper to a paper standard. Copper cash became merely supplementary coins, while gold and silver were relegated to the status of ordinary commodities. The legal value of the standard currency was purely fictitious, whereas that of the supplementary coins represented real value. Owing to the scarcity of copper, however, only a limited amount [of supplementary coins] was minted by the government, and only the inferior copper cash minted by private persons increased in quantity. On the other hand the paper currency, though issued by the government, was not limited in amount by the currency regulations, and was not convertible. Consequently there was a steady increase in the amount of paper notes issued, while the supplementary coins, being a good commodity with real value, were driven off the market.

// These developments led to a steady increase in commodity prices. The official price list shows that one tael of silver was valued at eighty strings in paper notes, and that 1,000 copper cash were also worth eighty strings; this means the paper currency had depreciated eighty times in value [since 1375]. The fall in the value of paper money was accompanied by the rise in prices of all goods. However, the price rises were not exactly in proportion to the rise of the ratio between copper and paper currency. In some instances the cost of commodities nominally increased, whereas actually they had fallen below the original cost. The following is an obvious example of this: The official price list states, "1 catty of copper, crude or refined, is worth 4 strings in paper currency." According to the currency regulations of 1368, one copper cash was worth 0.1 ounce of copper; 1 catty [i.e. 16 ounces] of copper, therefore, would have been worth 160 copper cash. It follows that without a fall in the value of notes, one catty of copper would also have been worth 160 cash in paper currency, and the price of 4 strings [4,000 cash] given in the list would mean that the cost of copper increased twenty-five times. According to the price table, however, 4 strings in paper currency had a real value of only 50 copper cash. In other words, one catty of copper was worth only 50 cash, which was certainly much below the original cost. We can conclude, therefore, that once a currency system fell into confusion all commodity prices would no longer behave naturally but would become very chaotic, which would deeply affect the lives of the people. //

I present below some sample items from Asai's official price list, to which, reckoning one tael of silver and 1,000 copper cash as both equal to 80 strings in paper currency, I have added information on the prices in terms of silver and copper.

Commodity	Price in paper notes (strings)	Price in copper (cash)	Price in silver (taels)
Metals:			
Gold, 1 ounce	400	5,000	5
Silver, 1 tael	80	1,000	
Copper cash, per 1,000	80		1
Copper, crude and refined, 1 catty	4	50	0.05
Iron, 1 catty	1	12.5	0.0125
Textiles:			
Silk gauze, 1 bolt	80	1,000	1
Silk damask, 1 bolt	120	1,500	1.5
Silk brocade,* per foot	8	100	0.1
Cotton cloth, 1 bolt	20	250	0.25
Linen cloth, 1 bolt	8	100	0.10
Flax, 1 catty	500 cash [1/2 string]	6.25	0.00625
Cereals:			
Rice, 1 tan 石	25	312.5	0.3125
Wheat, 1 tan	25	250	0.25
Barley, 1 tan	10	125	0.125
Millet, 1 tan	18	225	0.225
[Wheat] flour, 1 catty	500 cash	6.25	0.00625
Livestock:			
1 horse	800	10,000	10
1 mule	500	6,250	6.25
1 donkey	250	3,125	3.125
1 water buffalo	300	3,750	3.75
1 large hog	80	1,000	1
1 ox hide	24	300	0.3
Horse meat, beef, mutton, pork, etc., 1 catty	1	12.5	0.0125

*We follow the Institutes of Ming in correcting Li Chien-nung's entry of "Silk brocade, 1 bolt, 80 strings 1,000 cash, 1 oz."

Commodity	Price in paper notes (strings)	Price in copper (cash)	Price in silver (taels)
Fruits and Vegetables:			
Peaches, pears, per 100	2	25	0.025
30 persimmons*	1	12.5	0.0125
Vegetables, per 100 catties	2	25	0.025
Clothing:			
1 gauze hat	20	250	0.25
1 felt hat	4	50	0.05
1 doeskin boot	24	300	0.30
1 used cotton garment	5	62.5	0.0625
1 new cotton garment	16	200	0.20
1 new linen garment	10	125	0.125

According to the above table, one bolt of cotton cloth cost only
250 copper cash or 0.25 tael of silver; one tan of rice, only
312.5 copper cash or 0.3125 tael of silver; and one catty of beef,
only 12.5 copper cash or 0.0125 tael of silver. These figures
would seem to be unreasonably low, even for the old days of lower
costs of living. Since price fluctuations had become erratic, however, the people did not at all feel that the cost of living was low.
Those who depended on wages for a living found that their wages
did not increase as rapidly as the prices of things they had to buy
with depreciated paper currency. Those whose income was based
on the sale of products were also dissatisfied at receiving payment in depreciated currency. This led to government interference
in prices.

Traditional Confucian theory seems to have considered price-
fixing a proper function of the government. The Rites of Chou contains this statement: "When there is a natural calamity, selling
at high prices should be prohibited, so that prices will remain
stable. This should be applied also to scarce goods throughout the
year." Actually, however, there seem not to have been many
instances of the government's exercising this power until the Sung
and Yüan dynasties, when government price regulations began to

---

*We follow the Institutes of Ming in correcting the author's "tangerines."

appear frequently in the records. The reason for this government
interference was the irregular price rises caused by the depreciation of paper currency. "Official prices" were mentioned in
records for 1239; in 1265 the lowering of prices at Lin-an Prefecture [i.e. Hangchow, capital of Southern Sung] through the introduction into the market of 300,000 copper cash was ordered by
the Sung government; and in 1264 Emperor Shih-tsu of Yüan also
had ordered the regulation of prices through the establishment of
Treasuries for Price Stabilization in the various provinces. It
should be noted that the control of prices in these instances was
not done through an official price list, but by recalling the surplus
amount of paper notes in circulation and effecting a fall in prices.

In the Ming dynasty, however, the paper currency was incon-
vertible and was issued in unlimited amounts, so that price regulation had to be done entirely through governmental authority. In
1368, owing to the inflation caused by the bad fiscal policy of late
Yüan, "it was ordered that commodity prices should be periodically revaluated and fixed," and henceforth this became the set
system. The Hsü T'ung-k'ao 續通考 contains many references to
the application of this policy throughout the Ming period. It is recorded, for example, that prefectural, circuit, and district authorities examined and reported on the current market prices during the first ten days of each month, keeping watch on the maintenance of a fixed price level, and strictly forbidding any change
of price. In 1552 the readjustment of prices was ordered to be undertaken once every six months. In 1570 "the periodic readjustment of prices" was proposed by the Board of Finance as one of
the ways to alleviate the difficulties of merchants, the suggestion
being that the readjustments should take place in the fifth and
eighth months of each year so that the assessment of taxes could
be made on the basis of seasonal prices; the suggestion was approved.

From the above it would seem that the main aim of price controls in Ming was to prevent officials from keeping prices at arbitrarily low rates, and merchants from raising prices at will; it
had no apparent connection with the question of paper currency.
From the repeated orders and proposals for the establishment of
price readjustment, however, we can conclude that the officials
and the merchants were mutually engaged in cheating. The merchants often were actually unable to keep within the official price
quotations, while the officials frequently coerced the merchants.
There was often a discrepancy between the actual price and official price of commodities. This discrepancy was probably due to
the inconvertibility of the "precious notes." The merchants calcu-

lated the prices in terms of hard currency and invariably felt that
the commodity prices were too low; the officials calculated in
terms of paper notes, and invariably felt that prices were too
high. Hence commodity prices became a matter of contention between officials and merchants.

The precise date of the official list given above cannot be exactly determined, but after comparing it with certain information
in Hsü T'ung-k'ao we can conclude that it represents official prices
during early Ming, not long after the introduction of the paper currency. A passage in Hsü T'ung-k'ao recording prices for 1407
shows the same figures as our table for gold and silver, but contains some differences in the prices of rice and silk textiles. This
indicates that even at such an early date discrepancies had begun
to appear between official and actual prices. The same source
shows that twenty years later, in 1426, the discrepancies had become still greater. In that year the Board of Finance readjusted
all prices in terms of paper notes, so that an ounce of silver was
equal to 2,000 strings in paper currency; an ounce of gold, 8,000
strings; a chicken or a duck, 30 strings; the prices of many other
unenumerated goods were increased fivefold. Accordingly, on the
basis of the original ratio among paper, silver, and copper cash,
the price of a fowl was then ten or twenty times that in modern
Shanghai, which would be truly alarming. On the basis of the new
ratio of one ounce of silver to 2,000 strings of notes, however,
the actual price of a fowl was only 0.015 oz. of silver, or 15 copper cash, which was pitifully low. So long as the paper currency
was in force, there inevitably existed this tremendous gap between
the official and actual prices. Consequently the official price list
became a permanent source of suffering during the Ming dynasty.

3. General Effects of Paper Currency on the
Life of the Officials and the People

Aside from the difficulties arising from a depreciating currency and official price-fixing, as described above, there were
several other ways by which the paper money acted as a means
for the exploitation of the people. These prevailed for some two
centuries after the reign of the first emperor of Ming. They included the following:

(i) Convictions for Using Prohibited Media of Exchange

When the paper currency was first introduced only the use of
gold and silver was prohibited; copper coins were one form of legal

tender, being used alongside the paper notes. The people's prefer-
ence for copper over paper money, however, soon led to the prohibition of the use of the former. Thus in 1394:

> Edict to the Board of Finance: Let the proper government
> agencies recall all [copper] cash into the government and
> exchange it with the same amount of paper currency; copper
> coins should henceforth be banned from circulation. All cop-
> per coins owned by soldiers, civilians, and merchants must
> be delivered to the government within half a month. Those
> who dare clandestinely use or bury them shall be convicted.

Again in 1403:

> The use of gold or silver as the medium of exchange is pro-
> hibited. Those transgressing against this shall be adjudged
> guilty of a major crime. Anyone who provides information
> leading to their capture shall be rewarded with the gold or
> silver involved in the case.

In the following year those convicted of the infraction of this law
were ordered to have their death sentences commuted to the exiling of the whole family to Hsin-chou [in modern Jehol]. In 1428
a government order ruled as follows:

> Those who refuse to use the paper notes shall be fined 1,000
> strings for every string refused. The relatives, neighbors,
> and neighborhood heads who are cognizant of these matters
> but do not report them shall be fined 100 strings for every
> string so refused. Those who clandestinely carry on business
> behind closed doors, and those who raise commodity prices,
> shall be fined 10,000 strings; the relatives, neighbors, and
> neighborhood heads who conceal such information shall be
> fined 1,000 strings.

Nevertheless by 1448 the use of copper coins had become prevalent, the rate of exchange being two copper cash for one string.
Palace Guards were therefore sent to inspect the markets in the
capital; anyone found using copper cash in the transactions was
fined ten times [the sum involved in the original transaction]. Actually, however, these restrictions were not effective. On the
contrary, most business transactions were conducted with silver
or copper currency. Corrupt officials seized upon this as an opportunity for blackmail. [The late-Ming scholar] Ku Yen-wu
[1613-1682] records many instances of such malpractices on the

part of unscrupulous officials which resulted in exile or imprisonment of the accused people.

(ii) Imposition of Heavy Taxes

These taxes were of three kinds: the household salt tax in notes,
the additional levies on shops and market stalls, and miscellaneous
taxes and tolls payable in notes. The first of these was initiated in
1404 on the suggestion of Censor Ch'en Ying, who sought to reduce
the amount of paper money in circulation by levying a monthly per
capita tax on salt consumption. The rate was set at one string in
paper notes per adult, on the basis of the consumption of one catty
of salt per month; minors were assessed half this amount. This
measure failed to reduce the amount of paper notes in circulation,
however, because the government continued to print more money,
while this household salt tax became a general poll tax. At first
the government accepted both old and new notes for such tax payments, but in 1468 the people were required to pay in silver or
copper cash. This was considered by contemporaries to be a great
economic evil.

The additional levies on shops and market stalls were introduced as a temporary measure in 1425. It was hoped that the very
old bills among the notes thus obtained by the government could
be destroyed, and that the amount of notes in circulation could
thereby be reduced. The authorities had promised that these levies
would be abolished when paper currency became firmly established
as a medium of exchange. This was never realized, however, and
instead of being abolished the levies were subsequently increased
fivefold.

The miscellaneous taxes and tolls were introduced in 1429.
They involved the payment of taxes on a large variety of enterprises, including truck gardens, orchards, warehouses, inns, oil
factories, and mills. Tolls were exacted on all mule-, donkey-,
and ox-carts and boats used for transporting goods. Once introduced, these levies invariably became permanent burdens; toll
houses especially became a fixed item in the fiscal system.

The above taxes were all introduced with the alleged objective
of reducing the amount of paper currency in circulation. If the
government really had such an intention, however, why did it not
commute the existing taxes in kind into payment in paper money,
rather than institute these additional taxes? Further, why did the
government continue to issue more notes? Finally, when it became
apparent that the surplus of paper currency could not be thus reduced, why were the new taxes not abolished, but instead collected

in hard currency? After 1488 commutation of taxes into silver became the usual practice. The erstwhile prohibited media of exchange--silver and gold--now became a necessity for the tax-payers. Paper currency became worthless, though nominally it was still not abolished (officials were paid in paper currency; see below), and the additional tax burdens also remained. No wonder Ku Yenwu inveighed bitterly against the Ming fiscal system.

(iii) Illegal Extortions through the Exchange of Old and New Notes

In 1376 a "paper currency conversion system" was initiated. This was the process by which people could exchange old worn-out notes for new ones from the government, which charged a fee of 30 cash per string of paper notes for this service. By this method the government itself actually destroyed the credit of the paper currency, as forcing those who sought to exchange old notes to suffer a loss of 30 cash per string was tantamount to announcing the instability of the paper currency. The conversion system was soon discontinued owing to the frequent occurrence of malpractices, such as people offering counterfeit old notes in exchange for new ones. Nevertheless, the people generally began to discriminate between old and new notes; the former often came to have a value of only half of the latter. Tax collectors in many places thereupon refused to accept old notes as tax payments; yet when the revenue was sent to the central government it consisted entirely of old notes. This meant that the tax-payers were assessed double the legal quota while the national government received only half the revenue. From 1393 on there were repeated decrees forbidding the tax collectors to refuse old notes, but these orders were not effective. By the middle of the fifteenth century it had become an established rule that "taxes must be paid in new notes," and in 1480 the Board of Finance memorialized that tax officials should be ordered to deliver all their collections in new notes.

Extortions reached another high point with the introduction of commutation of tax payments into silver. In 1487 it was reported that while the paper notes in circulation were worth less than one copper cash per string, when the people paid taxes the exchange rate was set at 0.025 ounce of silver (that is, 25 copper cash) per string. In addition, there was another form of extortion known as "compulsory sale of notes." When paper money had depreciated to the point where 1,000 strings were worth only 0.4 or 0.5 ounce of silver, influential personages in the capital often exported it to the provinces and prefectures, and openly asked the local officials to force its sale at the rate of five ounces of silver per 1,000 strings, thus reaping a tenfold profit. This practice was prohibited in 1477, but subsequent repetitions of the injunction show that the sale of paper notes continued in spite of the prohibition.

(iv) Diminution of Official Salaries

During the Hung-wu reign [1368-1398] officials were paid in rice, and occasionally in cash or paper currency; 1,000 cash or one string of paper money was the equivalent of one tan of rice. In the reign of Emperor Ch'eng-tsu [1403-1424] only the nobility were paid entirely in rice; civil and military officials were paid partly in rice and partly in paper money, the commutation rate being set at one tan of rice for 10 strings of paper currency. The actual price of rice at this time, however, had risen to 20 or 30 strings per tan. The rate was subsequently readjusted several times, but by the Cheng-t'ung period [1436-1449] the proportion of rice to paper currency in the officials' salaries decreased, while the value of the paper money also declined. By late fifteenth century one tan of rice in the salary scale was worth only 14 or 15 copper cash [when paid in paper currency], which probably represented the lowest official salaries in history. The situation was thus described by Wang Hung-hsü [1645-1723] in the section on "Food and Money" in his Draft Ming History:

> In the reign of Emperor Mu-tsung [1567-1572], although paper money had fallen into disuse for nearly a hundred years, and taxes were seldom collected in paper notes, yet officials still continued to receive their salaries in paper money just as before. When the government treasuries did not have enough of it to pay the salaries, merchants were encouraged to step in and provide it, or it might be purchased in the capital. When no notes were available the payments, amounting to hundreds of thousands [of strings], would be suspended. It was only in the reign of Emperor Shen-tsung [1573-1619] that salaries became payable in silver so as to make up for the back payments.

Such whittling away of official salaries in effect compelled the officials to engage in corrupt practices in order to maintain themselves. These practices included the imposition of extra exactions on the tolls, buying from the people at unreasonably low official prices, and so on.

(v) Effects on Criminal Justice

According to the Ming History, there were two kinds of redemption of punishments, the statutory and the customary. While
the charges for the former were fixed and unchangeable, those
for the latter were raised or lowered in accordance with the circumstances. After the Ch'eng-hua period [1465-1487] payments
for redemption were made only in terms of paper currency, and
as a result of the depreciation of paper money the rates for the
regular redemption became much lighter than those for the customary redemption, although originally they were much heavier
than the latter. Thus it appears that in the Ming dynasty paper
currency brought deprivation and suffering to all but the criminals.

4. Contemporary Thought Regarding Ming Paper Currency

After several abortive attempts the manufacture of paper money
was finally stopped by the government in 1450. Its circulation continued into the sixteenth century, however, and did not entirely
cease until after 1573. By then the notes had become worthless,
although up to that time the government had persisted in using it
for such purposes as payment of official salaries. But in 1643,
during the last reign of Ming, certain officials, pressed by the
government's financial straits, suggested issuing paper currency
anew as a means of creating government income. This suggestion
was put into practice, and the issuance of paper notes did not
cease until Peking was about to fall to the rebels. We may say
that the Ming dynasty rose and fell with the rise and decline of
paper currency.

The amazing feature in Ming currency policy from the time of
the first emperor on is the fact that, in spite of a rich background
since the ninth century, no one seems to have understood the basic
principles of paper money. No one, in the varied controversies
concerning paper currency during the two and a half centuries between 1375 and 1643, appears to have grasped the fact that the
basis of paper money was "credit", and that the fundamental criterion for the establishment of credit was the convertibility of the
paper money into hard currency, or into goods equivalent to such
hard currency in value. The Ming policy-makers thought that the
establishment of a valid paper currency depended solely on government "regulations." Yet the government itself was unable to
act according to these regulations, and when they failed to hold
up looked upon their collapse as a mysterious phenomenon. This
lack of understanding is illustrated by the following colloquy in

the course of a controversy in 1643 over the question of the rein-
troduction of paper money, a move favored by the emperor but
opposed by members of the Grand Secretariat:

>   Secretariat: "Even though the people are stupid, who
> would be willing to exchange a tael of silver for a piece of
> paper?"
>   Emperor: "Well, then, why was it possible [to introduce
> paper money] in the reign of the Exalted Emperor [i.e. Hung-
> wu]?"
>   Secretariat: "The Exalted Emperor ruled according to
> the way of the gods.* He used paper money only for the grant-
> ing of rewards and payment of official salaries, not for army
> pay or other things."
>   Emperor: "All we need is strict regulations."
>   Secretariat: "It will be difficult to carry out mere regu-
> lations."

Although the members of the Grand Secretariat realized that it
was difficult to put "mere regulations" into practice, they were
unable to explain the whys and wherefores. Emperor Ch'ung-chen
therefore finally forced the adoption of the paper currency.

Throughout the Ming dynasty only four persons stand out as
holding noteworthy views on paper currency. One of these is Huang
Fu, Junior Guardian of the Heir-Apparent during the reign of Emperor Ying-tsung [1436-1449], who expressed the following views:

> One tael of silver was valued at three to five strings [in paper
> currency] during the Hung-wu reign, but now it is valued at
> over 1,000 strings. This is indeed the nadir of the paper
> money system. [The government] should appropriate a cer-
> tain amount of government silver, send agents with it to the
> capitals [of Peking and Nanking] and all densely populated
> areas in the provinces, and redeem the old notes according
> to the market rate of exchange. [The redeemed notes] should
> be sent to the capital at the end of the year. When the amount
> of old notes [in circulation] has been reduced, [the govern-
> ment] should then issue new notes to a suitable amount, and
> recall the silver to the capital.

---

*This is a literal rendering of the phrase shen-tao she-chiao 神道設教, which
because of its implication of reliance on mysterious and inexplicable precepts, has
come to be used as a euphemism for "fooling the people."

Huang Fu's ideas stand out in contrast to the views of Ming officials, who were only concerned with defrauding the people of their
silver with paper money. Although he advocated the convertibility of old notes into silver, he was still unable to expound fully the
basic principles involved in the establishment of a system of convertibility. Furthermore, his views were directly opposite to
those of contemporary officials. His proposal was therefore referred to the Board of Finance for decision, and was there rejected.

Another noteworthy thinker was Ch'iu Chün, Grand Secretary
during the reign of Emperor Hsiao-tsung [1488-1505]. He deplored
the mismanagement of paper currency during Chin and Yüan as
having alienated the people and caused the fall of the dynasties,
and held that the evil of paper money lay in its over-supply and
lack of basic standard, just as counterfeiting was the pitfall for
copper coins. Ch'iu's proposal was that there should be in simultaneous use three kinds of legal tender: silver as Class I money,
paper currency as Class II, and copper coins as Class III. The
last two should be used as the common media of exchange, but
with their values set by silver as the standard. 0.01 tael of silver was to be the equivalent of 10 copper cash. New paper notes
were to be valued at 10 cash per string; used but unmutilated ones,
5 cash per string; creased ones, 3 cash per string; and worn-out
ones with only the denomination legible, 1 cash. Silver was to be
used only when the sum involved was 10 taels or more.

Ch'iu was seeking to replace the paper standard of Ming with
a silver standard, so that both paper money and copper cash
would be relegated to the status of supplementary currency. However, the gradations in the value of paper money and the limitations on the use of silver to sums of 10 taels or more show that
it was not a thorough silver standard system that he proposed,
and that his views were seriously limited by the contemporary
monetary confusion.

Third on our list is Ku Yen-wu, a scholar who witnessed the
fall of Ming. In his Jih-chih-lu 日知錄 Ku attacked the paper
currency policy since the beginning of the dynasty as an attempt
"to discard that which was hard and durable, and use that which
was soft and perishable. Since this [policy] was against all reason,
it inevitably became inoperative." Thus, Ku Yen-wu regarded
paper money as something that could by no means be introduced.
But in that case how was the successful circulation of "exchange
medium" during Sung to be explained? Ku said it was because in
Sung the hard money was copper coins, which were extremely
heavy and cumbersome, whereas in Ming the hard money was

silver, which was light and convenient to use, so that, government regulations notwithstanding, the paper money could not be properly introduced. By this contention, however, he still fails to explain the simultaneous circulation of silver and paper money in the Yüan dynasty. Obviously Ku Yen-wu was not able to get at the principles underlying the operation of paper currency.

The last on our list is Yeh Tzu-ch'i of early Ming. Born toward the end of the Yüan dynasty, Yeh was, like Ku Yen-wu, a scholar who had little to do with Ming politics. His comments on the question of paper currency are as follows:

> If paper currency is to be established there must be cash money to serve as its basis; just as in the tea and salt industries use is made of vouchers which are exchangeable on delivery for tea or salt. If paper currency were to operate in a like manner, how could there be any question of its efficacy? Previously [i.e. during the Yüan dynasty], when the system was changed, there should have been established in the prefects and districts treasuries where certain amounts of cash were stored, and the method of cash vouchers should have been followed. [....] By this method, when a voucher [i.e. paper note] is presented, cash should be paid; when a voucher is issued, then cash should be recalled. Let the cash be the mother and the voucher the child, and let there be mutual balance between the two so as to regulate [the prices of] all commodities in the Empire.

Failure to institute such a system, Yeh holds, and reliance on strict legal sanctions instead was a cause for the fall of the Yüan dynasty.

Yeh appears to have been the most enlightened of Ming writers on the subject of paper currency. Though he directly mentioned only the Yüan dynasty, he was actually hinting to the Ming authorities as to the proper method to adopt. Unfortunately, his words fell on deaf ears, and Ming monetary policy embarked upon more than two centuries of errors.

By early Ch'ing paper currency had come to be regarded as a sign of maladministration. Thereupon the system of paper money, which had had an early beginning in China, came to a temporary end.

NOTES

李劍農, 明代的一個官定物價表與不換紙幣, 社會科學季刊
Li Chien-nung, "Ming-tai-ti i-ko kuan-ting wu-chia-piao yü pu-huan chih-pi," Quarterly Journal of Social Science (Wuhan University), I (1930), 501-526.

The principal sources used in this article are Ming shih, Draft Ming History (Ming shih-kao 明史稿), Hsü T'ung-k'ao 續通考, and writings by contemporary individuals such as Ku Yen-wu and Ch'iu Chün. The author does not cite the specific sources for most of his many quotations. The Japanese title of the work by Asai Torao 淺井虎夫 is Shina hōsei shi 支那法制史.

We have presented only about one-third of the items given in Asai's price list.

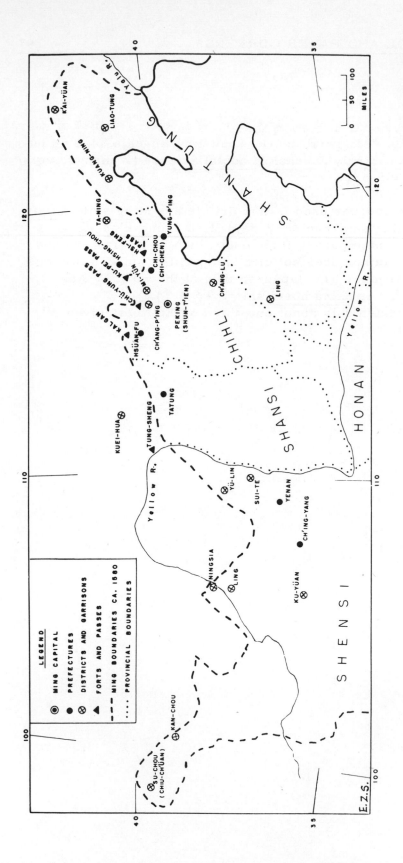

Map 6. Northern frontiers of Ming dynasty

LEGEND

⊚ MING CAPITAL
● PREFECTURES
⊗ DISTRICTS AND GARRISONS
▲ FORTS AND PASSES
- - - MING BOUNDARIES CA. 1580
· · · · PROVINCIAL BOUNDARIES

K'AI-YÜAN

LIAO-TUNG

KUANG-NING

TA-NING

HSING-CHOU
HSI-FÊNG PASS

KU-PEI PASS
CHI-CHOU
YUNG-P'ING
CHI-CHEN
(CHI-CHEN)

CHU-YUNG PASS
MI-YÜN

KALGAN
CH'ANG-P'ING
PEKING
(SHUN-T'IEN)

HSÜAN-FU

CH'ANG-LU

LING

CHIHLI

KUEI-HUA

YUNG-SHÊNG

TATUNG

SHANSI

HONAN

Yellow R.

Yellow R.

YÜ-LIN

SUI-TE
YENAN

CH'ING-YANG

NINGSIA

LING

KU-YÜAN

SHENSI

KAN-CHOU

SU-CHOU
(CHIU-CH'ÜAN)

E.Z.S.

SHANTUNG

MILES
0 50 100

40

35

120

110

100

21

THE MING SYSTEM OF MERCHANT COLONIZATION

by

WANG CH'UNG-WU

1. Merchant Colonization and the "Salt Exchange" System

In frontier areas it was impossible for the garrison colonies to be self-sufficient. The deficits therefore had to be made up by the transportation of provisions by the peasantry, a service which was called People's Grain Delivery. The undeveloped state of communications in early times made it especially necessary to devise comparatively economical means of transportation. Apart from the People's Grain Delivery, there were three methods of transporting grain:

(a) Delivery of grain by convicts: In the course of carrying out colonization by the people, the government had instituted convict settlements. Later, owing to the shortage of supplies in the frontier areas , it had the convicts deliver grain. By the Cheng-t'ung period [1436-1449] the "Ordinances for the Delivery of Rice by Convicts" had become especially severe.

(b) Rewards of official positions for those who delivered rice: This is the so-called Cap and Sash Grain Contribution. In the Ching-t'ai period [1450-1456], for example, when a drought in several prefectures in Shansi affected the grain supplies for the troops, the well-to-do were exhorted to contribute grain, legally defined rewards being offered for presenting grain at specific points. For example, in the case of those who transported beans to Hsüan-fu [modern Hsüan-hua in Chahar], a contribution of 1,000 tan 石 was rewarded with the military rank of Chief Banner; 800 tan, Small Banner; and 90 tan, Captain. In the Hung-chih period [1488-1505] those who contributed 100 tan of rice or 16 taels of silver at Yenan [in Shensi] or Ch'ing-yang [in Kansu] were rewarded with the privilege of becoming expectant officials without submitting to examination. These and other instances of rewards for the transportation of supplies probably succeeded in their purpose.

(c) "Salt Exchange": This was a system in which salt merchants

transported grain to the frontier areas and in return received certificates with which they obtained salt. The section on "Food and
Money" in the Ming History states:

> In the salt system of the Ming dynasty, nothing surpassed the
> "Salt Exchange." In the third year of Hung-wu [1370], Shansi
> Province reported: "Grain for Tatung [in northern Shansi],
> when transported from Ling District [in Shantung] to the T'ai-
> ho Range [in northern Shansi], involves long distances and
> heavy expenses. We petition that merchants be permitted to
> deliver grain with compensation at the rate of one small Huai
> salt certificate* for every tan of grain delivered at Tatung
> Granary, or for every 1.3 tan delivered at T'ai-yüan Granary.
> After the sale [of grain to the government] has been completed,
> the merchants take the certificates given them to the offices
> where [the salt] is located and present them [in exchange for
> salt]. In this way, the expenses of transportation will be econo-
> mized and the supply of grain at the frontier will be sufficient."
> The emperor approved this. The merchants were summoned to
> deliver grain in return for salt; this was called "Salt Exchange."
> Later most of the frontier areas of the provinces followed
> suit in order to build up military supplies. The salt system
> and frontier plans advanced on the basis of mutual assistance.

This system was taken over by other frontier provinces as a
means of combating the food deficit in their areas. Initially the salt
merchants had merely been asked to deliver grain to the frontier.
Very soon in early Ming, however, most of them began to bring
new land under cultivation in the border areas and to supply the grain
locally. This was the so-called "merchant colonization," which was
instituted during the Hung-wu and Yung-lo periods [1368-1424].

The system of merchant colonization was of help to military
colonization and frontier defense in three ways:

(a) It supplied the soldiers with grain, something which the
troops could not adequately accomplish themselves. From the government's point of view, this saved on the transportation of grain.
From the point of view of the merchants themselves, investing part
of their wealth in assembling migrants to go and bring new land under cultivation enabled them "to obtain the advantage of compensation in salt without the disadvantage of the transporting of grain."

---

*According to the treatise on "Food and Money" in the Ming History, a "large
certificate" (ta yin 大引) was good for 400 catties of salt, and a "small certificate" (hsiao yin 小引) for 200 catties.

(b) The peasants who opened up the land, being chiefly unemployed migrants, were thus able to obtain employment, thereby
directly reducing the number of unemployed and indirectly avoiding disturbances in the country.

(c) The grain supply on the frontier increased as a result of the
merchant colonization, so that when the soldiers lacked supplies,
they could buy grain with money. Grain prices also would not increase, and the market could not be manipulated by powerful individuals.

2. Expansion of Merchant Colonization and
Contributions of Grain by "Salt Exchange"

The "Salt Exchange" system stated in northern Shansi and
spread from there to Ningsia and Szechwan in 1373, to Yunnan in
1389, and to Kweichow in 1419. During the Hsüan-te period [1426-
1435] the system of merchant colonization was gradually extended
into all the northern garrison areas. Subsequently it also spread
into Manchuria and into the various frontier garrison areas of
Shensi. In a few exceptional cases the system also penetrated into
some districts in the interior of the country.

It should be noted that the ratio between grain paid in and salt
given in return varied according to the quality of the salt and from
one period to another. The Veritable Records of Ming contain information indicating the various destinations of the grain, the
sources of the salt given in return, and the ratio between the two
commodities. An examination of this information reveals the following points:

(a) The salt of the Huai River area was the best, followed by
that of Chekiang, Ch'ang-lu [in Hopei], and other areas. Hence
Huai salt fetched the highest amounts of grain. The Huai River region was the biggest producer of salt, and the Huai salt merchants
were the most powerful. This explains why the Huai merchants
later requested that the payment of grain for salt be commuted into payment in silver.

(b) In general the ratio between grain and salt gradually increased. In 1433, for example, one yin 引 [four piculs] of Huai
salt required a payment of only 4.5-5.0 pecks of rice, but by 1435
it took 9.0-9.5 pecks. As a result there were frequent petitions
reporting that the salt merchants were less interested because of
the lower profits and requesting that the proportion of grain relative to salt be reduced. The petitions were successful. In 1450 the
Veritable Records of Ming reported:

Previously, when the merchants, in response to imperial
summons, delivered grain to Lung-ch'ing Granary in Mi-yün
[in northern Hopei] in return for Huai salt, for each yin of
salt they paid 8 pecks of rice and 5 pecks of beans, or 40
bales of hay. At Ku-pei Pass [in northern Hopei] the rates
per yin of salt were 7 pecks of rice and 3 pecks of beans, or
35 bales of hay. Now these rates are considered too high and
have been reduced. With respect to transactions at Lung-
ch'ing Granary in Mi-yün, there has been a reduction of 1 peck
each for rice and beans, and of 10 bales for hay. At Ku-pei
Pass there has been a reduction of 5 pecks for rice and 1
peck for beans, and of 10 bales for hay.

Other reductions are also noted in the records. I suspect, however,
that these reductions were exceptional and ephemeral. The general
pattern was still one of increase. After the Ching-t'ai period [1450-
1456] military colonization gradually disintegrated, and the system
of grain deliveries by "Salt Exchange" became one of the most important means of supplying the troops. This naturally could not but
contribute to increasing the amount of grain which had to be paid
for salt. The more the grain payments increased, the fewer were
those willing to engage in "Salt Exchange." Here we can see the
circumstances leading to the gradual decline of merchant colonization.

3. Yeh Ch'i and the "Salt Exchange" System

Mention of merchant colonization and the "Salt Exchange" system
immediately evokes the memory of Yeh Ch'i, President of the Board
of Finance during the Hung-chih period and the first to advocate payment in silver instead of grain. People subsequently misinterpreted
this action, believing that the collapse of military colonization resulted from the abolition of merchant colonization, and that the system of payment in silver was sufficient to cause, in the words of
the Ming History, "the abandonment of merchant colonization, the
sky-rocketing of grain prices, and the increasing depletion of frontier supplies." As a matter of fact, this is an unjust accusation
against Yeh Ch'i.

Critics of Yeh Ch'i charge that his reason for commuting grain
payments into silver was to benefit merchants who came from his
own area in the Huai region and were his cronies and relatives.
Yet the Ming History records a number of items which attest to
his probity. Moreover, the change was not recommended by Yeh
Ch'i alone, but by other officials as well, including one from

southern Kiangsu who of course was not a fellow provincial of the
Huai merchants.

The aspersions against Yeh Ch'i can also be refuted by an
analysis of the chronology of the change. Well before his time
there were cases of payment in silver rather than grain. The official change-over, initiated in 1492, merely represented a formali-
zation by Yeh Ch'i of what had already become widespread in in-
formal practice.

Finally, there was the factor of objective necessity. Most of
the late Ming emperors were inept rulers, spendthrifts who knew
nothing of financial matters and suffered from financial difficulties.
With the change to silver payments for salt, however, the Ming
History notes that "The price of grain became double that in the
early part of the dynasty....and the Imperial Granary accumulated
up to a million taels of silver." Before the Ching-t'ai period one
yin of Huai salt required a payment of at most not more than 1.5
tan of rice; at the time of the commutation into payment by silver
in 1492, one tan of grain was worth only 0.2 tael of silver, whereas after the change the merchants had to pay 0.3 to 0.4 tael per
yin. Obviously it was the government that profited. From the merchants' point of view the previous system had become unbearable
because of official corruption, protracted delays in issuance of
salt according to the certificates, and other evils. The commutation into payment in silver was of mutual benefit to the government,
which doubled its receipts of silver, and to the merchants, who
"no longer suffered delays in getting salt."

4. Decline of the System of Merchant Colonization

The commutation of grain deliveries to payment in silver resulted in the decline of the system of merchant colonization. From
this stemmed "the sky-rocketing of grain prices and the increasing
depletion of frontier supplies." Frontier defenses were affected in
two ways:

(a) Grain prices on the frontiers gradually increased. The
Board of Finance shipped silver instead of rice to the frontier, but
since military rations depended on rice, the effect could only be a
rise in prices. The situation at Yü-lin [in northern Shensi] is an
example. Previously, when merchant colonization was well developed there, a tael of silver could buy two to three tan [i.e. 20-
30 pecks] of rice. After the commutation, however, the land was
abandoned, and a tael of silver could buy only .8-.9 pecks of rice
in bountiful years, and as little as .5-.6 pecks in lean years. In
infertile areas, where the harvests were smallest and crop failures

most frequent, the soldiers nominally were supposed to receive
a monthly grain ration of one picul but actually received only 2 -
3 pecks in kind, or 7-8 pecks in commutation.* One peck in kind
was worth .15 or .16 tael of silver, and one peck in commutation
was worth .07 tael. Thus two pecks in commutation was less than
one peck in kind. Hence, in the words of a Ming writer, "the im-
poverished soldiers wore ragged uniforms, lived in tumble-down
barracks, and ate only three or four bowls of watery gruel a day.
If they did get enough to go to sleep with a full stomach, they
would boast of this as quite a feat."

(b) The amount of silver exported to the frontier gradually increased. The rise in prices following the shift from grain payments to silver payments forced the government to send large
amounts of silver to the frontier to pay for the increasing cost of
grain. During the Hung-chih and Cheng-te periods [1488-1521],
the amount of silver sent to the frontier for food purchases was
only 400,000-odd taels. It increased to 590,000 at the beginning
of the Chia-ching period [1522-1566], to 1,000,000 after 1539, to
2,200,000 in 1549, to 2,400,000 in 1559, to 2,500,000 in 1562,
and finally to 2,800,000 at the beginning of the Lung-ch'ing period
[1567-1572], a four-fold increase in less than forty-five years.
The accompanying table shows the increase in the amount of silver sent to the northern frontier regions for food purchases. In
some cases the increase ran to as much as twenty-five times the
earlier amount.

From the middle of the Ming period on, the problem of food
supplies for the frontier areas became extremely acute. The harsh
measures which followed accelerated the collapse of the Ming dynasty.

The reader will probably ask at this point why the system of
merchant colonization collapsed, and why, after its disintegration,
it could not be restored. There were four reasons:

(a) Once any system has collapsed it is very difficult to restore.
Moreover, the commuting of grain payments into silver enabled
the merchants to avoid the hardship of transportation and the government to obtain more silver, so that despite the harm resulting
from the collapse of merchant colonization, it was difficult to restore the old system.

(b) Powerful individuals upset the salt system and made it impossible for the merchants to engage in "Salt Exchange." At the
beginning of the Ming dynasty only the merchants and the common

*Presumably the commuted payment was in the form of paper money or, more
likely, some sort of script nominally equal to a specified quantity of grain.

Deliveries of Silver to Frontier Areas
(in taels)

Place	Amount sent before 1522	Amount sent during Lung-ch'ing period [1567-1572]	Increase
Chi-chen [in northern Hopei]	67,000	389,000	312,000
Mi-yün [in northern Hopei]	15,000	394,000	379,000
Yung-p'ing [in northeastern Hopei]	29,000	246,000	217,000
Hsüan-fu [in Chahar]	51,000	333,000	282,000
Tatung [in northern Shansi]	50,000	420,000	370,040
Shansi*	200,000	213,000	13,000
Yenan [in Shensi]	100,000	367,000	267,000

*See the note on page 309.

people were permitted to engage in such activities. Anyone in the
family of an official of the fourth grade or higher was not permitted
to compete with the common people for profits. During the Ching-
t'ai period, however, the Mongol incursions and the lack of food
supplies on the northern frontier evoked the following edict: "Families of military personnel and civilian officials are permitted without discrimination, in food deficit areas beyond the frontiers, to
engage in "Salt Exchange" so as to obtain salt by certificates from
the salt comptrollers of Huai, Che[kiang], and Ch'ang-lu." Prior
to this there were already some leading magnates in the garrison
areas who, according to an entry in the Veritable Records of Ming
for 1435, "freely allowed their servants and retainers to upset the
salt system, engage in private deals involving hundreds of boat-
loads in each case, and practice armed robbery everywhere they
went, so that the circuit inspectors and government troops did not
dare make inquiries." Now with the relaxation in the prohibitions,
officials and powerful civilians, on hearing of delivering grain in
the "Salt Exchange," sent their servants to engage in grain purchases on the frontier. In addition they deliberately declared that
the way was too long and the transportation too difficult, and demanded a reduction in the amount of grain to be paid for the salt.
Furthermore, they raised the minimum requirement of grain deliveries and made it impossible for small merchants to engage in
"Salt Exchange." The Ming History says: "Purchases on the frontier were invariably made in terms of a thousand piculs of grain
and ten thousand bales of fodder. As a result the families of middle
officials and military officers were able to monopolize the profits."
The corruption of the powerful magnates increased during the
Hung-chih and Cheng-te periods. In the end they resorted to the
practice of contracting for the government salt certificates and
then selling these at a high price to the merchants. Thus they could
obtain big profits without transporting grain to the frontier or buying it there. The general run of merchants, who were without
power or capital, could only humble themselves to buy the salt certificates from the magnates in the hope of getting no more than a
pittance of profits. Thus the salt system was thrown into confusion,
and merchant colonization of course was even more out of the
question.

(c) The increasing cost of salt certificates made it gradually
more difficult for the merchants to obtain a profit. Before the
Ching-t'ai period, as mentioned above in Section 2, there was already a tendency in this direction. Later it became even more pronounced. The situation was aggravated by all manner of oppressive
and corrupt practices on the part of the officials. Under such

conditions, the merchants were of course unwilling to make deliveries of grain, and the system of garrison colonization was therefore abandoned.

(d) The sale of "surplus salt" at depressed prices made the merchants unwilling to deal in other "regular" salt. The distinction
between the two kinds of salt is indicated in the following passage
by a late Ming writer, Shen Mou-hsiao:

> In the system at the beginning of the dynasty, the entire salt
> production was placed under [government] control so as to
> assist the grain supplies on the frontier. Hence the salt ob-
> tained by frontier merchants with official certificates was
> called "government salt." Salt not covered by the certificates
> was frequently bought from the surplus of the small salterns
> by the authorities, who stored it up in various markets to
> await the arrival of the merchants. This was called "sur-
> plus salt," but it amounted to the same thing as government
> salt.... Apart from this, there was no other salt.

This surplus salt had been taken over by the government lest the
merchants traffic in it. The original intention was fine. But later,
owing to the fact that surplus salt was very cheap and its sale
brought many advantages, it was sold in large quantities and
squeezed out the regular salt.

Surplus salt sold illegally by private individuals was called
"private salt," a thing which was strictly forbidden by the Ming
policy of nationalization of the salt industry. A decree ordered
that those who dealt in "private salt" were to be put to death by
strangulation. As a result traffic in this sort of salt was a rare occurrence at the beginning of the dynasty. Later, however, with the
local authorities unable to buy the surplus salt [for the government]
owing to the collapse of the currency system, and with the concur-
rent ban on the private traffic in surplus salt, there resulted on
the one hand a shortage of salt for the people's consumption and
a rise in its price, and on the other hand extreme distress among
the salt-makers whose livelihood was based on surplus salt. This
further increased the traffic in private salt. As one writer put it,
"To avoid the evils of the regular levies merchants could not but
traffic in private salt. Deprived of the profits from surplus salt,
the salt-makers could not but sell privately in order to make a
living."

As the government became corrupt and the salt prohibitions
were relaxed, the official inspectors of private salt entered into
corrupt deals with the merchants. What used to be surplus salt was

now entirely transformed into private salt. Because of this the
merchants who dealt in legal salt by the "Salt Exchange" system
became even fewer in number. The system of merchant colonization, therefore, also could not be restored.

NOTES

王崇武，明代的商屯制度，禹貢
Wang Ch'ung-wu, "Ming-tai-ti shang-t'un chih-tu," <u>Yü-kung</u>,
V, 12 (August 6, 1936), 1-15.

In an introductory note the author remarks that this article is
one chapter in his draft <u>Ming-tai-ti t'un-t'ien chih-tu</u> 明代的
屯田制度 (The Ming System of Colonization). He also states that
there were three forms of colonization in Ming times--by the army,
by the people, and by merchants.

22

FRONTIER HORSE MARKETS IN THE MING DYNASTY

by

HOU JEN-CHIH

PART I. INTRODUCTION

1. Origins of Horse Markets in the Ming Dynasty

The first horse markets in Ming were established in 1406 in the Liao-tung region [southern Manchuria] as a means of dealing with the barbarian tribes in that area. The horse market at Tatung [in Shansi] was established for the first time in 1438. After a lapse it was re-established, together with one at Hsüan-fu [southern Cha-har], in 1551, but the two did not last for more than a year. It was toward the end of the Lung-ch'ing reign [1567-1572], when [the Mongol chieftain] Anda offered to present tribute to China, that the markets at Hsüan-fu and Tatung, together with one in Shansi, were re-opened.* From then on for some sixty years horse markets continued in operation along the northern frontiers. They exercised a great influence on the course of Ming frontier relations.

The numerous military campaigns of early Ming demanded large supplies of horses, most of which came from the northern frontier peoples. The formal institution of a market place for the purchase of horses by the Chinese government was first discussed in 1405, following a request from the people of the Fu-yü Garrison

---

*During part of the Ming dynasty there were, as noted below at the beginning of section 2, chiu pien 九邊 "nine frontier areas" along the northern border. (Actually the total number, and the individual places, are given differently by various sources.) The present article limits its attention to three such areas, those designated by the names Hsüan-fu, Tatung, and Shansi, which thus have a special connotation not carried by the customary usage of these names. For example, in the present article "Shansi" refers to the frontier area of that name, and not to the identically-named province either of Ming times or of today.

Under the frontier area was the wei 衛 "garrison," a term designating both the military force and the territory under its control--e.g. Ta-t'ung tso-wei "Tatung Left Garrison" and Ta-t'ung yu-wei "Tatung Right Garrison."

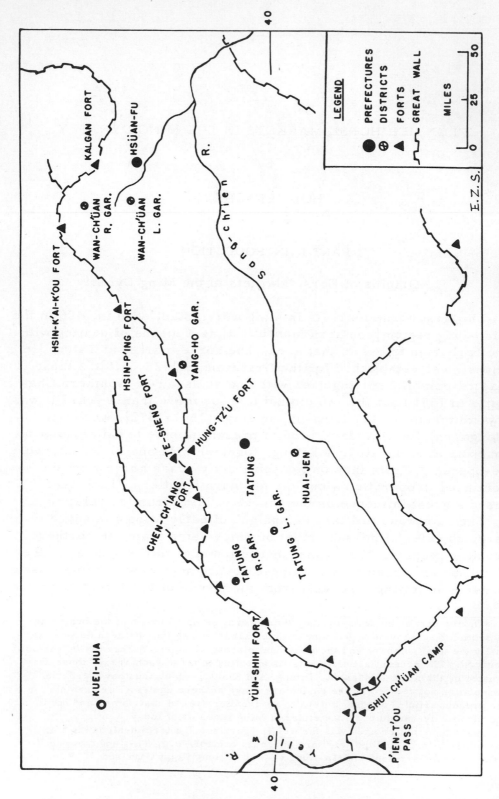

LEGEND

●	PREFECTURES
⊕	DISTRICTS
▲	FORTS
╱╲╱	GREAT WALL

MILES

0   25   50

KALGAN FORT

● HSÜAN-FU

HSIN-K'AI-K'OU FORT

⊕ WAN-CH'ÜAN R. GAR.

⊕ WAN-CH'ÜAN L. GAR.

HSIN-P'ING FORT

⊕ YANG-HO GAR.

TE-SHENG FORT

HUNG-TZ'Ü FORT

CHEN-CH'IANG FORT

● TATUNG

⊕ TATUNG R.GAR.

⊕ TATUNG L. GAR.

⊕ HUAI-JEN

○ KUEI-HUA

YÜN-SHIH FORT

SHUI-CH'ÜAN CAMP

P'IEN-T'OU PASS

So-ch'ien R.

Yellow R.

40

40

E.Z.S.

Map 7. Northern horse markets of Ming

[in Manchuria] for permission to sell their horses at the capital
[i.e. Peking]. The decision was made to set up markets not in the
capital, but at Kuang-ning and K'ai-yüan [in Manchuria]; these
were later known as the Liaotung Horse Markets. Henceforth the
term "horse markets" had not only a commercial connotation, but
also a political significance, since it was the means by which the
sovereign-tributary relationship between China and the frontier
peoples was manifested. In other words, the Ming horse markets
were a political measure for the control of the frontier peoples.
As the [Ming work] Hsü T'ung-k'ao has aptly stated: "In early Ming
horse markets were established in the east, and tea markets in
the west, so that the frontiers could be controlled and expenses
of border garrisons reduced."

2. Northern Frontier Establishments and Border Troubles

Frontier troubles, especially Mongol incursions, were a major
problem throughout the Ming dynasty. The northern boundary of
the empire extended from the Yalu River in the east to Chiu-ch'üan
[in Kansu] in the west. Along it were established nine frontier
areas, which were, from east to west, Liaotung [southern Man-
churia]; Chi-chou [or Chi-chen in northern Hopei]; Hsüan-fu
[near Kalgan] in Chahar; Tatung; Yen-Sui [i.e. the area comprising Yenan and Sui-te, in Shensi]; three fortified passes in Shansi;
Ku-yüan in Shensi; Ningsia; and Kan-Su [i.e. the area comprising
Kan-chou and Su-chou in Kansu]. Later the strong-points of Ta-
ning [near Peking] and of Tung-sheng [west of Tatung] were added
to serve as buffers for Hsüan-fu and Tatung, in the eastern and
western parts respectively of the chain of defenses. Between 1411
and 1430, however, territories some 300 li wide were lost in the
east; this included the fall of Ta-ning to the Urianghai tribe. Subsequently Tung-sheng was also lost in the west. As a result the
Hsüan-fu, Tatung, and Shansi frontier areas were subjected to border invasions together with their attendant problems.
    After the fall of the Yüan dynasty the Mongols maintained them-
selves to the north of China. The most powerful tribes, which included the Tartars in the east and the Oirats in the west, dominated
the others.* In 1409 the chiefs of the Oirats came to pay tribute to

---

*During the Ming dynasty the name Ta-tan (Tartars) generally designated the
northeastern Khalkha Mongols in distinction from the Oirats, living southeast of
them. (Wolfgang Franke, Addenda and Corrigenda to Pokotilov's History of the
Eastern Mongols during the Ming Dynasty. Studia Serica, Series A, No. 3.
[Chengtu and Peiping, 1949], p. 21).

the Ming government, and were invested with princely titles in return. The investiture of the Tartar chiefs took place in 1413 and
1423. The Ming government was unable, however, to check the
frequent rebellions or to damage seriously the power of these two
major tribes. By the Hsüan-te period [1426-1435] the Oirats had
achieved hegemony north of the Chinese border, and in the 1430's
began to ask for the opening of markets where they could sell their
horses to the Chinese. This was granted by Ming in 1438, but the
Mongols were forbidden to purchase weapons, copper, or iron from
China.

Dissatisfied with the low prices offered by a Chinese eunuch
for their horses in 1449, the Oirats, under the leadership of Esen,
staged a major invasion across the border, smashing the forts
around Hsüan-fu and Tatung and reaching the vicinity of the capital. In the Ching-t'ai reign [1450-56] the Oirats again concluded
peace and sent tribute to Ming. In 1452 Oirat envoys were given a
banquet at the Board of Rites [in Peking], and were allowed to sell
horses. A passage in the "Biography of Anda" in Military Exploits
of the Wan-li Period describes the situation as follows:

> When [the Oirats] came to pay tribute, the envoys numbered
> as many as 3,000 and more. This caused hardship to the
> frontier population... In the first month of the following year
> (1453) a banquet was given at the Board of Rites for 2,876
> Oirat envoys, including Chajan and others. Of these, twenty-
> two chieftains, chief envoys, and deputy envoys were ordered
> by imperial decree to be given gold and silver according to
> their ranks. The gifts were dispensed by generals, high com-
> manders, guard commanders, post commanders, and other
> officials who had been appointed to the task. Others [of the
> Oirats] were all given silk, boots, and hats. The gifts were
> worth more than 100,000 [taels?].

These periodic tribute missions and horse sales were interrupted in the T'ien-shun and Ch'eng-hua periods [1457-1487] owing to the unsettled political conditions among the Mongol tribes.
Border relations between the Ming and the Mongols consisted of
periods of strain interspersed either with brief years of tribute
and trade, or with frequent invasions, the seriousness of which
was not truthfully reported to the Ming central government.

The beginning of the Chia-ching reign [1522-1566] saw the rise
of Anda in Inner Mongolia. Together with his elder brother Gun
Bilig Mergen Jinong, Anda was able to devastate most of the border

regions from Yü-lin [in Shansi] in the west through Tatung to Hsüan-
fu in the east, the campaigns of 1540 and 1542 being particularly
disastrous for the Chinese population. It is estimated that within a
period of one month in 1542 Anda's forces subjugated and looted ten
"garrisons" and thirty-eight prefectures and districts; killed or
carried off over 200,000 people and 2,000,000 heads of cattle,
horses, sheep, and hogs; and seized a proportionate amount of
clothing and gold and silver. Some 10,000 units of private and public houses were burned, and several hundred thousand ch'ing of
agricultural land was laid waste. A consequence of this campaign
was that the forts at Tatung were lost to the invaders, a fact which
greatly increased the danger of the situation.

PART II. HORSE MARKETS IN THE CHIA-CHING PERIOD

1. Anda's Repeated Requests for Tribute
Relations and His Invasion of 1550

Anda led his forces in an expedition against Tatung in the autumn
of 1550. Ch'ou Luan, the commanding general of Hsüan-fu and
Tatung, succeeded in persuading Anda, by means of bribery and
the promise of trade, to change the objective of his attack. Thereupon Anda's troops swept eastward, charged inside the Ku-pei Pass
[on the Great Wall north of Peking], plundered cities in northern
Chihli [i.e. Hopei], and laid seige to Peking for three days before
retreating. This was the historic invasion of 1550. It was the cul-
mination of years of negotiations and unsettled relations between
the Mongols and the Ming government.

Following his earlier invasion of Shansi in 1540 Anda had repeatedly requested permission to pay tribute to Ming. In 1541 he
sent his Chinese aide Shih T'ien-chüeh on a mission to Yang-ho
[northeast of Tatung] for this purpose. Upon learning of it, however,
the Board of War rejected the request on the grounds that "barbarians are full of cunning tricks and cannot be trusted," and instead
set a price on Anda's head. This so incensed Anda that he carried
out another invasion, which penetrated the frontiers. In the following year Shih T'ien-chüeh was sent at the head of some Mongol envoys on a similar mission. This time the Mongol emissaries were
killed by the governor at Tatung, and Shih was taken captive and
sent to Peking, where he was beheaded. These events resulted in
Anda's devastating invasion of 1542 mentioned above. A third mission was sent by Anda in 1546, but the envoys again met death at
Tatung. Weng Wan-ta, the governor-general [of the whole area],
objected strongly to such treatment of the Mongol emissaries, but
to no avail.

More missions requesting the setting up of tribute relations
were sent by Anda, but the local officials did not dare even to report them to the central government. The efforts in 1547 and 1548
were reported to Peking by Weng Wan-ta, who was seriously concerned with establishing peaceful relations with Anda, while China
strengthened her frontier defenses, but his importunities brought
only reprimands from the emperor, and ultimately his own dismissal from the post. Proposals for paying tribute hence temporarily came to a halt.

Various reasons prompted Anda to seek a tribute relationship
with Ming. According to the "Biography of Weng Wan-ta" in the
Ming History, these were, first, to obtain Chinese silk cloth,
which could not be gotten in sufficient amounts in the border raids,
and second, to form an alliance with China in opposition to one of
his rivals. Weng Wan-ta was fully cognizant of these factors, and
urged the Ming government to utilize to its own advantage the internal split among the barbarians and their desire for gain, but
his counsels found no sympathetic audience at court in Peking,
where the predominating influence at the time stemmed from the
advocates of war.

Now in 1550, when Anda turned his invading forces eastward
after having been bribed by Ch'ou Luan, the latter presented to the
throne the following memorial for the opening of horse markets:

Hsüan [-fu] and Ta [-tung] are the localities where border
conflicts have been most severe. This arises from the fact
that the enemy's bases are all located inside the border,
and that our garrison troops have been in the habit of passing
in and out among them and trading with them. With the passage of time close friendships have developed, so that the
bandits [i.e. the Mongols] have come to know all about the
strength and weakness of the Chinese forces. Chou Shang-
wen, the former commanding general, also clandestinely allowed his followers to trade with the bandits, who, in addition,
often employed fugitives and deserters. In sum, frontier defenses have reached a hopeless state.

With the increase of their [i.e. the Mongols'] population
they have had to depend on China for every kind of supply.
When unable to obtain what they need, they stage an invasion.
Thus, they have raided the frontier year after year, and always with profit. In past days, when tribute relations were
not permitted [by the central government, Chou] Shang-wen
allowed them to trade when they were submissive, following
which the border became quieter as they were able to get

what they desired. Now, rather than let frontier officials illegally establish such relationships and reap the profits, why
not have the Court initiate this step so that the favor will
stem from above? Even now trade is being carried on at the
garrisons of Liao [-tung] Left [Garrison], Kan-Su, and Hsi-
feng Pass [in Hopei]. If Your Majesty would graciously consent to proclaim to the border people that they will be allowed
to sell horses at the various garrison areas, they will become
China's shields for generations to come, and frontier conflicts
will thereby be eliminated.

The proposal was favorably received by the emperor. But before any decision could be reached by the Board [of War], Anda's
invading forces had already penetrated to the outskirts of Peking.
Ch'ou Luan was commissioned as the supreme commander of all
the forces marshalled in the capital against the Mongols. It turned
out, however, that his own troops were the most undisciplined,
pillaging the nearby villages disguised as invaders. Anda was able
to reach one of the Peking city gates, take hostages, and present,
as his price for ending hostilities, the demand that permission be
given for three thousand Mongols to enter Peking for tribute purposes. The emperor consulted with the high officials, including
the grand secretary, Yen Sung, and the president of the Board of
Rites, Hsü Chieh. It was his opinion that "We should not stint on
furs, money, pearls, and gems [to give to the invaders], if it is
for the good of the country." Anda's request for paying tribute was
ultimately rejected, however, on the grounds that three thousand
Mongol emissaries inside the capital might prove unmanageable,
and that they might turn out to be a Trojan horse for a later attack
by Anda. Fortunately the latter, satiated with his victories and
plundering, withdrew of his own accord on the following day. As
a result of the withdrawal by Anda and his men the matter was
brought to a peaceful close.

2. Initiation of Horse Markets at Hsüan-fu and Tatung

Ch'ou Luan continued to rise in power after the withdrawal of
Anda in 1550, gaining the complete confidence of the emperor. In
1551 Anda renewed his request for the establishment of markets.
As an earnest of his intentions he delivered the chieftain Ulji as
a hostage, and voluntarily arrested two Chinese turncoats. The
request was forwarded to Peking by Su Yu, the governor-general
of Hsüan-fu and Tatung. At the same time Su Yu made the following recommendation:

We should maintain our vigilance so as to demonstrate our
control [over the barbarians]. While keeping our defense works
built up, we shou'd let them gather the people of the various
tribes at Hsüan-fu, Tatung, Yen[-Sui], and Ning [sia] in order
to engage in trade. We can exchange our cloth and grain for
their cattle, sheep, mules, and horses. Thus their desire will
be satisfied, and our frontier defenses can be strengthened.

At court this memorial was given hearty support by Ch'ou Luan,
who also memorialized in favor of opening markets for trade, and
compared such undertakings with the markets existing at Liaotung.
He proposed that the high provincial authorities should announce
to the tribes the opening of horse markets in the Tatung garrison
area, that the Board of War should appropriate 100,000 taels of
silver to purchase silk cloth for the trade, and that there should
be four periods of trade per year. The same procedure was to apply to the other garrison areas, such as Hsüan-fu, Yen-Sui, and
Ningsia, according to the discretion of the local officials.

In his advocacy of horse markets Ch'ou Luan was supported by
Chao Ching, president of the Board of War. The emperor consulted
the grand secretary, Yen Sung, who thought four trading periods
a year too frequent, and suggested that they be reduced to two, one
in spring and the other in autumn. This was approved. A decree of
April 9, 1551, ordered the opening of horse markets, first at
Tatung, then at Hsüan-fu, and appointed Shih Tao, a secretary in
the Board of War, as general supervisor of trade matters at Tatung.
The Board of War appropriated 100,000 taels for this purpose.
The policy of Ch'ou Luan and Yen Sung was in the ascendancy, and
opposition to this horse trade was effectively suppressed in the
government.

The Tatung horse market was opened in the fourth month [May 6-
June 3] of the same year at Chen-ch'iang Fort,* which was located
eighty li to the north of the city and was a new fort built only in 1545.

Anda arrived with his followers for the opening of the market,
which lasted four days until all the silk cloth had been disposed of.

---

*Chen-ch'iang Pao literally means "Subduing-the-Barbarians Fort." As the
names of the Great Wall forts offer an interesting sidelight on China's frontier
relations, we note here the literal meanings of the names for several other forts
mentioned in the present article: Chang-chia-k'ou Pao "Chang-Family-Pass
Fort" (present Kalgan), Hsin-k'ai-k'ou Pao "Newly-Opened-Pass-Fort," Hsin-
p'ing Pao "Newly Pacified Fort," Hung-tz'u Pao "Great Bounty Fort," Shui-
ch'üan Ying "Water-Spring Camp," Te-sheng Pao "Victory Fort," Yün-shih Pao
"Clouds-Stone Fort," Sha-hu Pao "Kill-the-Barbarians Fort," Mieh-hu Pao
"Exterminate-the-Barbarians Fort."

This was followed by a feast [given by the Chinese] in accordance
with the requirements of propriety. Anda presented nine horses
as tribute, together with a memorial, written in Mongol, attesting
his loyalty. In return he was given a lined red brocade gown, a
large hat topped with a gold button, and a gold sash. Anda's adopted
son Toqto received a lined red brocade gown; four others, including an envoy and the hostage Ulji, each received a blue brocade
gown. In addition Anda was presented with four pieces of multi-
colored silk cloth.

In the following month the Hsüan-fu horse market was inaugu-
rated at Hsin-k'ai-k'ou Fort, some 40 li northwest of the city of
Wan-ch'üan Right Garrison. This fort was built in 1435 and occupied a strategic and much assaulted position close to the border.
The tribes of five chieftains--Bayasqal [a younger brother of An-
da], Sengge Dügüreng [or Huang Taiji, Anda's eldest son], Bayo
[a grandson], Bulang Taji [?], and Uighurchin Taiji [a grandson]
--came to trade at this market.

Of the 100,000 taels appropriated for the horse markets, 60,000
were assigned to Tatung and 40,000 to Hsüan-fu. At Tatung the
transactions included 4,740 bolts of silk, which cost 8,893 taels,
and 7,000 bolts of cotton cloth. In exchange the Chinese obtained
a total of 4,771 horses at a cost of [approximately] ten taels apiece.
Total expenditures at Tatung amounted to 44,032 taels. The remaining sum was used in gifts and feasts [for the Mongols]. No details are available for the Hsüan-fu market.

In the same year two more horse markets were established, one
in the garrison areas of Yen-Sui for Noyandara Jinong [a nephew
of Anda], and one in Ningsia for Baisangghur Lang Taiji [a brother
of Noyandara]. These operated along the same lines as the markets at Tatung and Hsüan-fu.

Data in the Institutes of Ming indicate that when the horse markets were opened, strict regulations were set up for their control.
Among other things, only authorized persons were allowed to par-
ticipate in the transactions during the market days, and private
trade was banned between Chinese and Mongols outside the market
periods. Nevertheless, according to the "Biography of Ch'ou Luan"
in the Draft Ming History, Anda's people behaved in an unruly and
military fashion from the start, even threatening to stage an invasion of Tatung Left Garrison. Soon Anda even requested the
opening of markets for the sale of Mongol sheep and cattle. [The
comptroller of the markets] Shih Tao, presented the case as follows:

Recently [....] with sincere earnestness Toqto, pointing out
that the wealthy among the barbarians are exchanging their

horses for textiles, has asked whether the poor among them could be permitted to obtain rice and wheat in return for cattle and sheep, which are their only property. Your Minister thinks that about two- or three-tenths of these barbarians are rich, while eight- or nine-tenths are poor. If we do not consent to this request, the poor will undoubtedly be pinched by hunger and cold, and will violently break their bonds. This will prove detrimental to [our] national security.

The proposal met with objections from Yen Sung and Su Yu, and even Ch'ou Luan did not dare lend it support. Consequently it was rejected. Shih Tao also was recalled from his post soon after.

At that time, however, the Mongols were already waiting at the Tatung border to exchange their sheep and cattle for grain. When they were not permitted to do so they began to attack the frontier. Then followed a period of several months in which invasion and plundering of the frontier were interspersed with the presentation of tribute horses by Anda and his brother-in-law Bujige. At the Ming court, on the other hand, the pendulum of opinion was swinging toward opposition to the horse trade, and the Mongols' successful incursions were laid to the relaxation of border defenses since the opening of the horse markets. While Ch'ou Luan tried to redeem himself by offering to fight the Mongols beyond the border, Hsü Jen, the commanding general at Tatung, was restraining his troops from clashing with the tribes-people on the grounds that trading relations had now been established. As a result the Mongols were able to penetrate the frontier and reach as far south as Huai-jen [south of Tatung]. Frontier defenses had reached a low point, and under these circumstances horse markets became anathema in Peking. In the third month of 1552 the Tatung market was closed by decree.

The Hsüan-fu market was allowed to continue, chiefly because capable administration there had succeeded in bringing a measure of peace to this part of the frontier. There was even talk of increasing the periods of exchange during the year. Later in 1552, however, when Ch'ou Luan, unable to stop the invading forces at Chi-chou, fell from power and died, the entire idea of horse markets also fell into disfavor in the Ming government. In the autumn of that year, therefore, all frontier horse markets were ordered closed. This presumably included the market at Hsüan-fu.

PART III. HORSE MARKETS IN THE LUNG-CH'ING PERIOD

1. Northern Frontier Expenditures in
the Early Years of Lung-ch'ing

Anda's power continued to increase after 1552. Aided by a number of rebel Chinese, who were made chiefs by Anda, the latter's
forces were able to conquer large territories in Shansi early in
the Lung-ch'ing period, killing and pillaging as they went. Such
frontier warfare increased the burden of Ming government expenditures beyond the annual income. According to a passage in the
Veritable Records of Ming, at the end of 1569, when an inventory
was taken of the treasury, it was found that (a) of the 1,725,600
taels obtained through "merchant colonization" during the first
three years of the reign, only some 109,900 taels now remained
after appropriations for frontier troop provisions, while the payments to the garrisons for the current year were not yet completed.
(b) From the various regular sources of revenue, such as the poll
tax, land tax, salt gabelle, and transit dues, over 9,290,000 taels
had been expended since the first year of the reign, and there remained in the treasury 2,700,000 taels. However, the present
needs of the frontier forces amounted to over 3,000,000, so that
the income was inadequate to meet the expenditures.

The increased cost of the frontier defenses arose from the fact
that additional garrison areas had been created to cope with the intensified threat of Mongol invasions, and from the consequent increase in the number of troops employed to guard these areas.
The soldiers' pay, and the transportation of provisions for the men,
became major problems of government finance.

A memorial of 1570 by Chang Shou-chih, president of the Board
of Finance, described the situation in some detail. Frontier expenditures had increased from 590,000 taels per year in 1539 to
the current more than 2,800,000 taels per year, with those for
certain areas showing a spectacular rise. At Hsüan-fu, for example, the expenses for the regular armies stationed there were
20,000 taels in 1563, but now they amounted to 120,000 taels.
Chang hinted broadly that not all the troops reported by the garrison commanders existed other than on paper; but however this
might be, that the government was in financial straits was an un-
disputed fact.

At this juncture Anda's grandson came to offer surrender. Ably
handled by the frontier officials, this turned out to be the beginning of another period of tribute relations, and the financial difficulties were temporarily lessened for the Ming dynasty.

2. History of the Tribute of Anda

(i) The Surrender of Bahanaji

When Anda appropriated as his own concubine his daughter's daughter, called Third Lady, who was originally betrothed to a certain Ordos Mongol, and replaced her with a secondary wife belonging to Bahanaji, his favorite grandson, the latter took umbrage and decided to answer the call for surrender issued by Wang Ch'ung-ku, the governor-general of Hsüan-fu and Tatung. His group of around a dozen persons, including his old servant Alige, arrived at a fort west of Tatung on October 18, 1570.

Fang Feng-shih, the governor at Tatung, was disposed to utilize this opportunity for the opening of negotiations with Anda. Bahanaji and his party were met by 500 Chinese cavalry troops and brought to Tatung on the 22nd. After interrogation that took place immediately, Fang wrote to Wang Ch'ung-ku as follows:

> The surrendered barbarian Bahanaji [....] is motivated by no reason other than his anger at Anda for taking away his betrothed and giving her to the Ordos. It seems to be quite true that this is the reason for his surrender. He is only eighteen years old, seems to be of a simple and innocent mind, and acts on the advice of his servant Alige. We are here provided with a great bargaining power. As he has arrived [of his own will], we should treat him well so as to keep him content. Twice I have received reports from our scouts that Anda is determined to invade the Left and Right Garrisons [of Tatung] and demand the release of his grandson. [....] It appears that the plan of trading with [the Mongols] which I previously mentioned to you can be put into effect. Would you consent to having it put into practice now, with the proper persons chosen to handle it? The barbarians [i.e. Bahanaji and entourage] are still unsettled in mind. I shall keep them here in the garrison city a few more days, obtain more information from them, and then send them on to your office. [....] I hope you will kindly advise me.

Before reports could be received from Fang and Wang, however, news of Bahanaji's surrender had already reached Peking. This elicited some inquiries from grand secretary Chang Chü-cheng, who together with another grand secretary was sympathetic to the views of Fang and Wang. A policy of acceptance of the surrender

and using Bahanaji as a lever of bargaining was worked out through
correspondence among these four. They were able to overcome opposition from other officials and obtain imperial approval. Thereupon an edict conferred on Bahanaji the title of guard commander,
and on Alige that of post commander, and also bestowed upon each
a red brocade gown. The garrison authorities were ordered to
treat them well, and Wang Ch'ung-ku was charged with working
out a suitable plan for the control of the barbarians.

(ii) Bargaining for the Extradition of Chinese Rebels

When Anda heard of the desertion of Bahanaji he immediately
turned back from a western expedition, and with the aid of a son
and nephew sent a three-pronged attack against the Chinese frontier to back up his demand for the release of his grandson. This
fitted perfectly into the plan of the Chinese frontier officials. Fang
Feng-shih sent emissaries to the field, stopped the Mongol advance,
and asked Anda to deliver the Chinese rebels in his camp in exchange for his grandson and as a token of his good faith. The tortu-
ous negotiations were described in detail in a letter from Fang to
Chang Chü-cheng. The crux of the question was the exchange of
the Chinese in Anda's force for Bahanaji; this was something on
which Anda could not quickly come to a decision. Fang's messengers were able to ward off an attack by Anda's son, Huang Taiji,
who promised: "I shall not plunder your territory. As I have
gained nothing on this trip, however, I shall go east toward Hsüan-
fu and cross the border at Kalgan, so that I can seize some food
en route." Actually he was later turned back by the eastern garrison troops, and had to make his exit through the western passes.

Fang and Chang agreed that Bahanaji must be used as a lever
to bargain for the extradition of the Chinese rebels. To this Anda
finally acceded after nearly two months of negotiations. Then the
plan was memorialized by Wang Ch'ung-ku, who declared it was
better policy to take this opportunity to pacify and win the support
of Anda through the granting of titles and the permission to trade,
as he then had a following of over 100,000 men and was an influential factor among the northern frontier peoples. Imperial assent
was given his proposal.

In letters written by Chang Chü-cheng to Wang Ch'ung-ku the
method of exchange was set forth. One of the letters reads in part
as follows:

> The silk cloth [needed for the ceremonies of exchange]
> has already been appropriated from the Palace Treasury and

is being sent to you post haste. Carry out the plan as soon as
it arrives, so as to prevent the barbarians from changing
their minds through prolonged waiting. When the young chief
[i.e. Bahanaji] leaves he should be treated with great favor.
Inform Fang Chin-hu [i.e. Fang Feng-shih] that Bahanaji
should be given all the things that he has been using, and
should be generously feasted and presented with gifts. He is
also human and cannot help but be grateful....
      As to the [Chinese] rebels, they should be sent to the capi-
tal for execution, after which their heads are to be exhibited
along the nine frontier areas as a warning to others. [You
should] first move Bahanaji close to the border, have the
rebels sent in first, and then release him. Should they [i.e.
Anda's men] try to recover the hostages by force, decapitate
Bahanaji forthwith and display his head to them. Then close
up your city gates and fight. They will be in the wrong and
we in the right, and we shall certainly win the battle. As to
Alige, by no means permit him to go back [with Bahanaji].
Detain this man. He will prove to be of great use in the future.

      Criticism of the policy of conciliation existed both in and outside
the government, but it was overcome by the combined efforts of
the officials in favor of the policy, all of whom gave it earnest support. On December 16, 1570, an emissary from Anda delivered
the nine rebels to Wang and Fang at Yün-shih Fort [on the Great
Wall west of Tatung], and in return Bahanaji was sent back to the
Mongols. Reluctant to leave, he swore never to rise against China.
With him went also his [first] wife, but Alige and two messengers
from Anda remained behind as hostages. The nine rebels were
sent to Peking, where a Presentation of Prisoners Ceremony was
performed, after which they were publicly executed. Wang Ch'ung-
ku, Fang Feng-shih, and others involved in the negotiations all received promotions.

(iii) Investitures and Payment of Tributes

      After the return of Bahanaji, Anda despatched a messenger with
his thanks and with a request to be given a title and to establish
tribute and trading relations. He also foreswore invading China in
the future.
      In reply Wang Ch'ung-ku asked that in addition to Anda's own
people, others, such as Bayasqal's (beyond the Hsüan-fu border)
and Noyandara Jinong's (in the Yellow River area), also pay tribute, thus extending China's control over most of the border. With

the exception of [Anda's third cousin] Tümen Jashaghtu [beyond
Ch'ang-p'ing, northeast of Peking], Anda and the others all con-
sented to the proposal, and each sent eighteen envoys with cre-
dentials. Wang Ch'ung-ku thereupon memorialized the matter, suggesting that tribute and commerce should be established, and that
the Ming forces should desist from burning the pastures and raiding the Mongols' home camps.

This proposal raised a mighty furor at Court. If China stopped
burning and raiding when the Mongols merely sought peace, asked
the Board of War, what was she to do if they requested the non-
fortification of the frontiers? Furthermore, the problem of establishing markets required even more careful consideration, as they
had been banned under the previous reign [Chia-ching]. The advocates of the tribute and trade policy, however, strenuously pressed
their point. Chang Chü-cheng drew attention to the advantages that
would accrue from such a policy, such as reduction in defense
expenditures, the possibility of China's maneuvering amid the internal conflicts in Anda's clan, etc. Wang Ch'ung-ku emphasized
the fact that this time Anda was asking for entitlement and trade,
which made the circumstances different from the tributes of the
Chia-ching period, when China had to accede to the Mongol requests
under the threat of invading armies.

Wang listed eight matters for consideration in connection with
the setting up of tribute relations. The more important of these
are given below together with his own comments on them:

// (a) Granting of titles and official positions: As the chief Anda
occupies the senior position among all the barbarians, he should
be granted the title of Prince so that he can assume the leadership
over his junior relatives and function as the shield of [our] country.
His near relatives, such as Bayasqal, Noyandara Jinong, and
Huang Taiji, should be granted the title of general; forty-six lesser relatives should be given the title of guard commander; and
a dozen or so sons-in-law should be given the title of post commander. They should all be given official caps and garments so
that they may know the proper conduct of subordinates. This is
subjugation of the stubborn barbarians through the instrumentality
of titles and decorations.

// (b) Fixing the amount of tribute to be paid: There should be one
tribute annually. Anda's quota should be ten horses [accompanied
by] ten barbarian envoys; that of Bayasqal, Noyandara Jinong, and
Huang Taiji, eight horses and four envoys each; and that of the

other chiefs, a number varying in accordance with the size of their
tribe. In toto the annual number should not exceed 500 horses and
150 envoys. Let the horses be divided into three grades. Thirty of
the best grade should be presented for Palace use, but the rest
should be paid for according to the worth of each horse. Old and
lean ones should not be accepted as tribute. Each year sixty of the
barbarian [envoys] should be allowed to enter the capital, and the
rest should be made to wait at the border. When the envoys depart
they should be allowed to use the proceeds from the horse sales to
purchase textiles for presentation as gifts for their chiefs.

//(c) Deciding on the dates and route of tribute: The tribute and
trade should take place in the spring, when the horses are weak,
and when all the barbarians arrive for His Majesty's birthday cele-
brations. The horses and the loyalty memorials are to be inspected
and admitted at the Tatung Left Garrison. Those [of the envoys]
who are to remain at the border should be billeted in the various
towns. Those who are to go to the capital should be escorted there
by officers, along the route of Chü-yung Pass and Ch'ang-p'ing to
Peking, where they should lodge at the Bureau of Barbarian Affairs. When their business is completed they should be escorted
back by the same officers and along the same route.

//(d) Deciding on the opening of markets: The northern barbarians depend entirely on China for their supply of cooking pots, iron,
and textiles. Now that they have foresworn invasion of China, their
envoys have requested the opening of markets for trade so as to
prevent the occurrence of theft and robbery. The method of commercial exchange should follow that established for the northern
tributes in the early part of the Hung-chih period [1488 ff.] (see
below, section iii, "Locations and Regulations of the Horse Markets"). Should the barbarians create any border disturbances when
the exchange is over, Anda and the other chiefs are to be held
responsible.//

(e) Deciding on operating expenses: Heretofore large sums have
been spent annually in the upkeep of defense works, troop provisions, and awards and compensations for soldiers who killed
Mongols or were killed by them in minor clashes. Now these sums
can be greatly reduced, and the amount saved can be assigned for
use in rewarding the Mongol envoys and guards at the markets.
If this proves insufficient, then more should be appropriated from
the funds for militia provisions at the various garrisons. Surplus
funds should be carried over for use in the following year.

The foregoing proposals were referred by the throne to the
Board of War for consideration. A decision was not reached until
after more than two months' deliberation among the major metro-

politan officials. At one point in the discussions it was found that
there were twenty-two persons for the proposals, seventeen against,
and five for the investiture plan but against the opening of markets.
In the main the opponents of the proposals based their objections
on the ground that military preparedness should not be relaxed on
the frontiers, that investiture would increase Anda's prestige
among the Mongol tribes, and that to permit the entrance of Mongols into China would fan their greed and create more trouble.
Finally the supporters of the investiture and trade proposals had
to bring out data concerning the investiture by Emperor Ch'eng-
tsu [1403-1424] of the Oirat and Tartar princes to clinch their
argument. With the Board of War thus convinced, the investiture
and establishment of tribute was then decided upon.

In the third month [March 25-April 23] of 1571 an edict conferred on Anda the title of Submit-to-Righteousness Prince, together with the gift of a dragon robe, bolts of colored silk, and an
imperial decree. In the next month other chiefs were also given
titles, which included two adjutant generals, ten guard adjutants,
nineteen guard lieutenants, eighteen post commanders, twelve post
adjutants, and a number of captains.

Investitures of Anda and the leaders of three other major tribes
took place at Te-sheng Fort outside Tatung in the fifth month of
the same year. Wang Ch'ung-ku and others sent two military officers to the scene to proclaim twelve imperial edicts to the Mongols. After this four Mongol leaders swore an oath on behalf of
Anda. The oath ran as follows:

> Listen to me, you 800,000 troops of China and you 400,000
> northern barbarians, listen all of you and hear my laws:
> When our infants grow into strong men, and our colts grow
> into big horses, neither shall ever invade China. Should any
> prince enter the [Chinese] border and do evil, he will be
> stripped of his soldiers and horses and deprived of his ad-
> ministrative powers. Should any individual barbarian do evil,
> his wife and children and all his sheep, cattle, and horses
> will be taken away and given to other barbarians.

Such an oath indicates that Anda had embarked upon the tribute relationship in sincerity.

In the sixth month Anda and other chiefs sent in a tribute of 509
horses. Thirty of the best, together with a memorial expressing
loyalty and a saddle wrought in silver, were presented by envoys
as tribute to the emperor. The remaining horses were distributed
among the Hsüan-fu, Tatung, and Shansi garrisons. The Mongol

envoys all received rewards. In appreciation Anda further sent in thirteen Chinese rebels still in his camp, which action drew high praise from the throne. The rebels were executed by decree.

Thenceforth Anda, who in his declining years turned to Buddhism and abjured killing and pillaging, carefully kept peace with China. After 1573 Wang Ch'ung-ku became president of the Board of War. Fang Feng-shih succeeded him as governor-general of Hsüan-fu and Tatung, and in turn was followed by Wu Tui and Cheng Lo, who managed the frontiers ably, so that the Mongol tribute and trade continued without a break. Among the Mongols, the consort of Anda known as Third Lady was particularly helpful in the protection of the Chinese frontier. Anda died in the winter of 1581-82. He was succeeded by his son Huang Taiji, who through marrying Third Lady was able to exert control over all the tribes. Early in 1586 Huang Taiji also died and was succeeded by his son Shelige. Third Lady, with a following of some 10,000 troops, built for herself a city [in present Suiyuan] and lived apart. The Ming government bestowed upon the city the name of Kuei-hua [meaning "Converted to Civilization"]. Governor-General Cheng Lo, believing that Third Lady was the real power able to control the tribes, succeeded in bringing about her marriage with Shelige. In 1587 the latter was invested as Submit-to-Righteousness Prince, and Third Lady as Loyal and Submissive Lady. Shelige's death in 1616 was followed by intra-tribal disputes over the leadership. Although in 1613 Shelige's eldest grandson was able to receive Ming investiture by virtue of his marrying Third Lady, the latter died shortly afterward, and the new chief's jurisdiction actually did not extend far. In the meantime the tribute relations had enabled the frontier population to live in peace for some sixty years.

3. Locations and Regulations of the Horse Markets

(i) Locations of Markets

In 1571 four markets were opened: at Kalgan Fort in Hsüan-fu; Hsin-p'ing Fort and Te-sheng Fort in Tatung; and Shui-ch'üan Camp in Shansi. Business was transacted once a year at each fort to the accompaniment of feasts and rewards for the Mongols. The following are brief sketches of the market towns.

(a) Kalgan Fort: This was situated sixty li to the northwest of Hsüan-fu. It was first built in 1429 with a circumference of four li; but it was subsequently extended, and its walls were faced with bricks in 1574. It had risen because of its convenient position as a trading site, and apparently remained a simple frontier town down to the opening of the seventeenth century. Fortifications and new official buildings were added in 1613, and from then on the town served as an important center for the Mongol trade and tribute throughout the Ch'ing dynasty.

(b) Hsin-p'ing Fort: This was located about 100 li to the northeast of the city of Yang-ho Garrison, which was under the jurisdiction of Tatung. It was first built in 1546. It occupied a very strategic location on the border mountains. The market was set up two li west of the fort, close by the Great Wall.

(c) Te-sheng Fort: This was situated some 80 li north of Tatung. It was built in 1548. Actually the horse market was set up at Chen-ch'iang Fort, only two li to the west of Te-sheng Fort. Twenty li to the south of the latter was Hung-tz'u Fort, where the governor took up his residence every year during market days for convenience in exercising control.

(d) Shui-ch'üan Camp: This fort, which lay sixty li northeast of P'ien-[t'ou] Pass, was built in 1435. The horse market was set up outside a pass about two li to the northeast of Shui-ch'üan Camp. There were three check points facing out to handle the entrance and egress of the Mongols, and one check point facing inward that served as a demarcation between Chinese and Mongols at the pass.

In a report of 1571 Wang Ch'ung-ku listed the results of the exchange in the first horse markets that year as follows:

Te-sheng Fort, Tatung (market dates: June 20-July 5).
    Official market: [participants:] tribesmen of the Submit-to-
        Righteousness Prince Anda. 1,370 horses were sold
        for 10,545 taels.
    Private market: 6,000 heads of horses, mules, donkeys,
        cattle and sheep were sold.
    Expenditure for gifts and rewards: 981 taels.
Hsin-p'ing Fort, Tatung (August 4-15).
    Official market: tribesmen of Huang Taiji, Bayo, and Labugh
        Taiji [a younger brother of Anda]. 726 horses were sold
        for 4,253 taels.
    Private market: 3,000 heads of horses, mules, cattle, and
        sheep were sold.
    Expenditure for gifts and rewards: 561 taels.
Kalgan Fort, Hsüan-fu (July 15-28).
    Official market: tribesmen of Bayasqal and Engke Daiching
        Taiji [a nephew of Anda]. 1,993 horses sold for 15,277
        taels.
    Private market: 9,000 heads of horses, mules, cattle and
        sheep were sold.
    Expenditures for gifts and rewards: 800 taels.

Shui-ch'üan Camp, Shansi (September 3-18).
    Official market: tribesmen of Anda, Doro Tüman [a second
        cousin of Anda], and Wei-wu-shen [?]. 2,941 horses were
        sold for 26,400 taels.
    Private market: 4,000 heads of horses, mules, cattle and
        sheep were sold.
    Expenditures for gifts and rewards: 1,500 taels.

Henceforth it became the custom for the frontier authorities to
report on the results of the horse markets in the ninth month of
each year. In addition in 1571 the authorities opened one horse market on the Shensi frontier, three in Ningsia, and two in Kan-Su.
These operated along the same lines as the Hsüan-fu, Tatung and
Shansi markets.

Subsequently other markets were added along the frontier. These
included a large market and six small markets at forts situated
along the Great Wall to the east and west of Tatung. The "large
market" was of the kind described above. The "small markets"
were places which were set up to enable Mongols living near the
frontier to come and trade once or twice a month; they involved
no provision for feasts or rewards. Though the precise dates of
the opening of these markets are not known, evidence in the Veritable Records of Ming leads us to the conclusion that they were
probably instituted in either 1572 or 1573.

(ii) Regulations of the Horse Markets

According to regulations promulgated by the Board of War at
the beginning of the horse markets, the total number of barbarian
envoys in each tribute mission was not to exceed 150, and the number of horses, 500. The envoys were to stay at the frontier and
were not required to go to Peking, the thirty tribute horses for the
emperor being sent on by officers assigned by the governor and
governor-general. The cost of the horses was to be defrayed partly
by appropriations from the Board of War, and partly by the transfer of the horse-replacement and militia provision funds at the various garrisons. For a month beginning with the opening day, 300
Mongol and 500 Chinese soldiers were to be stationed at the market. The articles of exchange were gold, silver, cattle, horses,
hides, and horse tails on the part of the Mongols, and satin, silk,
cotton cloth, needles and thread, and so forth, on the part of the
Chinese. The sale of iron cooking pots, saltpetre, and steel or
iron was strictly forbidden. In 1572 the sale of copper cooking pots
to the families of Mongol chiefs was allowed. The ban on iron pots
was lifted later when Fang Feng-shih became the governor-general

of Hsüan-fu and Tatung, but the number exported was restricted
to 500 pots per year.

As to the horses, regulations of 1573 provided that the sturdy
steeds were to be retained for military use in the garrison area in
which they were purchased, and that the rest were to be transferred
for sale by the local authorities. The 1,900 or so horses procured
each year at the Shansi market were to be sent through the courier
service in that region for use in the garrison area, at the official
price of twelve taels per head. In 1575 the average number of
horses to be obtained and the amount of money to be spent in the
purchase of goods for obtaining the horses were fixed as follows
for the three markets:

	Hsüan-fu	Tatung	Shansi
horses (heads)	18,000	10,000	6,000
money (taels)	120,000	70,000	40,000

Of the sums needed, the Board of War was to appropriate, in the
first month of each year, 12,000 taels each for Hsüan-fu and Tatung, and 10,000 taels for Shansi. The rest of the amounts needed
was to be made up by the militia and horse replacement funds at
the local garrison.

In 1608, with the investment of Boshughtu Jinong [a great-grand-
nephew of Anda] as the Submit-to-Righteousness Prince, new regulations were promulgated that included these five points:

(a) Chinese were allowed to sell to the Mongols only textiles
and food-stuffs. All other commodities were contraband. Any military officer who clandestinely sold saddles to the Mongols was to
be judged guilty of association with the barbarians and punished
accordingly.

(b) On market days the garrison officers were to order interpreters to tell the barbarians not to include among their horses
any that were ailing, maimed, dying, or too young to eat feed. Disregard of this injunction was to be dealt with in appropriate fashion.

(c) Business was to be conducted with dispatch, so that the barbarians would not have the opportunity of tarrying at the spot.

(d) Once the trade regulations had been fixed, the least increase
in the number of horses or in price was to be strictly forbidden.

(e) The interpreters were to be held responsible for keeping
the Mongol envoys at the markets within the proper number, and
for the presentation of cattle and horses to the Chinese commissioners.

Apparently, after some forty years in operation the horse markets were maintained along the general lines first set up, with only minor deviations in detail. Although gifts to the Mongols often

exceeded the customary amount, the whole system nevertheles resulted in greatly reducing Ming government expenditures for the frontiers.

4. Conclusion

When the tribute relationship with Anda was first established, Ming officials were still afraid of the consequences of reduced frontier defenses; hence many continued to urge vigilance. With the passing of time, however, the Chinese began to relax their attention; nevertheless, owing to the non-aggressiveness of the Mongols by that time, the frontier remained quiet for sixty-odd years. A late Ming governor-general described the scene along the borders in this period as one of "abundant goods and peaceful people, with merchants gathered from all directions, just as in China Proper."

Danger appeared from another quarter, however, in the form of the Chahar khanate. Its leader, Lindan Khan, having been stopped in his eastward ventures by the newly risen power of the Manchus under Nurhachi, turned his attention southward. Employing the threat of force and the excuse of helping Ming to fight the Manchus, he was able to exact heavy money gifts from the Ming government. In 1628 the Chahar forces invaded the Hsüan-fu and Tatung areas, plundering and killing as they went. A total of over 2,000 frontier inhabitants were killed, not including the unidentified, more than 1,000 persons were wounded or captured, and tens of thousands of heads of livestock were lost. Thus were the fruits of sixty years of peaceful frontier relations wiped out. The confusion in Ming frontier policy at this time was soon followed by the fall of the dynasty itself.

NOTES

侯仁之，明代宣大山西三鎮馬市考，　燕京學報
Hou Jen-chih, "Ming-tai Hsüan Ta Shan-hsi san-chen ma-shih k'ao," Yen-ching Journal of Chinese Studies, no. 23 (1938), 183-237.

The major sources used by the author are Ming shih, Ming shih-kao, Ming shih-lu, Hsü T'ung-k'ao, Wan-li wu-kung-lu 萬曆 武功錄, San-yün ch'ou-chu k'ao 三雲籌俎考, and the collected works of contemporary personages directly involved in the matter of horse markets, such as Chang Chü-cheng's Complete Works

(Ch'üan shu 全書) and the Ta-yin-lou chi 大隱樓集of Fang Feng-
shih. A large number of other works were also consulted, including Ming-shih chi-shih pen-mo, Ku Yen-wu's 顧炎武 T'ien-hsia
chün-kuo li-ping shu 天下郡國利病書, and local gazetteers.

Our identification of Mongol names is based chiefly on Henri
Serruys, "Pei-lou fong-sou, Les coutumes des esclaves septen-
trionaux," Monumenta Serica, 10 (1945), 117-208, and Wolfgang
Franke, Addenda and Corrigenda to Pokotilov's History of the
Eastern Mongols during the Ming Dynasty (Chengtu and Peiping,
1949). In the following romanized list of names mentioned by Hou
Jen-chih, unasterisked items indicate identifications and transcriptions derived from Serruys or Franke, single-asterisked items
indicate identifications from the same sources but tentative transcriptions suggested by our Mongol colleague, Mr. John Hangin,
and double-asterisked items indicate transcriptions suggested by
Mr. Hangin for names for which further identification was not
possible:

1.	A-li-ko	Alige** (servant of Bahanaji)
2.	Ao-erh-tu-ssu	an Ordos
3.	Ch'a-chan	Chajan** (Oirat envoy)
4.	Chi-nang	Gun Bilig Mergen Jinong (elder brother of Anda)
5.	Chi-neng	Noyandara Jinong (a son of preceding)
6.	Hu-la-chi	Ulji** (a chieftain)
7.	Hu-tun-t'u	Lindan Khan (Mongol khan, died 1634)
8.	Hsin-ai	Sengge Dügüreng (Anda's eldest son)
9.	Huang t'ai-chi	Huang Taiji (same person as preceding)
10.	K'un-tu-li-ha	Bayasqal (a grandson of Anda)
11.	Lang t'ai-chi	Baisangghur Lang Taiji (a brother of no. 5)
12.	Lao-pa-tu	another name for no. 11
13.	Pa-han-na-chi	Bahanaji* (a grandson of Anda)
14.	Pa-tu-erh	another name for no. 10
15.	Pai-yao	Bayo* (a grandson of Anda)
16.	Po-yao	another name for preceding
17.	Pu-chi-ko	Bujige* (a brother-in-law of Anda)
18.	Pu-lang t'ai-chi	Bulang Taiji**
19.	Pu-shih-t'u	Boshughtu Jinong (a great-grand-nephew of Anda)

20. She-li-k'o — Shelige* (a son of Huang Taiji)
21. To-lo t'u-man — Duro Tümen* (a second cousin of Anda)
22. T'o-t'o — Toqto (Anda's adopted son)
23. T'u-man — Tümen Jashaghtu (a third cousin of Anda)
24. Wei-wu-erh-shen t'ai-chi — Uighurchin Taiji (a grandson of Anda)
25. Wu-shen — Labugh Taiji (a younger brother of Anda)
26. Yeh-hsien — Esen (an Oirat chieftain)
27. Yung-shao-pu ta-ch'eng — Engke Daiching Taiji (a nephew of Anda)

MANCHU-CHINESE SOCIAL AND ECONOMIC CONFLICTS IN EARLY CH'ING

by

MA FENG-CH'EN

1. Introduction

The military conquest of China by the Manchus brought political tension to the Chinese scene. In addition, the different stages of development of the Manchu and Chinese economies also resulted in conflict, in which the Manchus utilized their superior political status to strike out at the social and economic organizations of the Chinese. After adjustments were made, however, it turned out that the Chinese economic form still predominated.

What were the post-conquest changes that took place in Manchu society which contributed to the social and economic conflicts with the Chinese? There seem to have been five major changes: (a) Land system: In Manchuria the amount of land was practically unlimited. Land was distributed by the authorities to the people, and bad land in the allotments was exchangeable for that of a better grade. But on arriving in China Proper, the Manchus found that the land around Peking was all privately owned, and was not as fertile as that in Manchuria. For the Manchus, then, the land situation deteriorated in regard both to quantity and quality. (b) Livelihood: In Manchuria agriculture was supplemented by hunting and digging for ginseng, but around Peking neither of these was possible. The "hunting expeditions" of the Ch'ing emperors were for the purpose of "preserving the military tradition" and not for economic production. Hence the Manchus' source of income was further reduced. (c) Aims of warfare: Before the conquest the Manchus fought, especially in their incursions into China Proper, for economic gain; gold, silver, livestock, and prisoners taken along the way were distributed to the troops. After the conquest they fought for the "pacification of the country in order to secure the foundation of the empire"; hence the aim was changed from the economic to the political. The term of service of Manchu soldiers also was extended

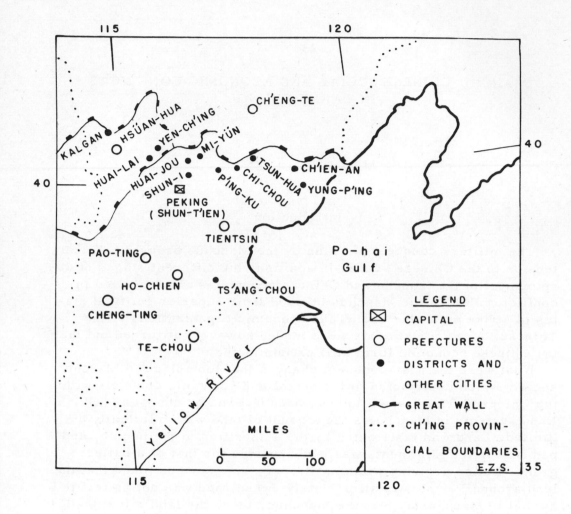

Map 8. The area of Manchu-Chinese conflicts in early Ch'ing

from a short to a long period of time. These factors made for still greater changes in Manchu society and economy. (d) Labor force: Before the conquest the slavery system began to break down, so that the Manchus were losing an important source of labor supply. Furthermore, they were inferior to their Chinese neighbors in agricultural techniques, so that it was difficult for them to compete successfully with the latter. (e) Lastly, money economy was more advanced in Peking than in Manchuria, and commodity prices in the former were much higher than those in the latter. This not only accentuated the Manchu's problem of livelihood, but also was a key issue in the adjustment of early Manchu-Chinese economic conflicts.

Thus, the military and political successes of the Manchus against the Chinese at the beginning of the dynasty cost them dearly in economic terms. After the conquest their economic status declined. At the same time the dislocations caused by adjustment to the new environment created economic problems. Yet, like the nations of more modern times, the Manchu rulers of early Ch'ing were able to resort to political means to cure their economic ills, as by taking land privately owned by the Chinese and giving it to Manchus. The reason for this step was that it was necessary for the settling of the princes, meritorious officers, soldiers, and so forth. But actions of this sort opened the way to social and economic conflicts with the Chinese over such questions as enclosure of land, Chinese adherents of the Manchus, and fugitives from the banners. In the final outcome the Manchu way of life failed to prevail. In 1655, when it was suggested that reforms in the Manchu economy should be planned in a way so as to fit better into the Chinese scene, Emperor Shun-chih highly approved of the idea, and later changes were made along this line.

2. Enclosure of Land

The term "enclosure" needs to be explained, because the phrase "enclosure by galloping" is often heard. If the demarcation of land to be enclosed was done by galloping on horseback, then the amount obtained by Manchus would have been limitless in terms of mou. We can demonstrate with negative evidence that such was not the method of enclosing land. First, it was clearly provided in the statutes of 1645 that each able-bodied Manchu subordinate to an official from a Prince down should be given six shang 晌 of land in lieu of food rations; again, in 1649 and 1650 revisions were made in the numbers of shang to be allotted each man. This indicates that the land was enclosed by measurements of area rather than by riding. Second, the origin of the term "enclosure" can be found in

the Manchu practice of measuring Banner land with a string, a procedure which was known as "enclosure."

The significance of land enclosure as a form of economic change
was important. It meant the promotion of a system of public landownership in a society where land was privately owned. The reason
why the Manchus were able to do this was of course the strength of
their political hegemony.

The process began with an edict of January 20, 1645, ordering
the Board of Finance to conduct a thorough investigation of the land
in the prefectures and districts in the vicinity of Peking. Included
in the investigation was land whose owners were actually present
as well as land whose owners had died or fled in the recent fighting.
The owner-occupied land was re-assigned to the present owners
according to the number of persons in each household, while all
the ownerless land was distributed among the princes, officers, and
soldiers from Manchuria. Before this the occupation of ownerless
land by Manchus had already been going on to a certain extent.

It was suggested, however, that lest intermingling lead to fric-
tion with the Chinese, the Manchus should have their allotments
set apart in a separate area, so that each group could live in peace
without close contact with the other, and taxes on both Manchu and
Chinese properties could be more effectively controlled by the respective authorities. Therefore the order was issued for the survey of all land, and for the segregation of Manchus and Chinese.

It appears that two distinct procedures, one for Manchus and one
for Chinese, were involved in the act of enclosure. With regard to
the Manchus, the government distributed to them all the ownerless
land, as well as the land [earlier] taken from Chinese owners.
With regard to the Chinese, in cases where it was possible to seg-
regate Manchus and Chinese, land held by an owner was reallotted
to the original owner according to a per capita scale; in other
cases the Chinese were moved and compensated with land in some
other place. An edict of 1645 ordered that the compensation in land
and houses must be carried out speedily and fairly. However, it
was quite obvious that certain ill-effects resulted from enclosing
privately owned land.

There were differences in the nature of the losses suffered by
the Chinese: (a) When land was re-allotted to the original Chinese
owner, each allotment was limited to a specific amount. (b) For
those who received compensation elsewhere, the amount received
was probably not equivalent to the original property. The sudden
uprooting and resettlement were an added misery, and many persons thus became homeless and unemployed. (c) Garrison colonists became vagrants after losing their land. (d) For those living

in an area which was not subject to enclosure but which received
the influx of people assigned there by the process of compensation,
the result was a diminution in the amount of their landed property.
On the other hand, not all those given compensation could effectively possess the assigned land, owing to original local rights of
ownership. In addition to the above, such factors as the loss of personal property in the process of moving, the lack of ploughing animals, tools, and seeds in the new environment, the strangeness of
the locality, and the untimely season when the removals took place,
all produced widespread suffering. Although before long the Manchu emperor announced the remittance of some of the taxation for
the alleviation of the people, it was but a temporary measure and
could not heal the real wound. The remitted amount--whether an
entire year's dues for those who received compensation, or half
a year's dues for those who got re-allotments--could not cancel
the losses sustained in this upheaval. The misery of the Chinese
was further intensified by the unruly conduct of the Manchus, who
were not subject to control of the local authorities.

In cases where enclosures took place in the areas near the capital, so that the Manchus might keep within easy touch with one
another, the Chinese owners would be sent to some distant place
for compensation. Then their misfortune would be multiplied many
times. A contemporary, Yüan Mou-te, described the flight of such
people as follows: The places to which these evicted persons were
sent were sometimes three or four hundred li, sometimes as far
as seven or eight hundred li away. Since they were apt to find
neither shelter nor farm equipment in the new locality [if once they
moved there], the dispossessed were [often] compelled to let the
land which they had been assigned remain under cultivation by their
present holders [while they hoped to benefit from this relationship
through rent*]. If the present holders were fair-minded, the dispossessed would have had a chance of making a livelihood. But
truth was often to the contrary. Those who had the dispossessed
persons assigned to their land proved to be the local hoodlums, who
were habitually unfair and who were connected with the minor local
government functionaries, so that they could avoid rent payment
through innumerable devices. Furthermore, many of the dispossessed lacked the wherewithal to undertake the long journeys, and
were forced to go into debt or even resort to begging. Some former

---

*This point is not explicitly stated by the author here quoted, but that such was
the case can be proved by corroboration of the Institutes of the K'ang-hsi Reign,
chüan 2, pp. 29-30, and Imperial Ch'ing Memorials, chüan 9, memorial of 1656
by Tu Shuang, which gives a clearer picture of the same situation as described
by Yüan.

landowners, unable to meet the payments on taxes and debts, became vagrants; others starved to death on the road; still others
were brutally beaten or got bogged down in lengthy litigation. The
last-mentioned was a widespread evil in itself, with many ex-
owners the victims of official extortion while their cases were con-
tinually delayed, or just simply shelved.

Such being the effect of enclosure on the Chinese population, it
is no wonder that in a contemporary enumeration of the ten miseries of the people, "enclosures" headed the list. The mere mention of the enclosure of land or occupation of houses was enough
to produce ruffled tempers.

Large-scale enclosures took place three times in early Ch'ing
--at the beginning of 1645, at the beginning of 1646, and in the
second month of 1647. In the last year it was also decreed that the
enclosures of land should henceforth cease. The historical records
provide data on the amount of land enclosed, the localities in
which this took place, and the kind of land given in compensation.
We are informed, for example, that in Shun-i, Huai-jou, Mi-yün,
and P'ing-ku, four districts close to Peking, 60,705 shang of land
were enclosed, and the expropriated owners were sent to occupy
ownerless garrison land in other parts of the same province. Some
of the land to which the expropriatees were sent had previously
been enclosed by the Manchus, who on finding that it was of an inferior quality reassigned it to this use. In all the amount of land
enclosed as a result of the three decrees was 993,707 shang.

The enclosed land was distributed as manorial estates or as
commoners' holdings. The former were granted to members of
the imperial clan and of the Eight Banners, and the latter were
granted to commoners. The sizes of the grants varied in different years. The total land received by royal members of the Eight
Banners amounted to 22,309 shang. The common members of the
Banners were granted land on the basis either of rank or of official position. Officials appointed to provincial posts and administrators of imperial and princely households also were recipients
of land grants.

The commoners' holdings were distributed as follows: In 1645
it was ordered that all able-bodied men who were subordinates of
officials from princes down should each be given six shang of land
in lieu of food rations. In 1647 a rescript ordered the freezing of
the size of commoners' holdings at the present state. At the same
time, however, extra grants equivalent to ten men's shares were
assigned to each company commander, because originally not
enough land had been given out as commoners' holdings. In 1649
the rate was fixed at five shang for each new arrival, which was
reaffirmed in 1650 and applied to both previous and new arrivals.

The territories involved in the three enclosure acts were the following prefectures with some sixty-odd districts under their jurisdiction: Shun-t'ien, Tientsin, Pao-ting, Ho-chien, Ts'ang-chou, Yung-p'ing, Hsüan-hua, Chen-ting [later renamed Cheng-ting], and Te-chou. In addition the land in more than twenty other districts or military administrative areas was also involved. The territory extended from Ch'eng-te [in Jehol] and Kalgan [in Chahar] beyond the Great Wall through Chihli and down to Shantung.

The aim of these enclosures and distribution of land was an attempt on the part of the Manchus to solve their problem with regard to the amount of land available. The results, however, were not satisfactory, either quantitatively or qualitatively. Not only were the territories of enclosure restricted to the 500-li area around Peking, but the problem of agricultural techniques also presented a great difficulty to the Manchus, because in the latter respect the Manchus were quite backward. Many of them therefore complained that the land was poor and difficult to cultivate. Consequently a plan was devised by the Court of Censors whereby all land allotted to [units of] less than four able-bodied men was turned back to the government in return for a monthly allowance of money and grain for subsistence. The better grades of land were then assigned to those who had complained of the poor quality of their holdings, and the rest was given back to the local Chinese population. The local Chinese who received the poor grade land were divided into two groups with two different kinds of tenure. Those in one group paid labor service and taxes but were exempt from enclosure of their land; the others worked as rent-paying tenants on land which was subject to enclosure when the occasion called for it. The actual cultivation of the land, in any event, had reverted to the Chinese. By returning the land to the Chinese the Manchus had thus avoided solving the problem of the quality of Manchu-held land simply by eliminating the problem itself, which was an indication of their defeat in this respect. At the same time the hardship suffered by the Chinese was incidentally somewhat alleviated.

In addition to the above device, the Ch'ing government also exchanged the Manchus' poor land for that of a better grade. The method provided that, with regard to the villages under Banner administration which had received poor land, in those with less than one hundred able-bodied men, the latter were to remain on the land, but in those with over one hundred such men they were allowed to move to another place. About 132,250 shang of land was enclosed in Shun-t'ien, Pao-ting, Ho-chien, and Yung-p'ing to exchange for poor land in the territories of the Yellow Bordered, Full White, Full Red, and Blue Bordered banners. The allotment was five shang for each able-bodied man.

In 1666 a survey was made of the land of all eight Banners, and a considerable number of exchanges were made in those banners where more than half of all of the land was unsuited to cultivation. The worst case was the Yellow Bordered Banner, where 40,600 able-bodied men were reassigned to 203,000 shang of land in Chi-chou, Tsun-hua, and Ch'ien-an; this land was taken from the allotments in the Full White Banner and from local people's land, surplus land, land for colonization, and land of the dependent Chinese. Any deficiency was to be made up by taking the local people's land in Yen-ch'ing. A similar large-scale shifting occurred in the Full White Banner; this involved 22,361 able-bodied men and 11,805 shang of land.

Needless to say, the effect of such land exchanges on the local economy was no less profound than that of enclosures. Exchanges were reduced to some extent in 1667 and were ended by imperial decree in 1706. Various additional abuses began to appear in such processes as enclosing for new arrivals from nomad areas, for making up deficits in allotments, and so forth, as a result of which local functionaries or gentry encroached on the people's good land. This constituted a serious disturbance to the local population. The frequency of edicts between 1647 and 1685 prohibiting the enclosure of the property of local Chinese testifies to the persistence of the evil. It could not be stopped by the mere issuance of decrees even after 1685.

In short, the Manchus' problem as to the quality of land could not be solved by the policy of exchange, and at the same time the economic losses of the Chinese population were increased many times.

3. Chinese Adherents of the Manchus

Chinese who joined the Manchu Banners as adherents were called t'ou-ch'ung 投充, a term which was once defined by Emperor Shun-chih as meaning "slaves." According to a decree of 1648, such Chinese could be bought and sold by their master, since they were considered the slaves of the Manchus. It would seem that the system of adherents after the Conquest was a modified extension of the pre-Conquest slavery system. A similar system had already existed in pre-Conquest days, when, according to a memorial, "poor people who lacked oxen, farming tools, and seeds worked the fields for the well-to-do families." These tenant-farmers were exempted from all labor service. Later the institutionalization of this practice became known as t'ou-ch'ung. The practice assumed added importance after the Conquest owing to

two factors, namely the decline in the original Manchu slavery system and the special position of the Chinese population.

The decline of the Manchu slavery system was indicated by several phenomena, such as the end of the practice of enslaving war
captives, who were the chief sources of slaves in pre-Conquest
days; the freeing of slaves who showed bravery in battle; the separation of slaves from productive work after the Conquest; and the
desertion of thousands of Chinese slaves, originally war captives
of Manchu raids, after the Conquest.

However, since slavery was an important element in Manchu
economy, its decline was soon replaced by a substitute, that is the
system of adherents. That this system was considered a necessity
by the Manchus is indicated by the inconsistency of the decrees in
alternately imposing and relaxing legal restrictions.

Of the Chinese who joined the Banners, some did so out of poverty, but others who were not poor also joined for various reasons.
One of these was the desire of the Chinese to avoid separation
from their land during enclosures. Another was the hope of obtaining the protection of the Banner administration; while unscrupulous
persons could thus obtain immunity for their crimes, many law-
abiding persons were also able to obtain redress for wrongs done
by the Banner, such as encroachment on their land. Other reasons
were fear of the "butchering" which was widely attributed to the
conquering Manchu armies, compulsion from the Manchus, and
desire to avoid payment of labor service.

The system of adherents was initiated during Prince Dorgun's
regency [1648-1650], when the Banners were permitted to receive
indigent Chinese and use them as servants. This practice in itself
would not have been enough to produce Manchu-Chinese conflicts,
were it not for several developments which ultimately engendered
conflict in the situation. These developments can be analyzed as
follows:

(a) Changes in the personnel joining the Banners: At first consisting only of the poor, the group gradually came to include landowners as well. As the status of the adherents was that of slaves,
this created a problem of the landowners who had placed themselves in servitude. The result was a change from landownership
to tenancy. The original holder of the land thus changed from a
landowner into a tenant farmer. The ownership of the land had now
passed into the hands of the Manchu master, to whom the tenant
had to pay rent. Initially these changes had a great effect on the individual but exercised only a limited influence on the scope of the
conflict with the Manchus. However, the effect on Chinese economy
and society widened when landless persons took to joining the

Banners with land belonging to others, or encroached on others'
land to make up for the small amount they had originally brought
with them when joining the Banner. Such practices deepened the
seriousness of the threat to the Chinese population.

(b) The scope of service of the adherents: At first the scope of
service was wide and ill-defined, consisting for the most part of
"such services as tilling the fields and herding horses," which we
may consider as the regular services. Those who tilled the fields
worked the land assigned to them and had to pay rent. In addition
some of the adherents were appointed estate managers either by
the Manchu nobleman whose estate they were connected with, or
by the authorities of the Banner in which they served. The estate
managers of the latter, being under the jurisdiction of the Banner,
were beyond the control of the local authorities. Their status was
the same as the Manchu servants in the Banners; both were known
as "retainers." The advantage to the Manchus of estate managers
of local origin was that the latter would be familiar with local conditions and could more easily manage rent collection. It was reported that at times the managers of estates even used their knowledge of the locality to help their employers encroach on the people's
land. In some cases, to be sure, these estate managers could do
things that worked to the advantage of the Chinese, such as aiding
followers to conceal the true amount of their landed property from
the Banner; sometimes several dozen ch'ing of land could thus be
clandestinely removed from taxation. On the whole, however,
this changed form of service had made of the Chinese adherents
of Manchus an evil force between the Manchus and Chinese segments of society, and in the end the Chinese were the losers.

(c) Emergence of a new evil force in society: This was due to
the fact that the adherents and their families constituted a special
group among the population who had the protection of the Manchu
Banner, and under this privilege many abuses took place.

(d) Combined evil of Manchus and Chinese: Often the Manchu
master and the Chinese adherent were accomplices in the perpetra-
tion of crimes. Though it is questionable whether the master always consciously participated in them, his protection of the adherents nevertheless had the same detrimental effect on the Chinese population.

4. Enslavement

An edict of 1647 prohibited the system of adherents. Its ultimate
effect was to change the form of joining Banners into the buying and
selling of slaves. That is, indigent Chinese who had no way of mak-

ing a living were permitted to sell themselves into a Banner. In essence this practice was not much different from the system of adherents in the latter's early stages, only the process of purchase
being added. In time, however, many persons thus sold into slavery
also became oppressors in their locality. Enslavement therefore
provided further opportunities for the continuation of Manchu-Chinese conflicts engendered by the Chinese joining the Banners.

The Manchu Court realized the ill-effects of such practices, and
in 1651 issued an edict enjoining the local officials to be vigilant
in suppressing the crimes of the adherents. Only a short time later,
however, this order was rescinded. This action was due to the
Court's desire to preserve Manchu economic interests. The result
was to heighten the social and economic conflicts with the Chinese
without helping the Manchus to preserve the former mainstay of
their economy--the system of slavery. In fact, with the Chinese
working on the land paying rent in kind--and later in money--to the
Manchus, the relation between Manchus and the land became more
and more remote. The relation between the Chinese adherent and
the Manchu master had become primarily a relation between landlord and tenant. In such a relationship there was no need for slavery
to exist.

5. Fugitives

The system of adherents was a way in which the Manchus sought
to replenish the slavery system from outside sources. The restrictions on fugitives instituted within the Banner, on the other hand,
were aimed at preventing the internal disintegration of slavery.

The question of fugitives had already become serious before the
Conquest, but was further magnified thereafter. This can be attributed to several causes. In the first place, their arrival within the
Great Wall acted as an incentive to the captured Chinese slaves to
desert and return to their original homes. Secondly, after reaching
home the fugitives could be securely hidden by their families. Finally, there were as yet no hard and fast rules for dealing with the
situation, a fact which encouraged the flight.

In answer to the situation the Manchus initiated various measures in order to prevent desertions. In 1651, for example, it was
ordered that Manchu masters were to give leaves to their Chinese
slaves for visits to their homes. An edict of 1646 had permitted
members of the families of Chinese slaves to join them in the Banners. Finally, laws were promulgated which would make use of the
resources of the government to curb desertion.

There were several changes in the fugitive laws. Those first

promulgated in 1644 held the neighbors and ward heads responsible
in reporting fugitives to the proper authorities; laxity in carrying
out this responsibility was to be severely punished. Shortly thereafter it was also decreed that all fugitives should be sent to Peking;
if those who were concealed and not sent in [by the authorities] were
discovered by their masters or reported by others, the local officials as well as those who had aided the fugitives were to be punished. The penalty for concealing fugitives was beheading of the
leading man of the family. The severity of this law led to unrest
and widespread revolts, whereupon the Court was temporarily in-
duced to reduce the penalty from beheading to whipping. With an
increase in the number of cases of fugitives, however, the laws
were again tightened in 1646. The new regulations included the following provisions: (a) The fugitive was to be returned to the master after receiving one hundred lashes. (b) As regards the persons
who aided a fugitive, those who were poor were to be awarded to
the complainant [i.e. the fugitive's master], while those who were
rich were to lose either half or the whole of their property to the
master. (c) The informer was to receive one-third of the property
of the defendant [i.e. the one guilty of concealing the fugitive] to
an amount not to exceed one hundred taels. (d) The defendant's
nine closest neighbors, ward head, and neighborhood head were all
to receive one hundred lashes and to be exiled to the frontiers.
(e) If the case was not first discovered by the local officials, the
latter were to be adjudged guilty of negligence of duty and to be demoted and transferred. Officials from the prefect up who failed to
examine and send back fugitives were to be punished according to
the number of escaped persons found in the territory under their
jurisdiction.

In addition to the above there were further devices which sought
to enlist the cooperation of those aiding the fugitives as well as of
the local personages and provincial authorities in suppressing
desertion. Further changes were instituted in 1649 and 1652 which
did away with execution and exile and lowered other penalties for
concealers of fugitives.

The fugitive laws were not included in the ordinary codes. After
the regulations were drawn up they were assigned to the Board of
War for implementation. Subsequently a Supervisory Office for the
Arresting of Fugitives was created in 1654, but it was abolished
in 1699, and from then on the matter was transferred to the jurisdiction of the Board of Punishments.

Of the various policies dealing with fugitives, the drawing up
of legal regulations was the first to be instituted. Then followed
the granting of permission for members of the slave's family to

join him. The granting of leaves was the last to take effect.

During the Shun-shih period [1644-1661], however, a certain change had taken place which affected the nature of the fugitive problem. Before the Conquest the fugitives were all captives taken in wars, and those giving aid to them actually were "concealers." But when the number of Chinese adherents of Manchus increased, the fugitives were no longer all old slaves. Moreover, after the practice was established of awarding concealers of fugitives to Bannermen, there was presented the possibility that the number of fugitives would be increased by these slaves and a wider circle of people would become involved. Finally, when leaves were granted to slaves it often happened that the "fugitives" were actually those taking advantage of leaves, and the "concealers" apprehended in such round-ups were often people wrongly accused of this crime. The result was a further widening of the effects of the fugitive problem. The effects were as follows:

(a) In the determination of concealers there was no inquiry into the circumstances. Regardless of whether it was a case of parents concealing children or children concealing parents, as might happen in times of disturbance and under the influence of natural instincts, all were adjudged equally guilty as those who acted with willful intent. The punishments for concealers were actually more severe than those for robbers and receivers of stolen goods.

(b) The confiscation of property and loss of free personal status was a penalty originally limited to rebels. Such a severe punishment was not even applicable to bandits. Yet it was meted out to concealers. Group responsibility, also, extended the legal dragnet, so that in the first decade or so of the dynasty some thousands of Chinese families died under the implementation of the law. The vicious circle was perpetuated by the creation of new fugitives in the persons of concealers awarded to Bannermen as slaves. When the death penalty for concealers was reduced to exile after 1649, they had to provide the travel expenses for their families, but it frequently happened that the sentence of exile was delayed and that wives who arrived to join their husbands were informed that the departure was put off until more prisoners were accumulated; sometimes the prisoners fell sick and died in prison.

(c) With the instituting of leaves for slaves an avenue was opened for unscrupulous slaves to blackmail their hosts or local authorities by falsely alleging that those on leave were actually fugitives. In these cases of "false escape" and "false concealment" the master of the adherent or slave sometimes connived with the "fugitive" in joint extortion of the Chinese. There were also Chinese who pretended to be fugitives and who, assisted by accomplices, succeeded

in blackmailing people from place to place. In cases where exposure was threatened, the accomplices would pretend to be the master of the "fugitives," thus lending support to the allegations of
the latter. In some cases just the threat of reporting a "fugitive"
to the local authorities sufficed to bring results in the blackmail.
Thus was added a further element of social disturbance by the
Chinese themselves.

(d) In the predominantly agricultural society of China crop failures constituted major catastrophes, and the care of famine refugees was an important function of the government. However, in
certain localities fugitives were known to have disguised themselves and their families as refugees, so that local authorities and
people became unwilling to give aid to refugee groups for fear of
possible complications. The result was increased suffering and
starvation among the real famine victims, many of whom became
brigands out of desperation.

The purpose of the prevention of fugitives was the preservation
of Manchu economic interests. In the process, however, the Chinese population, individually and collectively, underwent tremendous suffering. The problem of fugitives ranked second in the
people's list of ten miseries. Though the system of granting leaves
was originally devised as a means of pacifying the slaves, actually
it led to threats and blackmail for the local population, an outcome
unforeseen by the policy-makers.

Although the laws for the apprehension of fugitives were very
strict, it was still difficult to apply them effectively. In fact, their
very severity had made the task more difficult, since the people
would either refuse to conceal fugitives, or, once they had engaged
in concealment, would have to go to all limits to prevent detection.

The fugitive laws were devised because the Manchus considered
it necessary to stop the desertion of their slaves. Actually, with
the establishment of a new tenant tenure and the paying of rent to
Manchu landlords by Chinese tenants, slavery was no longer a necessity in Manchu economy. The Manchu emperors did not per-
ceive this change, however, and proceeded with the instituting of
fugitive laws. What these laws accomplished was not so much the
preservation of the system of slave production as the maintenance
of Manchu ownership of the Chinese slaves. Even in this ownership,
however, a number of changes occurred: (a) In 1649 relatives of
fugitives were permitted to redeem the latter with a ransom; in
1652 Chinese were permitted to ransom war captives. This was a
sign of the influence of money economy. (b) Slave-ownership began
to assume the aspects of a duty. This is to say, owners were held
responsible for the livelihood of the slaves, and those unable to

provide support would allow them to be ransomed or even go free
in case ransom was unobtainable. (c) Those slaves who worked on
the master's land on a rent-paying basis became in reality tenants,
and the status of slavery gradually disappeared with the lapse of
time. (d) The slaves became personal servants and retainers, but
even these were not engaged in production. (e) The last and worst
development was the business about "false escapes." The slaves
engaged in blackmail by pretending to be fugitives, and the masters
utilized their position as owner to good advantage.

In sum, the fugitive laws were not sufficient to prevent desertion, but more than adequate in disturbing the peace of the Chinese
population. It was instituted under circumstances in which slavery
was not only unnecessary, but ownership itself was rapidly declining. The fugitive question and the question of Chinese adherents
of the Manchus were but two phases of the same problem. Both
point to the economic and social conflicts that existed between the
Manchus and the Chinese.

6. Other Conflicts

The conflicts described above were those that involved the Chinese as members of an agrarian society. As a matter of fact, however, this did not exhaust the scope of Manchu-Chinese conflicts,
which occurred wherever there were clashes of economic interests.
The following are some examples:

(a) In the matter of trade and commercial establishments, if
post-Conquest Manchu commercial competition with the Chinese
had been conducted on a purely economic basis, there would not
have been much conflict in this respect. But many practices perpetrated by the Manchus and their adherents inevitably led to serious
conflicts. Some Manchus would issue proclamations which ordered
their adherents to occupy commercial establishments belonging to
others. Adherents sometimes indulged in such unfair practices as
gathering a gang together, stopping incoming merchandise on the
highway, and forcing a sale at low price. Lumber from Manchuria
was often controlled by high officials who cornered the supply, and
even government-controlled salt was smuggled and sold by persons
purporting to be adherents of the Manchus. Many were the unscrupulous merchants who encroached on others' businesses on the
strength of their Manchu backing. The sale of ginseng, a special
business of the Manchus, was another source of disturbance; the
problems created by the Manchu monopoly were not solved even
after the places of wholesale transactions had been limited to four
cities. Ordinary economic activities were not possible when some
of the participants enjoyed special privileges.

(b) Joining a Banner meant protection for wrong-doing. To be a Bannerman was to be above the control of ordinary law, and the system of adherents opened the door wide to racketeers. Whenever such a person's corrupt deeds were discovered, he would head for the capital and seek protection from some Manchu dignitary. The result was that criminals not only remained unpunished, but could also lord it over the local population in wealth and power. Assuming Manchu costumes and accents, these persons were beyond the reach of the officials, who dared not touch them.

(c) Disturbances were created by the "enclosure" of residential homes in Peking and by segregation of the population in different parts of the city. Enclosures of this kind were begun at the start of the Shun-chih reign; they were aimed at separating the Manchu troops and the Chinese people. Though some three-fifths of the city area was affected and people were moved around, there were still large numbers of Chinese and Manchus who lived intermingled in the same sections of the city. Numerous quarrels between the two groups ensued, with none to assume the responsibility. In 1648, therefore, it was further ordered that all Chinese officials, merchants, and common people, with the exception of adherents of Manchus, were to move to the southern section of the city by the end of the following year. Their original property was to be either demolished or sold. People who made pilgrimages to the temples in the city had to do so during the day, and were not allowed to stay overnight. Although in both 1644 and 1648 the government instituted certain remedial measures, such as remission of taxes for three years for those whose homes had been "enclosed," the Chinese suffered serious economic losses as a result of the actions of the Manchus.

Aside from segregation and the enclosure of houses, it was also ordered in 1645 that all Chinese who suffered from smallpox were to be banished forty li from the city. Unrestricted application of this rule led to eviction of those whose malady was not smallpox but ringworm or some other skin disease. The uprooted poor, unable to care for their families, often had to abandon their children by the roadside. Modification of this order was not able to erase the bad social effects it had produced at first.

(d) The presence of the Manchus engendered social instability. Since the Manchus were alien conquerors, many fantastic rumors continued to circulate as to what they were about to do. At one time it was rumored that the people were going to be exterminated, and at another that the city was going to be moved. A report in 1646 that the Manchus were about to round up all Buddhist images caused widespread destruction and loss in Buddhist images and ancestral portraits. Bands of unscrupulous persons robbed and plundered during the general unrest.

In addition other conflicts were caused by the changes in hair style and manner of dress. The disturbances went so far as to end in massacres at Chiang-yin and Chia-hsing [in Kiangsu]. These conflicts, though not economic in nature, nevertheless constituted serious social problems.

7. Adjustment of Conflicts

We must note, first of all, that the above conflicts were abnormal social phenomena caused by the Manchus' use of their superior political position to solve problems in their economy. Throughout these abnormal developments, however, a number of constant and normal factors also existed. These were the tendency toward private ownership of land, the importance of money economy, the superiority of agricultural techniques of the Chinese over those of the Manchus, and the assimilation of Manchus into the Chinese way of life, a process that was not halted by the conflicts.

The problem of adjustment lay in normalizing the abnormal phenomena. In this process of adjustment social and economic factors, rather than political, were of first importance, though this fact has frequently been ignored by people whose attention has been focused on the more obvious political aspect.

The adjustment of land enclosure problems had begun with the exchange of land in 1654, clear evidence that the enclosure system was in process of disintegration. Further, although the sale of Banner land to local Chinese was forbidden, within the Banner certain limited transactions in land were allowed, a fact which indicates the decline of the public ownership of land. Actually, despite legal prohibition some of the buyers of Banner land were found to be Chinese.

The Chinese were skilful in agricultural work, and many were encouraged to colonize unused land with a three-year exemption in taxes. Enclosures of land thus colonized occurred repeatedly. It was not until 1685 that such enclosures were permanently forbidden. While the Chinese worked hard, the Manchus became addicted to habits of extravagance and luxury, which together with the insufficiency of Manchu manpower made a change imperative in the public ownership of land.

Adjustments in the land enclosure problem were attempted by measures in the political and the social-economic spheres. As to the political sphere, decrees of 1647, 1653, and 1685 prohibited the enclosure respectively of landed property, lands and houses, and colonized land belonging to the Chinese population. These measures were not actually effective. Several other measures dealing with immediate and local problems clearly indicated the continued need for adjustments. In the social and economic sphere, where one of the major problems was the contention between Chinese tenant farmers and Manchu landlords, a decree of 1740 ordered that changes in the ownership of Banner land should not lead to dismissal of the original tenant farmers if the latter had made all necessary rent payments; otherwise the owner was to be indicted and punished. Rent increases and eviction of tenants were henceforth forbidden, except for the period when [the exceedingly corrupt] Ho-shen was a president of the Board of Finance [1776-1799]. Many Manchus mortgaged their land to Chinese when in need of money, so that by 1745 half or more of the Banner land was in the hands of the Chinese. Some of this land was redeemed by the government, but the tenants still were protected from eviction and rent increases.

For the Chinese tenants, the above developments amounted to a trend toward private ownership of land. In mortgage cases not only did they acquire de facto right of ownership, but also incidentally became exempt from taxation [because the land was nominally Banner land]. In addition, the Chinese were sometimes asked to colonize the Bannermen's allotments, or become tenants of Manchus, who paid rent and were free from enclosure acts. In all, the use of land fell increasingly into Chinese hands, and the land that remained under direct Manchu cultivation steadily dwindled.

Adjustment in the problem of Chinese adherents of Manchus and of fugitives was a dire necessity. The first step in this direction was taken in 1647, when an edict permanently forbade the system of adherents. The second step was to prevent the adherents from committing crimes. The third was to return the adherents to their status as free men.

The adjustments in the problem of fugitives also had several aspects: (a) The penalty for concealers was successively reduced from 1649 on. (b) The freeing of slaves decreased the potential sources of fugitives. (c) The prohibition of adherents, and the organization of additional Banner subdivisions [into which the slaves were incorporated], had a moderating effect on the slavery situation. (d) Concealers of fugitives were often able to avoid punishment by bribing the master of the fugitive; blackmail by fugitives also subsided with the gradual return of order to society. (e) Finally, the transfer of fugitive affairs in 1699 and 1700 from the Board of War to the Board of Punishments showed a relaxation in official severity, and also a lessening of the seriousness of the problem.

Conflicts in commercial undertakings evoked a series of edicts in 1644, 1660, and 1666 which aimed at curbing the abusive activities of Bannermen and their adherents. The most severe stricture came in 1679 with an edict curbing the activities of persons belonging to the households of Manchu noblemen; any such persons who monopolized businesses and encroached on others were punished with immediate execution. In 1722 retainers in noble households were forbidden to hoard straw and charcoal and sell them at high prices. The sale of ginseng was restricted from 1648 on to Peking alone, which eliminated somewhat the disturbances created by the sellers in the provinces.

The other conflicts, such as the use of Banners as protection by criminals, the smuggling of salt, and so on, gradually came to an end with the stabilization of the political situation and effective administrative control. The conflict brought about by enclosure of houses and segregation in Peking was passing in nature and involved only a small area. As time passed and the situation was stabilized, Manchus and Chinese came to live at peace with one another.

NOTES

馬奉琛, 清初滿漢社會經濟衝突之一般, 食貨

Ma Feng-ch'en, "Ching-ch'u Man-Han she-hui ching-chi ch'ung-t'u-chih i-pan," Shih-huo, IV, No. 6 (Aug. 16, 1936), 262-269; IV, No. 8 (Sept. 16, 1936), 349-356; IV, No. 9 (Oct. 1, 1936), 384-402.

The major sources used for this article are the collected statutes and memorials, including the Imperial Ch'ing Memorials (Huang-Ch'ing tso-i 皇清奏議), Tung-hua lu 東華錄, Records of the Eight Banners (Pa-ch'i t'ung-chih 八旗通志), Institutes of the Yung-cheng Reign (Yung-cheng hui-tien 雍正會典), and Founding of the Imperial Ch'ing Dynasty (Huang-Ch'ing k'ai-kuo fang-lüeh 皇清開國方略). Local gazetteers, such as that of Shun-t'ien Prefecture, as well as other compendiums were also used. The footnotes are placed in a thirteen-page appendix at the end of the article.

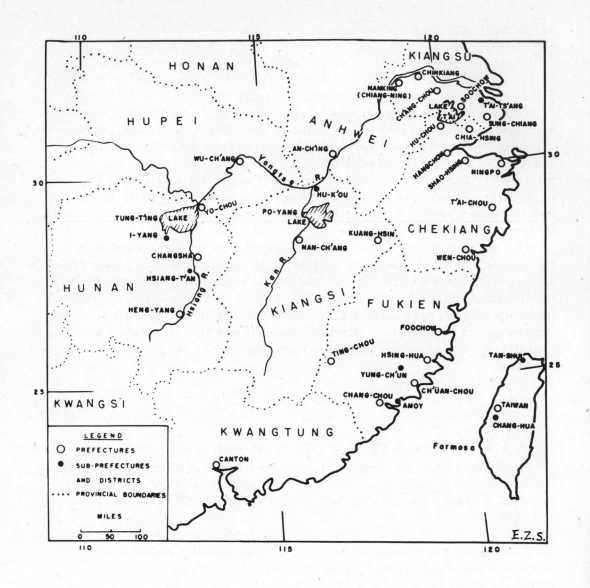

Map 9. Southeastern China in the Ch'ing dynasty

24

A SHIP'S VOYAGE FROM LUZON TO CHINA
IN THE EIGHTEENTH CENTURY

by

CHAO CH'ÜAN-CH'ENG

The proximity of the Malay Archipelago to Annam, Hainan Island, Formosa, and China Proper led to the growth of intercourse among these regions at an early date. Before the days of Magellan large numbers of Chinese from the coastal areas, especially Fukien, Kwangtung, and Kwangsi, were already settling in the Malay Archipelago. Such evidence points to the frequent communications between China and these islands. Though in the eighteenth century these areas had become colonies of the European powers, communications with China not only continued but were increased, thanks to the lifting of the ban on overseas trade by the Ch'ing government. The present study deals with a ship's voyage which is a dividing line for the new stage and at the same time is representative of the most common sort of maritime intercourse between China and Southeast Asia in the eighteenth century.

//The ship in question sailed from the Ilocos area in Luzon on July 18, 1749, with a crew of thirty-three men under Captain A-lun-shih. Her destination was Amoy, Fukien, where she was to take on a cargo of Yung-ch'un linen. The following cargo was brought along by the ship:

Rice	1,300 tan 石
Canvas	207 pieces
Ox hides	41 pieces
Lard	8 jars
Tobacco	8 chests
Betel nuts	60 packages
Sesame seeds	19 packages
Dried venison and dried beef	44 piculs
Sappanwood	38 piculs
Coconut meat	8 jars
Copper fragments	2 piculs
Silver dollars	3,900

∥After twenty-odd days of sailing, the ship and its crew reached
the sea off Amoy on August 8, when they suddenly ran into a storm.
They waited there for five days for the storm to pass, but on the
night of August 12 the ship was struck by a typhoon and lost its rud-
der. The crew quickly cut down the mainmast, but the ship continued to be blown off its course by the wind. It finally drifted to
the White Sands Reefs off Ta-hsi-ch'ien in northwestern Formosa,
and was wrecked there and sunk. None of the crew perished, but
all the cargo was lost in the sea except for a few items that were
salvaged from the water.∥

Now how were these men treated by the Chinese officials?

The spot where the Ilocos ship was wrecked lay to the north of
Tan-shui Sub-Prefecture, and was administrated by a Deputy
Magistrate, who also acted as an inspector of the coast. The first
person to take cognizance of the shipwreck, therefore, was this
Deputy Magistrate, who reported the case to Ch'en Yü-yu, the
Sub-Prefect of Tan-shui. The latter, upon receiving the report,
made an on-the-spot investigation himself, listed all the men and
salvaged items of the cargo, and asked the Deputy Magistrate to
accompany the crew members to Chang-hua District, together with
an official letter from Ch'en. Part of the letter went as follows:

> I have now made an inspection myself.....All the rice has
> been lost; the only things salvaged are some trunks and cloth-
> ing. I am now hiring carts and sending the shipwrecked bar-
> barians A-lun-shih and others on their way, each person hav-
> ing been given a food ration based on the length of the journey.
> I hereby notify you by this document [....] The District
> should immediately distribute firewood and rice, etc. to these
> thirty-four shipwrecked barbarians and find lodgings for them.
> Each item of their luggage and other belongings should be
> checked and carefully guarded so that no loss occurs. At the
> same time you are to hire carts, provide food rations, and
> send them forward [to Taiwan Prefecture] in the company of
> a subordinate, so that the shipwrecked barbarians will not be
> uncared for.

Accordingly, the District Magistrate of Chang-hua sent the crew
and their belongings to Taiwan Prefecture. There, in accordance
with the usual practice, the local authorities "checked the personnel, settled them in lodgings, distributed food rations, and dis-
patched guards to watch and protect them with care." Then "an official report was prepared, travelling papers were issued, boats
were arranged for, officers were appointed, and soldiers were

assigned," in preparation for sending the persons to Amoy. On September 15 the group set forth in three boats, accompanied by twelve guards and a man named Liu Ho. The latter, who could speak some foreign language and wanted to go to Luzon, joined the group as interpreter.

The office of the Marine Sub-Prefect of Amoy had been located at Amoy since 1686. His functions were: "to be in charge of the port and the merchants, to levy duties from sea-going merchant ships that pass through, to see to the transportation of rice, to supervise the distribution of military provisions, and to judge in local disputes and litigations." The case of the Ilocos ship, therefore, fell within the jurisdiction of the Amoy Sub-Prefect, Hsü Feng-yüan. Aside from feeding and guarding the shipwrecked personnel, the most important task of the Sub-Prefect was to obtain individual testimony from each of the crew. This was done with great care after ample preparations. In addition to Liu Ho, an interpreter named Ho Yu-te was also engaged to aid in translation. The following is the testimony given by the captain and the crew of the ship:

// Questions to Captain A-lun-shih: "What country are you the subject of? Did your ship belong to a barbarian king, or a barbarian official? What cargo did you bring? How many crew members are there for the entire ship? When did you start on this voyage from your country? Where were you planning to do business? When, where, and how were you ship-wrecked? Were there any deaths resulting from the wreck? How much of your goods has been salvaged?"

// Answers by A-lun-shih: "We, the humble barbarians, are all natives of Ilocos, in Luzon. This ship belonged to a barbarian official of Ilocos entitled A-li-chieh-mai-yu. I was assigned to be the captain. We brought with us 1,300 tan of rice, of which 150 tan were eaten by the crew on the way, 207 pieces of canvas, 41 pieces of ox-hide [.....] and 3,906 silver dollars, of which we used 36 dollars ourselves. There were thirty-four persons on board. We sailed from our country on July 18 with the intention of doing business in Amoy. [....] All the rice and goods were lost at sea, except for the following items which were salvaged: 13 small trunks, of which three contain 3,870 silver dollars and ten contain clothing; 5 trunks, two of which contain tobacco and 3 clothing; 4 bundles of canvas amounting to 100 [Chinese] feet; 9 rattan baskets of various sizes, containing old clothing; 10 big and small jars containing foodstuffs; 5 fowling pieces of different sizes and 3 swords; 2 ox-hide sacks; and bedding and articles of daily use. There were two head of cattle, but one died in Formosa and the other on the way to Amoy." //

A-lun-shih was further asked to give the names of the members
of the crew, which he did, together with the position and function
of each individual. The interrogation continued:

//Question: "You have come from Ilocos to trade at Amoy, and
you want to buy goods to take back with you. [We] shall now find a
substantial and reliable merchant for you, who will handle your
transactions. You should not deal privately with others, so that you
will not get cheated out of what you have. You are to make an itemized list of all your present belongings; we shall then place them
under seal and guard them for you."

//Answer: "We had originally wanted to do business at Amoy.
Now that our ship has been wrecked and our goods lost, we do not
have much money and are not planning to buy things. As to the
money, goods, and personal belongings that have been salvaged,
they have been forwarded to us from Formosa. Nothing has been
lost."

//Question: "Formosa has sent you to Amoy because your ship
was wrecked. It is still too early for ships to be going to the barbarian countries, and in the meantime you may stay in Amoy, but
at the end of the year, when there will be a ship sailing for Ilocos
in Luzon, you may embark and return home. While living in Amoy
you must be peaceful. You will be given a daily food ration."

//Answer: "[. . . .] We should appreciate the favor of an early
return to our country."//

The other members of the crew were then interrogated. They
gave their names and the duties of each on board the ship. From
their testimony it appears that the following officers and men
served under the captain: one first mate, who supervised the
watches and also acted as helmsman; one second mate, who helped
to steer the ship; one quartermaster in charge of the cargo; one
chief cook in charge of meals; one boatswain to oversee the sailors
and be in charge of the general affairs of the ship; one second boatswain to help the boatswain; two cabin-boys to serve the captain;
and twenty-five sailors.

After staying in Amoy for some five months, the crew was sent
back to Luzon on January 25, 1750, on board a Chinese ship that
was going to trade in Ilocos. During their stay the crew had been
given a daily allotment by the Amoy Sub-Prefecture consisting of
1 pint of rice and 10 cash "for salted vegetables" per person. At
the time of their return their belongings were given back to them,
and in addition each person was given a month's ration of rice, that
is 3 pecks, plus 4 taels of silver. The entire matter was memori-

alized by the Governor of Fukien on April 16, and was officially
ended on May 23, 1750.*

The following are a number of points which have emerged from
this episode and merit our attention:

(a) Kind of ships used: The kind of vessel used in the Luzon
trade was called by the Chinese a "double-plank ship," a name
given to all foreign ships. The exact origin of this term is not known,
although the ships so designated seem to have had certain definite
features in common. According to the Gazetteer of Amoy, the
largest of these "double-plank ships from Luzon" were square at
both the bow and the stern, and were some 100 feet long and 30 to
40 feet wide at the beam. Each was manned by over 100 sailors,
had a cargo capacity of some 20,000 tan, and could mount about a
dozen cannon on the first deck. The small ships measured some
80 feet long and 20 to 30 feet wide, were manned by 60 or 70 sailors, and could take around 10,000 tan of cargo. The ships' bottoms
were covered with copper sheeting as protection against reefs.
However, the very size of the larger ships just described seems
to indicate that they were a very advanced sort, probably not typical of the eighteenth century "double-plank ships." In contrast,
the Ilocos ship appears to have been more representative of the times.

(b) Organization of the ship's crew: Material is available as to
the organization of the crew on board Chinese sea-going vessels;
this material shows that under the captain were a purser, a navigator and a second navigator, a helmsman and a second helmsman,
and a number of other officers and sailors each with his own particular function. The testimony of the Ilocos crew now provide us
with reliable data on the organization of the ships' crew from the
Malay Archipelago. Of the thirty-four persons on board, seven
were officers, under whom there were two cabin-boys and twenty-
five sailors. The captain headed the officers, each of whom had
specific duties to perform, as previously described.

(c) Weapons carried: It does not seem likely that a typical vessel on the China Sea in the eighteenth century would possess the
larger number of firearms which are attested in local accounts for
a later period. Although the original complement of the Ilocos vessel is unknown, the weapons salvaged from the wreck consisted of
only five fowling pieces of various sizes and three swords. Judging from the small overall capacity of this particular vessel, the
original complement of arms was probably not very large. The Chinese government regulations on the armament of sea-going ships

---

*This presumably occurred when the memorial reporting the case reached the
emperor and was endorsed by him, marking the close of the matter.

of large size specified that "each ship is not to carry more than
the following: two cannon, eight fowling-pieces, ten short swords,
ten sets of bows and arrows, and thirty catties of gunpowder."
This also throws some light on the typical armament of eighteenth
century sailing ships from Southeast Asia.

(d) Goods exchanged: The aim of the voyage of the Ilocos ship
was to purchase Yung-ch'un linen in Fukien; most of the 3,900
silver dollars was probably intended for this purpose. Other trade
data for the years 1755, 1781, 1782, and 1783 reveal that the major Chinese exports to the Malay Archipelago consisted of textiles,
chinaware, paper, umbrellas, medicines, and other consumer
goods. The linen cloth sought by the Ilocos buyers fell within the
category of textiles. In the cargo brought over by the Ilocos ship,
betel nuts, sappanwood, and dried venison were some of the
most common imports from the Malay Archipelago. Data over an
extended period in the eighteenth century indicate that foodstuffs
were the most important imports, of which the most noteworthy
item was rice. The latter provided the main economic impetus to
the growth of trade between China and Southeast Asia, as many of
the coastal provinces in China were food-deficit areas and could
be greatly helped by imports from the countries to the south. The
rice deficit in China is indicated by the fact that there had long been
a strict ban on the export of rice from Kiangsu and Chekiang. A
limit was also set on the amount of rice carried by each sea-going
vessel; persons found guilty of carrying more than the legal amount
and selling it were punished with death by strangulation. The rice
supply of Fukien and Kwangtung was also insufficient. In contrast,
in the Southeast Asian countries there was such an abundant supply
that the price of Siamese rice fell to 0.3 tael per 100 catties during the Yung-cheng period [1723-1735], and the general price for
Southeast Asian rice during the Ch'ien-lung period [1736-1795] was
around 0.2 tael per standard tan. China's need for the surplus
rice of this region was instrumental in keeping the sea trade going. Hence, the ban on overseas trade established at the beginning
of the Ch'ing era was lifted in 1684; although reimposed in 1717,
it was again lifted after a few years. The problem was pertinently
stated in an official document of 1727:

> Governor-General Kao Ch'i-cho [1676-1738] of Fukien in his
> confidential memorial on the lifting of the sea ban pointed out
> that "The population is dense while the land is limited in the
> five prefectures of Foochow, Hsing-hua, Ch'üan-chou, Chang-
> chou, and Ting-chou, so that the rice produced there is in-
> sufficient to meet the demand. Most of the sea-going vessels
> bring back rice on their return. The lifting of the ban on over-

seas trade would therefore greatly benefit the people of the
coastal areas." Permission was granted to act as proposed.
Owing to the food deficit in Fukien and the tendency of the
unemployed there to become bandits, the ban was lifted in
this province.... However, the sea off Kiangsu and Chekiang
is adjacent to that off Fukien... Now that the ban has been
lifted in Fukien, but not in Kiangsu and Chekiang [....] in-
consistencies will certainly arise with respect to the patrol-
ling of the coast.... The proposal of the merchants of Kiangsu
and Chekiang that they be permitted to trade in the South Seas,
as is true in the case of the Fukien merchants, should be
accepted....

The cargo of rice carried by the Ilocos ship typified the general
situation of rice imports into China after the lifting of the ban.

(e) Amount of trade: According to a report by Ch'ing-fu, the
Governor-General of Kwangtung and Kwangsi [in 1741-1743], in
the eighteenth century a great many ships sailed for Southeast
Asia every year after the lifting of the ban, and many people were
employed as sailors, helmsmen, merchants' clerks, and so on.
The Bocca Tigris of Canton was an important port of call for all
Chinese overseas vessels, and the number of persons in Kwangtung who depended on overseas vessels for livelihood was estimated at several hundred thousand. The destinations of these ships
ranged from Annam, Cambodia, and Siam, to Songkla, Johore,
Malacca, Luzon, and other intermediate points.

In the eighteenth century Amoy was a flourishing port. Ships
called there on their Southeast Asian runs all year round, large
revenues were collected from this overseas commerce, and the
markets of Amoy were stocked with all kinds of goods. At the end
of the century Amoy still possessed eight hong merchant houses
and thirty-odd big and small business establishments [that dealt
in imports and exports]; some thousand foreign and Chinese vessels used the harbor [every year]. Subsequently, however, with
the opening of other ports, there was a sharp decrease in intercourse between Amoy and the Malay Archipelago, and the port entered a period of decline.

NOTES

趙泉澄, 十八世紀呂宋一咾哥航船來華記, 禹貢
Chao Ch'üan-ch'eng, "Shih-pa shih-chi Lü-sung I-lao-ko hang-ch'uan lai-Hua chi," <u>Yü-kung</u> VI, No. 11 (Feb. 1, 1937), 1-10.

Sources for this article are primarily the <u>Gazetteer of Amoy</u>, the <u>Gazetteer of Tan-shui</u>, and the Ch'ing government documents containing the testimonies of the crew. Also used are <u>Tung-hua-lu</u>, <u>Gazetteer of Ch'üan-chou</u>, and contemporary sources reproduced in the journal <u>Shih-liao hsün-k'an</u> [Historical Sources Ten-Day Journal 史料旬刊].

The names of the captain and crew, all of whom were presumably native Filipinos, have been rendered in our text by transliterations of the Chinese characters for the original names, as the latter are not available.

The terms describing the countries now generally known as Southeast Asia are rendered as follows: For <u>Nan-yang ch'ün-tao</u>, the geographical term "Malay Archipelago" is used; for <u>Nan-yang</u> in the author's text, "Southeast Asia"; for <u>Nan-yang</u> in quotations from eighteenth century works, the less modern-sounding and more literal equivalent "South Seas."

25

THE LAND TAX IN THE YANGTSE PROVINCES BEFORE AND AFTER THE TAIPING REBELLION

by

HSIA NAI

Introduction

In the crisis of the 1850's and 1860's the Ch'ing Court was able to overcome internal difficulties by employing both military and political tactics. The most important of the political measures concerned the question of land tax, which was a pressing problem in the provinces of the Yangtse valley occupied for the longest period by rebel forces during the Taiping Rebellion [1850-1864]. The Ch'ing government instituted both temporary exemptions of land tax and the more permanent measure of reduction of the tax rate in the six Yangtse provinces [Kiangsu, Chekiang, Kiangsi, Hupei, Hunan, and Anhwei]. The present study will deal with the causes, the actual implementation, and the effects of the tax reduction movement.

PART I. THE SITUATION BEFORE THE TAIPING REBELLION

1. Overcollections and Compulsory Commutation and Their Causes

The most important items of the land tax in the Yangtse provinces during the Ch'ing dynasty were the "rice tribute" and the "land-poll tax."* The rice tribute was payable either in kind or in money, and it was the practice of the tax collectors to collect

---

*At one time the Chinese fiscal system included two taxes called ti-fu 地賦 "land tax" and ting-fu 丁賦 "poll tax." In the Yung-cheng period [1723-1735] the ting-fu was incorporated into the ti-fu. The "poll" part of the tax was assessed at ten to twenty per cent of the amount of the land tax, and the combined tax was called ti-ting. We therefore render the latter as "land-poll tax," though it actually amounted only to a land tax, which landless persons were not required to pay.

above the amounts specified in the Complete Tax Regulations. For
payment in kind the collectors either charged more while measuring, or discounted what was collected. For the payment in money
they often fixed the price of rice higher than the market price; in
addition they might set the price of silver in terms of copper coins
at a higher rate than the market price, and make the tax-payer remit the tax in copper. The "land-poll tax" was officially payable
in silver, but the collectors compelled its payment in copper coins,
thus creating the same ills as in the commutation of the rice tribute. The people often had to pay several times the legal amount
of taxes.

This condition was prevalent in all the provinces. For example,
when the rice tribute was collected in Kiangsu it was calculated
at a compound discount, amounting first to 30 per cent and then to
an additional 20 per cent; that is, each picul was counted as less
than 0.6 picul. Sometimes this process was repeated, so that as
much as 2.5 or 2.6 tan 石 was necessary to meet the payment of
one tan. If the tribute was commuted to money payment, then the
price of rice was set at 8,000-10,000 cash or even more per tan,
while it was selling at 2,000 on the market. Chekiang presented a
similar situation. For the payment of each tan of the rice tribute
in the prefectures of Hangchow, Chia-hsing, and Hu-chou, for instance, it was necessary to pay the equivalent of 2 tan. The conditions were even worse in Anhwei, Kiangsi, Hupei and Hunan,
where the overcollection, according to contemporary reports,
was sometimes several times the legal amount.

What were the causes of such widespread overcollection and
compulsory commutation? The tax collectors no doubt squeezed
the people to fill their own pockets. Part of their loot, however,
had to be given as presents to their official superiors, and another
part had to be turned over to the local gentry. Thus, collectors,
superiors, and gentry formed a trinity with the common objective
of squeezing the peasantry.

The tax collectors were the first to handle the tax payments, and
hence many persons sought to obtain their profitable posts. An
edict of 1832 mentions how newly appointed prefects and district
magistrates were bribed to appoint certain persons to posts in the
tax and treasury departments; these persons would then use their
positions to perpetrate corrupt deeds. Feng Kuei-fen [1809-1874],
a contemporary specialist on the land tax in Kiangsu, held that
during each collection of rice tribute in that province the perquisites that could be obtained by the various levels of functionaries
were as follows: watchmen and tribute secretaries, as much as
10,000 taels each; some dozen scribes, a total of 20,000 to 30,000

taels; some 30 to 50 collection overseers, 200-300 taels each,
making a total of 10,000 to 20,000 taels; and 200 to 300 collectors,
100-200 taels each, making a total of 30,000 to 40,000 taels. As
to corrupt practices, Feng lists quite a number. Apart from the
discounting techniques, overcharges were exacted by methods with
such names as "seizing the pig," "sample price," and "premium."
In addition there were fees for transporting the rice, for examin-
ing the rice, for sifting the rice, for entrance to the granary, for
granary clerks, and so on. Still other methods of corruption which
directly injured the government revenue were described by [the
general and statesman] Hu Lin-i [1812-1861].

After lining their own pockets the collectors made presents of
money to the officials in the various levels of the local government. These presents were called "extra-legal fees"; those that
came from the rice tribute were known as "tribute perquisites."
In Hupei tribute perquisites were paid to every official from the
Grain Commissioner on down to the clerks and guards, the amounts
ranging from over 1,000 taels to a few dozen taels. It is estimated
that "extra-legal fees" were exacted in every district under more
than a hundred different names, in sums amounting to thousands
or tens of thousands of taels. In Hunan the categories of the perquisites were so numerous that the tax collectors were able to gain
a free hand in handling them. It was reported, also, that the overcollections in Anhwei had increased the originally low tax rates
several-fold, and that in Kiangsi the perquisites for a high superi-
or ranged between three or four thousand to eight or nine thousand
taels per annum, with the lower superiors getting proportionately
less on a descending scale. Among the items which made up these
funds were gate fees, holiday gifts, birthday presents, and gifts
for office furnishings and additional equipment. In addition it was
necessary also for the collectors to pay their colleagues on the
same level, as well as the office clerks and members of the various offices, and so on. The officials in Kiangsu and Chekiang also
depended on the rice tribute as a source for their various extra
exactions. The existence of these extra-legal fees, therefore, was
a major cause for the overcollection of the land tax in the six
Yangtse provinces.

The tax collectors and their superior officials were accomplices
in corruption. With the bribes in their pockets the superior officials were wont to see no evil, while the collectors, grateful for
their silence, willingly paid more bribes. The common people had
no way of redress. The local gentry, however, began to maneuver
for their share of the profit. Those who owned land--the "great
households" and "gentry households"--demanded lower tax assess-

ments. Those who did not own land acted as intermediaries between the government and the "small households" and in that capacity obtained a part of the latter's tax money. Some demanded payment from the tax collectors outright, and forced them to accede
to their demands on pain of exposure. The result was an increase
in the burden of the small taxpayer. Let us examine the situation
with regard to the gentry in each province.

(i) Kiangsu. All wealthy and influential families were "great
households." The rates of commutation were different for the
great households and the small ones, the gentry households paying 4,000 cash per tan, and the small households in the villages
10,000 per tan. There were also gradations within the two groups
of the gentry and common people. In the former the actual rate of
payment ranged between less than one tan to two tan for every tan
in the official assessment, and in the latter the range was from
under two tan to three or four. Unable to bear such burdens, those
of the common people who had the same surname as a large household would report their tax under the latter's name. These would
then collect the small family's tax, but turn over only part of it
to the government. Further, local "corrupt scholars" used to
blackmail the tax collectors and could only be bought off by money
payments, known as "litigation rice." In some localities where
there were three or four hundred such scholars the fee could reach
the staggering total sum of 20,000 or 30,000 taels.

(ii) Chekiang. As in Kiangsu, the great and small households
paid taxes at different rates. Further, the great households were
held responsible for only the official quota, while the small households were subject to extra levies besides the fixed amount. The
appending of the small households onto the great ones resulted in
the decrease in the number of the former.

(iii) Kiangsi. Small households in Hu-k'ou District whose official land-poll tax was less than 0.3 or 0.4 tael were assessed a
number of special levies different from the taxes paid by the great
households. In meeting the assessment for army provisions the
great households usually paid in kind, while the small ones paid
in money. There were gentry who acted as middlemen; they also
often received perquisites from the tax collectors.

(iv) Hupei. Small households paid the rice tribute in money.
The records show also that in the thirty-odd districts and prefectures liable for rice tribute such commutation was always made
in copper cash, never in silver. The great households, on the
other hand, paid in kind. From them the collecting clerks dared
not take more than the official amount. The corrupt gentry therefore became middlemen, taking their cut in the handling of the
taxes. They were called "locusts" by the common people.

(v) Hunan. The local authorities regarded the land-poll tax and the rice tribute as a source of profit, and the corrupt gentry took a share in blackmail, usually extorting large sums from them.

Detailed information on the situation in Anhwei is lacking. It probably was not different from the other provinces.

I have taken some care to describe the overcollection of land taxes, as it is only by culling the various sources that we can have some idea of the actual tax burden of the people. This cannot be gathered from such official works as the Complete Tax Regulations and Institutes and Regulations of the Board of Finance, which give only the official tax receipts.

2. Excessive Taxation in Kiangsu and Chekiang

By "excessive taxation" is meant here the extemely heavy official assessments of rice tribute that prevailed in Soochow, Sung-chiang, T'ai-ts'ang, Chinkiang, and Ch'ang-chou in Kiangsu Province, and Hangchow, Chia-hsing, and Hu-chou in Chekiang. It should be distinguished clearly from the "overcollection" or extralegal exactions discussed in the previous section.

The tax rate in "excessive taxation" was so heavy that it was often beyond the people's ability to pay. Li Hung-chang [1823-1901] noted that the term "excessive taxation" had appeared without censure in edicts and local gazetteers, a fact which suggested to him that there was room for reduction. In a memorial of Lin Tse-hsü [1785-1850], governor of Kiangsu in the mid-Tao-kuang period, the taxes paid by Soochow and the other four nearby areas was estimated to be three times that of Kiangsi province, and more than ten times that of Hupei and Hunan. The levies each year included more than 2,000,000 taels for the rice tribute and over 1,800,000 tan of rice for various other exactions. All this was from an area not over 500 li in circumference. A slight rise in the price of rice could increase the burden imperceptibly by one or two million taels. According to Tseng Kuo-fan [1811-1872], the average rice yield of this area was 1.5 to 2 tan per mou; after deducting the tenants' share and the taxes, the landowner's gross receipt did not exceed 0.2 tan pour mou.

The rice tribute quota for Hangchow, Chia-hsing, and Hu-chou in Chekiang was nearly as high as that for Soochow, Sung-chiang, and so forth. Out of the annual rice tribute quota of some 4,000,-000 tan for the whole country, Kiangsu and Chekiang were responsible for nearly 3,000,000, that is, three quarters of the total amount.

The excessive rates of taxation in Kiangsu and Chekiang, the origins of which have been discussed by various persons, stem from the fact that in these particular areas there were, up to the reign of Chia-ching [1522-1566] in the Ming dynasty, large amounts of government-owned land, from which were taken heavy dues for the treasury, while the tax on private land remained low. During the Chia-ching Period, however, the tax obligations of the government and private lands were averaged together and an equal tax rate was established. This greatly increased the tax burden of the people. Thus, the high tax rates for these two provinces were not based on the natural fertility of the soil, but rather on accidents of history. Despite the rich resources of Kiangsu and Chekiang, therefore, such heavy taxation must still be considered "excessive."

3. Need for Tax Reduction during the Tao-kuang and Hsien-feng Periods

The question arises as to why it was possible for the tax system to be maintained without change before the Hsien-feng period. There were two reasons for this. The first was economic. Between the K'ang-hsi [1662-1722] and Chia-ch'ing [1796-1820] reigns the country enjoyed relative peace and stability, so that the taxation, though heavy, could still be borne by the people of the rich Kiangsu and Chekiang provinces. This was the concensus of opinion of mid-nineteenth century officials like Kuo Sung-t'ao, Li Hung-chang, Tso Tsung-t'ang, and others.

The second reason was political. The Manchus' ruthless suppression of any sign of opposition in the early years of their rule had created a deep impression on the people, who preforce had to bear the exactions in silence. The Ch'ing government therefore had been able to obtain the heavy taxes on the basis of their military strength and entrenched political control.

But by the time of the Tao-kuang reign [1822-1850], the above two causes were no longer valid. In the first place, the people were no longer able to pay the taxes. According to a contemporary, Wang Ch'ing-yün [1798-1862], although the total quota for the land-poll tax for the six Yangtse provinces was 12,550,276 taels, the sum actually collected was only 11,020,240 taels in 1842, and it continued to decrease until in 1850 only 8,441,415 taels, or a mere two-thirds of the quota, were collected. Kiangsu, Chekiang, and Hupei were responsible for most of the arrears. A similar situation existed with regard to the rice tribute. In Kiangsu, for example, where the quota was 1,600,000 tan, the amount paid during the decade 1831-1841 was some 70 or 80 per cent of the quota; 1841-1851, 50 or 60 per cent; and 1851-1861, 40 per cent. The

quota for Chekiang was some 1,100,000 tan, but during the Tao-
kuang and early Hsien-feng periods the amount actually paid each
year was only 500,000 to 700,000 or 800,000 tan.

Now what had caused this sudden drop in the ability of the Yangtse provinces to pay taxes in the 1840's and 1850's? There appear
to have been three causes for this.

(i) Loss of agricultural productivity due to neglect of irrigation.
Corruption in Ch'ing officialdom became rampant toward the last
part of the eighteenth century; the local authorities concentrated
on self-enrichment at the expense of their public duties. Water
control thereby suffered. This led to disastrous floods and the
frequent remission of land taxes in the stricken areas. Floods accounted for the fact that Kiangsu, Chekiang, and Hupei were the
heaviest in arrears. While Lin Tse-hsü was the Governor of Kiangsu much attention was paid to water-control. For a time there was
substantial improvement, but there was a relapse into the former
state of neglect after Lin left the post. The great floods of 1823
and 1831 in Chekiang, as well as the great Hupei flood of 1832,
caused widespread havoc in these provinces and led to a decline
in grain production and tax collection. Floods were frequent also
in Hunan owing to neglect of the dykes.

(ii) Increase in the people's burden owing to the rise in the
price of silver during the Tao-kuang period. The common people's
medium of exchange was usually the copper cash. The peasant
received copper cash from the sale of farm products, but the land-
poll tax and the rice tribute commutations were computed on the
basis of silver. Coupled with the fall in agricultural productivity,
the people's ability to pay was drastically decreased. From the
1830's on the question of the rise of silver had become an important
concern of the high officials, who gave some detailed descriptions
of the effect of high silver prices on the small taxpayers. Tseng
Kuo-fan explained the situation clearly in a memorial of 1851:

(Taxes) are paid mostly in money, rarely in kind. Even
when the rice tribute is payable in kind, still the transport
charges and the land-poll tax must be paid in silver. The
common people's income from the fields is rice. When they
sell the rice for cash, the price is very low, and they are unhappy; then they exchange the cash for silver, but the price
of silver is very high, and again they are unhappy. In the
southeastern rice-producing areas the price of rice has for
centuries remained at around 3,000 cash per tan. In the old
days one tael was equal to 1,000 cash, so that each tan was
worth three taels. Nowadays one tael is equal to 2,000 cash,
so that each tan is worth only 1.5 taels. In the old days the

the tax on one <u>mou</u> of land could be amply met by the sale of
0.3 <u>tan</u> of rice, but nowadays more than 0.6 tan is needed to
pay the same tax. The government's revenue remains the
same, while the levies on the common people have imperceptibly doubled.

A similar report was made for Hunan province by Governor Lo
Ping-chang in 1858.

(iii) <u>Deepening of corruption</u> in the administration of tax and rice
<u>tribute</u>. The peasants sometimes were obliged to pay the overcol-
lection to the tax officials before the regular tax, so that the latter was often in arrears. It was reported in 1843 that the inability
to meet the tax assessment with their crops had compelled many
peasants to abandon their land.

In addition to the above, the following factors also contributed
to the fall in tax payments: (a) The low prices of agricultural products. Contemporary accounts indicate that the price of rice had
fallen by over one-half as compared to the eighteenth century.
Faced also with the rise of silver, the farmer often had to sell
five piculs of rice to get the money formerly obtainable with one
picul. (b) Decrease in the amount of cultivated land, the result of
the fall in income. It has been estimated that between 1812 and
1833, the cultivated area in the country had decreased by over
500,000 <u>ch'ing</u>. (c) Instability of family handicrafts, especially
cotton weaving, which since the Tao-kuang period had suffered
from competition with imported textiles.

Thus, the people were economically no longer able to bear the
land taxes; at the same time, the decline and weakening of the
Ch'ing dynasty were completely exposed after the White Lotus
uprising [1795-1803] and the Opium War [1839-1842]. The people,
no longer fearing the power of the government, began to resist the
heavy taxation. Their contempt for the Ch'ing rule is indicated by
their praise for the local militia in Kwangtung and Fukien during
the Opium War, and their sarcastic condemnation of the Manchu
military officers. The decline of the dynasty's power aggravated
for it the problem of revenues.

Such a situation called for a reduction in tax rates even before
the Taiping wars. There were a few enlightened officials who understood the sufferings of the common people. For instance, in
1833 Lin Tse-hsü, in answer to an edict criticizing the slow remittance of taxes from Kiangsu and other provinces, stated that
strict enforcement of tax collections might create trouble, and
that it was better for the government to be lenient for the time being. In fact, between 1817 and 1830 tax dues had been reduced by

large amounts for two areas in Kiangsu; but as such reductions
would not have easily been permitted by the Board of Finance, they
were officially called "postponement." In Hunan over-charges in
tax collection were weeded out by Lo Ping-chang when he was the
Governor of the province from 1850 on.

However, there were only very few such enlightened officials,
and their measures always halted when they were transferred to
other posts. The result was that the people began to resist tax collections. In the Yangtse provinces the movement gathered strength
even before the Taiping forces reached the region. In 1844 it was
reported that the uprisings in various districts in Hupei were
caused by the collection of the rice tribute, and by the attendant
overcollection. The smaller rebel groups resisted arrest, while
the larger ones killed officials and attacked cities. Other uprisings
of the same nature were reported from the Hukuang Provinces
[i.e. Hupei and Hunan] and from Chekiang. As the Taiping forces
pressed down the Yangtse valley, popular sentiment from Hupei
to Kiangsu became increasingly restless. Many more local uprisings occurred; these were scattered in different areas and in some
instances involved tens of thousands of aroused people. These uprisings consisted of non-payment of taxes, attacks on official residences, burning of government offices and collectors' boats, and
so on. The desperate situation worsened after the Taiping wars
had devastated the countryside. Hence all the provincial authorities in the Yangtse region included tax reduction in their programs
as they sought to put down the Taiping forces.

PART II. TAX REDUCTION DURING THE TAIPING REBELLION

1. Reasons for Tax Reduction

With the Taiping armies holding sway in the Yangtse provinces,
the matter of tax reduction could no longer be delayed. The following were the major causes that brought it about.

(i) Production broke down after the devastation of war, and the
government could not "dry the pond to get the fish." The destruction deeply impressed the high officials, who saw the need for a
reduction in tax rates. Lo Ping-chang, Hu Lin-i, Tseng Kuo-fan,
Ma Hsin-i, and Li Hung-chang all graphically described the desolation of the country. In Anhwei sometimes "no smoke was to be
seen for a hundred li." In Chekiang around Hangchow, Chia-hsing,
and Hu-chou often one could see no humans for scores of li, only
crumbled walls and ruined houses lying everywhere. In a report by
Li Hung-chang on the situation in Kiangsu he concluded that even

for the unscrupulous collectors the area of Sung-chiang, T'ai-
ts'ang, Soochow, and Ch'ang-chou now presented "no bones to
rack and no marrow to suck."

(ii) The dynasty wanted to lighten the burden of the people in the
hope of winning back popular support. The Taiping movement differed from previous rebellions in that it had an economic policy
with which to attract the people, and propagandized that it would
distribute the land according to the size of each family. In addition to the promulgation of the Land System of the Heavenly Kingdom, the Taiping regime also held forth before the people the
prospect of remission of three years' taxes. Such policies were
very effective, so that the approach of the Taiping forces was welcomed by the populace, while that of the government troops was
greeted with the stoppage of trade. The more far-sighted of the
Ch'ing officials, therefore, saw that in order to suppress the Taipings it was necessary to use both military and political means
simultaneously. When Hu Lin-i, for instance, retook Wu-ch'ang
and memorialized on reconstruction plans, he said that "civil administration and military affairs have ever been interdependent."
Though the officials did not dare say outright that the Taiping policies were winning the people's support, this nevertheless was im-
plicit in many of their statements. One after another they con-
tended that a reduction of taxes would rally the people to the government's side while depriving the rebels of support, and suggested its implementation in the Yangtse provinces.

(iii) The need for military supplies was urgent, and a lower tax
rate would increase the people's willingness to pay. During the
wars the people's ability to pay had decreased, and the authorities,
out of political considerations, were loath to press too hard. The
need for military supplies, however, continued to be pressing.
The only way out was to introduce tax reductions, so that the people would gladly pay their dues out of gratitude. From the point
of view of raising funds for military purposes the important thing
was that people should quickly pay their dues so as to enable the
government to cope with its crisis; whether or not the amounts
were reduced was of secondary importance. This was the view
held by the high officials, and some of them--such as Lo Ping-
chang in Hunan--were able to cite proofs in their own provinces
to demonstrate the thesis that tax reduction was a good way of re-
plenishing the government treasury.

(iv) The establishment of the likin enabled the government to
reduce the land tax without fear of a drastic drop in revenue. In
view of the need for large sums of money both for military and reconstruction purposes, it was clear that tax reduction could not

have taken place without some other source of large income. The
total government revenue before the reign of Hsien-feng averaged
some 40,000,000 taels per year, with the land-poll tax amounting
to two-thirds of the sum. The income from likin during 1869 was
over 10,000,000 taels. An examination of the dates shows that in
the Yangtse provinces the reduction of land tax in each province
invariably occurred after the introduction of likin there. For instance, likin was established in Kiangsu in 1853, and tax reduction took place in 1865; in Hupei the dates were 1855 and 1857 respectively; in Chekiang, 1864 and 1865. In Hunan tax reduction
followed the introduction of likin by six months in 1855. Such time
sequence indicates the relationship between the two.

Since likin was an indirect tax, it could more easily be foisted
on the people, the ultimate payers of all taxes, than could the direct land tax. The advocates of likin, however, were all wont to
justify the measure in terms of the traditional ideology of favoring agriculture and slighting commerce, holding that the establishment of likin would lighten the farmers' burden while making merchants pay their due share. Were these officials really ignorant
of the fact that the merchants could shift the burden of likin onto
the farmers' shoulders? But in any event, likin did directly aid the
implementation of tax reduction by providing the government with
an added source of income.

2. Nature of the Tax Reduction

The two following measures were adopted as antidotes to overcollection and excessive taxation:

(i) Overcollection was reduced so that only enough was taken to
cover the costs of local administration. Ideally speaking, reform
in this respect should have done away with any and all levies above
the official quota. The low official salaries, however, made this
impossible. The total collection after the reduction of overcharges,
therefore, was still somewhat above the government quota, since
it was necessary to let the local authorities retain certain amounts
to meet the expenditures of administration. In none of the provinces
were the overcharges entirely eliminated, but instead a small sum
was assessed with every picul of rice tribute or every tael of the
land-poll tax. For instance, in Kiangsi an additional 0.16 tael was
assessed for every tael due on the land-poll tax, and 0.27 tael for
every tan of the rice tribute; the sums realized were assigned to
defray the actual cost of local administration. Similar measures
were adopted in Anhwei, Kiangsu, and Chekiang. At the same time
local administrative costs also were pared down by the provincial

governors and governors-general, so that eventually a sizable sum
was saved.

(ii) The excessive tax rates in Kiangsu and Chekiang were reduced. It was difficult to obtain imperial approval for a general reduction of the official tax quota, because this, unlike the overcollections, which only affected the income of local functionaries,
would lead to a decrease of the revenue of the central government
itself. In the end only Kiangsu and Chekiang were given reductions
in the tax quota. The rate for Soochow, Sung-chiang, and T'ai-
ts'ang was reduced by one-third; Hangchow, Chia-hsing and Hu-
chou by eight-thirtieths; Ch'ang-chou and Chinkiang by one-tenth.

However, these methods were only attacks on symptoms, not
on causes. Therefore the two following policies were introduced
in order to stamp out the roots of tax corruption:

(i) Payment of perquisites to superior and other officials and
corrupt conduct of minor functionaries were strictly forbidden.
This was aimed at the elimination of overcollection by stopping the
practice at its source. Not only were perquisites banned in every
one of the Yangtse provinces, but the extortions and illegal activities of the lower officials were also prohibited.

(ii) The distinction between "great households" and "small households" was abolished. This was aimed at eliminating the corrupt
practices of the gentry, and at bringing an end to the inequality of
payments made by the two categories. For instance, when tax reduction was put into effect in Hupei in 1857, the distinction between
the great and small households was abolished. The same was true
of Kiangsu, Kiangsi, and Chekiang. The uniform rate applied both
to the basic tax rate and to the rate of commutation.

The above measures were side products of the tax reduction
movement, but they are noteworthy for two reasons. First, they
were measures that reached at the roots of the evil. Second, they
conformed quite closely to principles of finance. The elimination
of perquisites and bribes was equivalent to Adam Smith's "Principle of Economy," and the abolition of the categories of great
and small households to his "Principle of Equality."

3. The Course of the Tax Reduction

The tax reduction movement was introduced in the Yangtse provinces in the wake of the suppression of the Taiping forces there.
Accordingly it appeared in each province in this order: first in
Hunan, then Hupei and Kiangsi, then Anhwei, and lastly Chekiang
and Kiangsu.

(i) Hunan

With the taking of Yo-chou by government troops in August, 1854,
the Taiping forces in Hunan were completely defeated. Tax reduction was soon instituted by Governor Lo Ping-chang for a two-fold
purpose: to raise supplies for the campaign in neighboring provinces, and to win the support of the people, who were then agitat-
ing against the land tax and rice tributes. Lo was the chief execu-
tor of the tax reduction policy. The real power behind the scenes,
however, was Tso Tsung-t'ang, then one of Lo's advisors, who
planned and launched the program.

Tax reduction in Hunan was begun in 1855. According to Lo
Ping-chang's autobiography, there were large arrears in tax payments owing to the extremely low price of rice and the necessity
of paying in silver. In Hsiang-t'an, for example, where it was possible to collect some forty or fifty thousand taels of tax per year,
in 1854 only 4,000-odd taels were collected, and in 1855 no tax
whatever had been collected as late as the seventh month [July-
August]. The situation was changed when some local graduates
proposed a set of tax schedules to the authorities which revamped
the tax rates but kept the levy of certain sums for administrative
and military costs. Lo gave his approval to this plan. Subsequently
Changsha, I-yang, Hengyang, and other areas where the tax was
too heavy also adopted similar plans, all with satisfactory results.
In Hsiang-t'an over 100,000 taels were collected by January of
1856. In other prefectures where reduction also had taken place
the authorities were likewise able to make collections.

Not wishing to be restricted in his action at an early stage by
Court instructions, Lo Ping-chang did not report to Peking on the
reduction of tax rates until 1858, when he memorialized on both
the tax reduction and the introduction of likin in a memorial entitled "On the Raising of Military Funds in Hunan." In this he described the corrupt practices and bankruptcy that existed before,
the new measures instituted by him, and the satisfactory financial
and political results of his actions.

It is not possible to know the total amount of money involved in
the Hunan tax reductions. The sums varied locally, and the total
was not mentioned in Lo's memorials. Hsiang-t'an, for instance,
had its tax assessments reduced by approximately one-fourth.
This might prove to be a rather large percentage since the quota
for Hsiang-t'an was high. It can serve, however, as an indication
of the general picture.

Tax reduction in Hunan was followed by similar measures in
the other provinces, with some differences. Hupei differed from

Hunan in not adopting such measures until after the authorities had memorialized on it, but was similar to Hunan in giving much leeway also to local considerations. The Kiangsu authorities, on the other hand, drew up uniform regulations for the entire province, which many officials thought would be difficult to enforce over a long period.

(ii) Hupei

Wu-ch'ang was taken by government forces at the end of 1856. This marked the eclipse of the Taiping armies in Hupei along both banks of the Yangtse River. In the following year Hu Lin-i introduced a tax reduction program into the province.

While the primary aim of tax reduction in Hunan was the raising of military funds, that in Hupei was the winning of popular support. Not only was Hupei a strategically important area, but the population there was also even more rebellious than that of other provinces. One of the ways in which Hu rallied the people of Hupei was the lowering of the tax rates.

Hu Lin-i memorialized twice in 1857 on the need for eliminating over-collection, banning perquisites, making the rice tribute payable at a uniform rate by commutation, and drastically reducing excessive assessment. Hu reported that the overcollection was reduced by more than 1,400,000,000 cash.

As described by Hu in a memorial of 1858 on the results of tax reduction, the procedure was as follows: The gentry of the various localities drew up petitions in which they stated the amounts that could be reduced. The petitions were examined by the provincial authorities, who, taking into consideration local conditions, would either approve the proposals as correct or, if they thought the recommendations inadequate for certain localities, would increase the rate of reduction accordingly. This meant that the method adopted in Hupei was close to that in Hunan, that is, the reduction rates were determined for each locality separately on the basis of local conditions. Hu Lin-i reported that a total of over 200,000 taels in extra-legal fees and overcollections had been eliminated.

Hu was stringent in the application of his tax reduction measures, and made examples of recalcitrant officials by forthright punishments. Apparently the results were quite impressive.

(iii) Kiangsi

The Taiping forces in Kiangsi were defeated by Tseng Kuo-fan in the Fall of 1861. Subsequently tax reduction was instituted, pri-

marily for the purpose of raising funds for the military campaigns.
Li Huan, Grain Commissioner and Acting Provincial Treasurer of
Kiangsi, was placed in charge of the program.

The plan proposed by Li Huan and approved by Tseng was to set
a flat rate of payment for the entire province. The land-poll tax
was fixed at a lowered rate of 2,400 cash [per mou], including regular quota and wastage charges, and the rice tribute commutation
was fixed at 3,000 cash per tan, including all local administration
costs. The special characteristic of the Kiangsi plan was the uniformity of the reduced rates. For Kuang-hsin Prefecture, for
instance, where the over-collection had reached 14,000 cash per
tan of rice tribute, the new rate was also fixed initially at 3,000
cash. As the armies were in great need of funds, however, it was
proposed that Kuang-hsin be assessed an additional sum in tribute
commutation so that the reduction in income might not be so sharp.
Revisions were accordingly made in the following year after lengthy
deliberations among Tseng Kuo-fan, Li Huan, Tso Tsung-t'ang,
Shen Pao-chen, governor of Kiangsi from 1862, and Ting Jih-
ch'ang, then the district magistrate of Lu-ling who was also an advocate of tax reduction.

The final outcome was a three-point plan that would relieve the
people of an estimated 1,000,000-odd taels in tax payments, and
yield some 300,000 taels for military supplies. According to the
method of this plan, which was put into operation in the fifth month
[May-June], 1862, all land tax in the province was to be collected
in Kuping taels at a rate of 1.5 Kuping taels for every 1.1 taels
assessed. In regard to rice tribute, the commutation rate was set
at 1.9 taels per tan for Nan-ch'ang and nine other prefectures,
and at 3.0 taels per tan for Kuang-hsin. This was an attempt to
model on the local plan of Hunan. The general picture in Kiangsi
was still one of uniformity, however, for although Kuang-hsin was
at first assessed a higher rate, the difference had to be abandoned
later in the same year owing to the protests of the local population.

Tseng Kuo-fan later thought that the reduction of tax rates in
Kiangsi was too drastic, and that the uniform rate for the entire
province was a drawback in the successful operation of the reduction program. Furthermore, the fall in the price of silver in subsequent years also brought difficulties to the provincial authorities,
who were asked to collect in silver under the reduction plan, and
ultimately it was found necessary to abandon silver and return to
assessment in cash. Because of these difficulties no memorial was
sent up on the reduction program in Kiangsi until 1865, when Acting Governor Sun Ch'ang-fu reported on the satisfactory experi-
mental application of the plan. Imperial approval was thereupon

given. According to Sun Ch'ang-fu, the total revenue of Kiangsi from land tax and rice tribute commutation amounted to only some 3,000,000 taels. Yet the overcollections had been reduced by over 1,000,000 taels. This shows what a profound effect the reduction program must have had on the people of the province.

(iv) Anhwei

After the government forces had taken Anking [capital of Anhwei] in 1861, it was found that all tax records had disappeared. A "substitute tax" was therefore levied in place of the regular taxes. It was not until 1864, when the Taiping forces were completely subdued in Anhwei, that the regular land-poll tax and rice tribute were reinstituted. A tax reduction program was also initiated. Tseng Kuo-fan as Governor-General of Chiang-nan and Kiangsi was the final authority in the introduction of the reduction scheme, but the plan was drafted by the provincial Financial Commissioner Ma Hsin-i and Judicial Commissioner Ho Ching, and memorialized by Anhwei Governor Ch'iao Sung-nien. The reduction here involved the rate of commutation for rice tribute and the amount to be assessed. Ma and Ho proposed that an additional 1.2 tael per tan of rice tribute should be assessed aside from the official rate of 1.3 tael per tan, but that all other extra changes should be abolished; the amount in taels should then be changed into copper with rate of exchange varying in different localities. Tseng Kuo-fan, however, considered the rates still too high. According to Tseng's report the plan was put into operation only after the rate per tan had been reduced further by seven or eight hundred cash, bringing the rate to around 5,000 cash per tan in the majority of cases. The memorial on tax reduction stated that the final assessment would be sixty or seventy per cent of former rates, and that the amount of total reductions for the province would therefore be some 1,300,000,000 cash. Unfortunately no material is available on the actual application of the reduction program in Anhwei, so that a detailed study is impossible.

(v) Chekiang

Tax reduction in Chekiang was first suggested by Ting Shou-ch'ang in a memorial dated June 9, 1863. Ting mentioned two reasons for this, namely to win the support of the people, and to bring the official quota and actual payments to the same level. Previously actual payments had long lagged behind the nominal quota, and a reduction in rates would therefore benefit the people without

being detrimental to national income. Ting proposed that the rice
tributes of Soochow, Sung-chiang, Ch'ang-chou, Chinkiang, T'ai-
ch'ang [all in Kiangsu], Hangchow, Chia-hsing, and Hu-chou [all
in Chekiang] be reduced by one-third of the old rates. This met
with imperial approval, and Tso Tsung-t'ang was charged with the
implementation of the plan in the Chekiang areas. Toward the end
of 1863 Tso reported that since Hangchow, Chia-hsing, and Hu-
chou were still in Taiping hands the tax reductions could not be
carried out there, but that the same abuses existed in eastern
Chekiang and so the plan should be extended to that area. As an example he sent in the report on trial reductions in Wen-chou. A general reduction program was put under way following imperial approval of Tso's report.

From then on tax reduction in Chekiang spread to Ningpo, Shao-
hsing, and the other prefectures. Of the eleven prefectures in the
province only T'ai-chou was not included in the reduction program
by 1865. According to the memorials of those in charge, the overcollections in the ten prefectures were reduced by a total of 1,826,-
053,000 cash and 489,045 tan of rice. The method of reduction
consisted of three aspects: (a) All regular quotas had to be paid,
although the rice tribute rates for Hangchow, Chia-hsing, and Hu-
chou were reduced according to decree. (b) All extralegal fees
and perquisites were abolished. (c) The differentiation between
"great households" and "small households" was strictly forbidden.

In addition to the reduction of overcollection, that of the rice
tribute rates for Hangchow, Chia-hsing, and Hu-chou was also
instituted when these prefectures were retaken from the Taiping
forces. The general plan was to reduce the assessment on each
locality by a certain proportion of its original rates, the aim being a total reduction of eight-thirtieths of the original quota. The
amounts reduced from the rice tribute payments of the three prefectures were as follows:

Prefecture	Original Quota (in tan)	Reduction (in tan)	Percentage Reduction
Hangchow	163,565.99	25,735.49	15.8
Chia-hsing	492,276.10	145,416.30	29.5
Hu-chou	344,576.74	95,613.84	27.7

The total amount reduced was 266,765 tan, which was approximately 26 per cent of the original quota, that is a reduction of
eight-thirtieths. However, compared with the amount reduced on
overcollections this was by far the smaller sum. This shows that

the major part of tax reduction in Chekiang involved not rice tribute but overcollection.

(vi) Kiangsu

The subject of tax reduction in Kiangsu was first broached on
June 6 and 9, 1863 by metropolitan officials in memorials stress-
ing the people's urgent need for relief from the tax burden. By instituting reductions, it was held, the government could not only
avoid further rebellion but facilitate tax collections as well. At
the same time the provincial authorities also were urging tax reduction; this was supported by the local gentry as well. Among the
former were such persons as Fang Ch'uan-shu, Acting Prefect of
Sung-chiang, and Grain Commissioner Kuo Sung-t'ao, who in
early 1863 became active in planning a reduction program. They
were helped in their efforts by members of the Kiangsu gentry
like Wu Yün and Feng Kuei-fen, the latter an authority on land
taxes who was then serving as an advisor to Li Hung-chang. Li
delegated the responsibility of drawing up the tax reduction program to Kuo Sung-t'ao and Feng Kuei-fen. Urged on by Wu Yün,
these two finally sent in their memorial proposing tax reduction.
After listing the general causes that called for the initiation of
such a program in over-burdened Kiangsu, the memorial suggested
that the total rice tribute quota for the five prefectures of Soochow,
Sung-chiang, T'ai-ts'ang,* Ch'ang-chou, and Chinkiang be set at
around 1,000,000 tan per year. This would involve a cutting down
of the quota for the first three prefectures from 1,210,000 to some
500,000 tan; the old quota of 500,000 tan for Ch'ang-chou and
Chinkiang, considered quite low, would remain unchanged.

The preceding suggestion was considered too drastic by the Peking authorities and was subjected to revision. The final program,
as drawn up in 1865 by Feng Kuei-fen and Provincial Financial
Commissioner Liu Hsün-kao under the supervision of Li Hung-
chang and Tseng Kuo-fan, represented a compromise of diverse
opinions. The rice tribute of Soochow, Sung-chiang, and T'ai-
ts'ang was to be reduced by one-third as suggested by the Board
of Finance, instead of by the more drastic amount advocated by
Feng Kuei-fen. Ch'ang-chou and Chinkiang were to have their quota
reduced by one-tenth. It was also recommended that the land-poll
tax and the additional fees related to the rice tribute of the five
prefectures should also be reduced by two-tenths; this recommen-

*Although T'ai-ts'ang is referred to as a prefecture, it was actually a chih-li
chou 直隸州 , that is, a sub-prefecture under the direct control of the
provincial governor.

dation, however, was rejected by the Board of Finance. The tax reduction in Kiangsu therefore involved only the regular quotas of
rice tribute.

The procedure was as follows: (a) For Ch'ang-chou and Chinkiang, where the original assessments were relatively low, the
reduction was a flat 10 per cent. (b) For Soochow, Sung-chiang,
and T'ai-ts'ang, where the original assessments differed locally,
there was to be a graduated scale of reduction in proportion to the
original local rate. (c) Marginal coastal land within the three last
prefectures which did not produce rice were also granted a reduction. The total reduction for these three prefectures was, however, not to exceed one-third of the original quota.

According to the above plan, the amounts reduced in Kiangsu
were, in terms of tan, as follows:

Prefecture	Original Quota	Reduction
Ch'ang-chou	355,980.56	35,598.06
Chinkiang	214,735.07	21,473.50
Soochow	877,564.95	326,632.34
Sung-chiang	427,461.39	116,544.64
T'ai-ts'ang	153,432.74	42,878.00

In other words, the rates for Ch'ang-chou and Chinkiang were
reduced by one-tenth in each place, while the combined original
quota of 1,458,459 tan for the last three prefectures was reduced
by a total of 486,045.97 tan, that is one-third of the original quota.
The amount due from all five prefectures after the reduction was
1,486,048 tan, as against the original 2,029,174.72 tan.

In addition to this, reduction of overcollection was also separately undertaken from 1863 on. Attempts were made to deal with
such abuses as the distinction between great and small households,
differences in the rate of commutation, various perquisites, extra
payment for sea transportation, and so forth. For four of the five
prefectures an estimated total of 1,676,000 strings of cash and
374,600 tan of rice in overcollection was eliminated after the reform measures were put into effect.

Aside from the above five prefectures, tax reduction was also
instituted in the prefecture of Chiang-ning [Nanking]. This must
be treated separately because Chiang-ning, together with the prefectures of northern Kiangsu, were under the jurisdiction of different provincial administrative units during the Ch'ing dynasty.
After the defeat of the Taipings in 1864 a "substitute tax" was instituted for the Chiang-ning area, and the regular levies were not

re-introduced until 1874. Although in that year and the next the provincial authorities repeatedly urged a reduction of taxes here, the petitions were rejected by the Board of Finance, which went no further than to permit temporary reductions for two years. It was not until 1877 that a reduction of three-tenths in rice tribute was approved for five of the seven districts in Chiang-ning. Reductions in the excessive taxation in commutation of the two other districts were instituted in 1878 and 1880.

In sum, Kiangsu ranked first among the Yangtse provinces in the amount of reduction of rice tribute and overcollections. This was due to the fact that before the Taiping war it was the richest and the most heavily taxed province, and during the war it was the most devastated, so that the reductions here were greater than those in other provinces.

4. Results of Tax Reduction

How much had the tax reductions accomplished in lessening the people's burdens? According to data presented in the previous pages, the total sum of reductions in rice tribute and overcollection amounted to over 1,500,000 taels, more than 6,400,000 strings of cash, and over 1,700,000 tan of rice. This amounted to approximately 10,750,000 taels in terms of silver. Although the last figure can only be considered as a rough estimate due to local differences and fluctuations in the price of rice, it is sufficient to indicate the magnitude of the sums involved. If we also take into consideration the fact that the purchasing power of money at that time was three times that of today, then the significance of tax reductions to the people becomes evident. The reign of T'ung-chih has been known as the period of "Restoration." One of the economic bases of the Restoration was the tax reduction movement, which facilitated the recovery of the rural areas. However, the sums were primarily reduced from the perquisites and extralegal exactions of the officials, and except for 800,000 tan (the equivalent of about 1,000,000 taels) that were reduced from the official quota in Kiangsu and Chekiang, the government revenues were not affected.

Yet reduction in overcollections was something that could not be accomplished simply by the issuance of decrees. Not only would the local officials have to adhere strictly to the rules, but the higher authorities also would have to be vigilant in supervision. In the early stages of the tax reduction movements these conditions were satisfactorily met. However, even at that time Tseng Kuo-fan realized that "reduction of tax quotas can become an unefface-

able institution for a hundred generations, but reduction of overcollection cannot last for more than a decade." Soon it became apparent that officials were reverting to previous practices. Already
in 1867 an edict reprimanded local officials for not properly carrying out the reduction program. Between 1870 and 1885 many petitions were sent up by imperial censors and the Board of Finance requesting the elimination of perquisites and overcollection in the
Yangtse provinces, indicating the reappearance of the old abuses.
By the end of the Ch'ing dynasty these had still not been eradicated.

Not only did local corruption and overcollection re-emerge at
the end of the T'ung-chih period, but owing to financial difficulties
faced by the government even the official tax quota was increased
considerably during the next reign in the form of various additional
levies. Consequently the taxpayer's burden was greatly increased,
and the people became restless. It was not without reason that
H. B. Morse attributed the outbreak of the republican revolution
to the general discontent of the people against the Ch'ing government. The land tax was a direct levy, the effect of which was
most acutely felt by the people, and the fall of the Ch'ing dynasty
was certainly linked to the decline of the tax reduction movement.

Conclusion

The most noticeable feature of this tax reduction movement was
its emphasis on the elimination of overcollection and corruption,
so that the people's tax burdens were greatly decreased without
appreciably affecting the government revenue. The significance of
this movement to the history of late Ch'ing has generally been
neglected by historians.

A shortcoming of the movement was that rent reduction was not
instituted at the same time. Since tenancy prevailed in the Yangtse
provinces, a reduction in taxes without a decrease in rent could
benefit only the self-cultivating peasants and landlords, but would
leave the tenant farmers untouched. The reduction of rent was introduced only in Kiangsu, where, according to Feng Kuei-fen, it
was instituted after taxes were reduced. The reduction rate was
3 per cent for the first tan of rent per mou, and 50 per cent for
any additional fraction of a tan; the total rent was not to exceed
1.2 tan per mou. None of the five other Yangtse provinces, however, seemed to have followed suit.

Recently [in the 1930's] there has been much talk about reducing the extra levies on land. Government directives emphasizing
the abolition of "extortionate levies and miscellaneous taxes" and

the elimination of corruption and squeeze make the present efforts closely similar to the programs of the 1860's. In the provinces numerous additional levies, the proceeds of which have gone to fill the pockets of local officials and gentry, have been instituted under various names. This situation is also the same as that which prevailed in the nineteenth century.

The outcome of the present efforts will depend on a number of considerations: whether the government is truly determined to bring about tax reduction, whether the policies can be carried out locally, and how to fit the tax program into the overall picture of Chinese finance and rural reconstruction. Furthermore, tax-reduction benefits only self-cultivating farmers and landlords, but not the tenants, who constitute an increasing proportion of the rural population. In the future the government should also do something about the problem of rent reduction.

NOTES

夏鼐, 太平天國前後長江各省之田賦問題, 清華學報
Hsia Nai, "T'ai-p'ing t'ien-kuo ch'ien-hou ch'ang-chiang ko-sheng-chih t'ien-fu wen-t'i," The Tsing Hua Journal, X, 2 (April, 1935), 409-474.

This carefully done study is well documented, having over 240 footnotes. Another commendable feature is the addition of page references for works cited.

In Section 3, vi (Kiangsu) we have omitted the author's elaborate table showing the amount and rate of tax reduction in each district of the three prefectures of Soochow, Sung-chiang, and T'ai-ts'ang.

The author has drawn on a large number of contemporary sources, chief of which are the collected papers and memorials to Tseng Kuo-fan, Tso Tsung-t'ang, Hu Lin-i, Lo Ping-chang, Feng Kuei-fen, and Li Hung-chang. He also has relied heavily on the local gazetteers of the areas involved; on the History of Tax Reduction in Chekiang (Che-chiang chien-fu ch'üan-an 浙江減賦全案) and History of Tax Reduction in Kiangsu (Chiang-su chien-fu ch'üan-an 江蘇減賦全案); and on various essays, including those in Huang-ch'ao ching-shih-wen pien 皇朝經世文編 , and others by Wang Ch'ing-yün 王慶雲 . Other contemporary secondary works are also used, though not as extensively as the ones cited above.

INDEX

This Index also serves as a glossary of some of the Chinese names and special terms that have appeared in the articles.